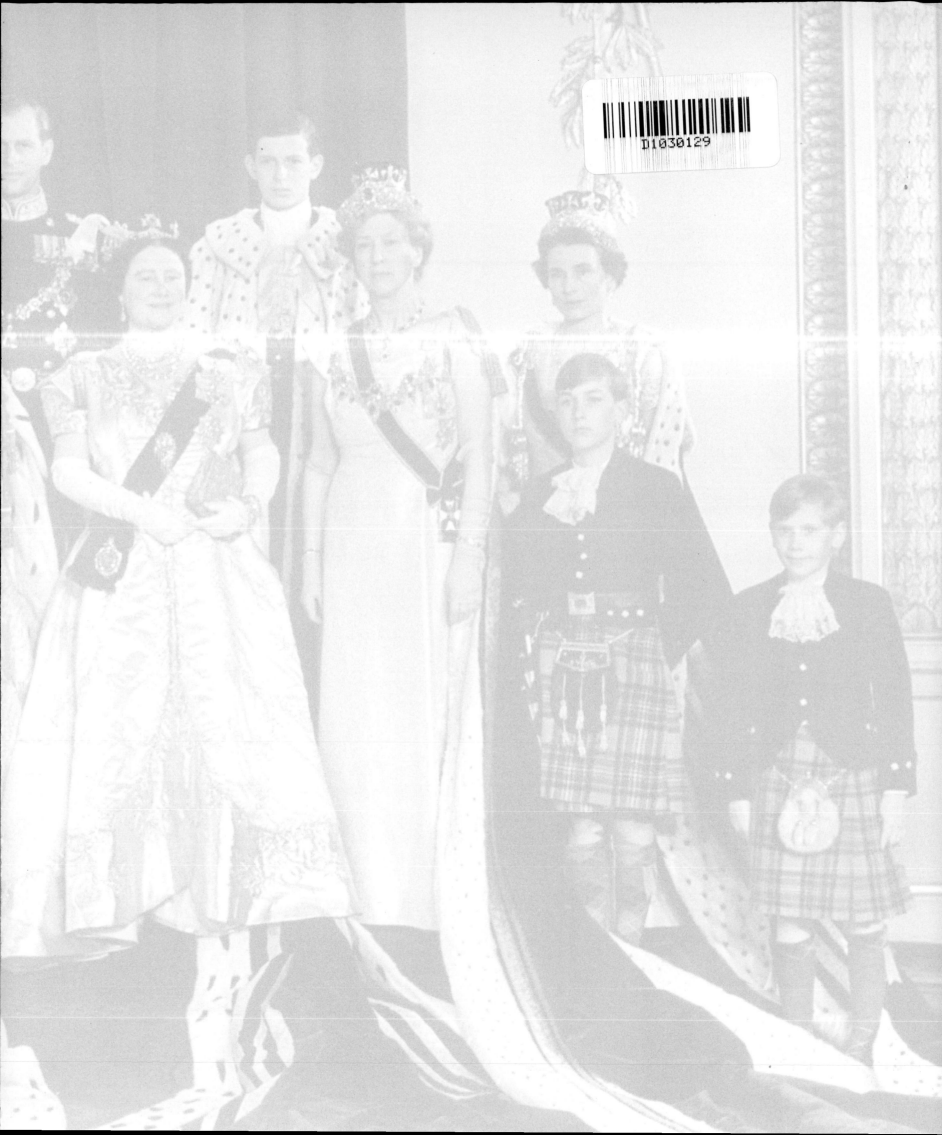

QUEEN ELIZABETH II
and the
ROYAL FAMILY

QUEEN
ELIZABETH II
and the
ROYAL FAMILY

DK UK

Senior Art Editor
Sharon Spencer

Senior Editor
Rob Houston

Design assistance
Alex Lloyd

Editors
Constance Novis, Helen Fewster

**Jacket Design
Development Manager**
Sophia MTT

US Editor
Margaret Parrish

Managing Art Editor
Michael Duffy

Managing Editor
Angeles Gavira Guerrero

Art Director
Karen Self

Producer, Pre-production
Francesca Wardell

Publisher
Liz Wheeler

Producer
Mary Slater

Publishing Director
Jonathan Metcalf

DK DELHI

Art Editors
Shreya Anand, Upasana Sharma

Senior Editors
Sreshtha Bhattacharya,
Anita Kakar

Jacket Designer
Suhita Dharamjit

Editors
Vibha Malhotra,
Priyaneet Singh

DTP Designers
Jaypal Chauhan, Nand Kishore Acharya

Picture Researcher
Sakshi Saluja

Managing Jackets Editor
Saloni Singh

Pre-production Manager
Balwant Singh

Production Manager
Pankaj Sharma

Managing Art Editor
Sudakshina Basu

Managing Editor
Rohan Sinha

First American Edition, 2015
Published in the United States by DK Publishing
345 Hudson Street, New York, New York 10014

A catalog record for this book is available from the Library of Congress.
ISBN 978-1-4654-3800-3

DK books are available at special discounts when purchased in bulk for
sales promotions, premiums, fund-raising, or educational use. For details,
contact: DK Publishing Special Markets, 345 Hudson Street, New York,
New York 10014
SpecialSales@dk.com

Printed in China

A WORLD OF IDEAS:
SEE ALL THERE IS TO KNOW

CONTENTS

1

THE BRITISH MONARCHY

2

3

4

QUEEN AND MOTHER
1960–1980   158

5

QUEEN AND GRANDMOTHER
1980–2000   196

6

CONSULTANT

Joe Little has been managing editor of *Majesty* magazine for 16 years. He has traveled extensively reporting on royal tours since his first overseas assignment covering Queen Elizabeth II's historic state visit to Russia in 1994. He was also in Ireland in 2011 to witness the warmth of the welcome for the Queen and Prince Philip. On many of the big royal occasions Joe assists the BBC in an advisory capacity; among the projects he has been involved with were the wedding of the Prince of Wales to Camilla Parker Bowles in 2005, the Queen's 80th birthday celebrations in the following year, Prince William and Catherine Middleton's nuptials and, most recently, Trooping the Color.

AUTHORS

Susan Kennedy formerly worked in publishing as an editor of encyclopedias and historical atlases. She has contributed to more than 15 books for adults and younger readers, and has a particular interest in history and modern culture.

Stewart Ross is a teacher, lecturer, and prize-winning author of historical books for adults and students. His books on British kings and queens include *The British Monarchy From Henry VIII*, *Monarchs of Scotland*, and *The Stewart Dynasty*.

R. G. Grant is a history writer who has published more than 30 books, many of them dealing with aspects of military conflict. He has written on the American Revolution, World War I, World War II, and the Vietnam War. He is author of DK's *Battle*, *Flight*, *Battle at Sea*, and *Soldier*.

Joel Levy is an author and journalist with a broad experience in writing about the past. Among his many books on history are the titles *History's Worst Battles*, *History's Greatest Discoveries*, and DK's *History Year by Year*.

Ros Belford is the author of numerous travel titles for DK, which combine her interest in history, geography, and biography with a love of travel. She is particularly interested in tracing the history of women—from ancient matriarchs to contemporary monarchs.

1
THE BRITISH MONARCHY
400–1911

« Gold coin of Elizabeth I picturing
a galleon and a Tudor rose

THE BRITISH MONARCHY
400–1911

400	1000	1100	1200	1300	1400

410
Rome abandons Britain; Romano-Britons must now defend themselves against Anglo-Saxon invaders as best they can.

597
St. Augustine arrives in the Kingdom of Kent with a mission to convert the southern English to Christianity.

793
Viking assaults on the English mainland begin.

≫ The Alfred jewel, late 9th century

871
Accession of Alfred to throne of Wessex, the only English kingdom not in Viking hands.

973
Coronation of Edgar as King of the English lays foundations of modern coronation ceremony.

⌃ Cnut the Great

1016
On death of King Ethelred the Unready, Cnut becomes first Norse King of England.

1018
Malcolm II, King of Scots, establishes his southern frontier on the Tweed River.

1042
Anglo-Saxon royal line returns with accession of Edward the Confessor.

1066
After slaying King Harold at Hastings, William Duke of Normandy takes the English crown.

1086
Results of survey of the realm are presented in the *Domesday Book*.

≪ Facsimile copy of the *Domesday Book*

1100
Accession of Henry I, who unites England and Normandy.

1135
After crown left to Queen Matilda, daughter of Henry I, Barons revolt in favor of King Stephen.

1154
Accession of Henry II, the first Plantagenet king, whose wife, Eleanor, brings him vast lands in France.

1170
Discord between the Church and State leads to the murder of Archbishop Thomas Becket in Canterbury Cathedral.

1189
Crusading and chivalrous hero Richard I, Lionheart, takes the crown.

1215
King John puts his seal to the *Magna Carta*, placing the crown beneath the law.

≫ The final version of the *Magna Carta*, issued in 1225

1265
Simon de Montfort invites "common" people to meet at the same time as Lords—the first Parliament.

1272
Accession of Edward I, "Hammer of the Scots," whose son will become first Prince of Wales.

1290
Death of Margaret "Maid of Norway" leaves Scottish throne vacant; Edward I asked to adjudicate, leading to the Scottish Wars of Independence.

1314
Scotland's Robert I (the Bruce) crushes the English army of Edward II at Bannockburn.

1337
Edward III attacks France, launching the series of conflicts known as the Hundred Years' War.

≫ Henry V of England

1381
Boy-king Richard II faces off with rebels in the Peasants' Revolt that followed labor shortages caused by the Black Death.

1399
Position of crown seriously undermined when Richard II is deposed and murdered by his cousin, Henry Bolingbroke, who becomes Henry IV.

1415
Henry V startles Europe with a remarkable victory over the French at Agincourt, paving the way for his son to be claimed King of France.

1455
Ineffective and incompetent government of Henry VI leads to outbreak of conflict known as Wars of the Roses between the houses of York and Lancaster.

1461
Edward of York becomes King Edward IV.

1485
Yorkist King Richard III is killed at the Battle of Bosworth, and Henry Tudor accedes to the throne as Henry VII.

Britain's monarchy stretches back further than almost any other similar institution. Over 1,500 years, between the Early Middle Ages and the early 20th century, its history was at best checkered. The position of British kings and queens of this period—some rogues, some average, a few genuinely heroic—rose from that of exalted tribal leaders to rulers appointed by God. Their role then changed slowly, and at times painfully, into that of living symbols, politically neutral personifications of their realm. This long and extraordinarily diverse tale mirrors that of the nation itself. Its keynote is the triumph of pragmatism—survival through adaptability.

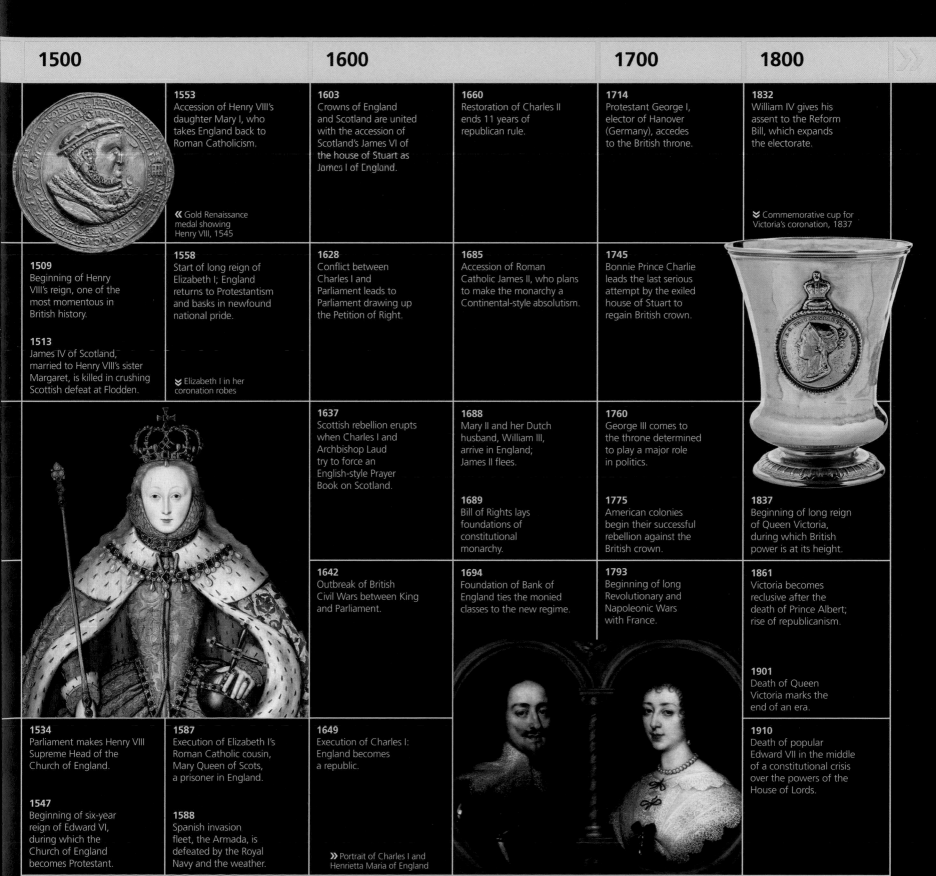

1500 | 1600 | 1700 | 1800 »»

1553
Accession of Henry VIII's daughter Mary I, who takes England back to Roman Catholicism.

1603
Crowns of England and Scotland are united with the accession of Scotland's James VI of the house of Stuart as James I of England.

1660
Restoration of Charles II ends 11 years of republican rule.

1714
Protestant George I, elector of Hanover (Germany), accedes to the British throne.

1832
William IV gives his assent to the Reform Bill, which expands the electorate.

« Gold Renaissance medal showing Henry VIII, 1545

⌄ Commemorative cup for Victoria's coronation, 1837

1509
Beginning of Henry VIII's reign, one of the most momentous in British history.

1513
James IV of Scotland, married to Henry VIII's sister Margaret, is killed in crushing Scottish defeat at Flodden.

1558
Start of long reign of Elizabeth I; England returns to Protestantism and basks in newfound national pride.

⌄ Elizabeth I in her coronation robes

1628
Conflict between Charles I and Parliament leads to Parliament drawing up the Petition of Right.

1685
Accession of Roman Catholic James II, who plans to make the monarchy a Continental-style absolutism.

1745
Bonnie Prince Charlie leads the last serious attempt by the exiled house of Stuart to regain British crown.

1637
Scottish rebellion erupts when Charles I and Archbishop Laud try to force an English-style Prayer Book on Scotland.

1688
Mary II and her Dutch husband, William III, arrive in England; James II flees.

1689
Bill of Rights lays foundations of constitutional monarchy.

1760
George III comes to the throne determined to play a major role in politics.

1775
American colonies begin their successful rebellion against the British crown.

1837
Beginning of long reign of Queen Victoria, during which British power is at its height.

1642
Outbreak of British Civil Wars between King and Parliament.

1694
Foundation of Bank of England ties the monied classes to the new regime.

1793
Beginning of long Revolutionary and Napoleonic Wars with France.

1861
Victoria becomes reclusive after the death of Prince Albert; rise of republicanism.

1901
Death of Queen Victoria marks the end of an era.

1534
Parliament makes Henry VIII Supreme Head of the Church of England.

1547
Beginning of six-year reign of Edward VI, during which the Church of England becomes Protestant.

1587
Execution of Elizabeth I's Roman Catholic cousin, Mary Queen of Scots, a prisoner in England.

1588
Spanish invasion fleet, the Armada, is defeated by the Royal Navy and the weather.

1649
Execution of Charles I: England becomes a republic.

»» Portrait of Charles I and Henrietta Maria of England

1910
Death of popular Edward VII in the middle of a constitutional crisis over the powers of the House of Lords.

The First English Kings

Between the accession of King Alfred in 871 and the Norman invasion of 1066, Anglo-Saxon and Norse monarchs forged several small kingdoms into a prosperous, orderly realm called England. It became one of the most tempting targets in Western Europe.

Following their invasion of 43 CE (see p.10), the Romans were the first to govern a unified England. Unity collapsed, however, when the legions departed at the beginning of the fifth century and southern Britain was invaded by Germanic tribes of Angles, Saxons, and Jutes.

Over the next three centuries, the many small Anglo-Saxon kingdoms coalesced into just a handful, the most prominent being Wessex, Mercia, and Northumbria.

BEFORE

Before unification into a single realm under kings of Wessex, Anglo-Saxon England comprised a multiplicity of small kingdoms.

THE HEPTARCHY
By the end of the **7th century << 10–11**, the many small tribal units of the **Angles, Saxons,** and **Jutes** had coalesced into seven major kingdoms. These were Wessex, Kent, Sussex, Essex, East Anglia, Mercia, and Northumbria. Kent had been the first to emerge and, owing partly to its close Continental connections, was for a long time the most sophisticated. By the 8th century, the Mercia of **King Offa** (757–796) was the dominant power.

TODAY A COUNTY, ONCE A KINGDOM
Some kingdoms, such as Kent, Essex, and Surrey, have survived as modern-day counties. Others, such as Hwicce (around Gloucester) and Deira (southeast Yorkshire), have disappeared entirely.

Conversion to Christianity after the arrival of St. Augustine's mission from Rome in 597 helped this unification process—a united Church welcomed partnership with broad-based secular powers, and enhanced royal authority with religious coronations. The monks who wrote the Anglo-Saxon Chronicle gave the title of "Bretwalda" to seven early Anglo-Saxon kings, implying that they had some sort of overlordship above their peers. The title was never a formal one, and final unification had to wait until the 10th century.

Alfred the Great

King Alfred of Wessex (849–899), reigned from 871 as the self-styled "King of the Anglo-Saxons" and the only English king to be given the epithet "Great." Alfred saved the Anglo-Saxon monarchy in the face of dire adversity. With some justification, he is generally seen as the first king of England. This role arose more by force of circumstance than deliberate policy, because, by the time of his accession, the greater part of England had been overrun by Viking invaders.

Alfred's landmark achievement was beating off the Danish Great Army, obliging its leader Guthrum to convert to Christianity in 879, and dividing England between Anglo-Saxon territory and the Scandinavian-held Danelaw. He strengthened his realm with fortified towns, known as burhs, enabling him to beat off later Viking attacks. A man of peace as well as war, England's first known literate monarch codified the law, encouraged literature, and even translated four Latin works into Old English.

Kings of England

Anglo-Saxon kings ruled as well as reigned, and Wessex was fortunate to be governed by a line of remarkable warrior-kings. Alfred's son Edward the Elder (reigned 899–924) as well as his grandsons, Athelstan, Edmund, and Eadred, expanded their rule north and east, thereby creating the Kingdom of England. While Edward's sister Ethelfleda (who ruled Mercia from 911–918) led

King Alfred's jewel
Inscribed "Alfred had me wrought," this remarkable treasure is more than 1,100 years old. The enamel figure on gold plate, covered by rock crystal and gold-framed, was probably originally used to tip a ceremonial wand.

the anti-Danish campaign in the Midlands, Edward the Elder took East Anglia and drove north to the Humber River. His son, Athelstan, who reigned from 924–939, then captured the Viking

> **"** This year, **Edgar,** *ruler of the English*, was **consecrated king** by a great assembly. **"**
>
> ANGLO-SAXON CHRONICLE, 973 CE

kingdom of York. By moving into Northumbria, he grew more powerful than any ruler since Roman times.

Edmund "The Magnificent," who reigned from 939–946, and Eadred, who followed Edmund and ruled until 955, tightened the grip on Northumbria further still. After a brief period of uncertainty, the crown passed in 959 to the sixteen-year-old Edgar the Peaceable (c.942–975). His coronation at Bath years later in 973, where he was anointed and received the allegiance of Britain's lesser kings, announced that the Kingdom of England was here to stay. Remarkably, modern British coronations follow the form that St. Dunstan devised for Edgar more than a millennium ago.

Ethelred the Unready

Brother succeeding brother is a reminder of the uncertain nature of the Anglo-Saxon royal succession. Close blood relationship was key, but nomination by the predecessor and approval by the nobility were also needed. Therefore, unsurprisingly, a

Viking vessel
The first English Kings lived when Vikings dominated many parts of the British Isles and northwest Europe. These seafarers set out from their homeland of Sweden, Denmark, and Norway, where this ship was buried.

The death of King Harold
The writing above this section of the famous Bayeux Tapestry reads, "King Harold is slain." The image and written sources suggest the last Anglo-Saxon king died when an arrow entered his brain through an eye socket.

reissued the laws of King Edgar, and extended his rule over both Denmark and Norway—all to no long-term avail. His strangely named sons, Harold Harefoot (1015–40), crowned in 1035, and Harthacnut (c.1018–42), crowned in 1040, both died young, and the crown reverted in 1043 to the Wessex line in the person of Edward the Confessor, son of Queen Emma and Ethelred the Unready.

St. Edward (England's only canonized monarch), had spent much of his early life in Normandy, and gained a respect for its people. He may or may not have been particularly holy. Whatever the reason for his sainthood, after a reign marked by tensions with the Godwin Earls of Wessex, Edward died childless. The English crown was up for grabs.

Cnut the Wise
A 14th-century image of King Cnut, England's first Danish monarch. The story of the King ordering back the sea is widely misunderstood: he used the incident to illustrate the powerlessness of an earthly monarch.

king's death often produced instability, sometimes marked by violence. Thus the reign of the ill-named and disliked Edward the Martyr (962–978), a son by Edgar's first wife, crowned in 962, ended when he was slain in Corfe Castle by the supporters of a son by Edgar's second wife. This son was the 12-year-old Ethelred (c.966–1016). Ethelred's name means "noble counsel" and his soubriquet "Unread" ("no counsel") was a play on words later mistranslated as "Unready." Edward was, in fact, prepared to face the renewed Norse attacks that began in 980, but he did not deal with them effectively. He organized a creditable military resistance and used the well-tried tactic (employed by no other than Alfred the Great) of paying the raiders

39,500 LB (17,900 KG) **The weight of silver paid by Ethelred to the Danes in 1012 to stop them from raiding England.**

"Danegeld" to encourage them to leave. However, he failed to unite the country behind him and, by the time of his death, much of England was once more in Danish hands.

England's crown up for grabs
Though he never boasted of being able to control the tide, as the much-told tale relates, Cnut the Dane (c.985–1035), crowned in 1016, proved to be one of England's more able early kings. He married Ethelred's widow, Emma of Normandy, dispersed rivals to his crown, listened to reliable aristocrats, kept on good terms with the Church,

AFTER »

The Anglo-Saxons left an enduring imprint on England's language, its culture, and its monarchy.

ENGLAND'S ANGLO-SAXON LEGACY
Most obviously, it is to the Germanic invaders that England (Angle-land) owes its very name and, thanks to the ambitions and talents of its kings, the eventual emergence of a single, monarchical state. England's Anglo-Saxon ancestors also left behind the framework of counties and diocese, and the idea of a jury.

A NEW LANGUAGE IS BORN
The core of the modern English language is made up of words that reach back to Anglo-Saxon times. However, the Viking and **Norman conquests 16–17** » transformed the grammar within which the words were used. By the **12th century 21** » a new Anglo-Saxon-Norse-Norman language, referred to as Middle English, had emerged, and is a language that modern English speakers can just about understand.

The **Bayeux Tapestry**

Probably made in Canterbury, England, the Bayeux Tapestry is both a spectacular work of art and a unique historical source. In a series of embroidered colored pictures, this 11th-century equivalent of a video tells the story of William the Conqueror's invasion of England and victory over King Harold at Hastings.

The events of 1066 changed forever the history of Britain and its monarchy. Historians can draw on a number of contemporary accounts of that momentous year, but no source can match the tapestry manufactured at the command of William the Conqueror's half-brother, Bishop Odo of Bayeux, to adorn his new cathedral at Bayeux, France.

Woven with dyed wool on linen cloth, the Bayeux Tapestry is a remarkable piece of Romanesque artwork, measuring approximately 230 ft (70 m) long and 20 in (50 cm) tall. Many skilled hands must have worked for several months to create a tapestry of this size. It comprises 58 continuous panels, each headed by Latin text explaining what is depicted. The message is unequivocal: Harold, the last Anglo-Saxon monarch, was a usurper, and God and right were on the side of William, Duke of Normandy, in his attempt to win the crown.

In addition to giving the Norman side of the story that culminated with the death of Harold and the defeat of his army on Senlac Hill outside Hastings on October 14, 1066, the tapestry is an invaluable insight into 11th-century life and customs. Its stylized images provide information on subjects such as weaponry, battle tactics, clothing, cooking, and boat-building.

The tapestry's history matches that of its dramatic subject. Having remained virtually unnoticed in Bayeux Cathedral for more than 500 years, the tapestry survived the 16th-century French Wars of Religion and began to attract interest in the early 18th century. French military leader Napoléon Bonaparte displayed it as propaganda when hoping to invade England, but locked it away again when his plan was called off. Strangely, Heinrich Himmler of Germany's Nazi Party coveted the tapestry as a record of "glorious Germanic history," and it was almost taken to Berlin in 1944. It was returned to Bayeux after World War II and is now on display in a special museum.

> **" The English** were in serious **difficulty** after they lost their king… but they still fought on… till the **day drew to a close."**
>
> **MASTER WACE**, NORMAN POET, FROM *ROMAN DE ROU*

Coronation of Harold II
This panel from the Bayeux Tapestry shows Harold II being offered the sword and scepter after being crowned the King of England in 1066. The Latin titulus or inscription reads, "Here sits Harold, King of England. Archbishop Stigand."

BEFORE

Before the Norman Conquest of 1066, most kings spoke Old English, the language of their subjects, and shared their customs and traditions.

IMPOSING FOREIGN MONARCHS
Harold I ≪ 12–13, the last Anglo-Saxon monarch, came from a Sussex family and was Earl of Wessex before being confirmed as king by the nation's elders. The Norman Conquest changed all this, imposing a foreign monarchy and aristocracy on a subservient people.

A NORTHERN EMPIRE
Foreign rule was not unknown in England. The North Sea Empire of King Cnut ≪ 12–13, had included Denmark, Norway, and part of Sweden.

The Normans

The Normans changed the realm of England forever. William I, William II, and Henry I secured its frontiers, reorganized its government, modernized its church, restructured its language, and remolded its architecture, enabling the state to survive the turmoil following Henry I's death.

On the death of Edward the Confessor (see pp.12–13), on January 5, 1066, three men claimed the English crown. Harold Godwinson (1022–66), Earl of Wessex, had received Edward's deathbed nomination, a wish confirmed by the Witan, a council of elders. The Duke of Normandy, William the Bastard (1028–87), claimed that in 1051 Edward had promised him the crown, and that during a visit to Normandy Harold had sworn to uphold this claim. The third candidate, citing an

> "[The King]… **compelled** … nobility … that, if he should die without **male** issue, they would… **accept his daughter.**"
>
> WILLIAM OF MALMESBURY, ON HENRY I, 1127

agreement made almost 30 years earlier, was King Harold III of Norway (1015–66), known as Harold Hadrada (which translates as "hard ruler").

Godwinson was crowned as Harold II on January 6, but his reign was to last only until October. On September 25, he traveled north and smashed Hadrada's invasion force at Stamford Bridge, killing its leader. Three days later, news came of Duke William's landing on the south coast. Covering 240 miles (386 km) in just 13 days, Harold hurried to face the new danger.

The two armies met on Senlac Hill outside Hastings. William's mounted knights prevailed. Harold was slain; the crown was now William's for the taking. Having burned and ravaged his way along the coast, he received the submission of London, and entered the city for his coronation on Christmas Day.

William the Conqueror

The seizure of England made William the Conqueror one of the most powerful men in northern Europe. However, power did not bring peace, and he spent much of his reign defending his possessions both in England and France.

Holding down an English population of between one and two million with just 10,000 Frenchmen was no easy task, and he faced revolts in each of the first four years of his reign. His response included the "Harrying of

100,000 The number of people who died of starvation during the Harrying of the North in 1069–70.

the North"—a set of campaigns in the winter of 1069–70 to subjugate the northern regions and eliminate the possibly of revolt in alliance with a

Church and state
This fanciful miniature from the 13th-century Latin chronicle *Flores Historiarum* (*Flowers of History*) depicts Henry I surrounded by churchmen, highlighting the mutual benefit of a good relationship between King and Church.

of ecclesiastical chroniclers, for Rufus quarreled fiercely with Archbishop Anselm of Canterbury. Foremost among the issues that divided them was the question of "lay investiture," the ceremony by which a new abbot or bishop received their office from the King. Anselm challenged this, claiming that the church was superior to any secular power. However, finding little support among his fellow clergy, Anselm went into exile in 1107.

Curthose objected, of course, and the war between the two lasted until Henry I's victory at Tinchebrai (1106) gave him possession of the Duchy of Normandy, and control over his brother. Though Henry I continued to fight off predators in the Duchy, Robert, at least, was in prison, where he spent the last 28 years of his unhappy life.

Possessing more diplomacy than his predecessor, Henry I agreed with Archbishop Anselm that, while the church could hold the theoretical power of investiture, the King would maintain real power. As the church possessed at least one-quarter of all England's wealth, no king could afford to give it total independence.

Henry I proved an sturdy upholder of law and order. His administrative reforms, associated with Bishop Roger of Salisbury, produced the first references to a key financial institution known as the Exchequer.

After the untimely death of Henry I's only legitimate son, Prince William, the succession question clouded the closing years of his reign. Henry I's anxiety proved fully justified when most of the barons refused to honor their oath to accept his daughter Matilda (see box) as sovereign; the ensuing 19 years were scarred by civil war and lawlessness.

Danish army. William paid the Danes to return home, but destroyed the stock and crops of the northern shires to starve the locals into submission. Further, he pursued a strategy of castle building, fierce reprisals, and seizing estates still in Anglo-Saxon hands. By appointing Frenchmen to important positions in church and state, he slowly brought the country under control.

Uneasy at their neighbor's new power, the King of France and Count of Anjou sought to discomfort and unsettle William in Normandy. The Conqueror's ambitious half-brother Odo and thin-skinned eldest son, Robert Curthose (meaning "Short Breeches"), also turned against William, obliging him to spend more time on the continent than in his new

kingdom. Possibly realizing the difficulty of ruling both Normandy and England, William bequeathed Normandy to Robert and England to his second son, William Rufus.

William Rufus

William II (1056–1100), who ruled England from 1087 until his death, was named "Rufus" thanks to his red hair or complexion, and was by some accounts a chivalrous warrior-king. He presided over a fashionable court where long hair was in vogue. Such a circumstance, coupled with the fact that he never married and produced no illegitimate children, has led some to believe he was gay. It is equally likely that any scandal attached to his name sprang from the imagination

When not squabbling with Anselm, Rufus had to deal with his own elder brother, Robert Curthose. Robert felt he had been short-changed when his father gave England to Rufus, and a long series of conflicts between the two brothers ended only when Robert joined a crusader army in 1096; Rufus lent him 10,000 marks for the venture, accepting Normandy as security. In 1100, the King was killed while hunting in the New Forest. An accident, said the court; divine justice, said the Church.

Henry I and Matilda

Rufus and Robert's much younger brother, Henry Beauclerc (1068–1135,) was the brightest and best educated of the Norman kings. He also had a reputation for ruthless brutality and lasciviousness, fathering at least 20 illegitimate children.

Upon Rufus's mysterious death, he immediately seized the Treasury at Winchester and two days later had himself crowned Henry I. Robert

AFTER »

After the Normans came the far more numerous Plantagenets, who held the throne in a long succession of 14 kings.

ESTABLISHING A NATION
Starting from the northern kingdom that had been secured by their predecessors, the **Plantagenet kings 20–21 »** expanded their realm into Ireland, completed the conquest of Wales, came close to adding Scotland to their domains, and challenged for supremacy in France.

AN END TO RULE BY FOREIGNERS
By the time of the reign of **Richard II 21 »**, the monarchy was fully reintegrated, with both the nation and the court using Middle English. This was the language of the poet Geoffrey Chaucer (1343–1400), known as the Father of English Literature.

The **Plantagenets**

The Plantagenets occupied the English throne from 1154–1399, longer than any other royal house. Under monarchs of varying ability, the family clung to power through such crises as the signing of the Magna Carta, the Black Death, and long wars with Scotland and in France.

BEFORE

The Plantagenet line can be traced to 821, to a couple named Tertullus and Petronilla, of Rennes, in Brittany.

COUNTS OF ANJOU AND PLANTAGENETS
Ingelger (c.850–899), son of Tertullus and Petronilla, became the first Count of Anjou (where the name "Angevin" stems from). The title passed to Fulk the Red and on to Geoffrey of Anjou (1113–51). His marriage to Matilda, daughter of **Henry I of England ‹‹ 16–17** and his wife of Anglo-Saxon descent, produced a bloodline combining Anjou, Normandy, and Wessex. However, the family did not use the Plantagenet surname for another 200 years.

The Plantagenet monarchy was one of extreme contrasts. The family gave England some of its most able kings: Henry II (1133–89); Edward I (1239–1307); Edward III (1312–77); and the great chivalric hero, Richard the Lionheart (1157–99), but also threw up the infamous John (1167–1216) and the tragically dim-witted Edward II (1284–1327).

The Angevin Empire
As Count of Anjou, the Plantagenet Henry II, son of Empress Matilda (see pp.16–17), was master of the Angevin Empire, which stretched from Hadrian's Wall to the Pyrenees. The lands had been acquired through marriage to Eleanor of Aquitaine (see pp.18–19) in 1152 and succession to the throne of England two years later.

A man of boundless energy, Henry II ruled from 1154–89, spending 20 years expanding his empire by occupying Ireland, driving into Wales, Scotland, and Brittany, and forcing the Count of Toulouse into submission. Meanwhile, at home, he regularized England's Common Law in a network of courts, and strengthened central government.

Coronation of Richard the Lionheart
This 14th-century illustration depicts the coronation of Richard the Lionheart on September 3, 1189, in Westminster Abbey, London. Richard lived much of his 10-year reign away from the country, spending only six months in England, according to some sources.

But it was all too good to last. The King's reputation was damaged when a conflict over the entitlements of the church led to the murder in 1170 of Thomas Becket, Archbishop of Canterbury, in the cathedral itself. The martyred Becket eventually gained sainthood while Henry's reputation plummeted still further. During his final years, he raised excessive taxes, made corrupt appointments, and faced a series of devastating rebellions led by his wife and truculent sons.

Lionheart and Lackland
Richard I, the Lionheart, who reigned from 1189–99, was a legend in his own lifetime. A generous yet fearless warrior who led the successful Third Crusade (1189–92), he also ensured England was well governed during his absence, and managed, more or less, to hang on to his massive Angevin inheritance. In the end, his bravery was his undoing: scorning to wear his chain mail, he was hit by a crossbow bolt during the siege of Châlus; the wound turned gangrenous and, having forgiven the lad who fired the bolt, he died in his mother Eleanor's arms. Even before he was crowned in 1199, the standing of King John (bitingly known as "Lackland" and "Softsword"), was tarnished

The body of Becket is laid to rest

Christ welcomes Becket into heaven

Murderous knights disturb Becket at prayer

Becket is assassinated while facing an altar in Canterbury Cathedral

French Reliquary Casket, 1180–90
Fragments of what were believed to be Becket's hair, clothing, and bones were contained in this casket, made in Limoges. The scene depicts the assassination of Becket, an event that shocked the Christian world, earned Becket martyrdom, and caused the cathedral to become a pilgrimage site.

"**Uneasy** lies the head that **wears** the **crown.**"
WILLIAM SHAKESPEARE, *HENRY IV, PART II*, 1597

by opportunistic rebellions against his ailing father, Henry II, and absent brother, Richard the Lionheart. As king, John fell out with the pope and with the baronage over his capricious behavior and loss of most of the Angevin Empire. As a result, a year before his death, John was obliged to sign the Magna Carta (Great Charter, see box) that put the monarch unequivocally under the law.

King and parliament
Ascending the throne in 1216 at the age of nine, the naive, peace-loving Henry III (1207–72) was out of his depth throughout his long and troubled reign. Attempts to win back lost French lands came to nothing and, in 1258, he was forced to accept limits on royal authority set out in the Provisions of Oxford. During the Barons' War (1264–68), Henry III's own brother-in-law, Simon de Montfort (see box), virtually took control of the throne, and Henry III held on to his position only thanks to the dashing exploits of Prince Edward, his son and heir.

Crowned in 1274, Edward I sought consent from the newly formed parliament to approve his taxation. He further enhanced parliament's standing by using it to promote statutes to clean up local government. All monarchs had been expected to govern with the consent of their peers since the 5th century. However, the emergence of the Commons meant that this consent might now stretch to all those with political and economic influence.

First mentioned in the 1230s, parliaments were large gatherings at court to discuss affairs of state and show support for government policy, especially taxation. In 1264, rebel leader Simon de Montfort 6th Earl of Leicester (c.1208–65) called a parliament attended by four knights from each shire. The following year, he invited two prominent citizens from major towns to join the knights of the shire (Commons), alongside barons and senior churchmen (Lords). The assembly possibly met in the Chapter House of Westminster Abbey (left). Soon, such parliamentary gatherings became the practice, giving rise to the claim that de Montfort's assembly marked the birth of modern parliaments.

Battle of Crécy from Froissart's Chronicle
This illustration from the 15th-century chronicle by Jean Froissart depicts a scene from the Battle of Crécy, fought during the Hundred Years' War. Edward III won a crushing victory over the French on August 26, 1346.

Edward I is primarily remembered as a warrior. In addition to going on crusade, he fought fierce (and costly) campaigns to hold on to Aquitaine. Nearer home, he subdued Wales, giving its people his eldest son as their prince, and made attempts to bring Scotland under the English crown. This left his pitifully inept son, Edward II, crowned in 1308, with a bitter legacy of debt and an unwinnable war with the Scots.

A lack of political competence and reliance on unsuitable male favorites drained any support Edward II might have had. The invasion in 1326 by his wife and her lover, Roger Mortimer, found the King virtually friendless. He was deposed and imprisoned in Berkeley Castle, where he was murdered most foully.

War, plague, and revolt
Edward III, crowned in 1327, restored Plantagenet prestige through military victories. In the early years of the Hundred Years' War (1337–1453), he vanquished the French at Crécy (1346)

and captured the French king at Poitiers (1356). Abandoning attempts to rule Scotland, he ushered in long years of domestic peace in England. Edward III also made use of Justices of the Peace—unpaid royal servants, such as knights, who, since 1195, had been responsible for maintaining law and order in their own locality. Edward III's encouragement of them strengthened the bond between king and gentry.

Working with parliament, Edward III's government had ridden out the pressing effects of the arrival in 1348 of a seaborne bubonic plague pandemic,

3,500,000 Estimated number of English deaths caused by Bubonic Plague (Black Death), 1348–49.

known as the Black Death. The disease caused a steep and sudden population decline, resulting in labor shortages, price rises, and social unrest.

Edward III's son, Edward, the Black Prince (1330–76), died before his father so Edward III's grandson, Richard II, (1367–1400) was crowned in 1377. Unfortunately, Richard's arrogant behavior sabotaged his grandfather's achievements. Having bravely outfaced the rebels in the 1381 Peasants' Revolt (see pp.22–23), Richard II developed an overinflated opinion of the status of monarchy, sharply at odds with the views of his people. He lost control of the government around 1387–88. Richard II's cousin, Henry Bolingbroke (1367–1413), crowned Henry IV in 1399 (see p.24), finally removed Richard II from the throne and had him thrown in prison, where he was murdered the following year.

In 1215, there was no adult member of royalty around who could oppose King John. As a result, on June 15 of that year, the King's baronial opponents forced him to sign the Magna Carta (Great Charter, below), a document asserting inalienable rights and basic liberties to be enjoyed by "all freemen of the realm." The Magna Carta served to inspire others rejecting high-handed royal behavior in the 17th century and, a century later, in the United States.

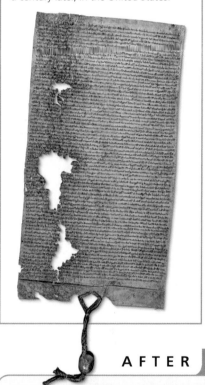

AFTER

During the troubled 15th century, when England was beset by troubles abroad and at home, the name "Plantagenet" acquired an almost mythical status.

EMPHASIZING HISTORIC LINKS
The family name "Plantagenet" was first adopted by **Richard of York 24–25** ≫, the great-grandson of Edward III. The father of the future **Edward IV 24–25** ≫ and **Richard III 24–25** ≫, and a key player in the so-called **Wars of the Roses 26–27** ≫, he probably called himself Plantagenet to emphasize his link to Geoffrey of Anjou and the 12th-century Royal Family. In the next century the name was retrospectively being applied to Henry II and all his descendants.

YORK'S POISONED CHALICE
Even though **Henry VII 28–29** ≫ was descended from the Plantagenets, he scorned to use the name adopted by his rivals in the House of York. Instead, he founded a new dynasty, **the Tudors 28–29** ≫.

The **Peasants' Revolt**

Arising out of the labor shortage following the Black Death, the Peasants' Revolt of 1381 tested the mettle of young Richard II. His brave but duplicitous behavior in the face of grave danger led to the suppression of the revolt.

The widespread mortality brought on by the Black Death, or plague, produced a shortage of labor. Accordingly, the simple law of supply and demand led to wage increases and calls for an end to the unpaid feudal labor required of serfs. A Statute of Laborers (1351) had some success in keeping wages at pre-plague levels, but discontent mounted as fresh outbreaks of the plague reduced the pool of labor still further. Meanwhile, England was engaged in the unsuccessful and badly run Hundred Years' War with France. In order to fund this prolonged battle, Richard II introduced several unfair taxes, including the poll tax of 1380, which was the final straw for the peasants.

Early in the summer of 1381, the people of Kent and Essex, two of England's more prosperous counties, rose in revolt. Lawyers and grasping landlords were slain, and legal documents burned, before the rebel army advanced to London. There, they joined the mob to open prisons and destroy the property of John of Gaunt, the King's uncle, and other unpopular magnates. The 14-year-old Richard II, stuck in the Tower of London with his ministers and a small troop of soldiers, watched in horror.

On June 14, Richard left the Tower with his bodyguard to talk to the opposition. He heard their demands and issued charters declaring the abolition of serfdom. On hearing this, many of the revolutionaries turned for home. Still, when the Tower's gates were opened to readmit the King, hundreds of rebels poured in. They dragged out and beheaded Lord Chancellor Simon Sudbury, Lord High Treasurer Robert Hales, and a handful of other officials. Richard met the remaining rebels at Smithfield the following day. After their charismatic leader, Wat Tyler, was killed in a scuffle, his followers dispersed. In the aftermath of the revolt, Richard revoked his concessions and ordered the rebel leaders to be rounded up and hanged.

" ... the time is come... in which ye may (if ye will) cast off the yoke of bondage, and recover liberty."

JOHN BALL, RADICAL ENGLISH PRIEST, IN A SERMON TO THE REVOLTING PEASANTS AT BLACKHEATH, JUNE 12, 1381

Pacifying the rebellious
This section from Jean Froissart's *Chronicles* depicts Richard II meeting the rebels in June 1381 to discuss their demands. The King waits in the boat while two negotiators speak to the crowd. In the background, rebels can be seen capturing the Tower of London.

Lancaster and York

The deposition of Richard II split the Plantagenets into factions, notably the Lancastrians and Yorkists. While their confrontations devastated much of the old aristocracy, thanks in part to the genius of William Shakespeare, they also gave us the monarchy's great hero, Henry V, and its villain, Richard III.

As England's wealth grew and its system of government became more sophisticated, the role of the monarch required an increasingly broad range of skills. He needed to balance the factions of powerful nobles, manage parliament, keep the gentry and merchant classes on his side, oversee the machinery of central government, and lead the country in times of war, even riding into battle. Men like Henry V (1387–1422), and, to a lesser extent, Edward IV (1442–83), handled the job well. For a man of lesser abilities, like the feeble Henry VI (1421–71), it was all too much. Without a strong monarch to restrain them, the ambitious aristocracy descended into an orgy of bloodletting.

Lancaster ascendant

Having seized the throne from Richard II and arranged for his murder, Henry Bolingbroke, Duke of Lancaster, was crowned Henry IV in 1399 (see p.21). He then spent the rest of his troubled reign fighting to hold on to his stolen prize. Rebellions came from the Earl of Huntingdon, Richard II's half-brother, and from the Percy Family of Northumberland, who had helped Henry IV to the crown. Scots and Welsh, eager to take advantage of England's troubles, made ready allies. Further difficulties arose from money squabbles with parliament, and from a radical new sect, known as Lollards, who wanted to reform western Christianity.

Once an admired crusader knight, Henry IV ended his days a sick and exhausted wreck. When he finally died in 1413, his son Henry V was crowned

BEFORE

The division of the houses of York and Lancaster can be traced back to 1386.

A KING DEPOSED, AN HEIR CHEATED
Richard II, son of **Edward III's ‹‹ 20–21** firstborn male, had no children. In 1386, he declared Roger Mortimer, Earl of March and a descendant of Edward III's second son, his heir. Henry Bolingbroke, Duke of Lancaster, and descended from Edward III's third son, deposed Richard II and took the throne as **Henry IV ‹‹ 21**. At this point, the Mortimer side of the family picked up the Duke of York title.

1ST EARL OF WARWICK 1428–71

RICHARD NEVILLE

Nicknamed "Kingmaker" a century after his death, Neville was an astute, wealthy man. In 1455, he sided with the Yorkists to defeat Henry VI. Six years later he helped Edward of York to the throne as Edward IV. In 1469, he captured the King, then let him go again. He rebelled once more in 1470 (joining with the Lancastrians), exiling Edward IV and restoring the now insane Henry VI. Neville's power-broking finally ended when Edward IV came back to England and slew him at the Battle of Barnet in 1471.

Contemporary portraits of contrasting kings
These portraits, taken from oil-on-panel paintings, depict Henry V, on the left, and Richard III. Henry V was a much admired monarch, while Richard III, final king of the House of York and the last of the Plantagenets, has few defenders.

king, and proved to be arguably England's most able monarch. A meticulous nationalist, he insisted that official documents were written in English, not French or Latin, and he encouraged the adoration of English saints, such as Thomas of Canterbury (see p.20) and Henry's holy predecessor, Edward the Confessor (see p.13).

In 1414, Henry V dealt swiftly and efficiently with a Lollard rising, and a plot to put Edmund Mortimer on the throne in 1415. He then decided to test his right to the French throne in battle. Henry's success is the stuff of legend. He trounced a much larger French force at Agincourt, conquered Normandy, and, by the Treaty of Troyes in 1420, was declared heir to the throne of France. Where this would have led, we shall never know; dysentery took his life on August 31, 1422.

Lancaster descendant

Henry's son by Catherine of Valois, daughter of Charles VI of France, was nine months old when he ascended the throne as Henry VI—the youngest age of succession of any English monarch. A few weeks later, he was declared King of France, but until Henry came of age in 1437, his uncle, John, Duke of Bedford, governed his realm as the head of a regency council.

Things went well until 1629, when visionary and military commander Joan of Arc (1412–31) instigated a French fight-back. Matters at home and abroad slipped from bad to worse when the pious, peace-loving, and wholly apolitical Henry VI took the reins of government into his own hands and, by 1453, the kingdom

Battle of Agincourt 1415
This illustration, taken from the 1484 manuscript "Vigils of King Charles VII" by Martial d'Auvergne, shows Henry V outnumbered by, yet victorious over, the French forces at Agincourt during the Hundred Years' War (1337–1453).

was in chaos. A serious rebellion led by Sussexman Jack Cade had been put down only with great bloodshed, and virtually all England's French possessions had been lost. The King, who had taken a hugely unpopular French wife, Margaret of Anjou, failed to control his squabbling lords. To cap it all, at this point Henry VI suffered a mental breakdown (possibly due to schizophrenia). Civil war flared and, in 1461, the 19-year-old Earl of March (1442–83), who, technically, had a better claim to the throne than Henry VI, was crowned Edward IV, while the deposed King was imprisoned in the Tower of London.

and never seen again. The slaughter of adult nobility was commonplace in the later 15th century, but the murder of children was not, and Gloucester, crowned Richard III in 1483, faced rebellions. He survived for only two years, then became the last English king to die in battle. The victor of the Battle of Bosworth, Henry Tudor (see pp.28–29), a grandson of Catherine of Valois, supposedly found Richard III's crown in a thorn bush and immediately put it on.

> ## "What **misery**… this region hath **suffered** by the **division** of Lancaster and York."
>
> EDWARD HALL, FROM HIS *CHRONICLE*, 1548

York divided

Edward IV was a tall, pleasure-loving warrior king who, having won his throne on the battlefield, in 1469–71 came close to losing it the same way. He fell out with the overmighty 1st Earl of Warwick (see box), who then dragged Henry VI out of the Tower and put him on the throne again. But the mentally deranged King inspired no one. After further conflict, Henry VI and his only son were murdered in 1471, and Edward IV retook his crown. He governed well and has sometimes

4 **The number of kings who were murdered or died a violent death between 1399–1485.**

been credited with founding a "new monarchy." But his marriage to a commoner, Elizabeth Woodville, stirred baronial resentment, and his early death brought more bloodshed.

Edward IV's son, the 12-year-old Edward V, reigned for 78 days in 1483 but was never crowned. He and his younger brother Richard of York were sent to the Tower by their uncle, Richard of Gloucester (1452–85),

AFTER

The death of Richard III opened the way for reconciliation between the houses of York and Lancaster.

TUDORS UNITE TWO HOUSES
Henry Tudor 28–29 》, Richard III's conqueror and a distant relative of the Lancasters, brought reconciliation. Now crowned as Henry VII, he married Richard III's niece, Elizabeth of York. Thus were the symbolic white rose of York and the red rose of Lancaster brought together to form the red-and-white rose of **The Tudors**.

THE KING IN THE CAR PARK
Richard III's remains were lost for 500 years. In 2013, however, after a dig in a car park once the site of Greyfriars Priory Church, it was confirmed with DNA evidence that the King had been rediscovered. Despite his reputation as a child-murderer, in 2015, thousands of people watched his body carried in procession to Leicester Cathedral to be reburied.

The **Wars** of the **Roses**

Between 1455 and 1487, England was afflicted with chronic instability as supporters of two rival branches of the royal House of Plantagenet fought for power, influence, and the greatest prize of all—the Crown.

At the heart of the conflict lay competition for the throne between descendants of Edward III's second and third sons, who belonged to the house of York (represented by the white rose) and Lancaster (represented by the red rose) respectively. The year 1455 is generally seen as the start of the wars, although violence had broken out before this. The throne was occupied by the Lancastrian, Henry VI, but due to his mental infirmity, Richard Duke of York acted as Lord Protector—the de facto ruler.

The term "war," in fact, inaccurately describes what followed. Over the next 30 years, there were only 60 weeks of campaigning. Other than at Towton, the armies were small and loss of life not particularly heavy. On the other hand, numerous nobles lost their lives, two kings were murdered, and a third died in battle.

The first phase of fighting (1455–1461) saw Henry VI fall into Yorkist hands. Margaret, his queen, raised an army and liberated him, but after the battle at Towton (1461), which was the bloodiest ever on British soil, Henry and Margaret fled to Scotland, leaving Edward IV to be crowned king. Henry was recaptured in 1465 and killed following the Battle of Tewkesbury (1471).

Edward IV's rule brought 12 years of peace. Fighting was rekindled after his death in 1483 when his brother Richard imprisoned and allegedly killed his 12-year-old son and heir, Edward V, and crowned himself Richard III. The coup was so badly received that when Henry Tudor (see pp.25, 28) landed with a small force in Wales, he gained enough support to defeat and kill Richard III in battle. As Henry VII, he defended his crown at the battle of Stoke (1487), which marked the end of the Wars of the Roses. Tudor propagandists later exaggerated the misery of the wars to strengthen loyalty to the new ruling family.

> **"**…what execrable plagues this famous region hath suffered by the **division and dissension** of the renowned houses of **Lancaster and York."**
>
> **EDWARD HALL,** LAWYER AND HISTORIAN, 1548

The Battle of Barnet
This 15th-century painting shows Edward IV (seen wearing a crown) piercing Richard Neville, leader of the Lancastrian army, with his lance at the crucial Battle of Barnet in 1471. This battle, along with the subsequent Battle of Tewkesbury, secured the throne for Edward IV.

The **Tudors**

The Tudors were the first recognizably modern royal dynasty, helping to explain their enduring popularity with novelists, playwrights, and filmmakers. Artists and writers have also been drawn to the immense personalities of Henry VIII and Elizabeth I, two giants on the tapestry of English monarchy.

Arguably the most colorful of all the royal dynasties, the Tudors steered the country through its transformation from a late medieval state to an early modern one, from 1485–1603. Moreover, the Tudors were fortunate that their period of power coincided with an unprecedented flowering of arts and culture, especially in literature and the theater, with which they have been associated ever since.

Episcopal flattery
Above the island castle of England, guarded by a dragon, lion, and greyhound (all Tudor symbols) the Bishop of Chichester's couplets praising Henry VIII lie between the roses of Lancaster, York, and Tudor.

◀◀ **BEFORE**

In the 814 years that elapsed from the accession of King Alfred in 871 to the arrival of the first Tudor monarch in 1485, the English throne had only once been occupied by a woman.

DISPUTED ACCESSION
Stephen of Blois ◀◀ 17 disputed the right of his cousin, **Matilda ◀◀ 17**, to accede to the throne. Though she fought back, Stephen seized the crown. Under the Tudors, the resistance to a female monarch receded when, for almost half the period of Tudor rule, a woman wore the English crown (**Mary I** and then **Elizabeth I**), setting a strong precedent.

Without a doubt, the England that Elizabeth I handed on to her Scottish successor in 1603 bore little resemblance to the England that her grandfather, Henry Tudor (1457–1509), had seized just 114 years earlier (see p.23).

Father and son

Crowned Henry VII in 1485, Henry Tudor laid the foundations of the renowned regime. It was not an easy task. The Yorkists (see pp.24–25) still hoped to make a comeback based on two pretenders: Lambert Simnel, who claimed to be a son of Edward IV's brother, and Perkin Warbeck, who said he was the younger of the two princes imprisoned in the Tower (see p.25). Simnel was eventually pardoned and permitted to work in the royal kitchens, but Warbeck was executed in 1497.

By encouraging trade and clamping down on overmighty subjects, by 1500, Henry VII's reign was relatively secure. He bolstered his position by the marriages of his daughter, Margaret, to James IV of Scotland (see p.31) and his son, Arthur, to the Spanish princess, Catherine of Aragon.

Few reigns were as dramatic as that of Henry VII's second son, Henry VIII (1491–1547), who became heir to the throne on the early death of Arthur in 1502.

Handsome, intelligent, well-educated, athletic, and musical, he ascended the throne as the ideal Renaissance prince. He left it 38 years later a bloated parody of his former self. With papal permission, he married Catherine, Arthur's widow, and while the highly skilled Cardinal Wolsey managed the day-to-day business of government, the young king enjoyed himself with a short war in France, tournaments, hunting, and music- and love-making. However, when Catherine bore a daughter, Mary, but not the longed-for son and

The epitome of majesty
This portrait of Henry VIII, age 49, was painted at the time of his marriage to Anne of Cleves by Hans Holbein the Younger. The message behind it is unequivocal: cross this man at your peril.

Ruins of Fountains Abbey, North Yorkshire
Ostensibly disillusioned with monastic behavior, Henry VIII and Thomas Cromwell dissolved the monasteries for fiscal gain. Fountains Abbey was the hub of a thriving Cistercian business enterprise.

Following the successes of the long reign of Elizabeth I, which glowed all the brighter in light of the ensuing turmoil, reservations about having a woman on the throne evaporated.

LONG LIVE THE QUEENS
In the 412 years between Elizabeth I's death and 2015, **four women have worn the crown** (Mary II, Anne, Victoria, and Elizabeth II) for a total of 144 years. The decision—enshrined in the **Succession to the Crown Act**—to give **males and females equal right of succession** from March 26, 2015 means that this statistic is likely to rise.

heir, Henry revealed the ruthlessness that would besmirch his reign. The Pope refused to grant him a divorce, so he employed a lawyer, Thomas Cromwell, to use Parliament to break with Rome and establish the Church of England, headed by the King. As England began its participation in the Protestant Reformation, all opposition was crushed, monasteries were dissolved, and their wealth diverted to the royal coffers.

Anne Boleyn, Henry's next wife, gave birth to another daughter, Elizabeth. Four more wives gave Henry just one son between them when, finally, in 1537, Jane Seymour produced Prince

fatally ill, Northumberland married his son to Lady Jane Grey, a great-niece of Henry VIII, and had her proclaimed queen. The coup was foiled by popular opinion—Northumberland was executed in 1553, as was Jane in 1554.

"Calais" engraved on her heart

Crowned Mary I in 1553, the Queen alienated many of her subjects with a campaign to restore Roman Catholicism that involved burning 300 Protestants. Her deeply unpopular marriage to a foreign king, Philip II of Spain, was childless. And finally, under her reign England's last possession on continental soil, Calais, was lost in an unnecessary

in every church in the land. How could she ever be replaced? An explicit reply never issued from Elizabeth I, but she shrewdly used her unmarried status and her nickname, the "Virgin Queen."

Elizabeth I's persecution of dissenters was moderate, too, and she executed Roman Catholics for the crime of treason, not for professing their faith.

Ably assisted by councillors, such as Sir William Cecil, Sir Nicholas Bacon, and Sir Francis Walsingham, when possible, she also avoided confrontation with her parliaments and in foreign affairs. An exception to this was when parliament threatened to withhold funds until her marriage was settled (see p.33). She let loose on them her formidable powers of rhetoric and made it clear that the well-being of her realm was her priority, and to marry or not was her private affair.

In the end, though, years of tension with the Roman Catholic powers of Spain and France spilled over into war.

1554 portrait of Queen Mary I
History is rarely kind to losers, and so it was with Mary Tudor, also known as Bloody Mary. Bigoted and devoid of charisma, she lacked the sensibility to realize how bitterly her people hated her austere Catholicism, her Spanish marriage, and—eventually—herself.

> "[King Henry VIII] is much **handsomer** than any sovereign in Christendom … **very fair** and his whole frame **admirably proportioned.**"

A VENETIAN VISITOR TO LONDON, 1519

Edward. However, Jane died days later. Further expensive wars with France and Scotland left the realm despoiled, exploited, and, by the time Henry VIII died, riven by religious strife. Edward VI (1537–53) was just 10 years old when his father passed away. Henry VIII had left government in the hands of his

12,000 The number of monks, canons, friars, and nuns thrown out of their dwellings when Henry VIII dissolved the monasteries.

son's maternal uncle, the Duke of Somerset, and a 16-man council. The Duke and Archbishop Thomas Cranmer sought to make the Church of England wholly Protestant, encouraging iconoclasm and sanctioning an English Prayer Book, causing much discontent.

In 1549, Somerset was removed from office by John Dudley. Now Duke of Northumberland, Dudley stabilized government finances and, encouraged by the young king, pressed ahead with the conversion of the country to Protestantism. When Edward VI became

war with France in support of Spain. As Mary I lay dying of stomach cancer, she declared that the word "Calais" would be found engraved on her heart.

The shift from Catholicism

If sterility was the keynote of the reign of Mary I, the reign of her sister, Elizabeth I (see pp.32–33), who ruled from 1558–1603, was caution. Raised in the Protestant faith, Elizabeth steered the Church of England away from Catholicism toward a moderate Protestantism that blended the new faith with Roman Catholic hallmarks, such as ecclesiastical vestments and bishops. England's relatively swift shift from Roman Catholic to Protestant had left many of her subjects mourning familiar practices and beliefs, above all, the cult of the Virgin Mary, whose statue had stood

Queen of the seas
This rare English gold coin dating to 1558–1603 bears an image of Elizabeth I and a warship. It was during the reign of the last Tudor monarch that England began to consider itself a major naval power.

The spark was ignited in 1587 when Elizabeth I executed her Roman Catholic cousin, Mary Queen of Scots (1542–87), for continually plotting to overthrow her.

The highlight of the Queen's reign came in 1588, when her navy, aided by stormy weather, prevented invasion by the supposedly invincible Spanish Armada. Thereafter, however, victories were difficult to come by. The Treasury was drained by costly campaigns at sea, in Ireland, and in support of European Protestantism. An economic downturn accompanied by meager harvests brought about widespread poverty. Together, these factors conspired to bring the reign of "Gloriana," also fondly known as "Good Queen Bess," to an end with a whimper rather than a blaze of glory.

DECISIVE MOMENT

THE CHURCH OF ENGLAND

In 1521, Pope Leo X gave Henry VIII the title *Fidei Defensor* (Defender of the Faith), the initial letters of which can still be seen on British coins. The accolade was in recognition of a book the King had written defending the position of the Roman Catholic Church. In the light of this, Henry's subsequent break with Rome and the establishment of the Church of England with himself as its Supreme Head, was all the more startling.

Indeed, the break with Rome was one of the few truly revolutionary events in English history. Henry VIII's move paved the way for English Protestantism and added considerably to his prestige.

As Supreme Head of the Church of England, a title conferred by the 1535 Act of Supremacy, Henry VIII acquired vast wealth and a quasi-spiritual authority. It was no coincidence that around the same time he was being addressed as "Your Majesty"—the first British monarch to be given this style.

Persecutor persecuted
Antoine Caron's painting records the arrest and execution for treason (1535) of Lord Chancellor Sir Thomas More. A highly respected scholar, More had also been a tireless pursuer of Protestants.

Born 1533 Died 1603

Elizabeth I

"I have the body but of a **weak and feeble woman**, but... the heart... of a king."

ELIZABETH I AT TILBURY, 1588

Queen Elizabeth I was born into a world of danger and intrigue. The birth of a daughter was a disappointment to her father, Henry VIII (see pp.28–29), and, by the time Elizabeth was two and a half years old, her mother, Anne Boleyn, was executed for adultery. Officially bastardized, Elizabeth learned not to draw attention to herself until her legitimacy was restored in 1543.

The next trauma occurred in 1547–49, when Thomas Seymour, three times her age, attempted to seduce her with the connivance of her stepmother, Catherine Parr. If this had any effect on Elizabeth's decision to shun marriage, we shall never know.

Journey from captivity to throne

Elizabeth's position was precarious during the reign of her Roman Catholic half-sister, Mary I (1516–58), and Elizabeth was imprisoned in the Tower of London on suspicion of complicity in plots to overthrow Mary. Nothing was proved, and so she was moved to less harsh custody in Woodstock, Oxfordshire. Happily for Elizabeth, the dying Mary recognized her as heir to the throne and she acceded peacefully in November 1558.

So who was this 25-year-old woman whom the people of London welcomed with unstinting joy as her coronation procession wound its way through

the streets to Westminster Abbey in January 1559? Contemporaries' overriding impression was one of majesty. Elizabeth, a born actor, carried herself like a queen. Stately and regal on all occasions, she could be capricious, waspish even. When annoyed, her comments were made all the sharper when delivered in her high, shrill voice. As she aged, she disguised the

Armada Portrait, 1588

This arresting portrayal, attributed to George Gower (1540–96), depicts Elizabeth I after her rout of the Spanish Armada. Surrounded by symbols of imperial majesty, she exudes power and magnificence.

English warships confront the Spanish Armada
The sea was described as "groaning under the weight" of the Spanish fleet, which had been sent to convey troops to attack and invade England in 1588. The Armada's decisive defeat was Elizabeth I's finest hour.

ravages of time and smallpox under a thick layer of ceruse (a poisonous makeup blend of white lead and vinegar), yet the queen was no painted doll. She rode fearlessly and with skill, frightening many with her daring. On the dance floor she was as nimble as she was tireless. Inside her active body lurked an equally active brain. Elizabeth received lessons from expert tutors in grammar, the various branches of mathematics, music, theology, history, philosophy, and literature. She was by all accounts an extremely quick learner and, by the age of 11, was fluent in French, Welsh, and Spanish, as well as Classical Latin and Greek.

"Beggar-woman and single"

After the 29-year-old Elizabeth had survived an attack of smallpox, many were certain that she would marry in order to secure the succession. Her reasons for never doing so remain something of a mystery. She observed from her sister's reign how marriage to a foreigner could alienate her subjects; she also knew that marriage to an Englishman would arouse jealousy and disputes. Thus, likely for a number of reasons, she chose to remain single, but this was risky. Had she died before 50, instability would have ensued while a successor was searched for, throwing the realm into turmoil.

In 1559, the queen came closest to marrying when she fell in love with Robert Dudley. When his wife, Amy, died after falling down stairs, however, tongues wagged that she been murdered to free her husband for Elizabeth. It was clearly impossible, under such circumstances, for a marriage to go ahead, but she remained close friends with Dudley for another 10 years.

Other candidates for Elizabeth's hand were very much political. Among those she considered, or pretended to consider, included Philip II of Spain (her sister's widower), King Eric XIV of Sweden, Archduke Charles of Austria, Duke Henry of Anjou, and Francis, his brother. But true to her words of 1563—"beggar-woman and single, far rather than queen and married"—she turned them all down. After all, she quipped, she was already married: to the people of England.

Her image as "Gloriana" was tied in with what is now seen as a Golden Age. Elizabeth I was at the heart of this national awakening, taking pride in the achievements of men like the naval commander Sir Francis Drake (c.1540–96), who circumnavigated the globe in a single expedition. She served as patron as well as inspiration in the literary arts, too. The English language had never before been as richly used as it was in the works of William Shakespeare (1564–1616), Christopher Marlowe (1471–77), and poet Edmund Spenser (1552/53–99), to name a few, who were working at the height of their creative powers.

Though her splendor was fading fast toward the end, she could still stir the hearts of her people. "Though God hath raised me high," she flattered in her final speech to Parliament, "yet this I count the glory of my crown, that I have reigned with your loves." Elizabeth I died a much-loved queen. The high level of public lamentation on her death was unprecedented.

Elizabeth I arrives at Nonsuch Palace, Surrey
Built by Henry VIII, sold by Mary I to the Earl of Arundel, and returned to Elizabeth I in 1590, Nonsuch Palace marks the peak of all Tudor building projects.

WRITER AND POET (1564–1616)

WILLIAM SHAKESPEARE

Son of a Roman Catholic Stratford-upon-Avon businessman, William Shakespeare was a member of the Lord Chamberlain's Men, Elizabeth I's favorite theater company. English theater flourished under Elizabeth I's patronage, and Shakespeare, considered the greatest writer in the English language, is known to have written at least 38 plays, and 154 sonnets and longer poems. His brilliant comedies, tragedies, and histories explore the universal human experience. His play, *Twelfth Night, or What You Will*, was written specifically to be performed at Elizabeth I's court for the close of the Christmas season, possibly in 1601.

Monarchs of Scotland

**That the land between the Shetland Isles and the Tees River became a single state owes
less to geography or anthropology than to the dynamism of some ambitious monarchs.
Over centuries, a succession of heroes and rogues forged the Scottish nation.**

« BEFORE

Though invaded by the Romans on
several occasions and subjected to
legion garrisons in the south and
east, Scotland never became part
of the Roman Empire.

MERGING PEOPLES
For much of the early medieval period, it was
a land of tribal regions and small realms, so
Scotland's emergence as a single kingdom was
slow. Among these small realms, it was the
Kingdom of the Dál Riata ("land of the
Scots") that absorbed all the others, including the
native Picts. A people shrouded in mystery,
the Picts slowly merged with the Scots of the
Dál Riata, and disappeared from history.

ENIGMATIC ORIGINS
The origin of the Scots (or Scotii) of Dál Riata
is unknown. They spoke the same Irish Gaelic
as the **Scotii of Ireland**, and shared a
cultural heritage. If they moved from Ireland to
the Western Isles of Scotland or not is unclear.

King Kenneth mac Alpin,
(c.841–859), and his successors
gradually extended the realm
of the Scots of Dàl Riata until it
covered most of present-day eastern
Scotland from the Tweed River to
the Central Highlands.

The making of a kingdom
The Alpin dynasty ended with
Malcolm II (1005–34), who, in 1019,
consolidated his southern frontier by
defeating Uhtred, Earl of Northumbria.
The new ruling house, Dunkeld, began
in 1034 with Duncan I (1001–40) and
continued in 1040 with Macbeth
(c.1005–57). Malcolm III (1034–93),

the next king, moved
Scotland closer to
mainstream Europe
through contact with
England's Norman
conquerors and
through his marriage
to Margaret, an Anglo-
Saxon princess who was
later made a saint. Four of
St. Margaret's sons wore the Scottish
crown in succession, but it was her
youngest child, David I, born in 1083,
and who ruled from 1124–53, who
was arguably the most capable of all
Scotland's monarchs. David I used
Anglo-Norman barons (including two

Great Seal of Alexander II
Rejecting monarchical solidarity,
Alexander II sided with the
barons who had rebelled
against England's King John
(see pp. 20–21) and, in 1216,
drove his forces as far south as
Dover on the Channel coast.

future Royal Families, the Bruces
and the Stewarts) to build up a
feudal-style regime. William I (1143–
1214), "the Lion," crowned in 1165,
continued this process and extended
royal authority into Galloway and the
far north. Alexander II (1198–1249),
who was crowned in 1214, defeated

Castle of history now a medieval ruin
The "Honors of Scotland," the oldest crown jewels
in the British Isles, were smuggled out of Dunnottar
Castle to keep them from the hands of Oliver
Cromwell's New Model Army (see pp.40–41).

King Haakon of Norway at Largs (1263) and three years later received the whole of the Western Isles into his kingdom. Thus, on the death of his son, Alexander III (1241–86), who had been crowned king at the age of 7, Scotland was a relatively unified and competently governed medieval state.

Sadly, Alexander III's death ushered in a crisis that nearly undid all the

The roots of the Stewart dynasty
Robert the Bruce, later Robert I, is shown with his first wife, Isabella of Mar. The dynasty was descended from the marriage of their daughter Marjorie to Walter Stewart, 6th High Steward of Scotland.

nation-building. When Alexander III's heir, his granddaughter, Margaret (1283–90), died en route to Scotland, the disputed succession was referred to Edward I of England (see p.21). Edward I chose John Balliol (c.1248–1314), who reigned as King of Scots from 1292–96. However, Edward I treated Balliol like a feudal subordinate. The Scots rebelled, but were soon crushed, and John was deposed and taken south.

During the ensuing 10-year interregnum, Scottish resistance to Edward I's wish to take over Scotland focussed first on William Wallace (whose ancestors had come to Scotland with the Stewarts), and then on Robert the Bruce (1274–1329).

21 The number of Scotland's 43 monarchs who died violent deaths between 841–1603.

Though he had previously sided with the English, in 1306, Bruce declared himself Robert I of Scotland. What happened next is as much legend as history. Edward I died on the way north to teach Bruce a lesson. The incompetent Edward II (see p.21) dithered and his army was soundly defeated by the Scots in 1314 at Bannockburn. Though England recognized Bruce's kingship in 1328, fighting again flared under Scotland's David II (1324–71), who was crowned in 1331, until Edward III (see p.21) was distracted by the Hundred Years' War.

The Stewarts

David II was succeeded by Robert II (1316–90), the son of Bruce's daughter, Marjorie, and Robert, 7th High Steward of Scotland. (The Royal Family still holds this title: Prince Charles is the 29th High Steward.) The reign of Robert II, crowned at age

Trappings of martyrdom
This is the prayer book and rosary used by the Roman Catholic Mary, Queen of Scots during the night before her execution in 1587 for plotting against her Protestant cousin, Elizabeth I.

Hollow spheres made of gold

Crucifix with pearl pendants

Hand-illuminated Book of Hours

54, was marked by rising lawlessness. Under Robert III (1337–1406), crowned in 1390, this escalated. His son, James I (1394–1437), was captured at age 12, shortly before Robert III's death and was held in prison for 18 years in England. The paternalistic James I, crowned in 1424, angered many with his high taxes and amassing of royal estates, and an angry knight killed him.

In 1437, age six, James II (1430–60) was crowned. He survived a turbulent minority, but came of age only to be blown to pieces when one of his own cannon exploded during the siege of Roxburgh Castle.

James III (1451–88), son of James II, was defeated and killed in Sauchieburn, outside Stirling, during a rebellion headed by his own son.

In James IV (1473–1513), crowned in 1488, Scotland finally found a king of international stature. A builder and a naval man, James IV's rich court thronged with artists. Sadly, he could not resist the traditional Scottish pastime of raiding England. In 1513, at Flodden, James IV was slain and his army was annihilated. Noble factions, both Catholic and Protestant—and mutually hostile—competed for control of the monarchy and the administration during the reigns of the next three Stewarts: James V (1513–42); Mary (1542–67); and James VI (1567–1625). When adult, James V restored firm

government. His Catholic daughter, Mary, Queen of Scots, lacked his skills and eventually lost her crown and her head (see p.29). Mary's son, James VI, (see pp.38–39) ruled Scotland with skill until 1603, when he inherited the English crown and moved to London as James I.

James of the Fiery Face
James II's nickname came from a large red birthmark on his face. Though it was said to indicate a fiery personality, the genial king was one of the most popular of the Stewart monarchs.

AFTER

After the union of the Scottish and English crowns under James VI and I, Scotland's monarch was based in a foreign land. Scottish independence came under increasing threat.

UNION WITH ENGLAND
By the later 17th century, Scottish business was unable to compete with England's commercial might. Eventually, in 1707, the Scottish parliament accepted the **Act of Union 39 ≫**, uniting the administrations of the two nations.

DEVOLVING POWER TO SCOTLAND
In the 20th century, a resurgence of Scottish nationalism led to a 1988 Scotland Act. Accepted by a referendum in Scotland, it devolved major powers to **a new Scottish parliament** and central administration.

Mary, Queen of Scots' bed chamber
Holyrood was the setting for one of history's most
famous murders. From the 18th century, fascinated
tourists began visiting the crime scene—the oak-
paneled rooms occupied by Mary, Queen of Scots.

ROYAL RESIDENCE

Holyroodhouse

The Palace of Holyroodhouse in Edinburgh was an important residence even before the union of the crowns in 1603. With previous inhabitants including Mary, Queen of Scots, it has been the scene of many turbulent events in the complex relationship between England and Scotland.

Holyrood was founded as an Augustinian abbey in 1128 by David I, son of St. Margaret of Scotland, an Anglo-Saxon princess who fled to Scotland after the Norman conquest. According to legend, it was built on the site where the King had a vision of the Cross—the "Holy Rood"—glowing between the antlers of a stag while out hunting on Holy Cross Day.

Towers and turmoil

When Edinburgh became the capital of Scotland in 1437, successive monarchs found the royal chambers at the abbey far more comfortable than Edinburgh Castle. Eager to impress his new queen, Margaret Tudor, daughter of Henry VII, James IV (1473–1513) had the abbey guesthouse converted into a palace. James also decided to develop the grounds: in 1507 a loch was drained to make space for gardens and sports such as tennis, hawking, and archery.

James V (1512–42) made further improvements, building new lodgings in a huge tower protected by a moat and drawbridge. His fortifications proved a shrewd investment: Holyrood was attacked and burned more than once during conflict with England throughout the 1540s, but the tower survived. It was there that in 1566 James V's daughter—Mary, Queen of Scots (1542–87)—witnessed the brutal murder of David Rizzio, her Italian secretary and rumored lover. Rizzio was stabbed 56 times by a group led by Mary's husband Lord Darnley, and it is claimed that his bloodstains can still be seen in the Northwest Tower today.

After her enforced abdication and flight to England in 1567, the palace became home to Mary's son, James VI, Scotland's first Protestant king. By the time he acceded to the English throne in 1603, the household had swollen to around 600. However, with the court's move to London, Holyrood faded in importance: Charles I was crowned King of Scotland there in 1633, but from 1646 the palace was entrusted to the care of the Duke of Hamilton (his descendents still hold the post of Keeper). Occupied by Cromwell during the Civil War, the building went up in flames again in 1650; what remained of the palace was used as a barracks.

Holyrood's fortunes revived after the restoration of the monarchy in 1660. Rebuilt in 1679 as an elegant, symmetrical Renaissance palace designed by the architect Sir William Bruce, its tumultuous history continued unabated. Charles II never stayed in the building he commissioned, but his brother, James VII and II, had strong connections. In 1686–87 James controversially set up a Jesuit College in the grounds and reintroduced Catholic worship to the abbey—which then became a target for the mob in the Glorious Revolution of 1688. In 1745, Holyroodhouse was again linked to the Jacobite cause (see p.40), when James's grandson, Bonnie Prince Charlie, held court there after seizing Edinburgh in an attempt to restore the Catholic line to the British throne.

Modern traditions

Despite its long association with the Royal Family, it was only in the 1920s that Holyroodhouse formally became its official residence in Scotland. The tradition of Holyrood Week—a summer celebration of Scottish history and culture—is a highlight of the royal year. With the Royal Company of Archers in attendance, the Queen entertains thousands of guests from all walks of Scottish life at garden parties and an investiture ceremony. The palace is open to visitors all year, unless the family is in residence.

Ceremonial displays

The baroque stairs, decorated with tapestries, frescoes, and plasterwork, lead to the State Apartments, where an investiture ceremony is held during Holyrood Week. Each year the week begins with the Lord Provost handing the key to the city of Edinburgh to the Queen.

THE GREAT STAIR

THE 16TH-CENTURY NORTHWEST TOWER

CEREMONY OF THE KEYS, 2014

<< 34–35

The Stuarts

Having ruled Scotland for 230 years, the Stewarts survived as monarchs of a joint kingdom for another 111 years. By the end of that time, their status had changed from a divinely appointed "loving father" of the people to a constitutional monarch with limited powers.

<< BEFORE

Before accession to the throne of England, the Stewarts had ruled a relatively small kingdom on the fringes of Europe.

SUDDEN AND UNEXPECTED DEATH
Violence was never far beneath the surface in Scotland, and numerous of **James VI's predecessors** << 34–35 came to untimely ends.

PINCHED BY PRIEST AND PURSE
A source of vexation for James VI had been his kingdom's austere **Presbyterian Church**, popularly known as the Kirk. Established in 1560, it was run by a General Assembly and had its own courts. James, who thought Presbyterianism incompatible with monarchy, won the right to appoint two bishops, but only with the Kirk's approval. Equally humiliating, Scottish kings were **embarrassingly poor**. Small wonder, then, that James could not believe his luck when, upon the death of **Elizabeth I** << 28–29, 32–33 into his lap dropped **the crown of England**.

> "The **authority** of a king is the **keystone** which closeth up the arch and order of **government**."
>
> THOMAS WENTWORTH, ENGLISH STATESMAN, 1628

James I
James VI of Scotland and I of England was arguably the most academic of all Britain's monarchs. His rigorous, brutal, but intellectually stimulating education inspired him to write a number of works, ranging from *Basilikon Doron* (1599) on kingship, to a treatise on witchcraft (entitled *Daemonologie*, 1597), and his celebrated anti-smoking propaganda, *A Counterblaste to Tobacco* (1604).

Not since the Normans (see pp.16–17) had a ruling dynasty made such a dramatic impact. It began when the first Stuart (or Stewart as the Scots prefer; the "u" spelling is a Frenchism) united the crown of Scotland with that of England: James VI became James I (1566–1625) of England because of his descent from Henry VIII's sister, Margaret (see p.28).

Forty years later, the two nations were torn by civil wars (see pp.40–41) that led to the trial and execution of Charles I (see box). An experiment with republicanism collapsed, as did an attempt by Charles II (1630–85) and the Roman Catholic James II (1633–88) to set up a European-style absolute monarchy. The outcome was a "Glorious Revolution," and the constitutional monarchy of the later Stuarts—Mary II (1662–94) and William III (1650–1702), and Anne (1665–1714).

The road to republicanism

James VI and I was an unusual figure, and a fascinating, if unattractive, tangle of contradictions. For a long time, partly thanks to character assassination by aggrieved courtiers, he was thought the "wisest fool in Christendom." Modern historians take a more kindly view. It is true that he argued with parliament, made a fool of himself over male favorites, and was useless with money. At the same time, he avoided war and gave the world the incomparable Authorized Version of the Bible. He also prevented an orgy of bloodshed between Roman Catholics

160,000 **Estimated number of Civil War casualties in England and Scotland.**

and Protestants in 1605 after a group of English Catholics was caught plotting to kill him by blowing up the House of Lords in the so-called Gunpowder Plot.

Charles I (1600–49), James VI and I's son, was crowned in 1626. In modern parlance he was a conviction politician. Sadly, he was not a great politician, and his convictions were those of a continental monarch, not a British one.

Two issues divided him from his people: his belief that he had been appointed King by God through the "Divine Right of Kings," and his lack of money and aversion to raising it by

THE EXECUTION OF KING CHARLES I

On January 30, 1649, the course of British history—and the history of the monarchy itself—changed forever with the execution in London of Charles I. After attempting to reach a negotiated settlement with a king described as "that man of blood," Oliver Cromwell and other Parliamentary leaders put Charles I on trial for High Treason.

The King rejected the authority of the court, but he was found guilty and executed, ushering in 11 years of republican rule.

Although the monarchy was restored in 1660, the shadow of the execution could not be wiped away. In the final instance, the monarch was subject to the will of the people, not a divinely appointed superhero.

The last Stuart sovereign
Through her close personal friendship with Sarah Churchill, wife of John Churchill, 1st Duke of Marlborough, Queen Anne inadvertently helped launch one of Britain's most celebrated political dynasties.

funding from France. However, a bigger problem for Charles II was his brother and heir, James, Duke of York (1633–1701), a man in his father's mold.

James horrified the political nation by converting to Roman Catholicism, a faith linked in the 17th-century mind with tyranny, gunpowder plots, arbitrary taxation, and every other conceivable wickedness. Crowned James II in 1685, his pursuit of pro-Catholic policies was the stuff of his subjects' worst nightmares. When his second wife, an Italian Catholic, gave birth to a son in 1688, raising the prospect of a line of Roman Catholic monarchs, religious leaders and members of parliament decided to oppose the King.

Constitutional monarchy

James II's two daughters by his first wife, Anne Hyde, were Protestant. It was Mary, the elder sister, to whom the opposition turned. In 1688, they invited her and her Dutch husband, William, back from the Netherlands where they lived, requesting also that they bring invasion forces to depose the King. William and Mary duly arrived and James fled to France. In 1689 his replacements were crowned Mary II and William III in what is known as the "Glorious Revolution." Their reign lasted until 1702.

The pragmatism of that bloodless revolution was enshrined in 1689 in a Bill of Rights establishing Britain's constitutional monarchy. The Crown was certainly not powerless, but royal and governmental expenditure were now separate, and the monarch was compelled to appoint ministers who had the backing of Parliament. This meant that England's commercial interests were now more in tune with those of the government and, as a result, the economy boomed.

Scotland, unable to compete with England's mercantile power, accepted the Act of Union (1707) joining English and Scottish parliaments together to form one Parliament of

Great Britain, based in London. The Act united England, Scotland, and Wales into Great Britain for the first time.

War with France resumed under Mary II's sister Anne, crowned in 1702. She was fortunate to find, in John Churchill, a military commander of exceptional ability whose victories on the continent were unmatched since Agincourt (see p.25). After nearly a century of turbulence, the surprising Stuart legacy turned out to be one of unprecedented stability and prosperity.

AFTER

conventional means. He made things worse when he tried to impose a prayer book on the Scots that was almost exactly the same as the English prayer book. The Scots rebelled and Charles I launched a military campaign against them that not only failed, but is thought to have led to a wider Civil War (see pp.40–41). The defeated king was put on trial and executed.

The specter of Catholic absolutism

Britain became a republic for 11 years (1649–60), most of them dominated by the towering figure of Oliver Cromwell (see pp.40–41). Though rejecting the crown, as Lord Protector, he was king in all but name. A successful one, too, who united the British Isles under a single government, earned it respect abroad, governed well, if sternly, and supported "liberty of conscience." On his death, however, there was no one

to step into Cromwell's giant shoes, and in 1660 Charles I's son, Charles II (1630–85) was invited to take up his late father's crown.

Charles II had hankerings for a Roman Catholic, absolutist monarchy but he kept them quiet. Like his father, he was irked by the need to rely on Parliament for money and got around the difficulty by negotiating secret

Little more than a century after Scotland's James VI had united the Scottish and English crowns, James II's Catholic faith lost the Stuarts almost everything they had gained.

ROVING COURT
Louis XIV allowed the **exiled James II** to set up court in a royal château near Paris. The French government found the Stuarts **politically awkward** and, on Louis XIV's death, Pope Clement XI rescued them and set up James II's son as "James III" in Rome.

FOCUS OF DISCONTENT
Though no longer resident in Great Britain, the Stuarts still had a number of supporters in England, Scotland, and Ireland. Known as **Jacobites 48 >>**, from *Jacobus* (Latin for James), they included those opposing the government, fervent Roman Catholics, and sentimental conservatives given to drinking toasts to the "kings over the water."

Gunpowder Plot conspirators
The infamous conspirators who planned to blow up James I are depicted here. The discovery of the plot on November 5, 1605, is still celebrated annually in the United Kingdom with fireworks and bonfires.

« BEFORE

After the end of the Wars of the Roses in 1487, England stayed clear of civil war for the next century and a half.

QUEEN'S CAUTION MAINTAINS PEACE
The **Tudors «< 28–29** experienced serious **rebellions**, notably the Pilgrimage of Grace (1536–37), Kett's Rebellion (1549), Wyatt's Rebellion (1554), and the Rising of the North (1569–70), but nothing on the scale of the French Wars of Religion (1562–98) or Europe's Thirty Years' War (1618–48). This contrast was largely thanks to effective local government and the cautious religious policy pursued by **Queen Elizabeth I «< 29** and **«< 32–33**.

11 YEARS' TYRANNY?
Between 1629–40 **Charles I «< 38–39** ruled without Parliament. This was perfectly legal, so many accepted it. But using the royal prerogative to raise funds (thereby bypassing the need for Parliament), made it tyrannous in the eyes of his enemies. Demanding Ship Money from inland counties, for example, when normally only coastal counties had paid, smacked of continental Catholic **absolutism**.

Battle of Marston Moor, 1644
The Civil War's biggest battle featured both Prince Rupert of the Rhine, the leading Royalist commander, and the "Ironsides" commander, Oliver Cromwell. Caused partly by the Prince's hot-headedness, victory fell to the latter.

Britain's Civil Wars

Between 1639–51, the British Isles were rocked by civil wars. Whether seen as a Great Rebellion, the Wars of the Three Kingdoms, or the first modern revolution, the conflicts altered the course of British history for ever and led to Britain's first and only experience of republican rule.

To understand the causes of the 17th-century civil wars, we need to remember that Charles I (see pp.38–39) was king of three realms: England, Scotland, and Ireland. We must also grasp how deeply people of the time felt about religion, especially about the Catholic–Protestant divide.

Very generally, Catholics considered Protestantism, especially Puritanism, dangerously anarchic as it put ultimate authority in the hands of each man and his Bible; Protestants, on the other hand, regarded Catholicism ("Popery") as the faith of tyrants who mistrusted the people and valued subservience above truth. England's Protestant Church was a compromise, making it a target for both Catholics and Puritans.

Scotland was mostly Presbyterian (a type of Protestantism), while Ireland was mostly Catholic. This powder keg of faiths required delicate handling to stop it from exploding. Sadly, for himself and his kingdoms, Charles I seemed incapable of understanding this.

LORD PROTECTOR, MILITARY AND POLITICAL LEADER (1599–1658)

OLIVER CROMWELL

Born into a family of minor gentry in Huntingdon, Cromwell converted to Puritanism in the 1630s. Elected to Parliament, during the Civil War he rose to prominence as an efficient military commander. He was the driving force behind the move to have Charles I executed. His swift conquests of Ireland and Scotland made him by far the most powerful man in the British Isles and, in 1653, he accepted the position of Lord Protector. However, the republican regime collapsed shortly after Cromwell's death.

Scotland's Prayer Book Rebellion
Charles I and Archbishop William Laud of Canterbury favored reforming the Church of England to place greater emphasis on ceremony, sanctity, and art. This alienated many English subjects, to whom the new policy looked like Catholicism by the back door; after all, Charles I had a Catholic wife. His high-handed behavior, attempting to rule without Parliament after 1629, and raising money by somewhat questionable means, only increased his opponents' worries.

New Model Army triumph
Parliament's reorganized New Model Army, commanded by Sir Thomas Fairfax, put the defeat of the Royalists beyond question when it annihilated Charles' army at the Battle of Naseby, June 1645.

> Though there were no more civil wars after those of the middle of the 17th century, there were more major battles fought on British soil.
>
> **WARS IN BRITAIN AND IRELAND**
> In 1685, a Protestant invasion by the Duke of Monmouth (1649–85), an illegitimate son of **Charles II 42 >>**, was crushed at Sedgemoor. After his flight from England, **James II << 38–39** was overcome in Ireland at the Battle of the Boyne in 1690. In 1715 and 1745, supporters of the **exiled Stuarts** were quelled only after bloody battles and, in 1746, the army of Bonnie Prince Charlie (1720–88) was famously destroyed at **Culloden 48 >>**. More recently, Ireland was torn by fighting between the Irish and the British (1919–21), and then experienced a full-scale civil war, 1922–23.

In 1637, when the King and Laud tried to impose an Anglican-style Prayer Book on Scotland, the Scots rejected it with violence and drew up a National Covenant to defend Presbyterianism. They obliged Charles I to find £850 a day to keep the Scottish army from descending into England. Raising a sum of that size, as the Scots knew, meant summoning Parliament.

Breakdown leads to impasse
Parliament passed a number of measures to curb royal power. These culminated in a Grand Remonstrance (1641), which listed all the opposition's grievances. At this point came news of the slaughter of thousands of Irish Protestants, victims of an uprising against the strict rule of Charles I's minister, Thomas Wentworth. An army had to be sent to Ireland, but who would command it? The Parliamentarians dared not give the King an army lest he use it against them; the King refused to surrender his prerogative power of commander-in-chief. When Charles I's attempted military coup failed, he left London to prepare for war.

The two sides were well matched, though Parliament controlled London and the navy. After 1643, Parliament also had the support of a Scottish Presbyterian army and, from 1644, its forces were reorganized into the best fighting force of its day: the New Model Army. The King had the backing of a number of wealthy aristocrats but, interestingly, several counties refused to take sides, and raised their own soldiers to keep out both King and Parliament.

Parliamentary victory
Charles' best hope was to strike first. After an indecisive battle at Edgehill, he tried to enter London but was turned back. The King's nephew, Prince Rupert, an experienced commander, achieved a number of successes in 1643. However, in 1644, he suffered a serious defeat at Marston Moor, in Yorkshire, where Oliver Cromwell's East Anglian "Ironsides" made a significant contribution to the Parliamentary victory.

In 1645, the New Model Army swamped the royalist forces at Naseby, and the royalists in Scotland were also defeated. Charles surrendered to the Scots, who handed him over to Parliament. As peace talks dragged on, the Parliamentarians divided between Presbyterians, allied to the Scots, and the more radical Independents of the New Model Army. The former wanted a national church along the lines of the Scottish Kirk; the latter believed each congregation should remain independent of any national church. Charles ineptly tried to play off one side against the other, but his slipperiness alienated both.

Cartwheels for ease of maneuverability

Cheap and lethal
Lightweight and easy to construct, falconets were the Civil Wars' most popular cannon. They fired a 1lb (0.45kg) shot approximately the same size and weight as a falcon, hence their name.

The bloody end
After the New Model Army crushed a royalist uprising of English and Scots, known as the Second Civil War (1648), Cromwell and other army leaders lost patience. A specially convened court found Charles I guilty of treason. On January 30, 1649, he was beheaded on a platform erected outside his father's Banqueting House in Whitehall.

The execution of the King did not bring the Civil War to an instant end. First, there was the question of Ireland. Crossing there in 1649, Cromwell slaughtered the people of Drogheda and Wexford to warn others against resistance. After this, the country was systematically brought back under English rule. Charles I's son, now Charles II (see pp.42–43), landed in Scotland. The Scots were irked at not having been consulted over the fate of Charles I, but their anger counted for nothing when their forces were destroyed by Cromwell at Dunbar (1650) and Worcester (1651), finally bringing the Civil Wars to a close.

> **" ... the smallest He that is in this kingdom hath a right as the greatest He."**
> THOMAS RAINBOROUGH, IN DEBATES HELD BY THE PARLIAMENTARY ARMY, 1647

The **Restoration**

The restoration of Charles II in 1660 marked the return of a crowned head of state. Parliament was now a fixture, and the settlement was an important step toward constitutional monarchy.

When Oliver Cromwell's son Richard was unwilling to continue his father's Protectorship (see pp.40–41), General George Monck arranged for the Long Parliament (elected in 1640) to dissolve itself and opened negotiations with Charles II, then in the Netherlands. Guided by Edward Hyde, the future Earl of Clarendon, Charles issued the Declaration of Breda offering a general pardon, a free parliament, and "liberty to tender consciences." On these terms, the v was welcomed home.

The Act of Indemnity and Oblivion forgave the past behavior of all except those who had signed Charles I's death warrant and a handful of others. The Restoration Parliament voted Charles II £1.2 million per year with which to run his court—an amount that would prove inadequate. All laws issued after 1641 were scrapped and confiscated land returned. However, land sales made during the interregnum (period between monarchs) to help the king remained valid.

While the Parliament had been in power, Puritanism had dominated—the excesses of the royals had been condemned and an austere lifestyle encouraged. However, the majority of the society was Anglican and held different views. The restoration of an Anglican monarch brought with it new laws that limited the rights of non-Anglicans. Puritans were labeled "Dissenters" and anti-Puritan sentiment spread throughout society. Theaters were reopened after an 18-year hiatus tforced by the former government, and women appeared on stage for the first time. To the delight of the rakish king, the new wave of Restoration comedies reached levels of bawdiness previously not allowed.

Restoration euphoria was too good to last. The settlement had left many former Royalists and Parliamentarians feeling aggrieved, and Charles was soon squabbling with his parliaments over money, his secret dealings with France, and the probable succession of his Catholic brother, James, Duke of York.

> **" The joy** was… so universal that **His Majesty** said… he **doubted** it had been **his own fault** he had been **absent…"**
>
> **EDWARD HYDE**, EARL OF CLARENDON, IN HIS *HISTORY OF THE REBELLION AND CIVIL WARS IN ENGLAND*

Charles II in royal regalia
This portrait was painted in a formal style to emphasize the continuity of the royal line. It depicts Charles II wearing the St. Edward's Crown and carrying the new orb and scepter commissioned after the earlier regalia was destroyed during the interregnum.

ROYAL RESIDENCE

Windsor Castle

The oldest inhabited castle in the world, Windsor has been the British monarchy's family home for just under 1,000 years. Some of the most resonant rituals and myths of royalty were created here. It is reputedly the Queen's favorite residence, and the symbolic heart of the monarchy.

According to legend Windsor Castle was built on the site of an old Celtic camp where King Arthur once lived. History tells a different, though scarcely less incredible, story. The castle dates back to the first precarious years of the Norman monarchy, a time when the King was in a constant power struggle with the barons, his command only as secure as his last victory.

Medieval fortress

Windsor was founded by William the Conqueror in 1070, four years after the Battle of Hastings, and was one of a ring of nine fortresses built to protect London from local Saxons. The site selected for the castle, above a bend in the Thames river near the village of Windlesora, was on the edge of Saxon territory. William appropriated the forest around it as a royal reserve and hunting ground to supply the castle with wood, deer, boar, and river fish.

The first fortress was a wooden motte and bailey, with three wards arranged around a central mound. In the 12th century, William's grandson, Henry II (1133–89), replaced the wooden palisade surrounding the fortress with a stone wall interspersed with square towers. He also built a stone keep on the irregular mound at the core of the castle—the now famous Round Tower.

These new fortifications were soon put to the test in 1214 during the insurrection of barons protesting at the ruthless taxation and limitless powers of the King. The following year a conference was held at Windsor, which culminated in King John (1167–1216). The following year a conference was held at Windsor, which culminated in the King being forced to agree to the restricted powers set out in the Magna Carta (see p.21).The document was sealed at Runnymede meadow, 3 miles (5km) along the Thames from Windsor.

Romantic traditions

It was in the next century, during the reign of Edward III (1312–77), that Windsor Castle began to emerge as the evocative symbol of ancient tradition, monarchy, and chivalry that it is today. Between 1350 and 1377 Edward spent £50,000 renovating the castle—the largest amount spent by any English medieval monarch on a single building, which may make Windsor England's most expensive secular building project of the Middle Ages. Partly financed by ransoms paid on prisoners taken at Edward's victories in France at the battles of Crécy, Calais, and Poitiers, Windsor Castle was transformed from a medieval fortress into a lavish Gothic palace, with a (literal) king's ransom spent on extravagant furnishings.

Many enduring royal rituals were also established at this time. Edward III revived the cult of King Arthur, and in 1344 created his own Round Table at Windsor. Traces of the structure—the centerpiece of a festival where 300 knights gathered to joust, feast, dance, and watch the reenactment of scenes from the stories of King Arthur—were discovered by archeologists in 2006. Inspired by Arthur, Edward created his own inner circle of knights, the Order of the Garter, and was instrumental in establishing St. George, who was in fact a Greek Christian from Palestine, as the patron saint of England. Windsor's chapel is dedicated to St. George, and images of the knightly saint destroying the dragon abound.

Lavish hospitality remained a feature of life at Windsor in the 15th century, despite the castle's relatively small size. In 1416 Henry V instructed the Dean and Chapter of Windsor to prepare their "logyns and mansions" to receive the multitude accompanying the Holy Roman Emperor Sigismund, who hoped to broker a peace between England and France by moderating the King's ambitions. Liberally entertained by Henry in London and in Windsor, Sigismund ended up installed as a knight in the Order of the Garter, and signed the Treaty of Canterbury, which supported English claims to France. »

THE LONG WALK

WINDSOR GREAT PARK

ST. GEORGE'S CHAPEL

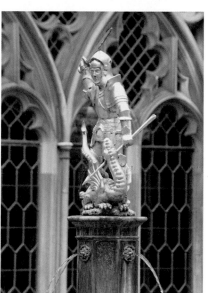

THE DEAN'S CLOISTER FOUNTAIN

Impressive surroundings

The castle is surrounded by Windsor Great Park—5,000 acres (2,000 hectares) of park land, including a deer park and some ancient oaks as old as the castle itself. Lined with London plane trees and horse chestnuts, the Long Walk cuts straight through the landscape for over 2½ miles (4km), and provides a magnificent and unforgettable approach to the castle. It was originally laid out by Charles II and planted with 1,652 elm trees; the carriage way was added by Queen Anne. Inside the castle walls, the red and gold uniforms of the Yeomen of the Guard, the oldest British military corps still in existence (here on the steps of St. George's Chapel), are a familiar sight—as is the recurring motif of St. George slaying the Dragon.

>> The Tudors made only minor additions and modifications to the castle, choosing instead to limit the size of their retinues at ever more extravagant Garter feasts. However, pressure on space increased under Elizabeth I, who used the castle to entertain diplomats, and became a source of friction in the early 17th century—when James I came to hunt at Windsor, his English and Scottish attendants would squabble over rooms.

> "It is the **most romantique castle** that is in the world."
>
> SAMUEL PEPYS, DIARIST, FEBRUARY 26, 1666

Charles I commissioned Inigo Jones to make improvements to the 14th-century apartments, but his plans were interrupted by the outbreak of Civil War. Instead the castle was commandeered by Oliver Cromwell for use as his headquarters and as a prison for captured royalist officers. Charles himself was held at Windsor for the last three weeks of his reign; after his execution his body was returned there by night, and buried without ceremony in a vault beneath St. George's Chapel.

Restoration
Determined to make Windsor a symbol of the restored monarchy, in 1668 Charles II appointed the architect Hugh May to supervise modernization. The Royal Apartments were the last word in Baroque extravagance: the opulent tapestries and textiles were so costly they were only exposed when the King and Queen were in residence to prevent the colors from fading. They remained virtually unchanged until George III decided it was time to give them a fashionable neoclassical restyle.

George IV, on the other hand, was aware of the symbolic power of the castle, and focused on enhancing the Gothic character of the exterior. He increased the height of the Round Tower and had medieval-looking towers and battlements built. Inside, he created a 551ft (168m) gallery—the Grand Corridor—and changed the interior décor to French Empire. By the time the King took up residence at the end of 1828, his improvements to the Castle had cost nearly £300,000 ($1,440,000).

Fortunately his successors felt there was little left to do, although Queen Victoria added a new private chapel, designed by Edward Blore, at the eastern end of St. George's Hall. It was here, on November 20, 1992, that fire broke out, and damaged or destroyed almost 20 percent of the castle area.

The long process of repair and restoration began immediately, with a Restoration Committee chaired by The Duke of Edinburgh. The areas that had been worst hit, such as St. George's Hall, were redesigned in a contemporary Gothic style, while others, such as the Grand Reception Room and State Dining Room, were restored to the condition in which George IV had left them. Within five years the restoration was complete, and the castle open to the public.

Interior features
Two of George IV's drawing rooms were painstakingly restored after the 1992 fire. St. George's Chapel (below)—one of England's finest Gothic churches, with magnificent fan vaults and heraldic standards belonging to the Queen, Prince of Wales, and the 24 Knights of the Garter—was untouched by the blaze.

GREEN DRAWING ROOM

CRIMSON DRAWING ROOM

FAN-VAULTED CEILING IN ST. GEORGE'S CHAPEL

St. George's Hall
Badly damaged in the 1992 fire, the castle's main reception room was rebuilt in a contemporary Gothic style. State banquets are held here with room to seat up to 160 guests.

The **Hanoverians**

In 1714, determined never again to have a Catholic monarch, the British offered the crown to a German prince from Hanover who was distantly related to James VI and I. Though power ultimately rested in Parliament, the Hanoverians still wielded significant political influence.

The German King
Crowned King in 1714 at the age of 54, George I was always more interested in the affairs of his native Hanover than those of his adopted country.

BEFORE

At the beginning of the 11th century, in the time of Edward the Confessor, a belief grew up that a touch from royalty could cure scrofula, an unsightly skin disease, popularly known as the King's Evil.

THE KING'S EVIL
Such was the demand for the healing powers of the anointed sovereign that ceremonies were held where a monarch laid a healing finger on hundreds of afflicted subjects. Gold coins, known as touchpieces, were handed out to those who received the royal remedy. In time, just touching a coin that had itself been in contact with a monarch was thought to be curative. By the 18th century, the belief was dying out, and **Queen Anne ‹‹ 38–39** was the last monarch to touch for the King's Evil.

The Battle of Culloden
In 1745, Charles Edward Stuart (or, Bonnie Prince Charlie) led the last Jacobite attempt to regain the throne. Landing in Scotland, he reached Derby before retreating to Scotland where, in 1746, his army was destroyed at Culloden.

William III and Mary II (see pp.38–39) were childless. Mary's sister, Queen Anne (crowned in 1702) had 16, all of whom predeceased her. To bypass the exiled Catholic Stuarts (see p.39), Parliament passed an Act of Settlement in 1701 stipulating that the sovereign must be Anglican; parliamentary consent was required for wars in defense of non-British territories; only British natives might hold office or receive grants of crown lands. Thus on Anne's death in 1714, the crown passed to George, Elector of Hanover, great-grandson of James VI and I (see pp.38–39). As Anne's closest living Protestant relative, his German birth was weighed up and deliberately overlooked.

With Parliament choosing the sovereign, belief in the Divine Right of Kings ended. The Hanoverians had been enthroned for purely pragmatic reasons and were expected not to thwart Parliament. However, their theoretical powers were considerable, and they influenced events through their right to choose the first minister. More significantly, in an age when many parliamentary seats were in the pockets of wealthy landlords, their political patronage could be crucial.

Kings and electors
The negatives of George I (1660–1727) are easy to list. He spoke little English, was more attached to his native Hanover than to Britain, publicly fell out with his son, and kept his wife under house arrest back in Germany on charges of adultery. He took his job of King seriously, however, attending cabinet meetings, refusing to be rattled by anti-Hanoverian xenophobia, and welcoming religious toleration. Above all, he did not try to push his authority too far, thereby establishing his family's status as acceptable heads of state.

More opinionated than his father, George II (1683–1760), reigned from 1727 and kept up the Hanoverian tradition of falling out with his son and heir, Frederick, Prince of Wales (d.1751). He also followed his father's example of relying on an oligarchy of

> **"It is the pride of kings which throws mankind into confusion."**
>
> TOM PAINE, *COMMON SENSE*, 1776

government ministers. Most prominent of these was Robert Walpole, generally recognized as Britain's first Prime Minister (in office 1721–42). George II took a close personal interest in two major European conflicts: the War of Austrian Succession (1740–48) and the Seven Years' War (1756–63). He was the last British king to lead men into battle (Dettingen, 1742), though he was criticized for doing so under the colors of Hanover, not Britain.

Family man and invalid

It is important to distinguish between George III (1738–1820) the family man and invalid, and the king who reigned from 1760. In the former role he attracts much sympathy; in the latter he was painfully out of his depth and lacked the wit to realize it, often with disastrous consequences.

George III treated his 15 children by his wife, Charlotte of Mecklenburg, much as he did his ministers: he sought goodness and obedience, and tried to direct them in the paths of virtue. This led to frequent confrontations with his dissolute eldest son, George (1762–1830), whom the King did not understand. Nor did he really understand much else that was going on around him—calls for reform of parliament and greater religious toleration, for instance, and the grievances of the American colonists who broke away from Britain in their War of Independence (1775–83).

The King suffered from porphyria, a kidney disorder with distressing symptoms that appeared as madness. He suffered breakdowns in 1765 and 1788 and, from 1811 onward, he was permanently incapacitated. Ironically, at a time when he was playing no part in affairs of state, he was at his most popular, thanks to Britain's successful wars against Napoleon (1803–14).

Pavilion of controversy
The merits of Brighton's flamboyant Royal Pavilion, designed in the Indo-Islamic style and started in 1787 as a seaside bolthole for the Prince of Wales, have always divided opinion.

Prince Regent in retrospect
Sir Thomas Lawrence's portrait of George IV as Prince Regent was painted two years after he ascended the throne. His regency (the time in 1811–20 when he acted as sovereign) resulted from his father's incapacity.

Hanoverian swansong

George IV, better known as the Prince Regent, a role he had enjoyed since 1811, reigned as King from 1820–30. Crowned at the age of 57, he was obese (nicknamed the "Prince of Whales"), sick, vain, extravagant, and lazy. He brought the monarchy to a new low.

Those seeking to defend him point to his patronage of the arts (a quality rarely seen in the modern British monarchy) and hold up London's

£240,000 **($1,100,000)** the total cost in pounds of the coronation of George IV in 1821.

Regent Street and the Royal Pavilion, Brighton, as examples of his precious architectural legacy. More valuable was his visit to Scotland in 1822, the first by a reigning British sovereign since Charles II (see pp.42–43), in 1650. George IV's visit played an important part in strengthening the bond between Scotland and England.

On George IV's death in 1830, the crown passed to his brother, William IV (1765–1837), who was age 64. Bluff and eccentric, he was known as "Sailor Bill" because he had served in the Royal Navy. In 1832, he reluctantly submitted to the will of the people and supported the passing of a bill to reform the electoral system, yet two years later he became the last monarch to appoint a Prime Minister (Lord Melbourne, in office 1834 and 1835–41) without Parliament's full support.

Like his brother George IV, William IV lived as husband and wife with a woman to whom he was not married and with whom he had many children. But the two legitimate daughters born to his wife, Queen Adelaide, both died young. As a result, William IV's crown passed to his 18-year-old niece, Victoria (see pp.50–61 and 66–67).

AFTER »

By the end of the Hanoverian era in 1901, any remaining mystique in the public's eye surrounding the monarchy had evaporated.

BAD EXAMPLE OF ROYALTY
Generations of family friction, eccentricity, and vulgar irresponsibility had left the Royal Family resembling other aristocratic dynasties whose fortunes had come through **accident of birth** rather than effort or talent. Many would have believed the touch of the drug-addicted Prince Regent more likely to spread disease than cure it.

STEP BY STEP
Though the monarchy was in urgent need of a make-over by the time of **Victoria's accession 54–55 »**, the path to popularity was not straightforward. For the first 20 years of her reign, Victoria, and to a greater extent her husband, **Prince Albert**, set new standards of sobriety and duty, and the monarchy's reputation rose. It then nosedived when the Queen withdrew from public life in 1861 after the **sudden death of Albert 60–61 »**. It had recovered by the end of her reign, and has largely retained public approval ever since.

Born 1819 Died 1901

Queen Victoria

> "I am very **young**… but I am sure… few have more… **real desire** to do what is **fit** and **right** than I have…"

QUEEN VICTORIA, IN HER DIARY, JUNE 20, 1837

By the end of her long life, Victoria had become Britain's longest-reigning monarch. She was the only child of the Duke of Kent, the fourth son of George III, and his German wife, Princess Victoria of Saxe-Coburg-Saalfeld. Thanks to Victoria's longevity and Britain's industrial, naval, and financial predominance globally throughout the 19th century, her name came to be applied to an entire era. Today, the adjective "Victorian" has contradictory implications. Positively, it is associated with diligence, self-reliance, thrift, and honesty: in a 1982 television interview, British Prime Minister Margaret Thatcher said, "Victorian values were the values when our country became great." Negatively, the term is equated with prudishness, narrow-mindedness, hypocrisy, and rigid inflexibility.

The Victorian paradox

Victoria was a fascinating bundle of contradictions, as was the age in which she lived. She welcomed the use of chloroform in childbirth but rejected electric light. She used the railroad extensively, but was terrified of high speeds and would never travel at more than 65 kph (50 mph). On other occasions, for instance, during the numerous attempts to assassinate her, she showed remarkable bravery.

In her personal life (see p.54) Victoria could be either warm and sympathetic or cold and distant. She took a close interest in all appointments to her several

Royal photo portrait, 1897
Victoria, Queen of the United Kingdom of Great Britain and Ireland from 1837, Empress of India from 1876, seen in the year of her Diamond Jubilee, marking 60 years on the throne.

Young Victoria
German court painter Franz Xaver Winterhalter (1805–73) first visited England in 1842 and painted the young Victoria's portrait. She had been queen for five years at this point, and married for two.

Gold bracelet
Presented to Victoria by Marie-Amélie, Queen of the French, in May 1852, the portraits depict Prince Albert and the four eldest of Queen Victoria's children. The sixth frame holds braided hair.

households yet, when her librarian tried to introduce his daughter to her on a royal visit to the library, she snubbed him with a curt, "I came to see the library." She liked children but hated being pregnant, disliked breastfeeding, and had little time for babies. To her older sons and daughters she was often an infuriating mother who rarely practiced what she preached.

Victoria referred to Albert, Prince Consort and her key advisor, as her "angel." But even Albert dared not approach her when she was in one of her notoriously furious tempers, and was on occasion reduced to passing her notes under her door. Albert, in ill health, traveled to visit his son who was in the grip of a scandal concerning an actress. Anxious and exhausted, Albert died of typhoid fever in 1861. Victoria blamed her eldest son, for her husband's early death, writing that thereafter, "I never can or shall look at him without a shudder."

Sometimes Victoria could be brusque and energetic, and at other times sentimental. After Albert's demise, Victoria had her husband's rooms in all of the royal palaces and castles maintained as they always had been, with towels and linen changed daily, and hot water for washing and shaving brought in each morning.

Ear trumpet
Victoria suffered some hearing impairment in later life and was given this silver-engraved ear trumpet in 1880.

Personal politics

As in her personal life, it is hard to find consistency in Victoria's political life. She respected hard work and was herself diligent. Then, after Albert's death, she shut herself away from public life, and on numerous occasions threatened to abdicate or take herself off to Australia. When in London or

Matriarch of Europe
Victoria surrounded by family. Her grandson, Kaiser Wilhelm II, sits at the bottom left while Czar Nicholas II of Russia and his wife Alexandra (Victoria's grand-daughter) stand behind the Kaiser. Albert, Prince of Wales, Victoria's eldest son, stands behind the Czar.

Windsor, she hankered after the peace of Balmoral, the castle in the Scottish Highlands she and Albert had built together; once there, she missed life down south.

By today's standards, Victoria's interference in politics would have been wholly unacceptable. However, in her day, such interventions fell just within the bounds of what was permissible.

The "three rights of the crown"—"to be consulted, to encourage, and to warn"—as espoused by English journalist and essayist Walter Bagehot (1826–77) were only just emerging at that time.

While believing she was above politics, Victoria fought to separate personal feelings from her official role. Being closely related to several European royal families put her in an uncomfortable position because, while the British government wanted to pursue foreign policies that increased Britain's power abroad, Victoria feared that such policies would undermine and humiliate the royal families elsewhere, leaving them vulnerable to being overthrown.

Public affection finally restored

Toward the end of her reign, when the greatly expanded franchise (the right to vote) was drawing the country

slowly toward democracy, Victoria's political influence waned. This was clearly illustrated in her relations with William Gladstone (1809–98), a British liberal politician who was the greatest political figure of his generation. She did not favor him, yet she reluctantly appointed him prime minister on four separate occasions. Nevertheless, she never once allowed the aged Gladstone to take a seat in her presence, and

40 The number of living grandchildren Victoria had at the time of her death

37 The number of living great-grandchildren Victoria had at the time of her death

complained, "He speaks to me as if I were a public meeting." What she seems to have resented most about the Liberal leader was his ability to carry the masses with him. As the "People's William," he posed a threat to the "People's Victoria."

Over time, the Queen's popularity grew, and the celebrations for her Jubilees of 1887 and 1897 were genuinely enthusiastic. When Victoria died in January 1901, she was the respected figurehead of a massive empire that was home to one person in four of the world's population. With Albert's help, she had restored the prestige of the British crown, set standards of behavior that would serve as a template for her successors, and (as much by luck and judgment) found a role for constitutional monarchy in an age of democracy.

TIMELINE

- **May 24, 1819** Alexandrina Victoria is born at Kensington Palace, London.

- **June 26, 1830** William IV assumes the throne. With no legitimate children to succeed him, his niece Victoria becomes heiress presumptive.

- **1830** The Regency Act says that Victoria may not become queen until she is 18.

- **May 24, 1837** Victoria turns 18 and becomes eligible to assume the throne should her uncle die.

- **June 20, 1837** Victoria becomes Queen of the United Kingdom of Great Britain and Ireland when William IV dies of heart failure.

- **June 28, 1838** Coronation ceremony at Westminster Abbey, London.

- **February 10, 1840** Victoria marries her cousin Prince Albert of Saxe-Coburg Gotha in the Chapel Royal at St. James's Palace, London.

- **May 6, 1840** Britain issues the world's first postage stamp, costing one penny, which bears the image of Queen Victoria.

- **June 10, 1840** Edward Oxford fires two bullets into the coach carrying the pregnant Victoria. It is the first of seven attempts on her life.

- **November 21, 1840** Victoria's first child, Princess Victoria Adelaide Mary Louisa, is born. Victoria and Albert will have a further eight children.

- **May 1, 1851** Victoria opens the Great Exhibition in Hyde Park, London, which showcases international culture and industry.

- **April 7, 1853** Chloroform is administered to Victoria in childbirth, lending credibility to its use as an anesthetic during labor.

- **November 17, 1855** Explorer Livingstone names the Victoria Falls on Africa's Zambezi River after the Queen.

- **1856** Balmoral Castle is completed.

- **June 26, 1857** Victoria Cross awarded for the first time; 62 soldiers and sailors receive it.

- **December 14, 1861** Devastated by the death of Albert, Victoria sinks into depression and withdraws from public life.

- **1870** The republican movement has strong support on account of the unsociable behavior of the "Widow of Windsor."

- **May 1, 1876** Prime Minister Benjamin Disraeli proclaims Victoria "Empress of India."

- **1887** Golden Jubilee marks 50th year of Victoria's reign. The celebrations help draw her back into public life.

- **September 23, 1896** Victoria's reign surpasses that of George III's as the longest in British history.

- **1897** Diamond Jubilee is marked by six days of celebrations in London and elsewhere, ending with a Review of the Fleet at Spithead.

- **January 22, 1901** Victoria dies of a cerebral hemorrhage at Osborne House, Isle of Wight, bringing to an end a reign of nearly 64 years.

VICTORIA CROSS

The archetypal Victorian family
Victoria and Albert pose for a photograph with their nine children in the 1861. The stiff poses are partly explained by the need to remain motionless while a photograph was being taken.

BEFORE

From 1714, the kings of Great Britain were also Electors of Hanover, which gave them the right, with eight others, to elect the Holy Roman Emperor.

CLOSE TIES WITH EUROPE

Elector of **Hanover << 48–49**, is a largely honorary title but, as long as the British king held this title, it tied Britain closely to European, especially German, politics. This tie also drew Britain into a continental land war during Napoleonic times (1799–1815). At the end of the conflict, Hanover became a kingdom, a development that gave three British monarchs, **George III**, **George IV**, and **William IV << 48–49**, a double crown.

LONG LIVE THE KING!

The monarchy, in the period before Victoria ascended the throne, had been largely secure due, in part, to the steadiness of the prevailing political system, and the longevity of the kings. From 1714–1837, there were only five monarchs, one of whom, George III, **reigned for nearly 60 years.**

Queen Victoria's coronation service
This painting by Charles Robert Leslie (1794–1859) shows the Queen toward the end of the service, kneeling to receive the Sacrament. She wears no jewels and the Crown has not yet been placed on her head.

Victoria becomes Queen

A botched coronation and a disagreement over her ladies in waiting did not augur well for the reign of the strong-willed young Queen Victoria. But marriage to her handsome, earnest-minded first cousin, Prince Albert of Saxe-Coburg-Gotha, gave her longed-for stability and domestic joy.

Victoria's father died when she was eight months old, and the fair-haired, blue-eyed princess spent most of her childhood in the seclusion of London's Kensington Palace. Her overprotective, ambitious mother, aided by Sir John Conroy, Victoria's mother's (possible) lover and personal adviser, brought up Victoria according to a meticulous, complex set of rules, which they named the "Kensington System" after the palace. The system was designed to make the princess an easily manipulated cypher.

Under the system, her every action was observed and recorded, and the young Victoria was even kept away from other children. Supported by her devoted governess Louise Lehzen, Victoria resisted strongly and, on the death of George IV (see p.49) in 1830, Victoria became heiress presumptive, prompting her renowned remark, "I will be good." Seven years later she acceded to the throne when her uncle William IV (see p.49) died without legitimate offspring. Until then, Victoria was made to sleep in her mother's room. However, on moving into Buckingham Palace—the first sovereign to take up residence there—she demanded a bedroom of her own. She also used her newfound authority to banish the hated Conroy from the royal household.

Coronation cup, 1838
This fine silver goblet was commissioned as a souvenir to mark the coronation of Queen Victoria. It has two applied plaques. One (left) shows the portrait bust of the Queen and the other a scene from the Coronation.

Coronation

The public immediately took to the 18-year-old Victoria. Her youth, purity, and piety were a refreshing contrast to the unseemly antics of her Hanoverian predecessors (see pp.48–49).

Nevertheless, she soon discovered the tribulations a sovereign must contend with, as her Uncle Leopold (1790–

Victoria's First Meeting with the Privy Council
Just hours after learning of William IV's death, Victoria held her first meeting with her councillors in the Red Saloon, Kensington Palace, at 11 A.M. on June 20, 1837. Age 18, she wrote that she was "not at all nervous."

1865) and later first king of the Belgians, warned her. Difficulties arose over her coronation. In the House of Commons, the traditionalist Tory party was accused of using the ceremony as propaganda to promote the monarchy, while Radicals said the £79,000 bill ($385,000) for the coronation, twice that of William IV's in 1831 (see pp.49), was wasteful and Britain would be better as a republic.

Complaints or no complaints, on June 28, 1838, the ceremony went ahead. It began with the longest procession the streets of London had seen since the return of Charles II in 1660 (see pp.41–43). Cheered by a crowd estimated to number around 400,000 ("millions of my loyal subjects... assembled in every spot,"

> "His ... **excessive** love and **affection** gave me feelings of **heavenly love** and **happiness.**"

QUEEN VICTORIA, IN HER DIARY, FEBRUARY 10, 1840

gushed Victoria later), the youthful Queen rode in the ornate Gold State Coach to Westminster Abbey.

At this point things began to go wrong. There had been no rehearsal, and no one was quite sure where to go or when. The music of a massive orchestra and choir was out of time because the choirmaster was forced to conduct from his seat at the organ.

The entire chaotic ceremony, which involved the Queen in two changes of formal attire, lasted a sleep-inducing five hours. The tedium was relieved only when an 82-year-old peer, appropriately named Lord Rolle, tripped and rolled down the chancel steps. When he had recovered, Victoria won the hearts of those present by getting up and coming down the steps to meet him so he didn't have to attempt the ascent again.

Early Difficulties

Victoria ultimately found happiness in her marriage. She first met her future husband, her cousin Prince Albert of Saxe-Coburg-Gotha (1819–61), in 1836. She was powerfully struck by his looks and serious yet sympathetic personality. They met again in 1839, and five days later, on October 15, Victoria proposed to him, and he accepted. It was a love match bonded by a strong physical attraction that enabled the couple to weather even the roughest emotional storms.

The wedding took place in the Chapel Royal at St. James's Palace, London, on February 10, 1840. As they had done for the coronation, excited crowds lined the streets to see the Queen travel from

300 The weight in pounds (or, 136 kg) of the cake baked for the wedding of Victoria and Albert. More than 1,000 guests each tasted a morsel.

Buckingham Palace to the chapel. Also, as at the coronation, the music was poor. But no one seemed to mind and, after an enormous wedding banquet in Buckingham Palace, the couple left for a honeymoon in Windsor Castle.

Victoria was soon pregnant. A daughter, Victoria (1840–1901), was born the same year on November 21. A further eight children followed: Albert Edward, Prince of Wales (1841–1910); Alice (1843–78); Alfred (1844–1900); Helena (1846–1923); Louise (1848–1939); Arthur (1850–1942), Leopold (1853–84); and Beatrice (1857–1944). Victoria's old governess and confidante Louise Lehzen ran the busy household until, after a heated quarrel in 1842 between Victoria and Albert, who detested Lehzen, she was given retirement. Despite such squalls, the relationship between the royal couple

AFTER ⟫

Under ancient German law codes, as Queen Victoria acceded to the throne, Britain's 123-year connection with Hanover ended. In the future, wars loomed.

LINKS WITH GERMANY LOOSEN
The Germanic kingdom's Semi-Salic law, dating back to the 6th century, **forbade female accession** to the throne as long as a male alternative existed. Accordingly, in 1837, Victoria's uncle, **Ernest Augustus**, the eldest surviving son of George III, took the crown of Hanover and left Britain to his niece.

FIRST STEP TOWARD WORLD WAR I
With the British monarch no longer **ruler of Hanover**, a close link with Germany was gone. This may be seen as the first step in a chain of events that led to Britain and Germany going to war. In 1914, German troops **advanced through Belgium**. Britain held that this infringed Belgium's neutrality, and **declared war** on Germany 79–81 ⟫.

deepened and Albert was soon his wife's wise adviser as well as her lover. When Victoria's pregnancies grew visible and prevented her from appearing in public ceremonies, it was Albert who assumed her duties. As their family expanded, the monarchy became more of a shared partnership between them. A part of Victoria always resented this sharing of power, but she usually welcomed it and even permitted Albert to dictate her political letters.

Queen Victoria in the crown jewels
After her coronation, Victoria is depicted in the regalia and vestments of a British monarch. The imperial state crown she wears is set with such gems as St. Edward's sapphire (front), which dates back to 1042.

Palazzo style
The gardens were also designed by Prince Albert and provide the perfect the setting for his Italian Renaissance villa with wide terraces that open out to glorious views of the sea.

ROYAL RESIDENCE

Osborne

Designed by Prince Albert in the style of an Italian Renaissance villa, the house at Osborne on the Isle of Wight, with its splendid views over the Solent, was intended to provide the Royal Family with a luxurious seaside retreat, well away from the pressures of court life.

Queen Victoria and Prince Albert bought the Osborne estate on the Isle of Wight in 1845. Owned by Lady Isabella Blachford, the estate was recommended to them by the Prime Minister, Sir Robert Peel. Victoria, who had fond memories of childhood holidays on an adjoining estate, declared "it is impossible to imagine a prettier spot." Albert was equally charmed by the site: it reminded him of the Bay of Naples which he had visited in 1838. The existing house, however, was too small for the royal couple, their growing family, and entourage, so work began immediately on a new building.

Ideal home

Inspired by his memories of Italy, Prince Albert worked closely with the property developer Thomas Cubitt to create an informal family home. The first part, the three-story Pavilion accommodating the private rooms of Queen Victoria and Prince Albert and the royal nurseries for their children, was completed in 1846. The Household Wing, providing rooms for members of the royal household, was finished in 1848. At this point the original house was demolished and replaced with the Main Wing, linked to the Household Wing by the Grand Corridor. The finished building was dominated by two Belvedere towers, with huge plate glass windows looking over the grounds to the sea.

Victoria and Albert gradually created their ideal world, building a model farm, estate cottages, lodges and dormitories, and a sea wall along the coast. The estate had terraced Italian gardens, and a private beach, where the children and their mother all learned to swim.

Hidden in the woods is a wooden chalet, the Swiss Cottage, where the royal children were taught household skills. The Princesses learned to bake and would occasionally serve tea to their parents and guests. They kept household accounts, which Albert inspected. The older boys, Bertie and Alfred, helped to lay the foundations. An entry in Queen Victoria's journal describes how Prince Alfred "worked as hard and steadily as a regular laborer"—and was paid by Albert at the same rate. Each child had their own garden plot where they cultivated fruit, vegetables, and flowers. Despite the miniature tools and monogrammed wheelbarrows, this was no mere game. The under-gardener assessed all the produce, and Albert paid the market price to the child who had grown it.

In the main house, the Queen received a panoply of distinguished guests: prime ministers Robert Peel, Benjamin Disraeli, and William Gladstone; inventor Alexander Graham Bell, who demonstrated the telephone at Osborne; and members of European royalty, including Emperor Napoleon III and Kaiser Wilhelm II.

After Albert's death, Victoria took refuge at Osborne, and eventually it became her preferred residence. In 1885 she agreed to the marriage of her youngest child, Beatrice, on condition she continued to live at Osborne. A new wing was built, with apartments for the Princess and her family, and an opulent reception room was added, encrusted with Mughal-inspired stucco-work, known as the Durbar Room.

Queen Victoria died in her bedroom at Osborne on January 22, 1901. Her children did not share her love for the house, and Edward VII presented it to the nation. After stints as a Naval College and convalescent home, the house is now run by English Heritage and is open throughout the year.

Informal seaside retreat

Private rooms like the nursery were all furnished with comfort in mind, but the Durbar Wing had a more impressive space for formal entertaining. Despite the privacy of the estate, Victoria was wheeled to the sea in her bathing machine when she wanted a swim.

QUEEN VICTORIA'S BATHING MACHINE

NURSERY BEDROOM

PEACOCK OVERMANTLE IN THE DURBAR ROOM

The **Great Exhibition**

Organized by the Royal Society for the Encouragement of Arts and strongly backed by Prince Albert, the Great Exhibition of the Works of Industry of all Nations, in Hyde Park, London, attracted 6.2 million visitors. It successfully promoted Britain's position as the world's leading industrial nation.

The proposal to hold an international exhibition in London to show off British ingenuity and promote harmony between nations came from Henry Cole, a civil servant and member of the Society of Arts, and was backed by Victoria's far-sighted husband, Prince Albert. The idea was not a new one. France had held an Industrial Exposition in Paris in 1844, and the concept had been copied in Madrid (1845), Brussels (1847), and Lisbon (1849). This put pressure on Britain, the undisputed leader of global finance and manufacturing, to organize something bigger and better than anything attempted before.

A royal commission looked into the matter and Lord Russell's Liberal government gave the project its backing. The committee charged with bringing the project to fruition by May 1, 1851, was chaired by the civil engineer William Cubitt. Alongside him sat Prince Albert, the celebrated civil engineers Isambard Kingdom Brunel and Robert Stephenson, and the architect Charles Barry. They struggled to find a suitable building plan until the well-known gardener Joseph Paxton came up with a design for an enormous greenhouse using cast plate glass, cast iron, and laminated wood. In just nine months the Crystal Palace, the world's largest glass structure, was built in Hyde Park, London, on time and on budget.

The 100,000 exhibits packed into the 25 acres (10 hectares) of floor space included the Koh-i-noor—then the world's largest diamond—a voting machine, a Colt revolver, and the first public conveniences. The Great Exhibition was an outstanding success, attracting an average daily attendance of 42,000 visitors and making a profit of £186,000 ($912,000)—money used to set up the Museum of Manufacturing (later known as the Victoria and Albert Museum) in Kensington. The Queen visited several times during its construction and almost daily once the Great Exhibition was open.

> "Its **grandeur** does not consist in *one* thing, but in the **unique assemblage of** *all* **things."**
>
> **CHARLOTTE BRONTË,** WRITER, IN A LETTER TO A FRIEND

The Crystal Palace
The Great Exhibition—housed in the spectacular Crystal Palace—showcased Britain as the "workshop of the world." It displayed an extraordinary array of innovative goods and machinery from Britain and its empire, as well as from other nations.

Empress of India

Victoria was delighted when the Royal Titles Act of 1876 gave official recognition to her status as an empress: she was now on a par with the German and Russian royal families. Nevertheless, in some circles the new nomenclature was seen as a somewhat vulgar European import.

Though India was regarded as the "jewel in the British Crown," until 1857 London governed it only indirectly. Day to day administration was shared between the East India Company and Indian princes. The arrangement fell apart during the extremely violent rebellion of 1857, also known as the Indian Mutiny, India's First War of Independence, and the Great Rebellion. The following year, the Government of India Act placed administration in the hands of the British government—the British monarch became India's Head of State.

By the time the Prince of Wales (later to become Edward VII) made his eight-month tour of India, beginning in October 1875, the subcontinent had settled down and the royal visit was a great success. This was in no small part due to his open-minded nature and refusal to accept the racism that many members of the Raj – the British government in India – practiced. Back home, the Conservative Prime Minister Benjamin Disraeli, the Queen's favorite, took advantage of the visit to introduce a Royal Titles Bill in 1876. He even persuaded Victoria to open Parliament in person for the first time since Prince Albert's death. The new law gave official sanction to her use of the title Empress of India, a move that would, Disraeli hoped, strengthen the bond between Britain and India. On January 1, 1877, Lord Lytton, Viceroy of India, marked the occasion with the Delhi Durbar, a spectacular celebration in the Indian capital.

Victoria had long been annoyed that the heads of the Russian and German royal families had sported a title she did not possess, and she warmly welcomed the elevation. She took to signing herself "V.R. & I.," *Victoria Regina et Imperatrix* (Victoria Queen and Empress).

> ## "I am an empress and in common conversation am sometimes called Empress of India."
>
> **QUEEN VICTORIA** TO SIR HENRY PONSONBY

Victoria Terminus
Now known as Chhatrapati Shivaji Terminus, this massive railroad station in Mumbai (formerly Bombay), India, was completed just in time to commemorate Victoria's Golden Jubilee in 1887. A monument to colonial rule, the edifice was built using locally procured materials, but fashioned in European style.

« BEFORE

The attitude of George III toward his American colonies, and their successful rebellion (1775–83) against him, taught Britain a valuable lesson.

AMERICAN WAR OF INDEPENDENCE
British North America had been subject to **English law** until the 18th century, but laws passed after 1763 to raise revenue for Britain united the American colonies in **acts of rebellion**. In reprisal, Britain passed yet more laws. The colonists rejected their legality, and political leaders wrote a **Declaration of Independence** in 1776. In the ensuing war, which ended in 1783, Britain lost its colony and the United States of America was born.

ASSET FOR THE MOTHER COUNTRY
From this time onward the men and women living in the **colonies**, especially those of European descent, were treated with greater respect than before. Even so, the colonies were still regarded as primarily existing for the **benefit of the mother country**, as providers of food and raw materials, as captive markets for British goods, and places where **surplus population** could go, and to which undesirables might be sent.

From **Empire** to **Commonwealth**

Victoria was figurehead of the largest, most diverse empire the world had ever seen. Efforts to bring its component nations closer together led to the creation of the Imperial Federation League and Colonial Conferences, from which today's Commonwealth of Nations emerged.

The huge British Empire headed by Queen Victoria (see pp.50–51) was an unusual entity—if it was an entity at all. Britain's global lands had been accumulated over a long time in a wide variety of ways. Some had been conquered, some purchased, some simply occupied, and others gained through negotiation (not always scrupulous) with previous owners.

Broadly speaking, the colonies were of two types. There were those like India and Kenya where the indigenous people made up the bulk of the population, and those like Australia and Canada where European settlers had swiftly overwhelmed the small indigenous populations. British territories in the Caribbean, such

as Trinidad and Jamaica, were different again. Here the indigenous peoples had been all but replaced by immigrants from Europe, West Africa (as slaves), and, latterly, Asia.

During the 19th century, the monarchy became the focal point for the swelling empire. In 1875–76, Queen Victoria's son, the Prince of Wales (see pp.72–73), made a highly successful tour of the

Safeguarding the empire
One way Britain protected its far-flung Empire was to increase the size of its Royal Navy. HMS *Dreadnought*, commissioned in 1906, became a tangible symbol of Britain's invincibility on the open seas.

subcontinent. During his visit, he showed Indians of every degree that they were the equals of his subjects at home. The tour also laid the ground for his mother to assume the title Empress of India in 1876 (see pp.62–63).

Empire under threat
There had always been many who felt uneasy about Britain's acquisition of an overseas empire. The rebellion of the American colonists in 1775–83 (see p.49), for instance, had attracted a number of

Indian princes at Edward VII's coronation
Few images reflect the monarch's role in old-style imperialism more than Albert Harris's painting of Edward VII receiving the Maharajas and other rulers of India's Princely States before his coronation.

The Colonial and Imperial Conferences were early indications of a change in attitude toward the colonies.

EMPIRE TO COMMONWEALTH
The word "commonwealth," widely used in the 16th century, had been revived in the 19th century as an alternative to "empire." By 1917, the South African leader Jan Smuts was talking of the "British Commonwealth of Nations." In 1949 the word "British" was axed and the modern Commonwealth of Nations, a voluntary association of 53 states, was born. **King George VI 94–95 ⟫** gladly acted as its figurehead, a role granted to his daughter, **Elizabeth II 134–135 ⟫** on her accession.

"**Africa** is still **lying ready** for us. It is **our duty** to **take** it."

CECIL JOHN RHODES, BRITISH IMPERIALIST, IN HIS "CONFESSION OF FAITH", JUNE 2, 1877

British supporters. Moreover, as the mother country edged toward a more representative form of government, rights were extended to the colonies of settlement. New Zealand became a self-governing member of the British Empire in 1852. Three years later, New South Wales established parliamentary rule over domestic matters, followed by Victoria, Tasmania and in 1856, South Australia. Queensland joined them in 1859, and Western Australia in 1890. Canada became the self-governing Dominion of Canada in 1867, and South Africa's Cape Colony started electing its own government in 1872.

"Scramble" for colonies
The mood of imperialism that swept through Europe in the 1880s led to a "scramble" for colonies in Africa, and heightened tension between the major powers. Britain's scattered empire was increasingly vulnerable. One response to the threat was to build up the Royal Navy. In 1889, Britain planned for 10 new battleships, 38 cruisers, and numerous smaller vessels in order that its navy would be larger than the fleets of any two other powers combined. A second response was to unite the peoples of the empire in an Imperial Federation League, or IFL. This was launched in 1884, and drew inspiration from the federal structure of the US and the way in which the Dominion of Canada had been organized. Supporters of the move were mainly Conservatives, although well-known Liberals such as the education reformer EM Forster also

joined. Its ultimate goal was to unite all Britain's colonies into a type of super-state under an imperial parliament. The plan was to start with Britain and the colonies of settlement, then expand into a kind of Anglo United Nations as other colonies joined. New technology, it was hoped, would overcome issues of geographical separation. IFL supporters argued that the alternative was imperial disintegration and decline.

The living symbol
This Empire Day postcard of 1907, designed for sending from the "mother country" to some corner of the empire, illustrates the monarch's key role in binding together Britain's far-flung colonies and dominions.

Meeting of equals
From the 1887 Colonial Conference onward, British ministers learned to negotiate and not simply to issue orders when meeting with the elected leaders of the dominions: all were subjects under the same monarch.

However, the proposal ignored the vast cultural differences between the peoples of the empire, the colonies' burgeoning nationalism, and Britain's unwillingness to be influenced, let alone dictated to, by colonials. Nevertheless, the proposal planted a seed that, as a very different type of plant, grew into one of the most inspiring institutions of the modern world: the Commonwealth of Nations, headed by Queen Elizabeth II.

First Colonial Conference
Called by the IFL and chaired by Prime Minister Lord Salisbury, the first Colonial Conference met in 1887 when representatives from all parts of the Empire were gathered in London for Victoria's Golden Jubilee (see pp.66–67). Over 100 delegates, including several prime ministers, attended, although India was not represented. The agenda mainly concerned defense. In return for a British pledge not to withdraw its naval presence unilaterally from the Pacific, Australia offered to pay £126,000 ($617,000) annually toward the maintenance of the Royal Navy's fleet in their part of the world. A trans-Pacific telegraph cable was proposed, and it was agreed that the Queen's official title should now read, "Queen of the United Kingdom of Great Britain, Ireland, and the Colonies, and all Dependencies thereof, and Empress of India."

Emergence of the Commonwealth
Further Colonial Conferences were held in 1894, 1897, and 1902. Between then and World War II, seven more meetings

or, Imperial Conferences, were held at irregular intervals. By 1936, this type of meeting was called a "Commonwealth of Nations," giving the dominions equal status to Britain within it.

The Colonial and Imperial Conferences were early indications of a British change in attitude toward the colonies. But while areas largely peopled by those of European descent had been granted self-government, other areas did not enjoy such new rights, and remained subjects of the Empire just as before.

In all cases, Britain had retained control over defense and foreign affairs, though its dealings with Australia and New Zealand in 1887 indicated that even in this field Britain's dominant position was open

£126,000 **($617,000)** **The amount of money Australia offered to pay toward its own defense at the 1887 Colonial Conference.**

to negotiation—another small but crucial step nearer a new relationship. Over the next 75 years, the concept of an interdependent partnership between free and independent peoples developed into the Commonwealth of Nations.

Australia's coat of arms
Though granted by George V in 1912, the design symbolizes the independent Commonwealth of Australia rather than the country's monarchy. Of the six state badges, only two feature a crown.

Victoria's Golden Jubilee memorabilia
This impressive array of tickets, invitations, and souvenir
programs illustrates how the celebrations captured
the public imagination, sweeping away any republican
sentiment lingering from the previous decade.

Special Service
at
St. Margaret's, Westminster,
on Sunday May 22nd 1887.
to commemorate the 50th year of the reign of
Her Majesty Queen Victoria.

J. Henniker   Heaton Esq M.P.

WESTMINSTER ABBEY.

Her Majesty's Jubilee Thanksgiving Service,
TUESDAY, 21st JUNE, 1887.

Admit Baron von Kreusser

The Police are requested to give every facility
to the Bearer of this Ticket.

Lathom
Lord Chamberlain.
[OVER.

Tuesday, 21st June, 1887.

Potages.
À la Tortue   Au Printanière
À la Crème de Riz

Poissons.
Whitebait
Les Filets de Soles farcis à l'Ancienne
Les Merlans frits

Entrées.
Les Petits Vol-au-vents à la Béchamel
Les Côtelettes d'Agneau, Pointes d'Asperges
Les Filets de Canetons aux Pois

Relevés.
Les Poulets à la Financière
Haunch of Venison   Roast Beef

Rôts.
Les Cailles bardées   Les Poulets

Entremets.
Les Haricots verts à la Poulette
Les Escaloppes de Foies-gras aux Truffes
Sprütz Gebackenes
La Crème de Riz au Jus aux Cerises
Les Choux glacés à la Duchesse

Side Table.
Cold Beef   Tongue   Cold Fowl

Programme.

BAND OF THE ROYAL MARINES, LIGHT INFANTRY,
(CHATHAM DIVISION.)

Victoria's Jubilees

Though never fond of pomp, Victoria went along with the jubilee festivities of 1887 and 1897, and was a gracious host to the European royalty who came to honor her. Both occasions were hugely popular triumphs of careful organization, setting a precedent for future events.

Queen Victoria's Golden Jubilee was as much a national event as a monarchical one. Great Britain was a wealthy and powerful nation, with the largest empire ever seen. When Queen Victoria reached the 50th year of her reign, the country reveled in its successes.

At first, the Queen was irritated by the thought of all the "hustle and bustle" involved in a jubilee. She was also aware that not that many years before, the monarchy—and Victoria in particular—had been deeply unpopular; even in 1887, crowds booed her when she visited London's East End. Eventually, she came to see that a jubilee might not be such a bad idea, and so the party was launched.

Invitations went out to Queen Victoria's extended family and to heads of state in every continent. Jubilee souvenirs were manufactured by the thousand. Worldwide, museums, bridges, streets, and even burial grounds were named or renamed in honor of the Queen and Empress.

The two days of official jubilee pageantry began on June 20. The first day saw a massive state luncheon. The next day, Victoria was driven in an open landau carriage to Westminster Abbey for a service of thanksgiving. She returned to Buckingham Palace for another luncheon, after which she waved to the cheering crowds from the palace balcony. A dinner took place that evening with representatives of every crowned head in Europe. Fireworks followed as bonfires flickered from hilltops across the land.

Given the success of the Golden Jubilee, there could be no doubt but that the 60th year of Victoria's reign would be celebrated similarly. After all, by 1897, she had reigned the longest of any monarch in British history. But the mood in the country had changed.

By now, the Queen herself was old and frail, tension with Germany and serious difficulties in Ireland and South Africa darkened the international situation, and doubts were growing about the morality of maintaining a subservient empire. To combat this, Colonial Secretary Joseph, with the Queen's approval, gave the 1897 jubilee a distinctly imperial twist.

Celebrations for the Diamond Jubilee took place on June 22. London was festooned with Union Jacks and the flags of other nations, and hawkers plied their souvenirs as hundreds of thousands took advantage of the national holiday to throng the streets along which the 17-carriage royal procession passed. Dressed in her customary black, the Queen was deeply moved as the crowds cheered and broke into spontaneous outbursts of "God Save the Queen."

The days that followed were filled with more parades, inspections, unveilings, addresses, and receptions. Victoria soldiered on through them, not always in the best of humor, but aware that it was her duty to attend. In response to countless expressions of affection and gratitude, including 1,310 congratulatory telegrams from all around the world, Victoria wrote a thank you letter to the people of Great Britain and sent a telegram to the Empire. "From my heart," it read, "I thank my beloved people. May God bless them."

Her old foe William Gladstone (see p.51) had hoped she would use her Diamond Jubilee to announce her abdication. Evidently, he had underestimated his adversary.

Ticket to view the Royal Procession, June 1897
Reserved seats were sold from which to watch the royal procession pass by. Victoria herself accepted only reluctantly the need for such "continental" fanfare.

BEFORE

Celebrations marking the fiftieth anniversary of previous monarchs had been decidedly low-key.

GOLDEN JUBILEE PRECEDENTS
The 50th anniversaries of both **Henry III ‹‹ 21** and **Edward III ‹‹ 21** had passed quietly. There was more enthusiasm in 1809, however, when a nation at war marked the Golden Jubilee of **George III ‹‹ 48–49** with country-wide festivities. Because of the King's illness, the Royal Family took part only by accompanying him to a private church service in Windsor, followed by a fireworks display.

> "No one **ever**… has met with such an **ovation** as was given to **me**."
>
> QUEEN VICTORIA, IN HER DIARY, JUNE 20, 1897

Victoria at St. Paul's Cathedral, June 22, 1897
Frailty left the Queen unable to climb the steps into the cathedral, so a short service of thanksgiving was held outside, which she watched from her open coach. The crowds' cheers in support of the Queen were deafening.

AFTER

More than a century would elapse before Britain would again enjoy the jubilee experience. The occasions, celebrated in 2002 and 2012, were run with superb efficiency and met with widespread enthusiasm.

LEARNING FROM THE PAST
Britain's unparalleled experience in organizing displays of monarchical grandeur ensured that **Queen Elizabeth II's Golden Jubilee 260–61 ››** and **Diamond Jubilee 282–83 ››** celebrations were better arranged and choreographed, and probably even more popular, than those of her illustrious forebears.

The Crown Jewels

The symbolic regalia worn by the monarch for the coronation and other state ceremonies, these have been kept in the Tower of London since the early 14th century, after a series of thefts from their first home in Westminster Abbey.

[1] **The Armills of Queen Elizabeth II** Created for the 1953 Coronation, these 22-carat gold bracelets were the gift of several Commonwealth nations. [2] **Coronation spoon and Ampulla** Holy oil is poured through the beak of the gold, eagle-shaped ampulla into the silver-gilt spoon to anoint the new monarch. The spoon was probably first used in 1199 at the Coronation service of King John. [3] **St. Edward's Crown** Created for the coronation of Charles II in 1661 (along with the Scepter with the Cross and the Sovereign's Orb, right), this replaced the medieval crown the Parliamentarians had melted down in 1649, and is used at the moment of coronation. Traditionally, the jewels adorning the crown were hired and returned but in

1911 it was permanently set with semiprecious stones, and now weighs 5lb (2.23kg). [4] **Queen Victoria's small diamond crown** This 4in- (10cm)- diameter diamond-encrusted crown was created at the Queen's own expense after the death of her husband, Prince Albert, and was designed to sit on top of the mourning veil she wore for the rest of her life. It was designed to be lightweight and comfortable. [5] **The Scepter with the Cross** This was redesigned in 1910 to house the Cullinan I Diamond. [6] **The Sovereign's Orb** Representing Christ's dominion over the world, the orb is placed in the monarch's right hand during the coronation service to symbolize his or her role as Defender of the Faith.

Jeweled
cross-patté
(footed cross)

Spherical gold
Monde

[3] ST. EDWARD'S CROWN

Red velvet lining

Tudor rose operates invisible
hinge and spring

[1] THE ARMILLS OF
QUEEN ELIZABETH II

Arch encrusted
with jewels

Head unscrews so
oil can be poured
into body

[2] CORONATION
SPOON AND AMPULLA

Crown is set with
440 gemstones

Solid gold
frame

Base (and wings)
added in 1661 for the
coronation of Charles II

Freshwater
pearl

Ermine cap
border

4 QUEEN VICTORIA'S SMALL DIAMOND CROWN

Removable openwork silver-frame arches make crown more versatile

Crown is set with 1,187 brilliant- and rose-cut diamonds in open-backed mounts

Velvet cap

5 THE SCEPTER WITH THE CROSS

Step-cut emerald

Faceted amethyst *Monde*

Sturdy enameled structure holds 530-carat (3.74oz/106g) diamond

Emerald sits at center of cross encrusted with rose-cut diamonds and decorated with pearls

Octagonal step-cut amethyst *Monde*

6 THE SOVEREIGN'S ORB

Drop-shaped Cullinan I diamond

Hollow gold sphere mounted with emeralds, rubies, sapphires, and diamonds set between single rows of pearls

Enameled collar covers a joint between sections of rod

End of an Era

By the time Victoria's 64-year reign came to an end, the majority of her millions of subjects worldwide had known no other monarch. Her passing was not just an important moment for the British crown; it marked the end of an era.

Contemporaries were convinced that the coincidence in 1901 of Victoria's death and the close of a century was deeply significant. For the journalist R. D. Blumenfeld, "perhaps the most glorious era in English history" had ended. Writing a short time afterward, H. G. Wells preferred to look forward: "the supreme dramatic phase in the story of England is about to come." Both men agreed on one thing, however: life would never be the same again.

The Diamond Jubilee was followed by three hard years. Victoria, painfully lame, was plagued by cataracts, and subject to memory lapses. Her affection for the Munshi (see p.61) unsettled palace life, and the death of her son-in-law, Emperor Friedrich II of Germany, troubled her. Nevertheless, she kept in touch with public affairs, inspecting troops from a wheelchair, and celebrating the victory at Omdurman in the Sudan. Accounts of this battle, however, suggested it was a one-sided massacre and nothing to celebrate. When a war against the Boers of South Africa was going badly, she remained obstinately optimistic and sent the soldiers chocolate. She kept her diary until her last days, and still bombarded politicians, soldiers, and naval officers with streams of letters.

The end finally came at Osborne House on the Isle of Wight. The family, including Kaiser Wilhelm, had gathered beforehand, and her son, the future Edward VII, was at her bedside. She had made the arrangements for her own funeral. Wrapped in her wedding veil, her body was taken to Windsor Castle. Here it was laid inside a half-ton coffin (actually there were three, one inside the other like Russian dolls) and carried on a gun carriage through the streets of the town for a service in St. George's Chapel on February 2. After lying in state for two days, the coffin was taken to Frogmore Mausoleum in Windsor Great Park, where Victoria was laid to rest beside her dear Albert.

For several days, the nation was gripped by a sense of profound shock as the reality of Victoria's passing sank in. In the words of Elizabeth Longford, "One phrase was on many lips—God help us."

"Today seems very curious—pubs shut… Streets seem deserted."

LONDONER J. C. DIX, WRITING IN A LETTER TO HIS BROTHER, FEBRUARY 2, 1901

History in the making
Silent crowds line the streets of Windsor as Queen Victoria's funeral cortège passes by on February 2, 1901. Because of a last-minute technical hitch, the gun-carriage bearing the coffin was hauled by a team of sailors rather than horses of the Royal Artillery.

Born **1841** Died 1910

Edward VII

" King Edward is the **first...** to be **attended** in his coronation by... **statesmen** from our self-governing colonies. "

THE TIMES, 1902

His Imperial Majesty King Edward VII
Though Edward VII's parents had forbidden him from joining the army, English painter and illustrator, Sir Luke Fildes, considered a military pose and uniform appropriate for the coronation portrait of the head of the world's most powerful empire.

Albert Edward was the second child and first son of Queen Victoria and Prince Albert (see pp.60–61). As a boy, he was subjected to a rigorous education designed by his father to make him the ideal modern constitutional monarch. It was not a success. Bertie was no scholar, and his failings in the classroom added to a sense of inadequacy engendered by his mother's dislike of small children.

After fruitless months at the universities of Edinburgh and Oxford, and excluded from a career in the army by his parents, the heir apparent developed a new style of royal visit. In his role as Prince of Wales, he toured overseas and attended important opening ceremonies at home. Three royal tours stand out.

Prince Albert Edward,
Edward Albert, Prince of Wales, and Princess Alexandra (1844–1925) are seen here with their first child, Prince Albert Victor (1864–92). The boy led a troubled life and died before both his parents.

The coronation that never was

These tickets were issued for the coronation in Westminster Abbey of Edward VII and Queen Alexandra, first planned for June 26, 1902, and for the procession two days later. Both were canceled due to the King's illness, and the coronation rearranged for August 9.

- **November 9, 1841** Queen Victoria gives birth to her first son, the Prince of Wales, in Buckingham Palace, London.

- **January 25, 1842** Given his father's name, the boy is christened as Albert Edward at St. George's Chapel, Windsor Castle.

- **1860** Albert Edward becomes the first heir to the British throne ever to visit North America.

- **1861** The Prince of Wales's affair with actress Nellie Clifden brings Prince Albert to Cambridge to remonstrate with his son; Victoria later blames the Prince's behavior for bringing on her husband's fatal illness.

- **1862** The Prince of Wales undertakes a popular tour of the Middle East.

- **1863** Marries Princess Alexandra of Denmark.

- **1870** The Prince of Wales is called as a witness in a high-profile divorce case

- **1871** National rejoicing at the recovery of the Prince of Wales from typhoid helps the Royal Family regain some lost popularity.

The first, a four-month trip round the United States and Canada, persuaded New Yorkers to say prayers for the British Royal Family for the first time since 1774. The 1875–76 visit to India prepared the ground for his mother's acceptance of the title Empress of India. His 1903 trip to Paris, made as King, helped promote good relations between Britain and its oldest enemy.

Playboy Prince

The Prince's easy, nonjudgmental manner won him many friends, though not all of them had gained his parents' approval. In 1863, at the age of 21, he married Princess Alexandra of Denmark. The relationship remained amicable and, even when Edward was involved with someone else, Alexandra chose not to protest. Queen Victoria, however, was less understanding. Where her husband Albert's life had been all science, politics, welfare, and earnest causes, her son's was all cigars, wine, shooting,

Delayed coronation

Albert Edward was 59 when he acceded to the throne as Edward VII. He was a highly popular figurehead and, to ensure every detail of his coronation was in place, the ceremony was postponed until June 26, 1902, more than a year after his accession. On June 24, however, the King underwent emergency surgery for acute appendicitis, and the coronation was delayed until August 9. Alexandra was crowned Queen immediately after the King. Despite the fact that some foreign delegations had returned home, it was a great success and set the tone for future coronations.

Uncle of Europe

Edward had never shown much interest in politics and Victoria had fed this apathy by denying him access to state papers until the 1890s. As King, Edward VII continued much as before. His most valuable role was

disadvantaged, but disliked radicalism. For example, he disapproved of giving women the vote in parliamentary elections, and was opposed to Irish Home Rule. His most active political participation was to promote the modernization of the armed forces.

At the very end of his life he was forced into the center of the political arena. In 1909, to pay for old age pensions and further battleship building, the Liberal firebrand chancellor Lloyd George proposed a 2 percent tax on those earning more than £5,000 ($24,500) a year. Defying parliamentary convention, the Conservative-dominated House of Lords rejected the proposal. This was a constitutional matter, so Edward had to be involved. He urged moderation, advising the Lords to accept a bill from the popularly elected House of Commons. The Conservatives refused and forced a general election. The new House of Commons then planned a law curbing the Lords' power of veto. Since the peers would never accept such a move, to get it through the House of Lords the King had to be prepared to appoint enough Liberal peers to outvote the Conservatives. Throughout the whole process, Edward VII sought compromise. In the end, he did not have to make the "disgusting" decision to create new peers. On May 6, 1910, he suffered a number of heart attacks and died. People mourned the first sovereign for centuries to have truly won their hearts. It is fitting testament to this affection that the years between Victoria's death and World War One are commonly referred to as "Edwardian."

CORONATION STATIONERY, 1902

- **1883** Demonstrating an interest in the arts, the Prince of Wales opens the Royal College of Music.

- **January 14, 1892** Death from influenza of the Prince of Wales' elder son, the controversial Prince Albert Victor, who some have claimed was Jack the Ripper. At the age of almost 50, the Prince of Wales is finally permitted to see Cabinet Papers.

- **January 22, 1901** Death of Queen Victoria and accession of Albert Edward, Prince of Wales, who chooses the title Edward VII.

- **August 9, 1902** After the King is successfully operated on for appendicitis, his coronation finally takes place in Westminster Abbey; Queen Alexandra is crowned alongside him.

- **1903** Edward VII makes a formal visit to Paris, where he is warmly welcomed.

- **1908** Controversially, the King summons the new Prime Minister, H. H. Asquith, all the way to Biarritz to have his post officially sanctioned. Edward VII undertakes an impressive state visit to Russia on behalf of Britain, helping ease tension between the two imperial powers.

- **1909–10** Edward VII urges compromise on the House of Commons, which is divided over the House of Lords' powers of legislative veto.

- **May 6, 1910** Edward VII dies of heart failure.

> ## "I thought **everyone must know** that a short jacket is... worn with a silk hat at a **private** view in the morning."

EDWARD VII TO HIS PRIVATE SECRETARY

horse-racing, and feasting; he was even named in court cases involving divorce and betting. Style mattered to him, too. It was Edward VII who started the fashion of leaving the bottom button of a vest undone. His less frivolous side led him to patronize the arts, including founding the Royal College of Music.

as an unofficial ambassador for peace abroad. Related to the Royal Families of Belgium, Bulgaria, Denmark, Spain Germany, Greece, Portugal, Norway, Romania, Russia, and Sweden, he used his position as "Uncle of Europe" to foster good relations. At home, the generous-hearted King favored alleviating the lot of the poor and

Royal hunter

King Edward VII, here posing with a shotgun, was a devotee of the hunt. Like many of his royal predecessors, his quarry included women as well as wild animals.

2

THE HOUSE OF WINDSOR
1911–1947

THE HOUSE OF WINDSOR
1911–1947

1911		1918		1923	

JUNE 24, 1911
George V is crowned.

AUGUST 4, 1914
Britain declares war on Germany.

≫George V Coronation cup

FEBRUARY 1918
The King gives Royal Assent to the Representation of the People Act giving women of property over 30 the vote.

JUNE 1921
Unemployment reaches 2.2 million.

APRIL 26, 1923
Albert, Duke of York, marries Elizabeth Bowes-Lyon at Westminster Abbey.

MAY 13, 1927
George V changes his title to King of the United Kingdom of Great Britain and Northern Ireland, acknowledging that the Irish Free State is no longer part of the kingdom.

≽ Marriage of The Duke and Duchess of York

DECEMBER 1914
Queen's Work for Women Fund created by Queen Mary to supply clothing for the army. George V visits British Field HQ on Western Front for the first time. German navy raids Scarborough, Hartlepool, and Whitby, killing 137 and injuring 592.

JULY 17, 1918
Czar Nicholas II and his family murdered by Bolshevik revolutionaries, sending shock waves through the Royal Families of Europe.

WEDDING GROUP.

THEIR HIGHNESSES – THE DUCHESS OF YORK. THE DUKE OF YORK. H.M. THE KING.

THE EARL OF STRATHMORE.

H.M. THE QUEEN.

MAY 7, 1915
Sinking of the *Lusitania* kills 1,198 civilians.

MAY 1916
Britain's wheat supply is depleted. The King entreats families to reduce bread consumption. The Women's Land Army is established to increase agricultural productivity.

NOVEMBER 11, 1918
Germany signs Armistice agreement with Britain. A letter from George V is reproduced and distributed to all returning prisoners of war—the first ever mass communication from a reigning monarch.

≽ Graves of soldiers, many of whom died in the Battle of the Somme, in Ovillers Military Cemetery in Picardie, northern France

JULY 1–NOVEMBER 18, 1916
Battle of the Somme. More than one million soldiers die.

NOVEMBER 11, 1920
King George V unveils the Cenotaph—a war memorial in Whitehall, London. The body of the Unknown Warrior—an unidentified British soldier who died in World War I—is buried at Westminster Abbey.

NOVEMBER 11, 1921
First Poppy Day—memorial day for soldiers who died in World War I—held.

APRIL 23, 1924
George V makes first ever royal radio broadcast, opening the British Empire Exhibition in a specially built stadium at Wembley.

JANUARY 16, 1926
BBC radio play about a workers' uprising in London causes panic.

1929
The BBC makes the first experimental TV transmission.

≪ Poppy commemorating World War 1

MAY 31, 1915
German Zeppelins bomb London.

JANUARY 9, 1916
Last British troops evacuated from Gallipoli, Turkey, as the Ottoman Empire triumphs.

MARCH 2, 1917
George V's cousin, Czar Nicholas II, abdicates.

JULY 17, 1917
George V issues proclamation changing name of British royal house from German-sounding Saxe-Coburg-Gotha to Windsor.

NOVEMBER 21, 1920
The Irish Republican Army (IRA) kills 14 British undercover agents in Dublin. In retaliation the Auxiliary Division of the Royal Irish Constabulary open fire on a crowd at a Gaelic Athletic Association Football match in Croke Park, killing 13 spectators and 1 player and wounding 60.

1922
Following World War I, British Empire is at its greatest ever extent, ruling over one-quarter of the world's population.

DECEMBER 1922
Irish Free State is formed with George V as its monarch. Northern Ireland parliament votes to remain part of United Kingdom.

APRIL 21, 1926
Birth of future Queen Elizabeth II.

MAY 3, 1926
General strike sweeps the nation, provoking fears of revolution.

DECEMBER 1930
Unemployment rises to 2.5 million.

The ancient certainties of Victorian and Edwardian life, when Britain was the center of a vast empire, and the divisions of class went largely unquestioned, were crumbling. The beginning of the modern era, these crucial decades were years of world war and revolution. They witnessed the collapse of the British Empire, the fall of many European monarchies, the rise of fascism and communism in Europe, and at home, the growth of Socialism and the women's movement. If the British monarchy was to survive, it was essential to adapt to the new realities and to mold a constitutional monarchy fit for a more egalitarian nation.

1931　　1938　　1943 »

1931
Edward, the eldest son of George V, organizes the National Relief Fund for Britain's many unemployed.

AUGUST 24, 1931
The Great Depression brings about a national crisis. On advice of George V, an all-party government is formed.

DECEMBER 11, 1931
Statute of Westminster is the first step in the transformation of the Empire into the Commonwealth.

OCTOBER 1932
Oswald Mosley founds British Fascist Party. Hunger March arrives in London from Scotland. Several violent clashes with police.

DECEMBER 25, 1932
George V delivers the first Royal Christmas Day message on BBC radio.

FEBRUARY 9, 1933
Oxford Union debating society passes a motion stating "This house will in no circumstances fight for its king and country."

AUGUST 12, 1933
Churchill makes first public speech on dangers of German re-armament.

JANUARY 21, 1934
Around 10,000 attend Mosley's British Union of Fascists rally in Birmingham.

JULY 11, 1934
A total of 41 squadrons added to RAF as part of new air defense program.

MAY 6, 1935
An ailing King George V celebrates his Silver Jubilee.

DECEMBER 10, 1935
English physicist James Chadwick wins Nobel Prize for discovery of the neutron.

JANUARY 20, 1936
King George V dies. Edward, Prince of Wales, succeeds as King Edward VIII.

⌄ Portrait of Edward VIII

MARCH 7, 1936
Germany re-occupies Rhineland, a demilitarized zone as per the treaty of Versailles.

OCTOBER 1936
Battle of Cable Street between British Union of Fascists and anti-fascist demonstrators. 207 unemployed miners march from Jarrow to London.

DECEMBER 10, 1936
Edward VIII abdicates. Prince Albert becomes King George VI.

MAY 12, 1937
George VI crowned.

JULY 9, 1938
Gas masks issued to all British civilians.

SEPTEMBER 29, 1938
Prime Minister Neville Chamberlain and Hitler sign the Munich Agreement, allowing Germany to annex parts of Czechoslovakia, which it calls the Sudetenland.

APRIL 27, 1939
National Conscription introduced—all men aged 21 and over have to undergo six months' military training.

JUNE 1939
George VI and Queen Elizabeth visit the US and Canada—whose support will be vital if there is war.

LATE AUGUST/EARLY SEPTEMBER 1939
Children are evacuated from cities throughout Britain; army and navy are mobilized; blackout is imposed across the country. Britain declares war on Germany on September 3.

⌄ King George VI and US President Franklin Roosevelt

JANUARY 1940
Britain calls up two million 19- to 27-year-olds for military service. Food rationing introduced.

» Ration pack supplied to British soldiers on active service

JUNE 4, 1940
Dunkirk evacuation ends. Churchill makes his "We shall fight on the beaches" speech.

JULY—OCTOBER 1940
The Battle of Britain, a German air campaign against Britain, begins. Germany launches the London Blitz—57 consecutive nights of bomb raids.

NOVEMBER–DECEMBER 1940
Blitz continues in industrial cities including Coventry, Birmingham. Manchester, and Liverpool, with hundreds of casualties.

1941
As the war spreads into the Middle East and Asia, the National Service Act is passed.

JANUARY 26, 1942
First US troops destined to fight in Europe arrive in Belfast.

FEBRUARY 25, 1942
15-year-old Princess Elizabeth registers for war service.

NOVEMBER 1942
Major Allied victory at 2nd Battle of Alamein, followed by Allied victory at Tobruk.

27 P/21
SPECIAL RATION TYPE
CONTENTS
BOILED SWEETS
FRUIT BAR
SWEET BISCUITS
OATMEAL MUNCH
CHEWING GUM
J.B.B. LTD. PKD.

MAY–SEPTEMBER 1943
Dambuster raids and Allied invasions of Sicily and mainland Italy boost morale.

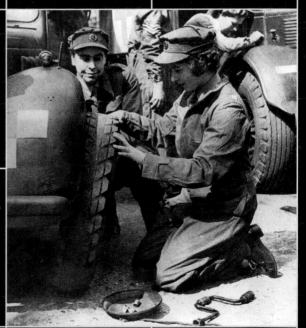

⌃ Elizabeth II aiding the war effort

NOVEMBER
Salisbury Plain and South Hams of Devon evacuated as preparations are made for the Normandy Landings.

JUNE 6
On D-Day, 155,000 Allied troops land on the beaches of Normandy.

MARCH–APRIL 1945
Last enemy action on British soil as a V-1 flying bomb strikes Datchworth, Hertfordshire. On April 15 British troops liberate the Bergen-Belsen concentration camp.

MAY 8, 1945
Churchill makes a victory speech and appears on the balcony of Buckingham Palace with the Royal Family. Street parties are held throughout the country to celebrate what was being referred to as Victory in Europe (VE) Day.

MAY 29, 1946
Princess Elizabeth and Philip Mountbatten are photographed together for the first time.

King George V
The King poses for an official portrait in his coronation robes. At heart, a man of simple tastes, George V submitted dutifully to the "fancy dress" required for royal ceremonial occasions.

Born 1865 Died 1936

George V

"You **can't shake hands** with a **clenched fist."**

GEORGE V, ON PEACEFUL NEGOTIATIONS DURING WORLD WAR I

nheriting the throne from his flamboyant, crowd-pleasing father Edward VII in 1910, King George V inevitably appeared uncharismatic by comparison. He was a dutiful character of simple tastes, behaving and dressing like an average English landowner. His favorite pursuits were hunting, sailing, and stamp-collecting. The responsibilities of his public role weighed upon him, and he far preferred a quiet private life. Yet this seemingly dull king proved the ideal monarch to lead his country through troubled times.

Career in the navy
As the second son of the Prince of Wales, George was not born to rule. He was trained for a career as a naval officer, while his elder brother Albert Victor was groomed as the future king. Prince George performed his naval functions competently, rising in rank on merit, and enjoyed the life at sea. This tranquil, relatively normal existence ended abruptly at his brother's untimely death in 1892.

Future king
At 26, George inherited his brother's role as the future king and also his brother's betrothed, Mary of Teck, known as "May." Despite the unfortunate circumstances leading

Strong ties
The young prince George is photographed with his mother Queen Alexandra. Edward VII and Alexandra were warm, loving parents, and George formed an especially close bond with his mother.

to their union, a solid love and respect developed between the couple after the wedding, if not before it. George was to be a faithful and devoted husband who depended heavily on his wife's support.

Family life
It was typical of George's modest tastes that he chose York Cottage in the grounds of the Sandringham estate as a family home. The royal couple had six children—David (born 1894), Albert (1895), Mary (1897), Henry (1900), George (1902), and John (1905), who was an epileptic and kept separate from the rest of the family, dying at age 13. As a father George was a strict disciplinarian and emotionally reserved. It has often been said that his sons were damaged by the fear he inspired. It is more likely, however, that they were hurt by their parents' frequent

absences because, after the accession of Edward VII in 1901, the royal couple were required to leave their children for six months at a time to make official visits to distant parts of the empire, including Australia and India. The children were raised by hired hands.

Accession to the throne
The death of Edward VII in May 1910 was a personal blow to George. "I have lost," he wrote in his diary, "the best of friends and the best of fathers." He took the throne in a period of acute political crisis, with a Liberal government in conflict with the Conservative-dominated House of Lords, suffragettes campaigning for votes for women, Irish nationalists pressing for Home Rule, and trade unionists threatening mass strikes. Fortunately Edward had taken care to educate his son in the business of monarchy and provide him with sensible advisors. George V performed his functions as a constitutional monarch with serious dedication. Although a conservative in politics as well as on moral issues, he scrupulously avoided partisan involvement in political issues, while attempting to exercise influence in favor of compromise and the peaceful resolution of disputes.

"Try living on **their wages** before you **judge** them."
GEORGE V, 1926

World War I
George V's role in World War I and its aftermath (see pp.80–81) won him widespread respect and affection among the British people, but the fall from power of his relatives Czar Nicholas II in Russia and Kaiser Wilhelm II in Germany were a sharp

reminder of the potential for popular disaffection. The monarchy would have to work to maintain its position as a focus for loyalty in the United Kingdom and the empire. Although much of the effort to popularize royalty devolved upon his eldest son, the charismatic Prince of Wales (see Edward VIII, pp.90–91), George V accepted the need to make contact with his people, most strikingly in the use of the new medium of radio (see pp.88–89). In 1924 he had the formal task of inviting newly elected Ramsay Macdonald to form Britain's first Labour government, an event regarded by many people at the time as heralding a social revolution. The King took a more relaxed view of Labour's rise to power. "They have different ideas to ours as

Family portrait
Photographed at Balmoral in 1906, George stands next to Mary, with baby John in her arms. The other children are, left to right, Princess Mary and the princes Harry, George, David (later Edward VIII), and Albert (George VI).

they are all socialists," he told his mother, "but they ought to be given a chance and ought to be treated fairly."

Illness and death
From the mid-1920s the King's health went into serious decline. Suffering from lung disease, he almost died in the fall of 1928 and the following year underwent two major operations. His grandchildren, including the future Elizabeth II, were a great comfort to him in his declining years. He showed them greater warmth than he had his own children. He disapproved of his eldest son, the Prince of Wales, much preferring his more dutiful second son. There is no doubt George V was out of step with his times. He was a narrow-minded conservative, disapproving of most innovative social customs, from divorce and cocktails to women smoking. But it was his respectability and simple decency that made him so well liked by his people. After his death in January 1936, more than 800,000 people filed past his body lying in state at Westminster Hall.

Imperial monarch
A souvenir postcard celebrating George V's coronation emphasizes the King's role as a focus for the loyalty of the far-flung British Empire and the different nations of the United Kingdom.

TIMELINE

- **June 3, 1865** Born at Marlborough House, London, second son of Edward, the Prince of Wales, and Alexandra.
- **January 1892** Becomes his father's heir after his elder brother dies; is made the Duke of York.
- **July 6, 1893** Marries Mary of Teck at St. James's Palace, London.
- **November 1901** Becomes the Prince of Wales when his father accedes to the throne.
- **May 6, 1910** Accedes to the throne on his father's death.
- **1911** Crowned in Westminster Abbey, London (June 22); formally presented as the Emperor of India at a Durbar in Delhi (December 12).
- **July 1914** Hosts an all-party conference in an attempt to resolve deadlock over Ireland's future.
- **August 4, 1914** Britain enters World War I.
- **October 1915** Injured by a fall from his horse while visiting British troops in France.
- **March 1917** Rejects asylum to Czar Nicholas II after the Czar abdicates the Russian throne.
- **July 17, 1917** Changes the name of the royal house from Saxe-Coburg-Gotha to Windsor.
- **November 11, 1918** Armistice ends the fighting in World War I.
- **November 11, 1920** Unveils the Cenotaph in Whitehall as a remembrance of the war dead.
- **June 22, 1921** Opens the first parliament of Northern Ireland at Stormont, Belfast.
- **April 23, 1924** At the opening of the British Empire Exhibition at Wembley, becomes the first monarch to speak on radio.
- **May 1926** During Britain's General Strike, urges the government to adopt a conciliatory approach to strikers.
- **1928** Becomes seriously ill because of lung disease, convalescent through to 1930.

THE CONVALESCENT KING WITH THE QUEEN

- **December 25, 1932** Makes the first royal Christmas radio broadcast to the nation.
- **1935** After 25 years on the throne, his Silver Jubilee is celebrated with widespread festivities.
- **January 20, 1936** Dies at Sandringham; interred at St. George's Chapel, Windsor Castle (January 28).

« BEFORE

With so many of Queen Victoria's descendants on European thrones, great power relationships were a family affair for the British monarchy.

EUROPE DIVIDED

By 1907, Europe was divided between the alliances of France, Russia, and Britain on one side, and Germany and Austria on the other. The British royals had cousins on both sides. Kaiser Wilhelm II was Victoria's grandson and Tzar Nicholas II was married to Victoria's granddaughter. The Royal Family disliked its German cousin, but maintained relations.

KING GEORGE V WITH KAISER WILHELM II

When Britain declared war on Germany, entering World War I on August 4, 1914, King George V and other members of the Royal Family had to appear on the balcony of Buckingham Palace to acknowledge cheering crowds. Like the majority of his subjects, however, King George was more horrified than enthused at the onset of war. His most immediate concern, expressed that evening in his diary, was for the safety of Prince Albert (the future George VI), who was serving as an officer in the Royal Navy.

Role of the Royals

Over the following four years the war expanded into a conflict of awesome dimensions, costing a million British and Commonwealth lives and requiring the mobilization of the entire resources of society. The role of a constitutional monarch in this "total war" had to be invented, as there was no precedent to follow. George V played no part in determining war strategy and had only a limited influence on senior appointments—in 1915 he supported moves to replace General Sir John French by General Douglas Haig as commander of British armies in France, but this was exceptional. Instead, the Royal Family focused on its ability to affect morale and inspire social solidarity.

George V was tireless in his duties. He made official visits to the Western Front in France, talking with generals, inspecting troops, awarding medals—he conferred 50,000 decorations with his own hands—and witnessing some of the devastation of trench warfare. Meeting the gravely wounded was the

Viewing the battlefield
George V surveys the devastation wreaked by the British victory at Messines in 1917. The Royal Family was fully aware of the harsh realities of the warfare in the trenches.

The Royals in Wartime

In 1914, four years after George V's accession, Britain was plunged into the most deadly conflict in its history. Throughout World War I, the Royal Family fulfilled its role as a focus for national unity and patriotism. Other European monarchies collapsed under the strain of war, but George V emerged more secure than ever in his people's affections.

Inspecting the troops
King George V meets British troops on a visit to the Western Front in France during World War I. The king traveled to the front five times in the course of the conflict.

"It is a **terrible catastrophe,** but it is **not our fault."**

GEORGE V, ON DECLARATION OF WAR, AUGUST 4, 1914

most painful royal duty—the king visited more than 300 hospitals in the course of the war. On one of his trips to the Western Front, in October 1915, he was injured by a fall from his horse, fracturing his pelvis, becoming himself a minor war casualty. He never fully recovered—the injury pained him for the rest of his life. When German Zeppelin airships and Gotha airplanes bombed London, King George and Queen Mary toured bomb-damaged areas. Recognizing the democratic nature of a conflict that involved the nation, they were careful to include factory districts and the working-class East End of London in their excursions.

The Royal Family could not, of course, in any real sense share the sufferings and deprivations of the British people at war, but symbolic gestures had impressive impact. In April 1915, when the government was pressing for potentially highly unpopular

limits on alcohol consumption, intended to increase the efficiency of industrial workers, George V himself "took the pledge," renouncing alcohol for the duration of the war. Few British workers followed his example, but it undoubtedly lessened the resentment brought about by blue laws.

Three of the royal children were old enough to participate in the war effort. The Prince of Wales (the future Edward VIII) served in the British Army as a staff officer, although he was barred from entering combat. Prince Albert did see action, taking part in the battle of Jutland in 1916 as a sub-lieutenant on board HMS *Collingwood*. Princess Mary, only 17 years old when the war began, promoted women's involvement in war work such as nursing in military hospitals and the "Land Girls" farm labor. She herself trained to become a nurse in the last year of the war.

Family ties

The Royal Family participated fully in the rabid anti-German sentiment generated by the war. The king wrote in his diary: "I shall never submit to those brutal Germans and I am sure the British nation is of the same opinion." Still, at a time when dogs known as German shepherds were being hastily renamed Alsatians and owners walking dachshunds were stoned in the street, the Royal Family was saddled with the embarrassingly Germanic name Saxe-Coburg-Gotha. Voices were occasionally heard insinuating that the royals were not truly British. Such comments incensed the King, who remarked: "I may be uninspiring, but I'll be damned if I'm alien." In July 1917, to settle the issue, he proclaimed a new dynastic name, adopting the unimpeachably English "Windsor."

In truth, only the most aggressive anti-royalists could imagine George V

Royal nurse
The young Princess Mary served as a part-time nurse in a London hospital in 1918. Gift boxes paid for by a fund bearing her name were distributed to all British soldiers and sailors at Christmas 1914.

PRINCESS MARY GIFT BOX

Call to arms
A poster calls for volunteers to join the British army. Every one of the 8 million British and imperial troops who fought in the war served officially in the name of the king.

and his family being complicit with Kaiser Wilhelm. In spring 1917, however, George's kinship with Tzar Nicholas II presented a more pressing problem. Forced to abdicate by a popular uprising at the start of the Russian Revolution, the Tzar sought to take his family into exile in Britain. The British government saw no objection, but George V and his advisors did. Knowing that a section of the British people viewed the Tzar as a tyrant and had welcomed his overthrow, they did not want the monarchy to risk unpopularity by being associated with him. The Tzar was thus denied refuge in Britain. When, the following year, he and his family were murdered by Bolshevik revolutionaries, George V felt both grief and guilt. Yet the judgment was surely correct that the association of the Royal Family with the Tzar might have alienated a part of the British working class.

At the Armistice in November 1918, the King found himself hailed by

cheering crowds, as he had been at the outbreak of war. His straightforward sense of duty and dogged courage had earned him widespread respect and admiration. Britain's wartime prime minister, David Lloyd George, later wrote: "One outstanding reason for the high level of loyalty and patriotic effort which the people of this country maintained was the attitude and conduct of King George."

AFTER ≫

World War I cast a long shadow over Britain in the 1920s and 1930s. The Royal Family stood out as guarantors of continuity in an uncertain, rapidly changing world.

REMEMBRANCE CEREMONIES
After the war there was a strongly felt need for regular remembrance of those who had sacrificed their lives. George V played a prominent role in the early remembrance ceremonies, laying the first wreath at the Cenotaph in November 1920.

MONARCHY AND NATIONHOOD
Participation in the war gave Commonwealth countries an increased sense of identity and nationhood. The monarchy became vital as a symbolic link between Britain and effectively independent Canada, Australia, and New Zealand.

Parliamentary procession
King George V and Queen Mary, seated in the
Gold State Coach, are at the heart of this solemn,
courtly procession on its way to the State Opening
of Parliament in 1924.

ROYAL RESIDENCE

Buckingham Palace

The official London residence of the British monarch since 1837, Buckingham Palace is also a working palace, where Queen Elizabeth carries out her ceremonial and official duties. It is the principal venue for state occasions and forms the backdrop to many national celebrations.

Buckingham Palace evolved out of the much smaller Buckingham House, built by the Duke of Buckingham in the early 18th century. A grand townhouse, which George III later bought for his wife, Queen Charlotte, it became known as the Queen's House, and 14 of George III's 15 children were born there.

Architect John Nash was responsible for modernizing and enlarging Buckingham House into a palace in the 1820s for George IV. The King wished to remodel London as a neoclassical city and he needed a palace that would reflect Britain's standing in the world. With Greek revival colonnades and pedimented porticoes enclosing a grand forecourt, and a magnificent, Roman-style triumphal arch for processions, his design was regarded as an architectural masterpiece. But Nash had vastly exceeded his budget and, after the King's death in 1830, he was dismissed for overspending.

Edward Blore was appointed as Nash's replacement. There was a lot of unfinished work for him to do, including outfitting the state apartments to Nash's designs. The new King, William IV, showed no interest in moving into the palace. In 1837 his successor, Queen Victoria, became the first monarch to use Buckingham Palace as her official residence in 1837.

The palace was certainly a theatrical setting for royal receptions, but the reality of living there turned out to be less luxurious. There were no bathrooms, so the Queen had to bathe in a portable bathtub, and the chimneys smoked so much that lighting fires was discouraged and the palace was freezing cold. The insufficient ventilation caused unpleasant odors, and when gas lamps were installed, there was serious concern about possible explosions. There were reports as well that the

staff, taking advantage of the teenage Queen, were lazy, and that the palace was filthy and neglected.

In February 1845, Blore was instructed to prepare plans for a new wing, in part to provide space for Victoria's growing family. This wing meant that the triumphal arch had to be moved to its present site near Speaker's Corner, where it became known as Marble Arch. But the most significant element of Blore's design was the central balcony on the new main façade, incorporated at Prince Albert's suggestion, and used for the first time in 1851 for the inauguration of the Great Exhibition. ❯❯

Marking the Queen's birthday

Trooping the Colour takes place on Horse Guards Parade, where the Queen inspects her troops. The procession begins and ends at Buckingham Palace. The ceremony also marks the sovereign's official birthday, a tradition that goes back to 1748.

CONCLUSION OF TROOPING THE COLOR AT BUCKINGHAM PALACE

Theatrical entrance

The state apartments are reached via the Grand Staircase—a theatrical design by Nash, with its gilded-bronze balustrade, illuminated by natural light through an engraved and etched glass dome.

» In Victoria's time the palace was a place of great entertainment. Famous contemporary musicians performed there, including Felix Mendelssohn and Johann Strauss II. There were extravagant costume balls, as well as more formal receptions and banquets.

When Queen Victoria was widowed in 1861 and withdrew from public life, she left Buckingham Palace, preferring

After Victoria's death, Buckingham Palace became a hub for the glamorous set that circled around Edward VII and Queen Alexandra. Debutante balls and lavish parties were held in opulent rooms redecorated in fashionable belle époque cream and gold. Under George V, the emphasis returned to official entertaining, though he did arrange a series of command performances

Despite all these improvement works, this was no fairy-tale palace, and in 1936, when George VI and Queen Elizabeth took up residence, they discovered a gloomy, dilapidated place with awkwardly placed electrical fixtures, endless corridors, and chilly rooms infested with mice.

Under the present Queen, the palace has been restored and the emphasis is firmly on its role as official residence and reception venue. Around 50,000 people visit the palace each year as guests at banquets, lunches, dinners, receptions, and garden parties.

Following the crisis provoked by the annus horribilis of 1992, Buckingham Palace has been at the forefront of initiatives to make the royal family seem more approachable. In 1993 the state rooms were opened to the public for the first time (initially to finance the restoration of Windsor Castle) and the palace has continued to open every summer. To date, more than six million people have visited.

Open to the public

Some tours of the palace include the White Drawing Room, the royal art collection, and the ballroom, with the table laid as if for a state banquet.

WHITE DRAWING ROOM

PICTURE GALLERY

Of the **775** rooms, **19** are state rooms, **52** royal/guest bedrooms, **188** staff bedrooms, **92** offices, and **78** bathrooms.

the relative intimacy of her other residences. The palace was seldom used, and, in response to the lack of royal interest, a note was found pinned to the railings in 1864, saying: "These commanding premises to be let or sold, in consequence of the late occupant's declining business."

of jazz musicians, including Louis Armstrong in 1932, while Queen Mary oversaw the restoration and extension of the royal collection of art.

Pollution, meanwhile, had decayed the original soft French stone of the façade, and, in 1913, it was replaced with white Portland stone.

THE BALLROOM

Pomp and ceremony
Designed by Nash, the Throne Room is perhaps the most majestic and dramatic of all the state rooms in Buckingham Palace. It is used for coronation and wedding photos, and to receive formal addresses.

The First King's Speech

George V became the first British monarch to make a studio broadcast when he addressed the people of his empire live on radio on Christmas Day 1932. The speech was heard by 20 million listeners in countries as distant as Canada, India, and Australia. Originally planned as a one-time event, the royal Christmas message became a tradition that is maintained today.

The British people first heard their King's voice on radio on April 23, 1924, when the fledgling British Broadcasting Company— then a private concern—transmitted the speech made by George V at the opening of the Empire Exhibition at Wembley Stadium. Since few people had wireless radios, the speeches were broadcast through loudspeakers in public places such as parks and department stores. In general though, George V was suspicious of radio, as of all other innovations, and was disinclined to involve himself in the new medium.

In 1932, the director-general of the now state-owned British Broadcasting Corporation (BBC), John Reith, needed a gimmick to launch the company's ambitious new Empire Service. He approached George V with a proposal for a Christmas broadcast and overcame the King's reluctance by giving him a guided tour of the BBC studios in London. The King was to speak from his home at Sandringham, an arrangement that required only the smallest possible disturbance of his routine. The text for the broadcast was written by aging novelist and poet Rudyard Kipling, the "bard of empire."

On Christmas Day, people across the world heard a firm, gentle voice begin: "I speak now from my home and from my heart to you all; to men and women so cut off by the snows, the desert, or the sea, that only voices out of the air can reach them." People did indeed find it magical that the King's voice could be heard in their living room. Focusing largely on the technological achievement of radio, the brief speech was judged an impressive success. Such was the popular enthusiasm that George V agreed to broadcast every year, with his last Christmas message transmitted in 1935, less than a month before his death.

> "To **all**—to **each**—I wish a **Happy Christmas.** God Bless You!"
>
> **GEORGE V,** ROYAL CHRISTMAS MESSAGE, 1932

George V on air
King George V gave his first radio message from an office at Sandringham that had been transformed for the occasion into a temporary studio. In this photograph, George V delivers his 1933 Christmas Day message from the same makeshift studio.

Born 1894 Died 1972

Edward VIII

"I... do **hereby declare** my **irrevocable determination** to **renounce** the **throne...**"

EDWARD VIII, IN HIS *INSTRUMENT OF ABDICATION*, DECEMBER 10, 1936

Young Edward
As a young man, the future Edward VIII was a stylish figure who charmed the people of Britain and the empire. However, his personality was not well suited to the formal responsibilities of kingship.

First son of the Duke of York, the future George V, Edward was christened Edward Albert Christian George Andrew Patrick David—Edward after his deceased uncle; Albert after Queen Victoria's long-mourned spouse; and George, Andrew, David, and Patrick after the four patron saints of England, Scotland, Wales, and Ireland, respectively. Within the family, he was always known as David.

Edward had a strict upbringing; he commented on it later: "The laws of behavior as revealed to a small boy tended to be ruled by a vast preponderance of 'don'ts.'" His relationship with his father was neither close nor comfortable. Following the family tradition, Edward entered naval college, but George V's accession to the throne in 1910 truncated his eldest son's naval career, since it was considered unsuitable for the Prince of Wales.

Edward showed early signs of rebellion against his assigned role in life shortly after his father's coronation in 1911. As a gesture designed to encourage Welsh loyalty to the crown, it was decided that Edward be formally invested as Prince of Wales at Caernarvon Castle. Since no such investiture had occurred for 600 years, a ceremony was invented with copious fanciful historical detail. The teenage Prince was required to wear a costume so ridiculous that, on the eve of the event, he declared he would refuse to take part. After a fierce argument with his father, the Prince relented and the ceremony went ahead without a hitch. However, the fuss was indicative of the Prince's potential discomfort with the kind of royal duties that George V unquestioningly accepted.

Edward served as an army officer in World War I. He was denied an active role by order of Lord Kitchener, the secretary of state for war, who held that although the Prince's death would be an acceptable loss, his capture by the enemy might prove a severe embarrassment. Despite reduction to a passive role, however, Edward's service as an aide-de-camp on the staff of the commander in chief in France and later as a staff officer in the Mediterranean zone was sufficient to support a claim to have "done his bit" for the war effort.

Popular prince

After the shock of the war, with its heavy death toll, there was an urgent need to promote the Royal Family as a focus for loyalty. Young, suave, and charming, Edward was put to work touring the empire. He was received

Prince of Wales
Edward was 17 years old at the time of his investiture as Prince of Wales in 1911. The Prince was forced to wear a fanciful pseudo-historical costume, which caused him great embarrassment.

with particular warmth in Britain's dominions, where he was seen as a refreshing change from the old-fashioned George V. At the British Empire Exhibition, held at Wembley in 1924, the Canadian pavilion exhibited a life-sized statue of Edward made of refrigerated butter. The prince was equally well-received by the British working class. He made well-publicized visits to industrial areas and promoted clubs for the unemployed, showing a comfortable and relaxed manner in the company of ordinary working men.

Unsuitable king

While Edward brought a welcome change to the image of British royalty in public, in private he behaved in a manner that appalled his father and worried the political elite. He mixed with the raffish, fashionable society of the 1920s and adopted its customs – drinking cocktails, dancing to jazz, and engaging in casual adultery. His affairs with married women, notably Freda Dudley Ward, Lady Furness, and finally, Wallis Simpson, were considered incompatible with the Royal Family's role as exemplars of the traditional moral order. A servile press kept the

Nazi visit
The Duke of Windsor inspects soldiers during his visit to Nazi Germany in 1937. The former king's close relations with the Nazi regime were a source of considerable disquiet for the British government.

social issues. He was critical of the government's complacent acceptance of high levels of unemployment in the 1930s, although his sympathies lay not with the socialists but with politician Oswald Mosley's Fascist

> ## "After I am **dead,** the boy will ruin himself in **12 months."**
>
> GEORGE V, SPEAKING OF HIS SON EDWARD TO PRIME MINISTER STANLEY BALDWIN

British people in ignorance of these liaisons, but in private, George V disapproved of his eldest son's manners and morals, openly preferring his second son, Albert.

The Prince of Wales must have already harbored doubts about the desirability of becoming king. When his father's illness obliged him to take over many of the King's functions in the late 1920s, he found the tasks tedious and performed them unreliably. He chafed at the restrictions placed upon his expression of views on political and

movement. Conservative politicians feared that, once on the throne, he might breach the rules of constitutional monarchy and intervene in politics to their detriment.

None of these issues were known to the British people, who embraced their new monarch with enthusiasm at his accession in January 1936. The abdication crisis (see pp.92–93), precipitated by Edward's strong determination to marry Wallis Simpson, brought about a sudden and sharp disillusionment. The

abdication was in part a coup by the political establishment to remove a ruler they distrusted, but also an escape route for a king who had no enthusiasm for the rituals and responsibilities of his role. The politicians of the "king's party" who tried to keep Edward on the throne found that the monarch himself was a lukewarm supporter of their cause. Finally, on December 10, 1936, Edward signed an instrument of abdication, becoming the only British king ever to renounce the throne voluntarily.

Life in exile

Created Duke of Windsor, Edward married Simpson and settled in France. Although he received a title and financial support, the Duke was effectively cut off from his family, who took a dim view of his behavior. The itch to intervene in public affairs led to an ill-judged visit by the Windsors to Nazi Germany in 1937, including a meeting with Hitler. After Britain and Germany went to war in 1939 the Duke was given employment with the British army in France, but rumors spread that the Windsors were engaged in traitorous contacts with the enemy.

After the fall of France, Prime Minister Winston Churchill, once one of Edward's strongest supporters, dispatched the Duke to the Bahamas—an exile lightly disguised by appointment to governorship of the islands. After the war, the Windsors returned to France, settling into the lifestyle of celebrity socialites. Over time, there was some defrosting of relations with the Royal Family and, at his death, Edward's body was brought back to England for interment in the Royal Burial Ground, Frogmore, at Windsor.

DUCHESS OF WINDSOR (1896–1986)

WALLIS SIMPSON

Born Bessie Wallis Warfield, Wallis Simpson grew up in Baltimore, Maryland. In the course of her first two marriages, to US Navy pilot Earl Spencer and American shipping executive Ernest Simpson, she became a socialite mixing in a decadent international set. After her marriage to Edward, she became Duchess of Windsor but was not allowed to be known as "Her Royal Highness." When she died in 1986 at her home in France, she was buried alongside Edward at the Royal Burial Ground.

(see pp.92–93)

TIMELINE

- **June 23, 1894** Born at the White Lodge, Richmond, Surrey.
- **1907–09** Attends Osborne Naval College and the Royal Naval College at Dartmouth.
- **May 6, 1910** Edward's father accedes to the throne as George V.
- **July 13, 1911** Invested as Prince of Wales at Caernarvon Castle.
- **1912–14** Attends Magdalene College, Oxford, where he excels at sports but does not earn a degree.
- **1914–18** Joins the Grenadier Guards and serves as a staff officer with the British army in France during World War I.
- **1916** Awarded the Military Cross for his role in World War I.
- **1919** Makes official visit to Canada and the US.
- **1920–21** Visits Australia, New Zealand, and India.
- **1924** Presides over the British Empire Exhibition.
- **1928–30** Performs many of the functions of a king during his father's illness and convalescence.
- **January 1931** Meets Wallis Simpson for the first time.
- **1934** Becomes involved with Wallis Simpson.
- **January 20, 1936** Accedes to the throne on the death of George V.
- **August–September 1936** Vacations with Wallis Simpson in the Mediterranean.
- **October 27, 1936** Simpson begins divorce proceedings against her second husband, Ernest Simpson.
- **November 16, 1936** The King informs Stanley Baldwin that he intends to marry Simpson, precipitating the abdication crisis.
- **December 10, 1936** Abdicates, renouncing the throne for himself and his descendants, and moves to France.

KING EDWARD VIII POSTAGE STAMP FROM 1936

- **June 3, 1937** Marries Wallis Simpson at the Chateau de Condé, near Tours, France.
- **October 1937** The Windsors make a visit to Nazi Germany, meeting Adolf Hitler.
- **September 1939** Outbreak of World War II; Edward is made a general and attached to the British military command in France.
- **June 1940** Flees France as it is overrun by German troops, and ends up in Portugal.
- **August 1940–March 1945** Sent by Winston Churchill to the Bahamas, where he serves as Governor.
- **1945** Returns to live in France, where he stays for the rest of his life.
- **May 28, 1972** Dies at his home in Paris.

Edward VIII's Abdication

The abdication crisis of 1936 is often seen as the romantic tragedy of a king who renounced the throne for love. But it was also a political plot in which a troublesome monarch was overthrown because he was considered unsuitable to reign.

Until December 1936, most of the British public had no idea that their monarchy was in crisis. Reports of Edward VIII's liaison with twice-divorced American socialite Wallis Simpson had appeared in foreign newspapers and magazines but were kept out of the British press. Instead, news focused on preparations for Edward's coronation, due to take place the following year. Britain's Conservative Prime Minister Stanley

BEFORE

When Edward VIII became king at age 41 on January 20, 1936, he seemed destined for a lengthy reign.

A PROMISING FUTURE
Edward was already well-known to the British people and the empire through his prominent role as **Prince of Wales ‹‹ 90–91**. A more charismatic figure than his father, he had been sent on **tours of the Commonwealth** in the 1920s to encourage loyalty to the crown. He had also made well-publicized visits to **Depression-hit industrial areas of Britain** to show royal concern for the hardships of the working class. Since 1934, however, Edward had been involved with a married American woman, Wallis Simpson—a relationship that would cost him the crown.

Baldwin had, from the outset, serious doubts about the new king. Edward's father George V had ruled as an impeccable constitutional monarch, avoiding any public expression of opinion on political matters. He had also established the moral rectitude of the Royal Family as an example to the nation. Baldwin correctly surmised that Edward was unlikely either to keep out of politics—he was known to sympathize with politician Oswald Moseley's British Union of Fascists—or set a suitable moral example. Baldwin's concern for Edward's liaison with Simpson was shared by other figures of the establishment, including the head of the Church of England, Cosmo Lang.

Breaking point
In October, Baldwin confronted the King with clippings from the foreign press reporting his summer vacation with Simpson in the Mediterranean. It was made clear to the King that the matter could not be kept under wraps indefinitely. Meanwhile, Simpson won

325 DAYS The duration of Edward VIII's reign.

a divorce ruling against her husband in a court in Ipswich, Suffolk, opening the way for a possible marriage to Edward. The drama came to a critical point at a meeting between the King and the Prime Minister on November 16.

Edward informed Baldwin that he intended to marry Simpson. Baldwin replied that having an American divorcée as queen would be unacceptable to the British people, the Commonwealth, and the Church of England. Edward said that, if this were the case, he would abdicate rather than renounce the marriage.

Two days later, visiting the Welsh valleys, an area of high unemployment,

Performing a king's duties
Surrounded by heralds, Edward prepares for the State Opening of Parliament at the House of Lords on November 3, 1936. This would be the first and last time that he would perform this ceremony.

the King commented in the presence of journalists that "something must be done" to find these people work. Widely reported in the press, this remark drew a favorable response as an expression of the King's concern for his people. Baldwin and his colleagues, however, interpreted it as a criticism of the government's economic policy and thus a wholly inappropriate intervention for a constitutional monarch.

As far as the British people were concerned, the abdication crisis began on December 3. The decision to go public was triggered by an outspoken attack on the King's morals by Alfred Blunt, the Bishop of Bradford. Suddenly the situation was blazoned in newspaper headlines and on billboards across the country. By the time this occurred, the issue had narrowed to a simple choice. Edward would not withdraw from his plan to marry, while Baldwin and the British establishment were determined there should never be a Queen Wallis. Still, it was suggested that the idea might be acceptable if the marriage was morganatic, that is, Simpson would not enjoy the title and privileges of a queen. However, this proposal gained little support in Parliament and was opposed by Commonwealth leaders in Canada and Australia. Baldwin therefore felt justified in rejecting the idea.

Stepping down
A diverse collection of politicians attempted to organize a last-ditch defense of the King. Edward's backers included Moseley's Fascists, press baron Max Aitken, and a small group of Conservative Members of Parliament led by future prime minister Winston Churchill. Although there was widespread sympathy for the King, Edward's supporters were unable to find adequate backing for a revolt

Official menu
This is the menu for the official dinner at Buckingham Palace after the State Opening of Parliament in November 1936. A week before this function took place, Wallis Simpson had filed for divorce, precipitating the abdication crisis.

against the government's stand. The King himself was stubborn in his commitment to Simpson and showed no desire to retain the throne. If anything, his brother, the Duke of York was more distressed at the prospect of gaining the crown than Edward was at losing it. Placed under intolerable pressure, Simpson offered to withdraw from her relationship with the King, but it made no difference. On December 10, Edward signed his abdication.

The following evening Edward, now the Duke of Windsor, made a moving, dignified radio broadcast from Windsor Castle, beginning: "At long last I am able to say a few words of my own." He declared his allegiance to his successor George VI and explained his inability to carry a king's "burden of responsibility." That night, Edward boarded a Royal Navy warship at Portsmouth and sailed for France and Wallis Simpson.

Edward's first radio broadcast
Edward VIII makes his first radio broadcast as king in March 1936. The next time he would address the nation and empire on radio would be in December to announce his abdication.

Wedding day
The Duke and Duchess of Windsor pose for photographs on their wedding day in June 1937 outside the Chateau de Condé in France. The Duke's family was not present at the ceremony.

> " I have found it **impossible** to… discharge **my duties as king**… without the **help and support** of **the woman I love.**"

EDWARD VIII, FROM HIS ABDICATION SPEECH, DECEMBER 1936

AFTER

George VI was crowned king on May 12, 1937, at the coronation that had been intended for Edward VIII. Meanwhile, Edward became a politically unsettling exile.

ROYAL EMBARRASSMENT
On June 3, 1937, **Edward married Simpson in France** and the couple settled there. The following October, they **visited Nazi Germany**, meeting Adolf Hitler. This became a serious embarrassment once Britain went to war with Germany in 1939.

THE WINDSORS VISIT BRITAIN IN 1967

RENEWING TIES
Edward returned to France after a five-year stint as **Governor the Bahamas,** and the couple settled into the lives of minor international celebrities. Their contacts with the Royal Family were distant—the Duke **attended George VI's funeral** in 1952, but not Elizabeth II's coronation the following year. From around 1965, the Windsors began to visit Britain at will and attended a number of royal occasions, including the centenary of Queen Mary's birth in 1967. The Queen visited the couple for the first time in France in 1972, shortly before the Duke's death.

CORONATION OF
THEIR MAJESTIES
KING GEORGE VI &
QUEEN ELIZABETH

BY Command of The King, the Earl Marshal
is directed to invite Her Royal Highness Princess Margaret Rose
to be present at the Abbey Church
of Westminster on the
12th day of May, 1937.
Norfolk.
Earl Marshal.

Crown stickers
These windshield stickers were used on royal cars during the 1930s. The black and white stickers were used for ordinary cars from the Royal Mews.

Coronation invite
Invitations to George VI's coronation were issued by the Earl Marshal—the 16th Duke of Norfolk Bernard Fitzalan-Howard. As chair of the coronations Executive Committee, he extended invitations to everyone from members of the Royal Family to trade union representatives.

After the coronation ceremony
On May 12, 1937, after his coronation ceremony at Westminster Abbey, King George VI and his family appeared on the balcony of Buckingham Palace to greet the crowd below. From left to right are: Queen Elizabeth, Princess Elizabeth, Queen Mary, Princess Margaret, and George VI.

The **Unexpected King**

The abdication had dealt a huge blow to the credibility of the monarchy. Throughout Europe, royal families had recently been toppled from their thrones, and at home, the familiar established order was questioned by many.

« BEFORE

Edward VIII's abdication brought into question the relevance of the monarchy as the embodiment of responsibility and virtue.

AN UNCERTAIN FUTURE
Edward VIII's abdication « 92–93 divided the nation, with traditionalists shocked at the dereliction of duty, and radicals declaring that the King should do whatever he wanted—largely because he was irrelevant. Consequently, when George VI inherited the throne, its future seemed uncertain.

RELUCTANT RULER
While Prince Albert and his family duly fulfilled their royal duties, they lived out of the spotlight. **Hampered by crushing shyness and a debilitating stammer**, Albert found public speaking a torment. After a particularly harrowing performance at Wembley in 1925, he began speech therapy.

George V had long harbored grave reservations about his first son Edward's ability to be king. The King had more faith in his second son, Prince Albert, and his granddaughter, Elizabeth's, abilities as potential monarchs. Despite this, the King had done nothing to prepare Albert for any kingly duties. Albert, who had always been overshadowed by his extrovert older brother Edward, was forced to step into his shoes after the abdication crisis (see pp.92–93). His coronation as George VI was held on the same day that had earlier been set aside to crown Edward. The *Illustrated London News* had already commissioned paintings of the event, and had to ask the artist to substitute Edward's face with George's.

Troubled times
This was an inauspicious time to be appointed king. Not only had the abdication dealt a huge blow to the credibility of the monarchy in England, but the familiar, established order was in question throughout Europe and the British Empire. In India and Ireland, there were cries for home rule and republicanism. Meanwhile, dictators were taking over Europe—Joseph Stalin was in power in the Soviet Union; Adolf Hitler had marched into the Rhineland; Francisco Franco had staged an uprising leading to civil war in Spain, and fascist Italy and Germany had forged an alliance. At home, unemployment was high, and rising tensions between the left and right wings had already led to civil unrest.

In this context, Edward—a playboy King who admired Hitler and cared more for his private life than his country—seemed not only to threaten the existence of the monarchy, but the very survival of democratic Europe.

An unlikely candidate
George VI, a shy and serious man with little self-confidence and a crippling speech impediment, seemed an unlikely candidate to reverse the fortunes of the monarchy and country. However, his

> **"Dickie, this is absolutely terrible. I never wanted this to happen; I'm quite unprepared for it… I've never even seen a State Paper."**
>
> GEORGE VI, TO LORD MOUNTBATTEN UPON HEARING OF HIS ACCESSION

modesty, determination, unshakable diligence, combined with an iron sense of duty enabled him to become a respected figurehead, who saved the reputation of the monarchy and earned the respect of both politicians and people.

Before the abdication, Prince Albert and his family lived a relatively quiet life, in between attending to various royal duties. Hampered by his stammer, Albert rarely spoke in public. According to royal biographer, Dermot Morrah, there were even moves among "some men of authority" to settle the crown instead on Albert's younger brother, the more charismatic Prince George, who had the added advantage of having already produced a male heir.

Albert and Elizabeth were deeply opposed to the abdication. They were furious with Edward and suspicious of Wallis Simpson. Both were reluctant to accede to the throne, but their sense of duty won over. George VI applied himself to his new role with tenacity, reading official papers, educating himself in constitutional matters, and working closely with his prime ministers. Inevitably, his inexperience and naivety showed at times, especially under the pressures leading up to World War II. Desperate to avoid another war, he backed Prime Minister Neville Chamberlain's policy of appeasing Hitler so fervently that many members of Parliament felt he was compromising his constitutional role of political impartiality.

Significant visit

Perhaps the most significant action of George VI, as Europe prepared for war, was the visit he made to the US in June 1939. Both President Franklin D. Roosevelt and the King were very aware of the importance of the visit. Roosevelt believed that war was imminent, and that "Great Britain would be our first line of defense." He stated that he would convince his country to drop its policy of isolationism. George knew that American help would be essential if the Allies were to win the war. After an informal picnic, the King and Roosevelt talked late into the night, with George taking meticulous notes, which he sent back to the British government. Among these notes he wrote: "If London was bombed, US would come in." By the following September, Britain was at war with Germany.

With the US president

George VI and US President Franklin Roosevelt travel from Union Station to the White House. This was one of the many meetings that helped foster the diplomatic relations necessary for the Allied Powers to weather and win World War II.

George VI went on to essay his kingly responsibilities with considerable success, on the personal front, his relationship with his elder brother was strained.

BENEFICIAL ALLIANCE

George VI's successful diplomacy in the US had significant returns. After Britain declared war on Germany, US President Roosevelt extended support by **repealing the arms embargo** so that arms could be sold to France and Britain. He then passed the **Lend Lease Act** permitting lending, leasing, selling, or bartering of arms, ammunition, and food to "any country whose defense the President deems vital to the defense of the US." America formally joined the conflict in December 1941.

Back home, George VI stayed in constant consultation with British Prime Minister **Neville**

Chamberlain 102–103 », and his successor, Winston Churchill, throughout the war.

FALLING OUT

Continued acrimony between George VI and his elder brother fueled the latter's fascination with Hitler, whom he met in 1937.

GEORGE VI WITH BRITISH PRIME MINISTER NEVILLE CHAMBERLAIN

Born 1895 Died 1952

George VI

"I pray to God… that **nothing** will **come between Bertie and Lilibet** and the **throne.**"

GEORGE V, ON HIS DEATHBED, 1936

Full dress uniform
George VI is pictured here in full dress coat in the rank of Admiral of the Fleet. He also wears a collar and badges of the order of the Thistle, and stars of the orders of the Garter and the Thistle.

Prince Albert, or Bertie—the second son of the Duke and Duchess of York—later crowned King George V and Queen Mary—was a shy, unassuming boy. He grew up in the shadow of his glamorous elder brother Edward. Albert was born in 1895 on the inauspicious day of the anniversary of the death of Queen Victoria's beloved husband Prince Albert—December 14 (see pp.60–61). This reportedly caused the Queen some distress. The news, two days later, that her new great-grandson was to be called Albert "that dear name which is a byword

for all that is great and good…" appeared to have offered her some solace.

The Duke of York and his family lived in York Cottage, a glum mock-Tudor villa on the Sandringham Estate. The future king, George V, was a severe father—a typical Victorian patriarch—and while his first son, Edward, thrived on rebellion against authority, Albert's self-confidence shriveled in the face of the constant cycle of reprimand and disapproval considered normal by parents of the era. As in most aristocratic—and many middle class—families of the time, the York children had very little contact with their parents. They lived in a separate part of the house with a battalion of nannies, nursemaids, and tutors, and were expected to stay there, except, according to the

Time with the Queen
Albert (seated on a cushion) is pictured here with his siblings—Mary (on the chair), Edward (standing), and Henry, as a baby—all gathered around their great-grandmother, Queen Victoria.

Countess of Airlie, when invited to their mother's boudoir after tea, or for "a less pleasurable interview with their father in his sitting room." The Countess, a close confidante of Albert's mother, the Duchess of York, was a frequent visitor to the house, "I never saw the children run along the corridors," she wrote, "they always walked sedately, generally shepherded by nurses or tutors." By contrast, their grandparents, Edward VII and Queen Alexandra, were effusive, fun, and relaxed—although considered far too indulgent by George and Mary—and they provided the children with some respite from the harsh regime of home.

Unpleasant childhood

Sandwiched between his charismatic golden-haired elder brother Edward, and his father's favorite (and only daughter) Mary, Albert seems at times to have been neglected—emotionally by his parents and physically by a nanny, who gave him so little to eat that he developed an intestinal condition that remained with him for the rest of his life. There are also reports of uncontrollable fits of rage at his older brother, most probably provoked by merciless teasing and taunting.

Sensitive, self-effacing, and insecure, Albert was forced to wear an iron leg brace to correct knock-knees, and it was made very clear to him that his natural left-handedness was a defect. The message to the child was clear: he was not good enough. Around the age of 7 or 8—the same time that he was being forced to write with his right hand—he developed a debilitating stammer.

Beating the hardships

Sent away to Naval College at the age of 14, Albert was small, timid, and had no experience of the world

Engagement

The future King George VI loved Elizabeth Bowes-Lyon deeply and became engaged to her in London on January 18, 1923. They married later in April in Westminster Abbey.

beyond the sheltered life at home at Sandringham. At first he was taunted and bullied: "It never did me any good to be a prince, I can tell you, and many was the time I wished I hadn't been. It was a pretty tough place." However, he soon began to make friends, winning people over with his lack of pretension and his sense of humor. He also showed a physical grit and determination that made him excel at sports.

Academically, Albert struggled, coming 68th in a class of 68 at his end-of-term exams. At his next school, the Naval College at Dartmouth, he was immediately assigned a young lieutenant as tutor and finally began to apply himself. At the end of the term his hard work was rewarded with a special gift from the lieutenant—a set of fake silver spoons, made of an amalgam that melted in a cup of tea. Bertie tried the trick at Sandringham, and it worked perfectly—although apparently his father George V was not amused.

"I'm only a **naval officer, it's the only thing I know.**"

PRINCE ALBERT, SOON TO BECOME GEORGE VI, TO LORD MOUNTBATTEN, 1936

The determination Albert had eventually demonstrated at school was soon to pay off in other ways. He fell in love with the young Elizabeth Bowes-Lyon, but felt completely out of his league. At ease socially, and with an engaging enthusiasm for life, she was one of the most popular girls of her day. "He's always talking about her," his mother remarked to Lady Airlie, "She seems a charming girl, but I don't know her very well." Having been assured by Lady Airlie, Mary of Teck (now Queen Mary) too became convinced that Elizabeth was the only woman who could make Albert happy. Elizabeth was cautious, however, and in the end, Albert had to ask her three times before

George Cross

King George VI created the British civilian and military medal, the George Cross, in 1940 for "acts of the greatest heroism or of the most conspicuous courage in circumstances of extreme danger."

she agreed to marry him. When she finally gave her consent, Albert sent his parents a telegram. The wording had been prearranged, and simply read, "All right. Bertie."

Marriage

The wedding was held on April 26, 1923, in Westminster Abbey. The newly formed British Broadcasting Company (BBC) requested permission to record and broadcast the event on radio, but the Abbey Chapter vetoed the idea. After the wedding—and a long trip to Africa—the couple settled down into a house on Piccadilly, where their two daughters, Elizabeth and Margaret Rose, were born. They lived the kind of life typical of the aristocracy of the time—comfortable and privileged, sheltered and yet fashionable, but by no means extravagant.

The abdication of Edward VIII was the end of life as the Yorks had known it. They left their family home on Piccadilly for Buckingham Palace, and the comfort of minor renown and routine royal duties for the pressures of office and worldwide fame. On May 12, 1937, the date initially intended for Edward VIII's coronation, Albert was crowned as King George VI.

People's king

At first glance, a man less suited to be king would be hard to imagine. He was sensible and agreeable but not quite the stuff of great monarchs. But George VI reigned at an extraordinary time, and it may have been his essential modesty and diffidence—combined with his grit and determination—that made him a monarch capable of guiding Britain through a period of war. He knew how to listen, and understood that he had a lot to learn. The people warmed to their unassuming king, moved by his speech difficulties and appreciating his evident humanity and dedication to duty. When it came to the day he had to inform the nation that it was at war via live radio broadcast (see pp.102–03), his words carried a human touch, uncommon in royal speeches of the time. He gave the impression there was no them and us, but simply "we."

TIMELINE

- **December 14, 1895** Born in York House on the Sandringham Estate, second son of Prince George, Duke of York, and Mary of Teck.
- **January 22, 1901** Death of Queen Victoria, who is succeeded by her son, King Edward VII. Prince Albert becomes third-in-line to the throne.
- **1909** Attends Royal Naval College at Osborne House (see pp.56–57) on the Isle of Wight.
- **June 22, 1911** Albert's parents, George and Mary of Teck, are crowned King and Queen.
- **1913–1916** Joins the Royal Navy and serves in World War I. Ill health forces him to retire from active service after the battle.
- **1918** Transfers to the recently established Royal Air Force and becomes the first member of the Royal Family to have a pilot's license.
- **1920** Leaves Cambridge University and begins to take on more functions. Visits to coal mines, factories, and railyards earn him the nickname "Industrial Prince." He meets Elizabeth Bowes-Lyon for the first time.
- **April 26, 1923** Marries Elizabeth Bowes-Lyon.
- **April 21, 1926** Elizabeth Alexandra Mary, the future Queen Elizabeth II, is born.
- **December 11, 1936** Abdication of Edward VIII; Albert becomes King. The Irish Free State removes all mention of the monarch from the Irish Constitution.
- **May 12, 1937** Coronation of George VI on the day previously intended for Edward VIII's coronation.
- **June 1939** Visits the US with Queen Elizabeth.
- **September 3, 1939** George VI announces over the radio that Britain is at war with Germany.
- **September 13, 1940** Buckingham Palace is bombed when the King and Queen are in residence.
- **1940–44** The King has weekly meetings with Prime Minister Winston Churchill. He visits troops overseas and gives support to those suffering at home.
- **May 8, 1945** Victory in Europe Day is celebrated. The Royal Family cheers the crowd standing outside Buckingham Palace from the balcony.
- **1947** Partition of India and creation of Pakistan. George is no longer Emperor of India, but becomes King of India and Pakistan.
- **1950** India becomes a republic within the Commonwealth. George is no longer King of India, but becomes Head of the Commonwealth.
- **September 1951** George VI has his left lung removed after the discovery of a malignant tumor.
- **February 6, 1952** Dies in bed of a coronary thrombosis at the age of 56.

STAMP PRINTED, BUT NOT ISSUED, TO COMMEMORATE EDWARD VIII'S CORONATION

Elizabeth and Margaret's Childhood

In April 1926, Britain was in crisis as a bitter miners' dispute threatened to erupt into a nationwide strike. Against this tumultuous backdrop, the news of the birth of Elizabeth—then, third in line to the throne—provided a welcome distraction.

On April 21, 1926, after a long and difficult labor, Elizabeth Bowes-Lyon—wife of Prince Albert—was about to be given a Caesarean section at the London house of her parents, the Earl and Countess of Strathmore. Elizabeth Alexandra Mary was born at 2:20 a.m. Shortly after the announcement of the birth was made,

an excited crowd gathered outside the house to watch the arrival of telegrams, gifts, and visitors.

Four days later, the miners' dispute culminated in a state of emergency being declared in the country. On May 3, a general strike was called. Industries and key services were frozen, and workers took to the streets. The strike lasted six days, yet public interest in the new baby persisted as crowds would gather outside Strathmores' house for a glimpse of the royal infant. On May 29, Elizabeth was christened at Buckingham Palace.

Popular baby

In January 1927, Elizabeth's father and mother left for a six-month-long royal visit to Australia. The baby was left in London in the care of nurses, nannies, and grandparents—normal practice among the upper classes of the time. But in the Australian press, fascination with the new baby was considerable, and "Betty," as she was dubbed, became the most famous baby in the world. Chocolates, china sets, hospital ward, and even an area in Antarctica were named after Elizabeth. She also appeared on a stamp in Newfoundland. Once her love of horses became known, Madame Tussaud's wax museum created a model of her on a pony.

Women's magazines speculated at length on Elizabeth's character. They reported that, at 21 months, she had stood on a table at a party at Sandringham, hurling crackers at the guests. Other reports stated that visitors to the family house at Piccadilly were likely to be bombarded with teddy bears flung down the stairwell. But as per popular press, the little scamp was also a golden-curled angel whose smile had greater power over her grandfather, King George V (see pp.78–79), more than anyone else in the kingdom. The Archbishop of Canterbury reported arriving at the palace to find the King

Princess's pets
Elizabeth poses with two corgis—her favorite breed of dog—at her home in Piccadilly, London, in July 1936. Elizabeth's first corgi, Dookie, was a gift from George VI in 1933 (see pp.108–109).

BEFORE

World War I plunged Britain into an economic crisis, with crippling national debt and high unemployment.

GOOD NEWS AT A DARK TIME
What began as a miners' dispute on the issue of poor wages and working hours was threatening to snowball into a general strike. Fearing social **anarchy and revolution,** the government mobilized soldiers and civilians to maintain order. Despite the crisis, **public interest** in the birth of a royal baby—the third in line to the throne—was huge. This was perhaps because it symbolized tradition and continuity at a time of great instability.

Wooden doll's house
This Tudor style doll's house was created in 1932 by Florence Palmer of Etchinghill for an exhibition. Elizabeth Bowes-Lyon acquired it for her daughters to play with.

pretending to be a horse, "shuffling on hands and knees along the floor while the little Princess led him by the beard."

Model siblings
In 1930, with the birth of Princess Margaret, the close-knit York family was complete. Elizabeth and her sister Margaret led a sheltered childhood. Occasional public appearances were much photographed and filmed by the press, with the princesses presented as role models for the nation's children. Mothers would attempt to copy for their daughters whatever the princesses were wearing.

Queen in waiting
The only true glimpse of young Elizabeth that has been made public is an essay she wrote on May 12, 1937, the day after her father's coronation. It reads: "At the end the service got rather boring as it was all prayers. Grannie [Queen Mary] and I were looking to see how many more pages to the end, and we turned one more and then I pointed to the word at the bottom of the page and it said 'Finis.' We both smiled at each other and turned back to the service." Elizabeth was already 11 when she wrote this. For the past five months, she had known that unless her parents had a son, she too would be monarch one day.

AFTER

After the abdication of Edward VIII, Elizabeth's father became king and she became next in line to the throne. Three years later, as Hitler threatened to conquer Europe, Britain declared war on Germany.

QUEEN IN THE MAKING
George VI had been completely unprepared for the **duties of monarchy** when he came to the throne, and was determined that Elizabeth be better equipped. He guided her through the complexities of royal duties and procedure as best he could, enlisting the help of experts, where necessary **106–107 »**. Monarchies were toppling across Europe, and the abdication had left the British public with little faith in the Royal Family. George VI believed that it was essential for Elizabeth to have an **unshakable sense of duty** if the British monarchy were to survive. During World War II Elizabeth followed the example of her parents, and took her first steps toward becoming a **figurehead for the nation 106–107 »**.

> " [Princess Elizabeth] is a **character.** She has an **air of authority** and **reflectiveness** astonishing in an infant."
>
> WINSTON CHURCHILL, DESCRIBING 2-YEAR-OLD ELIZABETH II, 1929

Coronation day
Princess Elizabeth stands with her mother on the balcony of Buckingham Palace on the day her parents were crowned King and Queen. The Princess wore a long dress, train, and coronet for the ceremony.

Princess Elizabeth (right) spends some quiet family
time with her pet dog, sister Princess Margaret,
and mother Queen Elizabeth in the grounds of
Windsor Castle in the summer of 1941.

The Royal Family in World War II

When Britain and France declared war on Germany on September 3, 1939, George VI was still establishing his role as king. Following the example set by his father in World War I, he focused on the role of Royal Family to boost morale and inspire social cohesion and national spirit.

In many ways the epitome of the reserved, dutiful family man, King George VI became an unlikely symbol of national resistance. For ordinary working- and middle-class British people, this serious, modest man who was happiest when at home with his wife and children, came to represent the values that Britain was fighting for. While a more glamorous, dashing king may have served only to emphasize the gulf between rich and poor, this hesitant man, ill at ease in the spotlight, was widely seen to have inspired a sense of common humanity.

school education made compulsory up to the age of 14. Newspaper circulation was on the increase, and—even more significant—almost every home in the country had a radio, and every town a movie theater. World War II was the first war in which politicians and the King could communicate directly with the populations, not only of Britain, but of the Commonwealth and even with what remained of the Empire.

On the day war was declared—September 3, 1939—George VI not only had to deliver the most important speech of his life, but had to do so live on radio. Anticipation was high,

that had been bombed, especially in the East End. The Palace also was hit many times by German bombs. On September 13, 1940, it suffered a direct hit when the King and Queen were in the Palace. Few workers were injured

King's speech
In the official photograph of the event, King George looks calm and regal in his naval uniform, sitting at his desk in front of a microphone. Actually, he delivered the speech standing in shirt sleeves at a lectern in a small room with the window open.

"I'm glad we've been bombed. It makes me feel I can look the East End in the face."

QUEEN ELIZABETH, AFTER THE BOMBING OF BUCKINGHAM PALACE

Society had changed since World War I. Britain had had its first Labour government, Ireland had declared itself an independent republic, women had won the vote and were increasingly going out to work, and society was more educated than ever before with

and throughout the country, streets emptied as the nation gathered around their radio sets. The stakes could not have been higher, and the King knew it. He delivered the speech, and the only person present in the room was his speech therapist Lionel Logue (see p.97). Lionel advised the King to forget about the audience and simply speak to him. The technique worked. For all his sobriety, George was the first people's king.

Bombing of Buckingham Palace
Throughout the war, King George and Queen Elizabeth ignored advice to move out of London to the safety of Windsor Castle. They mostly remained at Buckingham Palace, making regular visits to give support to communities,

Resilient in wartime
Queen Elizabeth and King George VI inspect the destruction at Buckingham Palace, following the German air raid during the Blitz, on September 10, 1940. They were not present in the Palace when it was bombed that day.

« BEFORE

George VI was still finding his feet as king after unexpectedly inheriting the throne following the abdication of his brother, Edward VIII.

CHANGING ORDER
World and social order was in a state of transition and crisis with the **collapse of many monarchies and fascist experiments in Europe.** The **British Empire** was in **decline,** while the **US was on the rise.**

and the chapel was destroyed. On the same day, the King and Queen visited West Ham in the East End. She later said, "I felt as if I was walking in a dead city... all the houses evacuated, and yet through the broken windows one saw all the poor little possessions... just as they were left."

The fact that the Royal Family had suffered too only endeared them more to the population. Like most people in Britain, George and Elizabeth lost relatives in the war. In 1942 the King's younger brother, Prince George, Duke of Kent, was killed.

Support to the war-torn nation

Weekly newsreels regularly included footage of the Royal Family—visiting bomb sites, munitions factories, hospitals, soup kitchens, troops—among the footage of war devastation. This footage was designed to raise people's morale. There were films, too, of George VI's several visits to troops on active service in France at the beginning of the war in 1939, and in North Africa in 1943, following the victory of El Alamein—a city in Egypt where Britain fought the Axis forces twice in World War II. In June 1944, 10 days after D-Day, he visited his army on the Normandy beaches, and later that year visited the troops in Italy and the Low Countries. Although not involved in strategy, he met Prime Minister Winston Churchill in private every Tuesday throughout the war, building up a relationship of mutual trust and respect—one of the closest relationships ever to exist between a prime minister and monarch.

JOIN THE ATS

All members of the Royal Family—including the children—were expected to set an example to the nation by contributing to the war effort. Princess Elizabeth not only made her first radio broadcast to the country's children at the age of 14 (see p.106), but sewed items for troops and raised funds with a Christmas pantomime. She joined the Auxiliary Territorial Service (ATS) later.

In recognition of the demands that modern warfare inflicted on ordinary people, the King decided to create medals to honor men and women—military and civilian—who had performed acts of outstanding courage. In 1942 the George Cross was awarded to the people of Malta in recognition of the bravery they displayed during the long siege by the Germans.

9 The number of times Buckingham Palace was directly bombed by German planes during World War II.

Victory day

It is perhaps an indication of the relationship that had grown through the war years between the Royal Family and the British public, that on May 8, 1945, on the night of Victory in Europe (VE) Day, after appearing on the balcony of Buckingham Palace to cheering crowds, the King agreed to his daughters' rather unexpected request. "We asked my parents if we could go out and see for ourselves," Elizabeth later revealed. Princess Elizabeth, 19, and her 14-year-old sister, Princess Margaret, with caps pulled down low over their eyes, mingled anonymously with the crowds. Describing it afterward, Elizabeth said, "We walked through the streets, a line of unknown people linking arms and walking down Whitehall, swept along on a tide of happiness and relief... I think it was one of the most memorable nights of my life."

Wartime campaign
British women who wanted to work for the army during World War II joined the Auxiliary Territorial Service (ATS). It had 200,000 members by the end of 1943. Princess Elizabeth served as a driver and a mechanic in the ATS.

AFTER

George VI became a highly respected monarch, but the stress of office had grave consequences for his health.

NEW WORLD ORGANIZATIONS
The beginnings of a new postwar world order with the **formation of the United Nations (UN)** in 1945 and the **North Atlantic Treaty Organisation (NATO)** in 1949. At home, legislation, including various acts setting up the welfare state, came into force, aiming at a healthier, better educated, and more socially equal Britain.

KING'S DECLINING HEALTH
King George VI always had a **delicate constitution**, and the **stress of office** – in particular, leading the nation during World War II – **severely affected** his fragile health. A heavy smoker, he was eventually **diagnosed with lung cancer.** The King suffered a **coronary thrombosis**, a fatal blood clot to the heart, **132 »** and died in his sleep in 1952 at the age of 56.

Working in the ATS
Princess Elizabeth learns to change a car wheel as a subaltern in the Auxiliary Territorial Service (ATS) in 1945. By the end of the war she was promoted to Junior Commander.

Visiting the war-affected
George VI and Elizabeth visit people in Sheffield made homeless after a German bombing raid during World War II—one of many initiatives the Royal Family undertook to boost public morale.

Elizabeth's Teenage Years

Although Elizabeth and Margaret were raised in a privileged and sheltered environment, their lives were turned upside down at a very young age by two major events—the abdication of Edward VIII and the outbreak of World War II.

After the abdication crisis (see pp.92–93) of 1936, Elizabeth's father became king and the family moved from their Piccadilly townhouse to Buckingham Palace. The Piccadilly house was hardly modest—it had 25 bedrooms and a staff of 16—but it was a thriving and much-loved family home, typical of the kind of London base maintained by wealthier members of the aristocracy. Marion Crawford (see pp.98–99),

(see pp.92–93)

(see pp.98–99)

governess to Elizabeth and Margaret for 16 years, remains the main source for information on the Princesses' lives at the time.

A new home

According to Crawford, there was nothing lovable about Buckingham Palace. It was bleak, vast, cold, and infested with rodents: "You may think a royal palace is the last word in up-to-date luxury but nothing could be further from the truth. Living at Buckingham Palace was rather like camping in a museum—one that's dropping to bits… that first night, the wind moaned in the chimneys like 1,000 ghosts. The palace had only recently had electricity installed… My bedroom light, for instance, could only be turned on and off by a switch two yards outside in the passage… Food had to come the better part of half-a-mile from the kitchens at the Buckingham Palace Road end to the dining room at the Constitution Hill end. We also needed the vermin man, who fought an endless battle against the mice with cardboard traps that had a lump of aniseed in the middle and treacle all around."

If Crawford's account is to be trusted, it was she who worried about the Princesses being too isolated, and suggested that they join the Girl Guides. The 1st Buckingham Palace Guide Company met for the first time on June 9, 1937. It comprised 20 members, all of whom were daughters of the aristocracy or members of the royal household and Palace staff. A Brownie pack—a Guiding group for girls ages 7 to 10 years old—was started for Margaret with 14 members.

Preparing to be Queen

George VI was determined that Elizabeth be better prepared for the duties of monarchy than he

Girl Guides

Dressed in Girl Guide uniforms, Elizabeth and Margaret prepare to release a carrier pigeon with a message to Chief Guide Lady Olave Baden-Powell on the occasion of her late husband's birthday in 1943.

Wartime broadcast

In 1940, Elizabeth made her first radio broadcast to the nation's children, many of whom had been evacuated. At the end, Margaret joined in too.

had been. He encouraged her to sit with him as he studied state papers (see p.130), and engaged Henry Marten, Vice-Provost of Eton College, to give her an intensive course of classes in constitutional history, the role of monarchy, and parliamentary procedure. Meanwhile, Margaret's education was less rigorous and regimented.

(see p.130)

Thanks to their parents' royal visits to Australia, New Zealand, Canada, and the US, the Princesses had the opportunity—rare at the time—to learn about foreign countries and cultures from people who had actually traveled. In 1939, on a tour of the US, Elizabeth's mother wrote to her describing a now famous picnic at President Franklin D. Roosevelt's home in New York State: "We all sat at little tables under the trees round the house, and had all our food on one plate—a little salmon, some turkey, some ham, lettuce, beans & HOT DOGS too!"

Occasionally, the girls accompanied their parents on royal visits. In July 1939, 13-year-old Elizabeth with her parents and sister, visited the Royal Naval College at Dartmouth. Prince Philip of Greece (see pp.124–25), a boisterous 18-year-old cadet, was given the task of looking after the girls. In her account of the meeting, Crawford said "He [Philip] played games with them [Elizabeth and Margaret], jumped over tennis nets, wolfed down plates of food and generally romped, ending by

(see pp.124–25)

rowing his boat after the departing Royal Yacht until the King had to bellow to him to go back." Elizabeth was apparently charmed.

War breaks out

A few months later, when war broke out, the King and Queen remained in London, while the girls were removed to Windsor Castle. It was a gloomy, eerie place—windows had been blacked out, paintings removed for safety, chandeliers suspended three inches above the ground so they wouldn't shatter in the case of a bomb, and furniture shrouded in sheets. The King kept pigs at one of the estate farms, and the girls tended an "allotment"—a plot of land for growing vegetables or flowers—and kept rabbits. Bathtubs at both Windsor and Buckingham Palace had a black line painted on them to ensure that no one bathed in more than 5 in (13 cm) of water. During air raids, shelter was taken in one of the castle dungeons, where beetles scuttled across the floor. However, the Princesses had the rare luxury of a bathroom in their air raid shelter. On one occasion, the librarian took the girls down to the vaults and

BEFORE

There was every reason to assume that Edward VIII would continue to be king and produce heirs of his own. It seemed very unlikely that Elizabeth would ever accede to the throne.

A PRIVILEGED PRINCESS

Elizabeth and Margaret led the kind of **sheltered, undemanding lives** considered appropriate for aristocratic girls—lives in which the greatest achievement was to some day marry well. Education was not taken very seriously—both girls were **homeschooled,** with dancing and riding as well as math and English on the curriculum. Lessons were often interrupted when the Princesses' mother thought of something more fun to do.

"Thousands of you... have had to leave your homes... My sister Margaret Rose and I **feel so much for you** as we know... what it means to be **away from those we love** most of all."

ELIZABETH II, FROM HER FIRST RADIO BROADCAST TO THE NATION'S CHILDREN, 1940

AFTER ≫

Prepared by her father, George VI, for her eventual role of monarch, Elizabeth grew up to be a serious young woman.

A DEDICATED QUEEN
Elizabeth was made deeply aware of the implications and **duties of monarchy** by her experience of World War II. In a **radio speech** broadcast throughout the Commonwealth from South Africa on her 21st birthday, she made a **solemn dedication:** "I declare before you that my whole life, whether it be long or short, shall be devoted to your service and the service of our great Imperial Commonwealth, to which we all belong. But I shall not have the strength to carry out this resolution unless you will join in it with me."

ELIZABETH AND PHILIP
After their 1939 meeting, Elizabeth and Philip would be thrown together on several other occasions **114–15** ≫, sowing the seeds for their **marriage 120–21, 266–67** ≫.

showed them the Crown Jewels (see pp.68–69), hidden in battered leather hatboxes stuffed with newspaper.

The girls continued their work as Girl Guides at Windsor during the war, and, like girls throughout the country, knitted and made brooches to be sold for the war effort. In 1940, they began to put on yearly plays to raise money to support the troops. The King saw the Princesses' efforts and quipped "At least if I am dethroned the girls will be able to earn their living." In October 1940, Princess Elizabeth, with Margaret by her side, made her first public speech—

a live radio broadcast to the nation's children, many of whom had been ordered to be evacuated.

Of the two children, Margaret was more funny, capricious, and naughty, and tended to attract all the attention. Elizabeth, on the other hand, was shy, serious, and socially ill at ease. She said of her sister: "It's so much easier when Margaret's there—everyone laughs at what Margaret says."

Forays outside Windsor were rare, although the girls did sometimes accompany their parents on public engagements. At age 15, Elizabeth joined the Auxiliary Territorial Service (ATS) as a volunteer, and learned to drive a truck and maintain an engine. Guiding continued to give the Princesses an occasional taste of normality. In 1944, the two were filmed

at camp, cleaning up, giggling in dugouts, and singing songs with the rest of the company, watched by their mother. The nation read with glee reports of the Queen drinking tea from a stained, chipped mug presented to her by Margaret.

On her 18th birthday in 1944, George VI appointed Elizabeth a Counsellor of State, making her responsible for performing his official duties at times when he was abroad or absent due to illness. This was no mere ceremonial task; shortly afterward, when the King was away in Italy, it was Elizabeth's duty as Counsellor to sign a reprieve for a murderer. The Princess had so far been sheltered from the less savory aspects of life, and was unprepared for the task and seemingly disturbed by it. She asked, "What makes people do such terrible things?" One ought to know! There must be some way to help them. I have so much to learn about people."

First official engagement
A special parade was organized at Windsor Castle to celebrate Elizabeth's 16th birthday—her first official engagement. The Princess newly appointed as colonel-in-chief of the Grenadier Guards, inspected the regiment.

Family Pets

The Royal Family's love of canines has a long history, with pet dogs, ranging from pugs to King Charles spaniels, appearing in royal portraits from the 17th century onward. Since the reign of Queen Victoria, royal dogs have had their own graveyard at Sandringham.

Elizabeth II is renowned for her love of corgis: the Crown coin that commemorated her Golden Jubilee shows her with a corgi. In 2012, three of her dogs, Monty, Holly, and Willow, featured in the opening ceremony for the Olympic Games.

The Queen's love of corgis began as a child. In 1933, her father bought one as a family pet. Although officially named Rozavel Golden Eagle, the household servants began calling him Dookie, a cheekily shortened version of "Duke". Since then Elizabeth has bred 30 corgis, most of them descended from her 18th birthday present, a corgi named Susan, who accompanied Queen Elizabeth and Prince Philip on their honeymoon in 1947. Although corgis remain her favorites, Elizabeth has also had labradors, a golden retriever, a cocker spaniel, a shih tzu, and has bred several dorgis, a corgi-dachshund cross.

The Royal Family's love of animals is not limited to dogs. Elizabeth is a skilled horsewoman and world-class race horse owner. At times, the Royal Family has been given rather unusual animals as presents. During World War II, Earl Mountbatten (see pp.192–93) showed up with a chameleon for Elizabeth and Margaret; in 1956, Soviet leader Nikita Krushchev gave a brown Syrian bear to six-year old Princess Anne; while in 1961, on a state visit to the Gambia, Elizabeth and Philip were presented with a baby crocodile—a gift for one-year-old Prince Andrew. The Queen's private secretary kept the baby crocodile in his bathtub until it could be donated to London Zoo.

The Queen's children and grandchildren have inherited her love of animals. They own dogs of various breeds and work as patrons for a wide range of animal charities.

> "The **Queen** carries a **magnet** when having clothes fitted… to **comb the room** for any **stray pins and needles** so the **dogs** don't hurt their **paws.**"
>
> **A ROYAL DRESSMAKER**, IN BRIAN HOEY'S *PETS BY ROYAL APPOINTMENT*

The Queen and her dogs
This picture of Elizabeth II was taken by photographer Lisa Sheridan in the gardens of Balmoral Castle in 1952. Sheridan became the Royal Family's most trusted photographer after a commission to photograph the royal corgis for a book on dogs in the early 1930s.

The **First Tour** in **Africa**

The British Empire was disintegrating. With India on the cusp of independence, attention fell on South Africa, with its prodigious sources of gold and diamonds. South Africa had backed Britain during the war, but Anti-British Afrikaners were on the ascendant, among them pro-Nazi racists.

The royal tour began with King George VI, Queen Elizabeth, and Princesses Elizabeth and Margaret boarding HMS *Vanguard*. News reels of the voyage include the princesses enthusiastically playing deck games with the sailors, arguably the most relaxed images of the Princess to have been made public. But once on land, the fun stopped.

They were welcomed by a crowd of more than 250,000 white South Africans on their arrival in Cape Town on February 17. Colorfully staged encounters with tribal kings followed, including an occasion on which the royal entourage was greeted by hundreds of Basuto tribesmen thundering through the dust on horseback. Commemorative stamps were issued and Princess Elizabeth received gifts of diamonds for her 21st birthday. But despite this elaborate show of South Africa as a model colony, the Royal Family was aware that the reality was very different.

Members of South Africa's Indian community in Natal boycotted the royal tour in protest of the Ghetto Act, designed to curtail Indian ownership of property in white areas. The Afrikaner press was also hostile. Detesting the overt signs of racial separation, and appalled by the authorities opposing him decorating black South Africans for war service, George VI found speech-making increasingly difficult. He referred to the officious Afrikaner police as Gestapo.

The Royal Family left for the UK on April 24. Within a year, South Africa had passed apartheid legislation. The impact of her disturbing visit endured, as Elizabeth would go on to show her support for anti-apartheid activist Nelson Mandela on several occasions. She went so far as to signal her distance from Margaret Thatcher when the British Prime Minister referred to Mandela as a terrorist.

> **"**In view of the **disabilities imposed** upon… **colored** peoples, it would be improper… to share the rejoicings of the white of South Africa.**"**
>
> **MAHATMA GANDHI,** ENDORSING THE BOYCOTT OF THE ROYAL TOUR

Into Africa
On March 22, 1947, the Royal Family visited the Natal National Park in South Africa. In addition to national parks, the Royal Family also took time to visit game reserves and the Victoria Falls. However, throughout the tour, they were keenly aware of the racial tensions plaguing the country.

BEFORE «

The first two decades of the 20th century saw many of Europe's monarchs toppled by war and revolution. Centuries of dynastic marriage had created a intricately interrelated web of royalty.

ROYAL MARRIAGES

In 1863 Queen Victoria arranged the marriage of her eldest son, the future Edward VII to Alexandra, eldest daughter of King Christian IX of Denmark. By the outbreak of World War I, the grandchildren of either Victoria or Christian occupied the thrones of the UK, Russia, Germany, Greece, Spain, Denmark, Norway, and Romania—**closely related monarchs** found themselves **on opposite sides.**

MATCHMAKER

Prince Philip's uncle, **Louis Mountbatten,** had done much to **engineer the match** between Elizabeth and Philip, to the extent that Philip wrote to him saying "Please, I beg of you not too much advice in an affair of the heart, or I shall be forced to do the wooing by proxy." Mountbatten had hoped for his name to be immortalized in the surnames of the would-be Queen's descendants.

> " His **wardrobe** was **scantier** than that of many a **bank clerk...** he had **only one civilian suit** and his **socks** were **full of darns.**"

JOHN DEAN, PHILIP'S VALET

Elizabeth as a bridesmaid

In October 1946, as speculation mounted about their relationship, Princess Elizabeth was bridesmaid and Prince Philip an usher at the wedding of Lord Mountbatten's daughter Patricia to Lord Brabourne.

Elizabeth and Philip

They seemed an unlikely couple—the shy, dutiful, and serious Princess Elizabeth and an exuberant, outspoken, and penniless exiled Prince Philip of Greece. Although third cousins, their childhoods could not have been more different.

At the age of 13, Elizabeth visited the Royal Naval College at Dartmouth with her parents and sister (see p.106). While there, she met her royal cousin, 18-year-old Prince Philip of Greece. The next time they met was when Philip came to watch the Princesses' performance in the annual Christmas pantomime (see p.107) at Windsor. Shortly afterward a photograph of the Prince appeared on Elizabeth's mantelpiece, and when her governess, Marion Crawford, warned that she was risking gossip, she changed it for one of Philip with a bushy beard. "There you are, Crawfie, I defy anyone to recognize him in this. He's completely incognito." Following the pantomime, they started writing regularly to one another, as Philip joined the Royal Navy as a cadet.

Apt match

The son of Prince Andrew of Greece and Princess Alice of Battenberg, Philip moved from place to place, after his family was exiled from Greece in 1922. Later, with Nazism on the rise, he left Germany for Scotland and became one of the first pupils to attend Gordonstoun school (see p.124, p.162). Philip seems to have taken delight in giving his address as "no fixed abode" in the visitors' books of the grand town mansions and country estates to which he was invited, often turning up only in what he was wearing—plus a razor.

Outspoken, self-reliant, and unrestrained, with a cheery sense of humor and uncrushable zest for life, Philip was no average young aristocrat. The general opinion was that he was "rather unpolished," rude, and overbearing. However, for Elizabeth, who was accustomed all her life to fawning and flattery, Philip's forthrightness and unconventionality came as a breath of fresh air.

War hero

In July 1943, during World War II, his ship, HMS *Wallace* took part in the Allied landings in Sicily. Off the coast of southeast Sicily, at the dead of night, the ship came under repeated bombardment. Prone and unprotected, the ship seemed doomed, until Philip came up with a plan to throw overboard a wooden raft with smoke floats to create the illusion of debris ablaze on the water. The German plane was fooled into attacking

At work
Prince Philip undertakes the role of an instructor at the Petty Officers' Training Center at Corsham, Wiltshire, between 1946 and 1947. He became engaged to Princess Elizabeth while working here.

> **"**Elizabeth **began** to **take more trouble** with her **appearance** and to play the tune **'**People Will Say We're In Love,' from *Oklahoma*.**"**

MARION CRAWFORD, ELIZABETH'S GOVERNESS

the decoy while the *Wallace* sailed to safety. This extraordinary initiative by Prince Philip helped save many lives.

Beginning of a long liaison

Back in London after the war, Philip and his black MG sports car became regular visitors to Buckingham Palace. The first occasion he seems to have invited himself, as he wrote to Elizabeth afterward apologizing for his "monumental cheek." "Yet however contrite I feel," he wrote, "there is always a small voice that keeps saying 'nothing ventured, nothing gained'— well I did venture and I gained a wonderful time." According to Crawford, Philip did most of his courtship in the old nursery, at tea time, with Margaret in attendance. She wrote, "Just as there was nothing polished about Philip, who often wandered about in his shirtsleeves, so there was nothing fancy about these meals: just fish and some sort of sweet, washed down with orangeade. After dinner, it would be high-jinks in the corridors as the three of them played ball (a good many lightbulbs suffered) and raced about like a bunch of high-spirited children."

Philip and Elizabeth did, however, occasionally go out together, but despite taking care always to be seen in company with other friends, speculation in the press became fevered. Visiting a factory at the age of 19, Elizabeth was hugely embarrassed when the crowd began asking "Where's Philip?" Shortly afterward, Philip was invited to Balmoral, where he seems to have shocked other guests by brashly going shooting with a borrowed gun, wearing flannel

Family portrait
The portrait of the Royal Family following the announcement of the engagement of Elizabeth to Philip Mountbatten features (from left to right): Elizabeth, Philip, Queen Elizabeth (later the Queen Mother), King George VI, and Margaret.

pants instead of plus fours (knickers). A footman revealed to the press that his "solitary naval valise" contained no spare shoes, pyjamas, or slippers and that his only walking shoes had to be taken to the local shoemaker to be repaired. It is believed that it was at Balmoral in 1946 that Philip proposed to Elizabeth and she accepted. Initially the King and Queen seemed to share the common misgivings about Philip. But as they got to know him, they grew to appreciate his direct manner, joshing humor, and love of the countryside. On one occasion Philip, wearing a borrowed kilt, curtseyed to the King, allegedly because the kilt was so short that it was the only way of maintaining modesty. Philip was fun, an extrovert, a good foil to Elizabeth's seriousness.

In early October 1946, at the wedding of Lord Mountbatten's daughter Patricia to Lord Brabourne at Romsey Abbey, the two got together again. Philip was an usher, and he

escorted the Royal Family from their car. The media caught Philip and Elizabeth looking at each other affectionately as she moved to remove her fur coat. With no official announcement of an engagement, the speculation in the media increased.

As a prelude to the impending engagement, Philip's uncle, Lord Mountbatten, had long campaigned for Philip to be naturalized. Mountbatten secured the agreement of Home Secretary and Prime Minister to Philip's naturalization in 1946. He was then known as Lieutenant Philip Mountbatten. Ironically, it turned out that the procedure had been unnecessary—a law of 1705 stated that descendents of Sophia of Hanover (mother of George I) were British.

Separated for a while

In early 1947, it was decreed that Elizabeth and her sister would accompany their parents on a trip to South Africa on what was to be a four-month royal tour (see pp.112–13). She would be 21 when she returned. The couple wrote to each other throughout their separation and Elizabeth put Philip's photograph on her dressing table during the trip. Elizabeth

returned, pale and thin, and so relieved to get back, that she danced a jig on the deck as the ship, HMS *Vanguard*, steamed into Portsmouth harbour.

On July 10, 1947, the long-awaited engagement of Princess Elizabeth and Philip Mountbatten was announced coinciding with a garden party being celebrated at Buckingham Palace.

Engagement announcement
Elizabeth and Philip stroll on the terrace at Buckingham Palace after the announcement of their engagement in July 1947. The engagement ring is a diamond solitaire set in platinum with five smaller diamonds on each side.

AFTER ≫

With the announcement of Princess Elizabeth and Prince Philip's engagement, public interest in the future Queen's consort abounded.

CONSPIRACY THEORY
As a descendent of the Greek-Danish royal dynasty, with his four sisters married to German aristocrats, it was inevitable that after **World War II,** conspiracy theories about the **pro-German** (and even pro-Nazi) sympathies of Philip would arise.

ELIZABETH II
1947–1960

« St. Edward's Crown, used during the
coronation of a new sovereign

ELIZABETH II

1947–1960

1947	1948	1950	1951	1952

APRIL 21
Elizabeth celebrates her 21st birthday with a Commonwealth broadcast.

JULY 10
Buckingham Palace announces the engagement of Princess Elizabeth to Prince Philip of Greece

⌄ Announcement of the engagement

JANUARY 30, 1948
Assassination of Mahatma Gandhi.

SEPTEMBER 6, 1948
Peter Townsend accompanies Princess Margaret to the coronation of Queen Juliana of the Netherlands.

APRIL 30, 1948
Silver wedding anniversary of George VI and Elizabeth.

JULY 29, 1948
London Olympics, which come to be known as the Austerity Games, commence.

NOVEMBER 14, 1948
Birth of Prince Charles.

JUNE
Korean War begins; over 100,000 British soldiers will serve with the multinational United Nations (UN) forces until 1953.

« Prince Charles's christening

MARCH
The Duke of Windsor publishes his memoirs: *A King's Story*.

MAY 3
George VI opens the Festival of Britain—a showcase for British enterprise and ingenuity.

JULY 7
The Duke of Edinburgh leaves the Royal Navy to focus on his duties as consort.

JANUARY 31
Elizabeth and Philip are waved off on tour of Africa by George VI.

FEBRUARY 6
George VI dies in his sleep at Sandringham, but Elizabeth is in Kenya and does not learn for several hours that she is now Queen.

FEBRUARY 16
Funeral of George VI, with coffin borne through London, then placed in a crypt at Windsor.

⌄ George's grieving widow and daughters

AUGUST 15
The King loses the title of Emperor of India, following July's India Independence Act; Pakistan becomes a separate nation.

NOVEMBER 20
Elizabeth marries Philip at Westminster Abbey.

MARCH 12, 1949
George VI undergoes an operation.

APRIL 28, 1949
Foundation of the modern Commonwealth with the London Declaration.

JULY 1949
Elizabeth and Philip move into Clarence House, which has been extensively refurbished.

NOVEMBER 1949
Elizabeth and Philip move to Malta where Philip is stationed with the Royal Navy.

AUGUST 15
Princess Anne is born.

NOVEMBER
Marion Crawford publishes *The Little Princesses*.

« Princess Elizabeth's wedding procession

DECEMBER 25
Stone of Scone, a block of red sandstone placed under the coronation chair in Westminister Abbey since 1296 and associated with Scottish nationhood, is stolen. It will be recovered four months later.

OCTOBER 26
Winston Churchill becomes British Prime Minister for the third time.

SEPTEMBER
George VI has a lung removed due to cancer.

NOVEMBER 4
Elizabeth attends State opening of Parliament, her first major state function.

» En route to State Opening of Parliament, 1952

118

The postwar years brought joy, tumult, and glory to the life of Elizabeth, as she celebrated marriage and motherhood, mourned the death of her father and grandmother, and dedicated herself to a life of service amid the pomp and circumstance of her coronation. In the years that followed she would travel the world, inspiring excitement and devotion from Fiji to Fife. She oversaw a period of transition for Britain's international status, all the while managing to balance the needs of her family with the demands of monarchy. Meanwhile, Elizabeth's sister Margaret wrestled with her own agonizing dilemma in choosing between love and duty.

1953

NOVEMBER
Elizabeth and Philip embark on a tour of the Commonwealth.

» Tea caddy commemorating Elizabeth's visit to Australia

MARCH 24
Death of dowager Queen Mary, age 85.

MAY 29
Conquest of Everest by Edmund Hilary and Tenzing Norgay.

« Elizabeth II's Coronation Day

JUNE 2
Coronation of Queen Elizabeth II at Westminster Abbey.

1954

JANUARY 12
Queen Elizabeth opens the New Zealand parliament.

APRIL 15
Queen Elizabeth and Philip return from Commonwealth tour.

MAY 6
English athlete Roger Bannister breaks the four-minute mile record.

IS SHE SAD?
SEVEN HOURS APART —THEN DINNER WITH PETER…

JULY 4
End of rationing in UK after over a decade of privation.

1955

FEBRUARY 17
UK announces it has the H-bomb.

APRIL 5
Sir Anthony Eden becomes PM after Churchill resigns due to ill health.

AUGUST 14
Annigoni portrait of the Queen draws massive crowds to the Royal Academy.

SEPTEMBER 18
UK annexes Rockall, a tiny speck of rock in the Atlantic Ocean, in order to preempt Soviet expansion in the region.

OCTOBER 31
Margaret announces that she will not marry Peter Townsend.

1956

MARCH 24, 1956
The Queen Mother's horse, Devon Loch, stumbles within feet of the finishing post in the Grand National.

APRIL 23, 1956
Nikita Kruschev, Soviet leader, visits the Queen at Windsor.

OCTOBER 1956
Anglo-French forces, which had attacked Egypt after it nationalized the Suez Canal, are forced to withdraw under international pressure. The debacle signals the end of Britain's imperial pretensions.

« Margaret's doomed romance in the news

DECEMBER 31, 1956
Prince Philip launches the Duke of Edinburgh Awards.

JANUARY 10, 1957
Harold Macmillan becomes Prime Minister after Anthony Eden's resignation causes constitutional crisis.

1956

MARCH 6, 1957
Gold Coast becomes first African colony to gain independence as Ghana.

OCTOBER 1957
Queen tours North America and meets President Eisenhower.

⌃ First televised Christmas message

DECEMBER 25, 1957
Queen Elizabeth delivers the first televised Christmas message.

1958

JULY 3, 1958
End of presenting debutantes at court; the last deb curtsies to the Queen at Holyrood, following the final Buckingham Palace ball in March.

JULY 26, 1958
Commonwealth Games begin at Cardiff, Wales; Charles is named Prince of Wales.

APRIL 1959
Queen Mother and Princess Margaret visit Pope John XXIII at the Vatican.

JUNE–AUGUST 1959
Queen and Prince Philip undertake the longest royal visit ever to Canada, partly to open the St. Lawrence Seaway.

»

BEFORE ◀◀

In 1947, two years after the end of the war, and in the wake of the harshest winter in living memory, Britain was held fast in the grip of austerity, with rationing getting worse rather than improving.

Most goods were rationed, with coupons needed to buy clothing, candy, sugar, gasoline, meat, cheese, butter, lard, margarine, tea, and soap. Gas was restricted by law to use for "essential motoring" and vacationing abroad was banned. Prime Minister Clement Attlee admitted, "I cannot say when we will emerge into easier times."

IN KEEPING WITH THE TIMES
In October 1947, **new restrictions came into force.** The weekly rationing of meat was reduced to a single shilling's worth, potatoes were restricted, and the clothing ration was cut. While 32 coupons had been available earlier, the allowance for the next five months was just 20 coupons. Against this backdrop, the relatively opulent event

CLOTHING RATION BOOK

planned for the Royal Wedding aroused **fierce resentment.** "Any banqueting and display of wealth at your daughter's wedding," the Camden Town branch of the Amalgamated Society Of Woodworkers warned the King, "will be an insult to the British people at the present time. You would be well advised to order a very quiet wedding in keeping with the times."

On the way to the abbey
The wedding procession advances toward Westminster Abbey. Travelling in the Irish State Coach at the head of the procession is Elizabeth, accompanied by her father dressed in his uniform as Admiral of the Fleet.

The **Wedding** of **Elizabeth** and **Philip**

Amid the gray austerity of postwar Britain the wedding of Princess Elizabeth to Philip Mountbatten offered a flash of color and gaiety, triggering a national and global outpouring of celebration... and fascination.

The engagement (see pp.114–15) of Princess Elizabeth to Philip Mountbatten was announced in July 1947, with the wedding planned for November. Despite a strong school of thought that the wedding should be low-key, keeping in mind the dismal state of national finances, the opposing faction won out. The royal wedding would be celebrated with royal pomp and circumstance, providing, Churchill declared, "a flash of color on the hard road we have to travel." But the King would bear the bulk of the cost, paying for it from the income from the Crown Estates.

High society
One minor obstacle was the groom's lack of estate; Philip had abandoned his Greek and Danish royal titles on becoming a naturalized British citizen. On the eve of the ceremony, King George VI bestowed upon him the honorific "His Royal Highness" and awarded him the Order of the Garter. On the wedding morning, he was created Duke of Edinburgh, Earl of Merioneth, and Baron Greenwich. The King remarked, "It is a great deal to give a man all at once, but I know Philip understands his responsibilities."

Wedding guests—an array of surviving royalty from around the world—stayed at Claridge's, including the Queen of

10,000 **The number of pearls imported from the US for Elizabeth's wedding dress.**

Spain, the King of Romania, the King and Queen of Denmark, and the Kings of Norway and Iraq. Philip Mountbatten had not one but two bachelor parties the night before the wedding, while the King hosted a dance at the palace for visiting royalty, which saw the Duke of Devonshire assaulted by an Indian rajah and the King himself lead a raucous conga line through the state apartments.

Like any villager in the Dales
On November 20, the princess emerged clothed in a beautiful ivory satin dress by Norman Hartnell. Like other brides, Elizabeth had been awarded extra clothing coupons to help her prepare, but unlike the others, she was able to rely on extravagant gifts from family and other sources. Her tiara was a gift from her grandmother. Her wedding ring was crafted from a piece of gold sent from Wales. "There is enough for two rings," she told Philip, "We can save a piece for Margaret."

Some 2,000 guests waited to greet her at Westminster Abbey. Conspicuous by their absence were Philip's sisters, tainted by Nazi connections, and the Duke and Duchess of Windsor, who were not invited (see pp.92–93). The service was intended to be as simple and unaffected as that of "any cottager who might be married in some small country church in the Dales this afternoon," gushed the Archbishop of Canterbury. A huge audience listened in on radio, and although highlights were televised, television set ownership across the country was minuscule at that time. Huge crowds surged down the Mall to call for the newlyweds, and especially the King, to come out and greet them.

Kept warm by a corgi
At the wedding meal for 150 close friends, the cake, made by McVities and Price, was 9ft (2.74m) high in four tiers and weighed 500lb (227kg). The princess changed into another Hartnell dress—a pale blue number described as "love in a mist"—and the couple was driven to Waterloo Station in an open

The grand cake
The decorations on the wedding cake included the coats of arms of both families, monograms of bride and groom, and regimental and naval badges.

carriage. Elizabeth kept warm with a hot water bottle underneath a rug on her lap and her favorite corgi, Susan, alongside her. From there, Philip and Elizabeth went by train to Winchester, to spend the first night of their honeymoon at Broadlands, the country home of Philip's uncle Lord Mountbatten.

After their honeymoon, their first home would be Windlesham Moor, in Surrey, while they waited for Clarence House to be refurbished (see pp.122–23). This grand but now rather dilapidated house was near to Buckingham Palace, allowing the King to keep his daughter close. At Windlesham Moor they sorted through the eclectic array of about 3,000 gifts they had received, which included 500 cans of pineapple from Queensland, a piece of lace made from yarn Gandhi had spun himself, and a rabbit tea cozy, two pieces of soggy toast, and a rock from Mt. Snowdon sent by an elderly Welshman.

"It is a far more **moving thing** to **give your daughter away** than to be married yourself."

KING GEORGE VI, TO THE ARCHBISHOP OF YORK, NOVEMBER 20, 1947

The newlyweds

Elizabeth and Philip are seen here posing for a photograph after the wedding. The princess's ivory duchess satin dress is embroidered with garlands of lily heads and white York roses with orange blossoms and ears of corn.

AFTER

The marriage of Elizabeth and Philip has withstood the constant scrutiny and pressures of royal obligations. But for some time after the wedding, the focus shifted to Princess Margaret.

SPOTLIGHT ON MARGARET

With Elizabeth now married, public and media attention soon began to focus on Margaret. On August 21, 1948, she celebrated her 18th birthday with an **official "coming out" onto the social scene.** For some time now the spotlight would be on the **beautiful and glamorous young princess and her prospects for marriage.**

ENDURING PARTNERSHIP

After their wedding, Philip, in a letter to his mother-in-law, stated that Elizabeth "is the only thing in this world which is absolutely real to me." Elizabeth and Philip would go on to celebrate their **silver anniversary** and, later, their **golden anniversary.** In 2007, they completed 60 years together, making the Queen the first British monarch to celebrate a **diamond wedding anniversary 266–67 ≫.** They celebrated their **blue sapphire—65th—wedding anniversary** in 2012.

SILVER ANNIVERSARY STAMP, 1972

In the library
Despite a refurbishment before Prince Charles took residency, on his insistence many of the contents in the House are arranged as they were in Queen Elizabeth's time, including her books in the library.

ROYAL RESIDENCE

Clarence House

This elegant Georgian residence is attached to St. James's Palace and shares its gardens. For more than 50 years it was the much-loved London home of the Queen Mother. It is now the official London residence of the Prince of Wales and Duchess of Cornwall.

In the late Georgian period, London had become one of the most influential cities in the world. It was, however, smelly, crowded, and disorganized. Determined to create a city whose architecture reflected its growing importance on the world stage, the Prince Regent, later George IV, hired three architects whose remit was to transform London. The most inspired of these was John Nash, who created iconic buildings such as Buckingham Palace and Marble Arch, and changed the face of the city forever with grand ceremonial boulevards such as the Mall and Regent Street.

One of the buildings he created along the Mall was Clarence House, built for the Duke of Clarence, who became King William IV on the death of his brother in 1830. A white stucco Classical mansion of three stories, it was a far more restrained and intimate building than Buckingham Palace. William was a man who shunned pretension and formality, and on his accession to the throne he decided to remain in Clarence House instead of moving to Buckingham Palace—simply adding a passage to connect it with the state apartments of St. James's Palace for ease of access.

Clarence House later became the home of Queen Victoria's mother, the Duchess of Kent, who added a conservatory, created a new private entrance from the Mall (the original entrance was from a public road), and replaced the house's somber crimson damasks with the pale painted wallpapers then in vogue. When the Duchess died, Queen Victoria's second son, Prince Alfred, Duke of Edinburgh, took up residence. After his marriage in 1874 to the Grand Duchess Marie Alexandrovna of Russia, the House was lavishly renovated, receiving a fourth story and an opulent Orthodox chapel (which no longer exists).

Headquarters of the British Red Cross and Order of St. John of Jerusalem during World War Two, Clarence House was again refurbished in the late 1940s to make it a family home for Princess Elizabeth, the Duke of Edinburgh, and the one-year-old Charles. They moved to Buckingham Palace after Elizabeth succeeded to the throne in 1952.

The Queen Mother

In the latter half of the 20th century, Clarence House became synonymous with Queen Elizabeth, the Queen Mother, who lived there for over 50 years. She was an enthusiastic hostess of luncheons, evening receptions, and afternoon teas; and an avid collector and patron of the arts. The house is still decorated with important objects and works of art.

Restoration

After the death of the Queen Mother in 2002, the house became the official residence of Prince Charles and his sons. It underwent essential renovation and redecoration, though great pains were taken by Prince Charles to use sustainable materials and to preserve the style and atmosphere created by his grandmother. Charles's main innovation was the formal, organic garden, which he designed himself in memory of the Queen Mother. It incorporates an ancient pear tree and a black mulberry reputed to have been planted in the time of James I.

Use today

Every year the Prince and the Duchess receive thousands of official guests from this country and overseas, and bring together people from all walks of life through seminars and receptions. On the initiative of Prince Charles, the house and its garden are open to the public for one month every summer.

House and home

Clarence House is said to have the atmosphere of a family home, despite its offices for staff and guards outside. The Garden Room, which leads out to the garden, was created by knocking two rooms together to provide a large entertaining space for Queen Elizabeth.

THE GARDEN ROOM'S 1945 PORTRAIT OF ELIZABETH

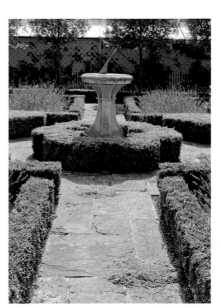

SUNDIAL IN THE FORMAL GARDEN

GUARD OUTSIDE CLARENCE HOUSE

Born 1921

The **Duke** of Edinburgh

"The **Queen** has the **quality** of tolerance in **abundance.**"

PRINCE PHILIP, 1997

In uniform
Philip, seen here wearing his naval uniform, had a fairly distinguished naval career. In 1942, at 21 years old, he became one of the youngest first lieutenants in the Royal Navy.

Born in a villa named Mon Repos on the island of Corfu in Greece, Philip was the product of the tangled 19th-century heritage of European royalty. His family was of German-Danish background, but by a quirk of dynastic fate, he was born a Prince of Greece as well as Denmark. Philip's full dynastic name at this point was Schleswig-Holstein-Sonderberg-Glucksburg.

Around the start of the 20th century, monarchies were being widely discarded by nationalist, republican, communist, and fascist movements. When Philip was just 18 months old, his father, Prince Andrew of Greece, and his mother, Princess Alice of Battenberg, were exiled to Paris and relieved of their crowns as a result of a coup. This made Philip, in the words of his official biographer, "nameless, stateless, and penniless" despite his noble birth.

Aged 7, Philip was sent to Surrey, England, to live with his maternal relatives, whose name he later adopted; in the wake of anti-German sentiments during World War I, Philip's grandfather Prince Louis Battenberg anglicized his name to Mountbatten on request of King George V, and in 1946, Philip followed suit. Meanwhile, back in 1933, just as Adolf Hitler came to power, Philip was sent to school at a castle in Germany. Although some members of his family—including his sisters—supported the Nazis, Philip had a distinctly antipathetic reaction to their ideology. Along with his inspirational headmaster, Kurt Hahn, he was chased out of Germany and relocated to Gordonstoun School in Scotland, where he excelled.

In the navy

As World War II loomed, Philip followed in the footsteps of his illustrious Mountbatten relatives by joining the Royal Navy via cadetship at the Royal Naval College, Dartmouth. In 1939, when George VI and Queen Elizabeth toured the college, Philip was asked to escort Princess Elizabeth, then only 13 years old, and her sister Margaret. Philip was Elizabeth's third cousin, since, like most European royalty, he could trace his descent back to Queen Victoria.

The Philip Movement

Philip is the object of veneration in one of the world's strangest religions, the Philip Movement, which emerged in the 1960s on the island of Tanna in the South Pacific. Worshipers regard the prince as a divine being and treasure the signed photos he has sent them.

Graduating at the top of his class in 1940, he embarked on a glittering though ultimately short-lived naval career. After marrying Elizabeth, Philip went on to take command of a ship of his own, but was forced to give up his career when the princess became Queen in 1952. Philip bitterly regretted his retirement from the service—"I'd much rather have stayed in the Navy, frankly," he said in 1992.

By royal appointment

The course of Philip's life changed forever when he struck up a romance with young Elizabeth, whose soft demeanour concealed a core of steel. At the time of the courtship, the young naval officer had a raffish reputation and a fast sports car to match, and there was both public and royal opposition to the pairing. However, Elizabeth's will would not be denied, and Philip soon became His Royal Highness The Duke of Edinburgh, Earl of Merioneth, and Baron Greenwich. Today he is the longest serving consort in British royal history, as well as the oldest ever male member of the British Royal Family.

Social blunders

Alongside his many years of faithful service as consort, Philip has also pursued passions of his own. He became a skillful carriage driver, helping to formulate the rules of the sport. He has also long nurtured an interest in wildlife—both hunting and conserving it. This contradiction was illustrated in 1961, when in the same year that he was made president of the new World Wide Fund for Nature (WWF), he sparked controversy by shooting a tiger in India. Controversy has, in fact, become one of Philip's trademarks, particularly his propensity for gaffes, or social blunders.

Four-in-hand
Philip, along with his groom and navigator, drives through a water obstacle at the Lowther Driving Trials in Cumbria in 2005.

On an official state visit to Papua New Guinea in 1988, he asked a British student who had trekked across the country, "You managed not to get eaten then?"; after the Royal Variety Performance in 1969 he famously asked singer Tom Jones, "What do you gargle with—pebbles?" He later added: "It is very difficult to see how it is possible to become immensely valuable by singing what I think are the most hideous songs." Philip is not, however, lacking in self-awareness: "Dontopedalogy is the science of opening your mouth and putting your foot in it," he once told the General Dental Council, "a science which I have practiced for a good many years."

Philip's monogram
Popular with European royalty since the Victorian era, monograms are used to identify and decorate a person's items. Philip's monogram graces everything from letterheads to handkerchiefs.

Encouraging the youth

One of Philip's most enduring contributions to public life has been his program for young people—the Duke of Edinburgh's (DofE) Award. The award grew out of the Prince's formative experiences with Kurt Hahn at Gordonstoun School. Hahn had initiated an awards program at the school to encourage young people to set and surpass their own targets for physical achievement, in line with his philosophy that while physical education is paramount, competition can be counterproductive. After the war, Hahn was eager to extend his program across Britain, and Philip helped him achieve his vision.

Philip said, "I could see that some such 'achievement-based' program, without requiring membership, might be a valuable tool for… the development of young people… to respond to Hahn's four major concerns about the development of young people… the decline of compassion, the decline of skills, the decline of physical fitness, and the decline of initiative." The program was launched in 1956, with Bronze, Silver, and Gold Awards. To earn them, boys needed to achieve targets in fields as diverse as physical fitness, volunteering, and expeditions. Two years later, a DofE program was introduced for girls. Philip described the development of the program: "I put together a group of women, and asked them to devise a similar program, which they thought would be appropriate for girls in the same age groups." The Awards soon went international, operating in 22 countries by 1966. Today, over 2 million Awards have been achieved in the UK alone, and over 7 million young people from 132 countries have taken part in the program since 1956.

> **"Prince Philip… has been a constant strength and guide."**
>
> QUEEN ELIZABETH, DIAMOND JUBILEE ADDRESS, MARCH 2012

TIMELINE

- **June 10, 1921** Born in Corfu, Greece.
- **1922** Coup d'etat sees Philip's family exiled to Paris.
- **1928** Philip is sent to live with the Mountbatten family in Surrey.
- **1933** Goes to Germany to study at a school run by Kurt Hahn.
- **1934** Joins Hahn at relocated school in Gordonstoun, Scotland.
- **1939** Becomes cadet at Royal Naval College, Dartmouth and escorts Elizabeth on a royal tour of the institution.
- **1940** Graduates at the top of his class and is awarded the King's Dirk and a prize for the best Cadet of his entry.
- **1940** Joins Royal Navy.
- **1941** Participates in the Battle of Cape Matapan and is mentioned in dispatches.
- **1943** Strikes up romance with Elizabeth after watching her in a royal pantomime.
- **1947** Marries Elizabeth after being created Duke of Edinburgh.
- **1947** Posted to Malta.
- **1952** Promoted to commander and given first command, but retires soon after from service.
- **February 1952** Breaks the news to Elizabeth that her father is dead.
- **1956** Founds the DofE award program.

PHILIP ADDRESSES WWF'S SECOND INTERNATIONAL CONGRESS IN 1970

- **1961** Becomes president of WWF.
- **1986** Lands in hot water on state visit to China after making a remark about "slitty eyes."
- **2001** Steps down as Chairman of DofE Award program after successfully managing it for nearly 50 years.
- **2002** Publishes letters between himself and Diana, Princess of Wales, to refute allegations that their relationship was strained.
- **2009** Becomes longest serving royal consort in British history.
- **2011** Turns 90 and steps down as patron of over a dozen organizations.

Born 1926

Elizabeth II, the Early Years

"I declare... that my **whole life,** whether it be long or short, shall be **devoted to your service.**"

ELIZABETH II, IN HER SPEECH ON HER 21ST BIRTHDAY, 1947

Learning to be queen
King George VI prepares his elder daughter Elizabeth for the role of queen. Here he is going through some state papers with her in a study at Windsor Castle in 1942.

To get a clear picture of the early years of Elizabeth II's reign, it is important to know that she was never intended to rule. Her childhood was sheltered and insular, and she had regular contact with her parents. Elizabeth and her sister Margaret lived in a little world of their own. In her 1950 book, *The Little Princesses*, Marion Crawford—"Crawfie," the governess who stewarded the education and early years of the lives of Elizabeth and Margaret, recalled that their nanny, Clara Wright (known as Alah) "had entire charge in those days of the children's out-of-school lives—their health, their baths, their clothes—while I had them from 9 to 5. (Alah) had to help her an under-nurse and a nursemaid."

In childhood Elizabeth was third in line to the throne, but since it was not her father but her uncle David who would inherit the crown as Edward VIII, few could have suspected that she would ever sit on it. Yet in late 1936 came the abdication of Edward VIII (see pp.92–93). "The shock of those terrible December days was literally stunning," recalled Queen Elizabeth, the Queen Mother. Her daughter was now destined to become queen. The new King George VI was very different in character from his flighty and self-indulgent brother, David. George VI and his wife would go on to instill their values in their daughter. The influence of her parents has been evident throughout her reign in her approach to the role of monarch, forming her overriding characteristics: an exceptional sense of public service married to traditional values.

Good works

Before Elizabeth took the throne would come the drama and challenges of World War II, with her own war service and an increasing public profile. In May 1944, Elizabeth gave a

Equestrian love
Elizabeth II is really fond of horses. In this photograph, she and the Queen Mother are admiring the greatest flat racehorse Sea Bird II winning the prestigious Epsom Derby in June 1965.

public address, to promote the Queen Elizabeth Hospital for Children in Hackney, east London, a charitable institution named after her mother. There she pledged her support for voluntary traditions at a time when the fashion was for ever-increasing state intervention in welfare. Thus she launched what has become a central feature of the royal project up to the present day: the role of "good works." Currently, the Crown's patronage list extends to more than 3,000 organizations—the Queen alone has 800. According to British historian David Cannadine: "charitable activity has become the place where the royal culture of hierarchical condescension, and the popular culture of social aspiration, have successfully merged."

Devoted to service

Another early clue to the type of queen Elizabeth would be, came in her 21st birthday broadcast to the Empire (see p.107), made in 1947. Recalling the dedication of her ancestors, she told the people she, too, would be devoted to their service. Duty has become perhaps the overarching principle of Elizabeth II's reign, but this in turn has led to some difficulties in balancing priorities, because alongside being the monarch of several nations and head of the Commonwealth, the Queen has also been a devoted wife, mother, daughter, and sister.

The two sides of Elizabeth have not always been easily reconciled. For instance, during her epic

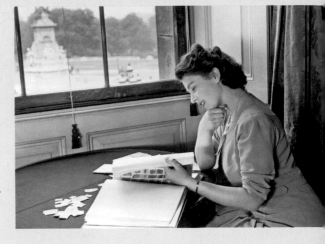

Sticking with tradition
With a passion for stamps running in the Royal Family, Elizabeth here is going through her collections in 1946. Her father George VI kept his stamps in blue binders, while her collection is kept in green books.

Commonwealth tour of 1953–54, she was away from her young children Charles and Anne for more than six months. This was followed in 1956 by a three-month period in which her husband Philip was absent putting the new yacht *HMY Britannia* through its sea trials, a separation that excited much speculation about their marriage. Moreover, when it came to her sister Margaret, and the agonizing choice she faced over marrying Group Captain Peter Townsend (see pp.154–55), the steeliest side of the young Queen's personality came to the fore. She bluntly refused to support Margaret in choosing love over duty.

A perfect balance

Yet against these examples of a harsh devotion to duty, can be set the overwhelming evidence of her devotion to family. The Queen's Christmas message of 1956 (see

"We should **remember** that in spite of all the scientific advances and **great** improvements in our **material welfare,** the family remains as the **focal point** of our **existence.**"

QUEEN ELIZABETH, CHRISTMAS MESSAGE, 1965

pp.156–57), for instance, included these touching words in respect of her husband's long absence: "You will understand me, therefore, when I tell you that of all the voices we have heard this afternoon none has given my children and my self greater joy than that of my husband." While they were still alive, Elizabeth would make sure to telephone her mother and sister every day.

There is a kind of conflict central to the persona of the Queen between her public face and her private demeanor. In public, she is widely perceived as reserved and aloof, but many accounts of her in private paint a picture of a woman with a robust sense of humor.

The Queen prefers to focus on her work. At 7 p.m. every weekday evening of the year, except Christmas and Easter Day, she receives a red despatch box of state papers to go through, which she needs to read and sign where necessary.

Racing mostly

The Queen has long had an abiding love of horses and horse racing. She runs a racing stable of her own and has had many classic winners. This love dates back to her teenage

years and was evidently a strong feature of her early reign; when asked what he and the Queen talked about at their weekly Tuesday meetings, Winston Churchill replied: "Racing mostly."

Private person

The Queen places a lot of value on her privacy, despite being the most famous and possibly most photographed woman in the world. This official photograph was released in January 1956 before her Nigeria tour.

ROYAL COAT OF ARMS OF THE UK

BEFORE

Three days before the Queen's first State Opening, the government was finalizing her speech. Traditionally, the speech was written on goat skin vellum with ink that took three days to dry. Once written, it could not easily be changed. Today sending the speech to the Palace for approval is still known as "going goat."

GUNPOWDER SEARCH
On the morning of the Queen's first State Opening, the **Yeoman of the Guard,** the Queen's personal bodyguard, performed a **ceremonial sweep** of the cellars of the palace—a nod to the **Gunpowder Plot of 1605 ⟪ 38–39.**

The Queen in Parliament and Politics

One of the first of Elizabeth II's duties as Queen was to attend the State Opening of Parliament. Loaded with pomp and pageantry, this event perfectly encapsulates the nature of the British constitution and the monarch's vital but precarious part in it.

The Queen is head of state of Britain and several other realms, and her role at the top of a constitutional monarchy is at the same time fundamentally symbolic, of vital importance, and extremely delicate. Simply by being at the top of the constitutional "pyramid" she helps to guarantee the rights and liberties of all her subjects, yet it is essential that she is scrupulously apolitical and visibly remains above

> ## "It is Her Majesty's pleasure that they [the Commons] attend her immediately in this house."
>
> GENTLEMAN USHER OF THE BLACK ROD TO PARLIAMENT, NOVEMBER 4, 1952

the political fray. In formal terms, she has the right to be consulted, to encourage, and to warn her ministers via regular audiences with the Prime Minister. Her duties include assenting to the passage of laws through Parliament, and consenting to the debate of bills that affect the Crown. She also has the responsibility for

proroguing or dissolving Parliament, and receives weekly briefings on parliamentary matters.

The Crown in Parliament
By far the Queen's best known and most visible role is to attend the annual State Opening of Parliament ceremony, the ritual that marks the start of a new parliamentary session. The Queen opens Parliament in person, and addresses both Houses with the Queen's Speech—a speech that lays out the legislative programme of her government over the forthcoming session. Neither House can proceed to public business until The Queen's Speech has been read. The ceremony articulates the delicate but time-hardened nature of the British constitution, and the Palace itself describes this as "the most colorful event of the parliamentary year [and] also the most important, because it brings together the three elements of the legislature [the House of Commons, the House of Lords, and the Queen]. The ceremony therefore represents the Crown in Parliament."

The theater begins before Her Majesty even leaves Buckingham Palace, where one of the government's chief whips (a Member of Parliament who serves, for these purposes, in the archaic office of Vice-Chamberlain of the Household) is offered by Parliament as a symbolic "hostage," to guarantee safe return of the sovereign. This ritual is a holdover from days when there was a genuine edge of jeopardy to relationships between the monarch and Parliament,

En route
Queen Elizabeth II, en route to her first State Opening of Parliament, is wearing the George IV State Diadem. She will change this on arriving at Westminster for the Imperial State Crown.

with memories still fresh of the regicide of 1649. Charles I was executed by Parliament after tensions over the constitutional relationship between King and legislature boiled over into Civil War (see pp.40–41). At modern state openings, the Vice-Chamberlain is delivered to Buckingham Palace and waits there until the monarch returns.

The royal regalia
While this goes on, the royal regalia are taken from Buckingham Palace to the Palace of Westminster, to be ready and waiting when the Queen arrives. Among them are the Imperial State Crown, which the Queen wears during the opening ceremony, the Cap of Maintenance, which was originally the lining for a crown—given as a gift from the Pope—and the Sword of State, originally made for Charles II, which symbolizes justice and mercy. The crown is taken to the Robing Room to await the Queen.

The Queen and the Duke of Edinburgh, escorted by the Household Cavalry, make the 12-minute journey between the palaces by State Coach, with the Queen wearing the George IV State Diadem. She is greeted with a fanfare by the State Trumpeters, and the Royal Standard is raised above the Palace of Westminster to signal that the Queen is in residence. The Queen proceeds to the Robing Room to put on the Imperial State Crown and the Robe of State. She then moves on to the House of Lords, heralded by another fanfare, via a staircase guarded by the "staircase party," a special detachment of the Household Cavalry, who are the only troops allowed to draw swords in the Houses of Parliament.

White wand and Black Rod
When the Queen reaches the House of Lords she says "My Lords, pray be seated," which triggers a sequence of events in which the Lord Great Chamberlain raises his white wand of office, a signal to the Gentleman Usher of the Black Rod (commonly known as Black Rod). He serves as the Queen's messenger in Parliament, and it is his job

to summon the Commons. This is followed by a great showpiece moment, in which Black Rod walks to the door of the House of Commons, which is

The Imperial State Crown
Originally made for Elizabeth II's father, this crown is worn on state occasions such as the State Opening of Parliament. It has three very large stones, and is set with 2,868 diamonds.

Sapphire, linking cross and fleur-de-lis

Ermine band

First time on film

The 1958 opening marked the first time in history that the sovereign was photographed reading the speech from the throne in the House of Lords. It was also the first time the ceremony was televised.

ceremonially shut in his face, to symbolize that the House of Commons is independent of the Crown. Black Rod knocks three times on the door before the command "Open the door" is given, and he is admitted to deliver the Queen's summons: "Mr. Speaker: the Queen commands this honorable house to attend Her Majesty immediately in the House of Peers." The Speaker and Black Rod then lead the MPs from the Commons to the Lords to hear the Queen's Speech.

A fixed point

The Queen's first State Opening came on November 4, 1952. It was her first major state event, attracting large crowds to watch as she arrived at Westminster. Wearing a specially made parliamentary robe of crimson velvet, decorated with gold lace and lined with ermine, she started her first Queen's Speech with a tribute to her late father. In 2014, she attended her 60th opening—a remarkable record, which has seen her miss just two: in 1959 when pregnant with Prince Andrew, and in 1963 when pregnant with Prince Edward. During her reign she has held weekly meetings with 12 prime ministers, outlasted 12 US presidents, and all the general secretaries of the Communist Party of the Soviet Union, witnessed white smoke coming from the Vatican six times, and seen the building and tearing down of the Berlin Wall. It is often said that one of the great values of her role as constitutional monarch is that she offers a fixed point, stable in a world of constant change.

Although the Queen is kept thoroughly informed about government business and politics, it is important that she does not get involved in making political decisions. When it looks as though she has or might, constitutional crisis threatens. Perhaps her greatest constitutional crisis came in January 1957 when Prime Minister Eden resigned in the wake of the Suez crisis (see pp.118–19) and the Queen had to exercise her royal prerogative, choosing between two candidates for his replacement. Informal soundings were taken by peers and the Queen was advised by Churchill; she chose Harold Macmillan over R. A. Butler, to the surprise of many. A similar situation arose again in 1963, when the Queen was once again advised to pass over Butler, this time in favor of Alec Douglas-Home.

Cabochon red spinel, known as the "Black Prince's Ruby"

Cushion-shaped Cullinan II diamond

AFTER »

After the Queen leaves Parliament to return to Buckingham Palace, the Royal Standard is replaced by the Union Flag over the Palace of Westminster.

THE OUTLAWRIES BILL

The parliamentary session **begins,** but instead of immediately moving to debate the Queen's Speech, both MPs and Lords introduce in their respective chambers what is known as the **Outlawries Bill,** a symbol of the autonomy of both houses from the monarch. **Purely ceremonial,** the bill is not taken forward and members are then able to debate the Queen's Speech and agree an "Address in Reply to Her Majesty's Gracious Speech."

Prime Minister's briefing

The Queen meets with her Prime Minister once a week. Here she is photographed meeting with Tony Blair in 2002. Her favorite prime minister was probably Winston Churchill— she even went to Downing Street for his farewell dinner.

The **Coronation Ceremony**

In a moving ceremony, replete with ancient traditions, Elizabeth offered solemn oaths, was anointed with holy oil, and received the crown of her ancestors. The service was laden with the physical and metaphorical weight of royal emblems.

As the coronation ceremony moved to its climax, Elizabeth, having arrived at the altar, was seated on the Chair of Estate, or the Coronation Chair. She read the coronation oath and took Holy Communion. The most significant part of the ceremony was the anointment. Hidden behind a silk canopy, the Queen was daubed with blessed holy oil, containing oil of orange, rose, musk, cinnamon, and ambergris—a rare material created in the digestive system of sperm whales. Traditionally, this oil was drawn from a supply dating back to previous sovereigns, but preparations for the 1953 coronation revealed that the last phial had been destroyed in bombing raids on London during World War II. Unfortunately, the pharmacy that made the oil had gone out of business, and it looked as though the recipe might have been lost. But the Coronation Commission was able to locate perhaps the last man from the pharmacy, an elderly person who had kept few ounces of the oil as memento, and he mixed up a batch.

After the annointment, the Queen was dressed in the imperial vestments and handed the trappings and regalia of state. She put on a cloth-of-gold robe, called the *Supertunica,* over the *Colobium Sindonis,* a loose linen tunic. She was then presented with the golden spurs, symbolic of chivalry, and a jeweled sword. These were followed by the armills (gold bracelets), representing sincerity and wisdom. Elizabeth then put on the cloth-of-gold Imperial Mantle robe and received the Sovereign's Orb and the two scepters: the Scepter with the Cross, symbolizing temporal power under God, and the Scepter with the Dove, representing equity and mercy. Finally, she was crowned with the solid gold St. Edward's Crown, although for the regalia portrait shown here, it was swapped for the Imperial State Crown.

"I here present unto you, Queen Elizabeth, your undoubted Queen."

GEOFFREY FISHER, ARCHBISHOP OF CANTERBURY, DURING ELIZABETH II'S CORONATION, JUNE 2, 1953

Iconic picture
This famous coronation portrait by photographer Cecil Beaton was shot inside Buckingham Palace after the Queen had returned from her coronation service. A painted backdrop of Henry VII's Lady Chapel in Westminster Abbey was used to create atmosphere.

NORWICH GATES, 1952

ST. MARY MAGDALENE'S CHURCH

ANMER HALL

SHOOTING PARTY, C.1910

ROYAL RESIDENCE

Sandringham

The house at Sandringham stands on a 20,000-acre (8,000-ha) estate in an area of outstanding natural beauty near the coast of Norfolk. It was bought by Queen Victoria in 1862 as a wedding present for the Prince of Wales, the future Edward VII, and his new bride, Princess Alexandra.

Although the Sandringham estate included a substantial Georgian mansion, it was too small for Albert and Alexandra, and they had it demolished. It was replaced in 1870 with a multiple-gable, red-brick, Jacobean-style country house.

The facilities were cutting-edge for the time, and included gas-lighting, flushing toilets, and a shower. There were large reception rooms for formal and family occasions, but the everyday living quarters were modest by comparison. Plenty of space was even provided for the family menagerie of dogs, cats, and horses.

Sandringham suited Princess Alexandra and her five children very well, which compensated in part for the long absences and infidelities of her husband. Geographically, it lies in a fascinating part of England. It was once part of Doggerland, the land bridge that linked Great Britain and Scandinavia before the last Ice Age. Its similarities to Princess Alexandra's native Denmark are therefore no coincidence, and it is perhaps why she felt at home here.

In 1886 Edward established the Royal Stud at Sandringham, and he soon became one of the most influential breeders in the country, producing two legendary racehorses: Persimmon, which won the famous

English races the St. Leger and the Derby in 1896, and Diamond Jubilee, which won the 1900 Triple Crown. The Prince plowed his prize money into the estate, creating a vast walled kitchen garden. This has been recently revived to produce vegetables for the Sandringham Visitor Center restaurant.

Both Albert and Alexandra were passionate about hunting on the Sandringham estate, so much so that in 1901, Albert, now crowned Edward VII, ordered all the clocks to be set half an hour ahead of GMT (Greenwich Mean Time), to increase the amount of daylight at the end of the day in winter for hunting. The tradition of "Sandringham Time" continued until 1936.

In 1932, under George V, a new Sandringham tradition was born: he made the first live radio broadcast to the Empire from the house on Christmas Day. Queen Elizabeth continued the tradition 20 years later, but made history again in 1957 when she invited the nation into the Library at Sandringham in the first live televised Christmas Day broadcast.

Private times

For Elizabeth, Sandringham holds particular significance. Her father, George VI, was born on the estate and he also died there. He grew up in one

of the estate houses, York Cottage, where his happiest times were spent with his grandparents. It was he who planted Sandringham's first apple orchards—the estate is now famous for its apple juices. He also turned a bomb crater on the estate, created during the first German Zeppelin raid in January 1915, into a duck pond.

Since her father's death, it has been the Queen's custom to spend the anniversary privately with her family on the estate.

Public viewings

Sandringham was first opened to the public in 1977. Between April and October, when the Royal Family is not in residence, several of the reception rooms on the ground floor are made accessible.

The decoration of the rooms and their furnishings have changed little from the time of Queen Alexandra and Queen Mary, wife of George V. Lavish gifts from members of the Russian and European royal families, who were frequent guests of the royals at Sandringham, are on display, including a Dresden porcelain chandelier and mirror frame from Kaiser Wilhelm I of Germany. **»**

Sandringham House
Dating from 1870, the country house built for Albert, the Prince of Wales, and Princess Alexandra was described by their friend Charles Carrington as "the most comfortable house in England."

DAIMLER MAIL PHAETON CAR

LADY AMHERST'S PHEASANT

Snapshots from the estate
Owned by the Royal Family for over 150 years, Sandringham has been a much-loved home to four British monarchs—and with the move of Prince William and his young family to Anmer Hall, a new generation are set to enjoy life on the estate. The Queen particularly likes to spend Christmas at Sandringham, and traditionally joins the celebration at the church of St. Mary Magdalene, within easy reach of the house. The spectacular wrought- and cast-iron Norwich Gates designed by Thomas Jekyll were a wedding gift to the future Edward VII from the County of Norfolk and City of Norwich. Edward (here seated at the wheel of the car) was very attached to the estate, and indulged his love of country pursuits by hosting regular shooting parties. Today visitors can inspect vintage royal vehicles at the Sandringham Museum, and stroll through the grounds, which are home to over 100 species of bird, including colorful pheasants.

>> The walls of these rooms are hung with family portraits by the leading court painters of the time. An important collection of oriental arms and armor is housed at Sandringham, brought back from the Far East and India in 1876, the year of Prince Albert's tour (see pp.72–73) and a special exhibition of them in the Ballroom is changed every year.

"Dear old Sandringham, **the place I love better** than anywhere in the world."

KING GEORGE V

The estate museum, in the former coach houses and stable block, holds an extraordinarily diverse collection. George V used the museum to gather together all his big game trophies from his other royal residences. There are vintage cars, the highlight being the Daimler Phaeton bought by Edward VII. He was the first British monarch to own a car—but it is not known whether he could drive.

Sandringham is run by the Royal Family as a modern estate. When the Queen acceded to the throne in 1952, Prince Philip was made responsible for its running, and it is only recently that the day-to-day management has begun to be handed over to Prince Charles. Most of the crops are still farmed conventionally, but there is a gradual move over to organic farming. Practices are designed to encourage as many species of wildlife as possible. With the Prince's eye always on conservation, more than 5,000 trees and several miles of hedges are planted each year, and 10 wetland areas have been created.

The estate features 198 acres (80ha) of orchards and soft fruits—including the black currants that Sandringham grows for the soft drink brand Ribena. A recent innovation beside the orchards is an experimental organic black truffle plantation. The ground conditions at Sandringham are thought to be ideal for oak and hazel trees infected with truffle spores, while it is hoped that staff at the Sandringham kennels will be able train truffle-hunting dogs.

Sandringham Country Park was first opened to the public in 1968. An area of woodland and open heath, it has been enlarged to cover 600 acres (240ha) and comes with two signed nature trails.

After Prince William announced his role with East Anglia's Air Ambulance in 2014, he and the Duchess of Cambridge decided to make Anmer Hall on the Sandringham estate their family home. The Georgian mansion was a wedding present, and a house William knows well from his childhood, when it was leased to his father's friend Hugh van Cutsem. They moved in after some refurbishment and additions, including a conservatory designed by architect Charles Morris, who also did work at Highgrove.

Vintage views of Sandringham

Photographs taken in the 1880s show grand rooms at Sandringham, such as the Saloon and the Dining Room, which were crammed with memorabilia from royal trips abroad as well as gifts from foreign dignitaries. Many of the interiors are lit by natural light streaming through bay windows: Queen Mary's desk, covered with family photographs, occupied a bright alcove.

THE DINING ROOM, 1880

THE SALOON, 1882

QUEEN'S MARY'S DESK

Frills and flounces
The Principal Drawing Room was photographed for *Country Life* in the early 1900s. Ornate plasterwork on the ceilings, walls, and doors, and the painted panels, can still be seen by visitors today.

An Anglican abroad
A goodwill ambassador to the Anglican world outside England, the Queen greets James Horstead, the Archbishop of West Africa, at a cathedral in Nigeria, in 1956.

The **Queen** as **Head** of the **Church**

The Queen has always taken her public role as head of the Church of England very seriously. In private she has nurtured an undemonstrative but abiding faith, as well as a commitment to ensure freedom of worship for all.

A mong the Queen's many titles is that of "Defender of the Faith and Supreme Governor of the Church of England," a role that is set out in the Preface to one of the foundational documents of the Church of England, where the Monarch is described as "being by God's Ordinance, according to Our just Title, Defender of the Faith and... Supreme Governor of the Church of England." The Queen also has a role in the Church of Scotland. Although she is simply an ordinary member and not supreme governor, she is required by the Treaty of Union of 1707

7 The number of Archbishops of Canterbury during Queen Elizabeth II's reign.

to preserve the Church of Scotland. Her role is central to the status of both these churches as "established churches," which means that they are regulated by British law.

The monarch's role in the Church of England is a direct consequence of Henry VIII's break with Rome in the 16th century, which led to a series of Parliamentary Acts in the 1530s.

GOLD MEDAL OF HENRY VIII

POWER TO THE MONARCHY
In 1534, Parliament proclaimed Henry the only supreme head of the Church of England, and in 1559 Parliament decreed an Act of Supremacy, declaring that Elizabeth I was the "only **Supreme Governor** of this realm and of all other highness' dominions and countries, as well in all spiritual or ecclesiastical things or causes, as temporal." The act was to "restore to the Crown the ancient jurisdiction over the estate ecclesiastical and abolishing all foreign powers repugnant to the same."

A significant portion of the Queen's coronation oath was given over to asserting this role. Among other things, the Queen swore "to maintain in the United Kingdom the Protestant Reformed Religion established by law... preserve inviolably the settlement of the Church of England... and government thereof, as by law established in England" to the utmost of her power. To the Queen these are not merely words, but a spiritual charge that she took to her heart. "The sense of spiritual exaltation that radiated from her was almost tangible to those of us who stood near her in the abbey," recalled Dermot Morrah, Arundel Herald Extraordinary, one of the principal organizers of the Coronation in 1953.

The Queen appoints and invests bishops (on the advice of the prime minister and Church Commission), and bishops and parish priests take an oath of allegiance to the Queen and need royal authority to resign. Much as with Parliament, the Queen opens the Synod (the governing assembly of the Church of England), and her assent is required for it to pass measures and canon legislature.

Defending the faith
On a more personal level, the Queen has a deep and abiding faith. Every Sunday, wherever she is, she attends church, including the private royal chapel in Windsor Great Park, St. Mary Magdalene at Sandringham, and Crathie Kirk at Balmoral. One commentator remarks that "Her every decision is informed by her faith." For instance, her former Domestic Chaplain Robin Woods, who describes the Queen as "a praying and

Papal visit
In September 2010, Pope Benedict XVI, on his first visit to the UK, met Queen Elizabeth in Holyroodhouse in Edinburgh, Scotland. He was received with a Royal Salute and a Guard of Honor.

A royal place of worship
The 19th-century Crathie Kirk near Braemar, Aberdeenshire, Scotland, has strong connections to Queen Victoria and to successive generations of the Royal Family who worship there when vacationing at Balmoral Castle.

believing woman," relates a story about the introduction of a new version of the Church of England prayer book in 1966. Before she signed off on the new version, Elizabeth called Woods, saying, "I don't think

Some experts are questioning the sustainability of the monarch's role as head of the Church of England, after the changes in the law in 2011 that made it legal for a royal to marry a Catholic.

FUTURE OF THE QUEEN'S ROLE
It is now theoretically possible for **the heir to the throne to marry a Catholic.** The political and constitutional reform committee commented: "The scenario does beg the question of whether it remains appropriate for the monarch to be required to be in communion with the Church of England."

I should sign something which will change the liturgy until at least we've prayed it through."

In a 2012 address at Lambeth Palace, the Queen gave an impassioned defence of the role and value of the Church of England: "The concept of our established Church is occasionally misunderstood and, I believe, commonly underappreciated... It certainly provides an identity and spiritual dimension for its own many adherents. But also, gently and assuredly, the Church of England has created an environment for other faith communities and indeed people of no faith to live freely."

> **" ...woven** into the **fabric** of this **country** the **Church** has helped to build a **better society."**
>
> THE QUEEN'S LAMBETH PALACE ADDRESS, 2012

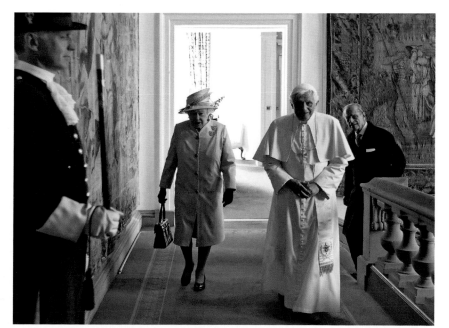

Travel and State Visits

Elizabeth II is probably one of the most recognizable women on the planet—partly because she has visited most of it. The Queen's constant tours enable her to connect personally with millions of people.

The Queen has traveled more widely than any other monarch. Her extraordinary history of official overseas visits dates back to 1947, when she was still a princess. That year, Elizabeth accompanied her parents on a tour of Rhodesia (now Zimbabwe) and South Africa, where she celebrated her 21st birthday in Cape Town, with a memorable radio broadcast to the Commonwealth

(see pp.106–107). In 1951, the princess and her husband Philip were sent on a five-week-long, coast-to-coast tour of Canada in place of the ailing George VI. However, it was only after Elizabeth's accession (see pp.132–33) and coronation (see pp.140–43) that her truly epic travel itinerary began.

First Commonwealth tour

One of Elizabeth's first duties as newly crowned queen was to undertake a grueling tour of the Commonwealth that had originally been planned for her father. She took off with Philip in 1953, leaving behind their two young children for a period of seven months. Her goal, she said to the people of the Commonwealth in a Christmas Day message broadcast from New Zealand, was "to show that the crown is not merely an abstract symbol of our unity, but a personal and living bond between you and me."

The highlight of the tour was the 1954 royal visit to Australia, which produced some extraordinary scenes. In

Commemorative tea caddy
The Queen's 1954 visit to Australia caused nationwide excitement. This octagonal tin of tea, with illustrations of Elizabeth and Philip on opposite sides, was specially produced to commemorate the visit.

« BEFORE

The prelude to the Queen's epic 1953–54 tour of the Commonwealth was her coronation tour of the British Isles, including visits to Scotland and Northern Ireland.

FIRST VISIT TO NORTHERN IRELAND
In July 1953, **Elizabeth visited Northern Ireland for the first time.** Accompanied by Philip, she traveled by train through the Ulster countryside and along the north coast. A public holiday was declared, and cheering crowds thronged to see the Queen. Conspicuous in the royal entourage was equerry **Peter Townsend,** brought along to put some distance between him and **Margaret 154–55 »**.

At sea
Captain Alan McNicoll shows Elizabeth around his ship, HMAS *Australia*, during her 1954 tour of Australia. This ship was part of the escort for the Royal Yacht carrying the Queen during the Australian leg of her coronation world tour.

Ballarat, in rural Victoria, more than 150,000 people lined the streets to get a glimpse of the Queen. "We shared in an elevating experience from which we should all emerge better citizens and better Britishers," gushed the *Ballarat Courier*—a local newspaper. At Melbourne Cricket Ground (one of the world's biggest sports stadiums), more than 100,000 children turned out to greet Elizabeth. Excitement turned to hysteria in other parts of the country: 2,000 people fainted while waiting to see the Queen outside Sydney's town hall, and women and children were trampled underfoot as a crowd surged to see the monarch in Lismore, northern New South Wales. It was estimated that some 10 million Australians—about 70 percent of the population—saw the Queen in person during the visit.

Coming home
Elizabeth's tour of the Commonwealth was scheduled to come to an end in May 1954. The Royal Yacht *Britannia*, built in 1953 by the prestigious Clyde shipyards of John Brown & Co. at a cost of more than £2 million ($5.6 million), was enlisted to bring the royal couple home. The yacht would carry Prince Charles and Princess Anne to the Mediterranean, where they would join their parents before sailing back to Britain. The family was reunited on May 1, when Elizabeth and Philip boarded the yacht at Tobruk, Libya.

On May 15, the Royal Family received a rapturous welcome as they sailed up the Thames River. Prime Minister Winston Churchill was also on the yacht, having boarded the previous day at Yarmouth, on the Isle of Wight. The twin arms of Tower Bridge were opened to their fullest extent to let the yacht through, and a huge banner bearing the words "Welcome Home" ran across the top of the bridge. A 41-gun salute thundered out from the Tower of London. After bringing the Queen's first Commonwealth tour to a successful conclusion, *Britannia* went on to cover more than a million miles in over 44 years of royal service.

Far and wide
The Queen's Commonwealth tour of 1953–54 was her longest. Since then, she has continued to tour extensively, travelling around 100,000 miles (160,000 km) per year for much of her reign, making at least one state visit a year. The rest of the Royal Family shares some of the burden with her. In her 1958 Christmas broadcast, after listing the Royal Family's

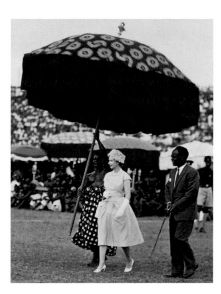

The Queen in Africa
Elizabeth is escorted to a dais under a large sunshade to view a parade at Kumasi Sports Stadium during a state visit to Ghana in November 1961. The Queen also visited Sierra Leone and Gambia the same year.

comprehensive travel plans for the year ahead, the Queen famously quipped, "Between us, we are going to many parts of the world. We have no plans for space travel—at the moment."

Historic firsts
During her reign, Elizabeth has visited more than 100 nations, and achieved many historic firsts. In 1986, she became the first reigning British monarch to visit China, and also made first state visits to Russia in October 1994, Brunei and Malaysia in 1998, and South Korea in 1999. In 1995, the Queen finally went back to South Africa for the first time since 1947, after the end of apartheid.

In 2011, Elizabeth became the first British monarch to visit the Republic of Ireland (see pp.270–71), making the first visit to southern parts of the island since the 1911 tour by her grandfather George V. At a state dinner held in her honor, the Queen reflected on the historic import of the occasion, talking of "the peace and understanding we now have between our two nations

> **43,617** The total distance in miles **(70,196 kilometers) covered by Elizabeth II during her 1953–54 tour of the Commonwealth.**

and between the communities within those two nations; a living testament to how much in common we have."

A royal ambassador
For much of her reign, the Queen has attended up to 10 official engagements a day when on tour, working up to 14 hours a day. It is perhaps not surprising, given the volume of arrangements and security involved, that tours take up to two years to organize. In recent times, the Queen's state visits have become shorter and less onerous.

Elizabeth is of remarkable value as an ambassador for Britain. A visit from the Queen helps the country exert influence, spread its culture and values, and advance its economic objectives. For instance, *Reader's Digest* magazine described the Queen's 1953–54 Commonwealth tour as "possibly the most ambitious and certainly the most successful piece of public relations ever attempted." A visit from the Queen carries unique prestige, due in part to the relative scarcity of ruling royal families since World War II. Lord Chalfont, who frequently served as the Queen's Minister in Attendance on state visits, noted: "The British monarchy occupies a unique band in the spectrum of international diplomacy… [the Queen] has for most people overseas that indefinable quality sometimes described [as] 'glamour.'"

AFTER

Accompanied by the Duke of Edinburgh, Elizabeth continues to undertake one or two official visits abroad each year.

ON BEHALF OF THE QUEEN
In recent times, the Queen has increasingly been **represented abroad by her family**—her son, Prince Charles, and grandchildren, Princes Harry and William **294–95 »**. The newest member of the Royal Family, Prince George, made his first visit abroad—a three-week tour of Australia and New Zealand **294–95 »** at only 8 months old.

Her Majesty's Yacht
The Royal Yacht *Britannia* is seen docked alongside the Victoria and Alfred Waterfront during Elizabeth's 1995 historic visit to South Africa after the abolishment of apartheid, or racial segregation. The yacht was decommissioned two years later.

Lovers on parade
A photo of young Princess Margaret, inspecting the troops at a ship launch in 1947, captures royal equerry Peter Townsend in the background. This was at the start of their relationship.

Margaret's Doomed Romance

The young Queen Elizabeth's fledgling rule soon faced a test that pitted changing social mores against the traditional conservatism of the monarchy, as Princess Margaret considered marrying a divorcee, Group Captain Peter Townsend.

"**We** were both exhausted… we felt mute and **numbed** at the **center** of this **maelstrom.**"

PETER TOWNSEND

On her 18th birthday, Princess Margaret enjoyed a glittering coming out. Her private life would now be the talk of the gossip columns, as commentators speculated over the identity of the most likely suitor for perhaps the most eligible woman in the world. The general view was that Margaret ran with a "fast" set: dashing young playboy aristocrats. But in truth she merely dallied with them, for her heart had long been set on an older, more serious figure: Group Captain Peter Townsend, a war hero whose daring exploits as a pilot during the Battle of Britain were legendary.

Out in the open

The outside world first became aware of the relationship between princess and equerry in 1953. On the day of Elizabeth's coronation (see pp.140–43), Margaret was seen picking a bit of fluff off Townsend's uniform, a gesture that spoke volumes. Their relationship immediately became a media circus, with sensational coverage that disturbed the Palace greatly. After Edward VIII's abdication crisis (see pp.90–91), the thought of another royal getting involved with a divorcee was unacceptable. Various steps were taken to separate the couple. In July 1953 Margaret was sent to accompany the Queen Mother on a tour of Southern Rhodesia (now part of Zimbabwe), while it had been arranged that Townsend would take a new job as the British Air Attache in Brussels. When Margaret learned that he would have left the UK by the time she returned, she collapsed. The Palace, including the Queen herself, were against the match, but when she reached the age of 25 Margaret would be able to marry without permission from the monarch.

Opposition to the marriage

As Margaret approached her 25th birthday, tension mounted. On October 14, the Palace issued a statement that no announcement concerning Princess Margaret's personal future was at present contemplated. Various constitutional and religious issues seemed to block any prospect of a union. Meanwhile Prime Minister Anthony Eden had told the Queen that any marriage between the two would not receive parliamentary sanction and that if it took place, a bill would be set out to deprive Princess Margaret of her rights of succession, her title, and her Civil List entitlement.

Hounded by the press

As speculation about their marriage mounted to fever pitch, Margaret and Townsend found themselves at the center of a media circus. Here the press wait for them to leave a dinner party in late October 1955.

Keeping her distance
Princess Margaret's visit to the West Indies in February 1955 was widely seen as an attempt to put some distance between herself and Peter Townsend. It did not work.

> **£6,000** **Annual income ($17,000) that Margaret would have lost had she married Townsend.**

For the love of Peter
Headlines from the *Daily Mirror*, dated October 19, 1955, give a flavor of the pervasive media coverage of Margaret's relationship.

The final decision

Margaret was faced with a stark choice: renounce the marriage, or renounce her royal life. At the end of October, she made her decision and informed the Archbishop of Canterbury, Dr. Geoffrey Fisher. On October 31, after a meeting with Townsend, she issued her statement: "I would like it to be known that I have decided not to marry Group Captain Peter Townsend." It was signed "Margaret" but had been written by Peter Townsend.

The **First Televised Christmas Message**

The Christmas broadcast had served to provide a powerful connection between the monarch and the people since the 1930s. In 1957, Elizabeth II was eager to use the latest technology to connect even more directly with the public.

On Christmas Day 1932, George V inaugurated one of the most deeply embedded of British yuletide customs—the royal Christmas message (see pp.88–89). The message was delivered via radio to millions of listeners. Elizabeth II continued this tradition, bringing to it her own love of television. She was a great fan of the new medium; after returning from her 1954 tour of the Commonwealth, she delayed appearing on the balcony of Buckingham Palace until she had finished watching English actress and singer Gracie Fields in the BBC's *Welcome Home Ball*. By 1960, there were 50 TV sets in the Palace.

The year 1957 would mark the 25th anniversary of the first Christmas broadcast on radio. Richard Webber, the BBC's head of outside broadcasting, recalled: "In television, we were keen to do everything that radio had done, so we asked the Palace if the Queen would consider reading the message live on television. She was a young monarch keen to enter into the spirit of the new era, and approved of the idea." The broadcast would be made live from the Long Library at Sandringham.

Elizabeth went from a single run-through into a live broadcast, in which she read from the teleprompter. She was filmed throughout by a single camera, which panned in during the speech. Toward the end of the broadcast, she was to quote some lines from English writer and preacher John Bunyan's *Pilgrim's Progress* and pick up a book as a prop. The Queen was the only one to notice that it was the wrong book, a detail that would not have been apparent to viewers, but she made sure that the correct volume was fetched from the library.

> "**I** should seem a rather **remote figure** to many of you… But now at least for a few minutes **I welcome you** into the **peace** of my own **home.**"
>
> **ELIZABETH II,** ROYAL CHRISTMAS MESSAGE, 1957

Gathering around to watch
Millions of viewers watched Elizabeth II's 1957 Christmas message. She struck a chord with her audience by saying: "My own family often gather round to watch television as they are this moment, and that is how I imagine you now."

4

QUEEN AND MOTHER

1960–1980

« Hybrid tea rose named "Silver Jubilee" in honor of Elizabeth II's 25 years on the throne

QUEEN AND MOTHER
1960–1980

1960	1962	1964	1966		1968

FEBRUARY 3, 1960
British Prime Minister Harold Macmillan makes his "winds of change" speech to the South African parliament, heralding the decolonization of Africa.

MARCH 10, 1964
Elizabeth II gives birth to her third son, Edward.

FEBRUARY
Prince Charles starts his two-term attendance at Geelong Grammar School in Australia.

DECEMBER 22, 1966
Rhodesia leaves the Commonwealth, having illegally declared independence the year before.

APRIL 20, 1968
Enoch Powell delivers his "rivers of blood" speech, warning of the dangers of increased immigration.

SEPTEMBER 27, 1968
US musical *Hair* opens in London following repeal of theater censorship the previous day.

FEBRUARY 19, 1960
Elizabeth II gives birth to her second son, Andrew.

MARCH 27, 1966
Football World Cup trophy, which was stolen in London, is found by a dog; England wins World Cup at Wembley on July 30, 1966.

« The Queen with Prince Andrew and the baby Prince Edward

MAY 28, 1967
Aviator and sailor Francis Chichester completes solo around-the-world sailing voyage.

JUNE 21, 1969
Royal Family documentary airs on BBC, followed by a second transmission on ITV a week later.

MAY 6, 1960
Princess Margaret marries Antony Armstrong-Jones, later created Earl of Snowdon.

OCTOBER 21, 1960
The Queen launches the UK's first nuclear submarine.

MAY 11, 1962
13-year-old Prince Charles starts at Gordonstoun School in Scotland.

AUGUST 6, 1962
Jamaica becomes independent.

JUNE 1963
Government minister John Profumo resigns after involvement in a sex scandal.

OCTOBER 15, 1964
The Labour party comes to power under Harold Wilson.

JANUARY 25, 1965
Churchill dies, state funeral follows six days later.

JUNE 1965
Queen presents Member of the Order of the British Empire (MBE) to each of the Beatles.

OCTOBER 21, 1966
Aberfan disaster in Wales; massive mudslide kills 116 children and 28 adults as it buries a school.

JULY 2, 1967
The Queen and Prince Philip visit Ottawa for the Canadian centennial.

⌃ An investiture chair

1960
Elizabeth allows her portrait to be used on currency for the first time.

OCTOBER 1963
When Prime Minister Harold MacMillan steps down due to ill health, the lack of a replacement sparks a constitutional crisis. The Queen is advised to appoint Alec Douglas-Home.

« £1 note; design first issued in 1960

JULY 4, 1967
England and Wales decriminalize male homosexuality.

JULY 1, 1969
Investiture of Charles as Prince of Wales at Caernarfon Castle.

SEPTEMBER 20, 1967
The Queen attends the launching ceremony of the ocean liner *Queen Elizabeth II (QE2)*.

AUGUST 1969
Northern Ireland riots mark climax of year of escalation of sectarian and nationalist conflict known as the Troubles.

MAY 31, 1961
South Africa leaves the Commonwealth after other nations reject its apartheid policy and white South Africans vote for a republic.

NOVEMBER 25, 1963
The Duke of Edinburgh represents the Queen at the funeral of assassinated US president John F Kennedy.

« Launch of the QE2

Two decades of upheaval and transition at home and abroad brought an era of rapid change to which the Royal Family managed to adapt, even as it expanded, with the Queen, Princess Margaret, and Princess Anne all having children. The Queen would face multiple challenges, including the widespread decolonization of former overseas territories, changing social mores at home, and the breakdown of her sister's marriage. The public would get its first intimate look at royal life, while national joy over the Silver Jubilee celebrations would soon be overshadowed by private tragedy as a terrorist atrocity struck close to the heart of the royals.

1970

JUNE 19, 1970
Ted Heath becomes Prime Minister after shock victory for Conservatives.

JULY 1970
Following visits to Fiji, Tonga, New Zealand, and Australia, Queen Elizabeth tours Canada; the following month Charles and Anne are guests of President Nixon in Washington.

JANUARY 1971
First Commonwealth Heads of Government meeting takes place in Singapore.

1971
Anne wins the European Eventing Championship, and later BBC Sports Personality of the Year.

FEBRUARY 15, 1971
Decimalization in UK and Ireland, with introduction of new money.

1972

JUNE 5, 1972
Funeral of the Queen's uncle, Duke of Windsor, formerly Edward VIII.

NOVEMBER 20, 1972
The Queen and Prince Philip celebrate their silver wedding anniversary.

JANUARY 1, 1973
The UK joins the European Economic Community (EEC).

NOVEMBER 14, 1973
Princess Anne marries Captain Mark Phillips.

1974

JANUARY 1974
Miner's strike forces Prime Minister Heath to introduce three-day week and leads to collapse of government and general election; this in turn results in hung parliament and fresh elections, returning Harold Wilson to power.

≈ Stamp commemorating the Queen and the Duke of Edinburgh's silver wedding anniversary

SILVER WEDDING 3P

MARCH 20, 1974
Attempt to kidnap Princess Anne is foiled.

NOVEMBER 11, 1975
Governor-General of Australia sparks a constitutional crisis when he fires the Australian prime minister.

1976

JANUARY 21, 1976
The Concorde begins transatlantic flights.

≫ Coin commemorating the Queen's Silver Jubilee

JANUARY–JUNE 1976
Cod War between the UK and Iceland erupts due to differences over fishing rights.

MARCH 19, 1976
Princess Margaret and her husband, the Earl of Snowdon, separate.

SUMMER 1976
A heatwave brings longest drought and hottest summer on record for the UK.

DECEMBER 31, 1976
The Prince's Trust—Prince Charles' charity for young people—is officially launched.

JUNE 6, 1977
The Queen's Silver Jubilee reaches a climax. The extended celebrations include home and foreign tours, Armada beacon chain, Thanksgiving Service at St. Paul's Cathedral, nationwide street parties, Thames River procession, and Jubilee walkway.

JUNE 15, 1977
Gleneagles Agreement marks the start of sports boycott of South Africa.

NOVEMBER 15, 1977
Princess Anne gives birth to Peter, her first child and the Queen's first grandchild.

1978

1978–1979
Widespread strikes by public-sector unions, together with the coldest winter in 16 years makes what the papers call "the winter of discontent."

JULY 25, 1978
World's first test-tube baby, Louise Brown, is born in Oldham, Greater Manchester.

MAY 1979
Margaret Thatcher becomes Prime Minister.

AUGUST 27, 1979
The IRA assassinates Earl Mountbatten along with three others.

≈ Mountbatten's funeral procession

NOVEMBER 21, 1979
Sir Anthony Blunt, the Queen's art adviser, is named as a Soviet spy and the fourth man in the Cambridge spy ring.

≪ The wedding of Princess Anne to Captain Mark Phillips

The **Childhood** of the Princes and **Princess**

The Queen's four children are not at all like each other, despite their similar upbringing. Part of this is probably due to their very different experiences in childhood, as well as the considerable age gap between them.

Mother and children
Queen Elizabeth with 4-year-old Andrew and the infant Edward, the youngest princes, photographed by Cecil Beaton in 1964.

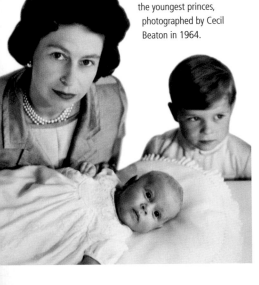

Few families of the postwar era have had to contend with anything like the level of scrutiny, fascination, adoration, and criticism that apply to the British Royal Family. These unique pressures and influences have shaped the four children of Queen Elizabeth II in different ways.

During the childhoods of Charles and Anne, their mother had only recently become Queen, a role that she embraced wholeheartedly. She dedicated herself to service, the Commonwealth, touring, and the daily business of monarchy, while at the same time deferring to her husband in matters of parenting. By the time Andrew and Edward came along in 1960 and 1964, the Queen was older, wiser, more assertive, and, according to various biographers and royal journalists, determined to provide a warmer and more maternal environment. This, along with significant innate differences in the siblings in temperament and intellect, and the wide gap in age, meant that Charles would have a very different experience from his younger brothers, and turn out to be a very different person from them.

Conflicting views on childhood

The early years of Charles and, to a lesser extent, Anne were characterized by a degree of emotional distance from their parents. It is worth noting, however, that Princess Anne vehemently disagrees with Charles's rather bleak assessment of his mother's lack of affection. "I'm not going to speak for anyone else," Anne told one interviewer, "but I simply don't believe there is any evidence whatsoever to suggest that she wasn't caring. It just beggars belief. We as children may have not been too demanding, in the sense that we understood what the limitations were in time and the responsibilities placed on her as monarch... but I don't believe that any of us, for a second, thought she didn't care for us in exactly

the same way as any other mother did. I just think it's extraordinary that anybody could construe that that might not be true."

Charles's education

Charles's father, Philip, was determined that the little prince should not be spoiled, but toughened up. Part of this would be achieved by his education, and he was sent to a series of suitable institutions. His first school was Hill House, where a 1957 report described him as, "A good, average schoolboy." Later that year he became a boarder at Cheam School, Headley, Hampshire. His parents were eager that he be treated like any other schoolboy, but the truth of his unique status would

slip out occasionally, such as the time when, wanting to write home, he enquired, "I know my mother is the Queen, but how do I put that on the envelope?"

In 1958, in a surprise move, the Queen announced that she was making her son the Prince of Wales:

> "We would like our **son** and **daughter** to **grow up as normally** as possible so that they will be able to **serve you** and the **Commonwealth** faithfully."
>
> ELIZABETH II, CHRISTMAS BROADCAST, 1958

Royal plaything
This miniature version of an Aston Martin DB5, famous from the James Bond movies, was presented to Prince Andrew in 1966 by the car company. It had rotating license plates and a functional smoke screen.

"This [has been] a memorable year for the principality... I have decided to mark it further by an act which will, I hope, give as much pleasure to all Welshmen as it does to me. I intend to create my son Charles Prince of Wales today."

Philip had absolutely no doubt that the proper destination for his son when he turned 13 would be Gordonstoun, the experimental school that had done so much to shape his own character. The children at

Gordonstoun endured a tough routine of cold showers and cross-country runs, intended to build character. Charles described the prospect as "pretty gruesome," and, reportedly, he was deeply unhappy during his time there, despite being made head boy. His stay at Gordonstoun was marked by one headline-grabbing incident when he got in trouble for ordering a cherry brandy at the age of 14, at a hotel in Stornaway. While Charles was in Scotland, back at Buckingham Palace his future was being mapped out, with a 1965 summit to plan

Bondi beach bum
Prince Charles, during his 1966 sojourn in Australia, smiles broadly as he is fitted with the distinctive bathing cap of the Sydney Surf Club, worn by lifeguards on Bondi Beach in Sydney. In this ceremony, he was made an honorary member of the club.

« BEFORE

Prince Charles's earliest years were rather lonely and he missed out on a close maternal relationship, since he saw his parents very little.

SOLITARY BIRTHDAY
Before Elizabeth acceded to the throne, she was already **leaving her children behind to go on long overseas tours.** When Philip was posted to Malta in 1949, Elizabeth, unencumbered by little Charles, had enjoyed a **carefree few months** there as an officer's wife. Charles celebrated his third birthday with a tea party at Buckingham Palace and a buggy ride around Green Park, while his parents were **away on a tour of Canada.**

GREETING WITH A HANDSHAKE
After Elizabeth came to the throne, she threw herself into the role, and five months after the coronation embarked on a tour that saw her **separated from her children for almost six months.** When the children and Elizabeth were reunited in Tobruk, in Libya, as the royal couple made their way back to Britain at the end of the tour, she **greeted Charles by shaking his hand.**

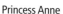

his higher education and career—a summit to which he was not invited. Soon Prince Charles had become the first heir to the throne to sit public examinations, winning a place at Trinity College, Cambridge.

Private Tutoring

Meanwhile, Anne's early childhood took place out of the public eye, with private tutoring. Mindful of the difficulties facing a young princess in terms of meeting other children, her aunt, Princess Margaret, prompted the formation of a new Buckingham Palace Brownie Pack—a unit of Girl Guides—with little Anne as a founding member. In 1963 Anne went to Benenden School, Kent, to board, and soon fell in love with the world of horse trials and eventing (see pp.186–87), winning her first trials in 1969.

Andrew and Edward

Prince Charles was big brother to two little princes, who would follow him to Gordonstoun. Andrew was educated by a governess up to the age of 8, keeping him close to home—a notable departure from the course followed with Charles—and then went to Heatherdown Preparatory School in Ascot before Gordonstoun. Edward was born in 1964, and for the first time, Prince Philip was present at the birth. Edward was a quiet child who loved listening to Swedish music group ABBA and Irish radio and TV personality Terry Wogan. While Andrew went straight into the navy, Edward was awarded a place at Jesus College, Cambridge, despite poor exam results, which sparked accusations of special treatment. After university he joined the Royal Marines as a university cadet but found the training too arduous and dropped out.

Princess Anne
A portrait of Princess Anne on her 19th birthday, by photographer Norman Parkinson, who also photographed her on her 21st birthday, her engagement, and her wedding.

In their childhood, Charles was a loving older brother to Anne, whose tomboy spirit and no-nonsense pluck he admired, but to Andrew and Edward he was a more remote figure, more like an uncle. Today the relationship between the royal siblings has somewhat cooled. According to a former aide, quoted by the London *Daily Telegraph*, in later life, "There was very little contact between them actually, save at family gatherings and events. Communication used to be dealt with by households—private secretaries. They were very un-close, leading independent lives."

AFTER

Prince Charles retains fond memories of the time he spent studying in Australia at the age of 17.

DOWN UNDER

From February to July 1966, **he spent two terms at Timbertop,** a remote campus of Geelong Church of England Grammar School in Melbourne, Australia. Despite the fact that Timbertop, too, was tough, it was **an experience the Prince enjoyed very much,** in contrast to his **miserable time at Gordonstoun.**

SHREDDED SHEEP

On one field trip to New Guinea, after seeing examples of the folk art of the Papuan people, the Prince expressed concern about **pre-industrial societies losing their traditional ways of life.** This experience gave him an introduction to the study of anthropology, which may have helped to foster some of his later concerns and pursuits. Charles also **tried his hand at sheepshearing,** but admitted to the press, "I made rather a mess of it and left a somewhat shredded sheep."

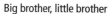

Big brother, little brother
Prince Charles entertains his little brother Edward, in a scene from the 1969 behind-the-scenes documentary film *Royal Family* (see pp.172–73). Edward is just 5 years old, while his big brother is nearly 21.

Against the Wall
During an 11-day tour of West Germany in 1965, the Queen and Prince Philip visited the Berlin Wall at Potsdamer Platz. Vast crowds turned out to see them.

Born 1948

The Prince of Wales

> "I only **take on** the most **difficult challenges**... to **raise aspirations**..."
>
> CHARLES, PRINCE OF WALES

Prince Charles's full title is His Royal Highness Prince Charles Philip Arthur George, Prince of Wales, KG, KT, GCB, OM, AK, QSO, PC, ADC, Earl of Chester, Duke of Cornwall, Duke of Rothesay, Earl of Carrick, Baron of Renfrew, Lord of the Isles, and Prince and Great Steward of Scotland. This may sound as if he is a bastion of tradition and an archetype of conservatism, and in many ways he is, but he also represents a new breed of royal. Charles is a royal in the classic tradition of engagement and service, but with a distinctive and modern twist. An academic and thoughtful man, he was the first heir to the throne to be sent to school, the first to take public exams, one of the few to go to university rather than straight into the military, and the first to get a degree.

Father and sons
Prince Charles is seen here with his young sons princes William and Harry at their Kensington home in 1985. As adults, the three are said to be very close and share several common interests.

Conservative radical

Charles's abiding concerns for the conservation of traditions and the environment became apparent early in his life. As a teenager attending school in Australia, he wrote an essay about the threat to traditional societies in New Guinea, while as an undergraduate at Cambridge, he proposed a telling motion to the university debating society in 1970: "This house believes that technological advance threatens the individuality of man and is becoming his master." Expressing concern about the march of technology, he confessed to be "in a slightly difficult position," as a result of his status. He still straddles uneasily the line between personal opinion and official impartiality.

Formative influences

Charles was close to his great-uncle Louis Mountbatten, and the pair had affectionate nicknames for one another: "honorary grandfather" and "honorary grandson." Charles had never gotten a chance to know his real grandfathers—King George VI died when Charles was 4 years old, and Prince Andrew of Greece and

Man of contradictions

In character, the Prince of Wales is humorous, self-deprecating, intelligent, and passionately engaged with a lot of issues, but also deeply insecure. He is pictured here looking very relaxed during a visit to Pakistan in 2006.

Red Crow
Prince Charles smokes a peace pipe—a ceremonial pipe—during a royal tour of Canada in 1977. During the visit, he was given the name "Red Crow," an Indian Chief of the Kainai tribe.

Denmark, passed away four years before Charles was born. He also had a difficult relationship with his father.

Mountbatten would later attempt to matchmake his granddaughter, Amanda Knatchbull, into the Royal Family, and he vigorously promoted the match to Charles. But the young Prince had little

marvelous... Fortunately I landed... I had visions of myself going round and round until eventually the fuel ran out."

As a father, Charles sought to bring up his children very differently from how he was brought up. He had a strong desire not to create the sense of distance and loneliness he experienced as a child.

Hobby horses
Although a military career was not for Charles, he did take to farming, particularly appropriate for one of Britain's largest landowners. As Duke

> "He has spent an awful lot of his life **searching for a role,** but I think he does now **feel fulfilled** pursuing his **various interests.**"
>
> PENNY JUNOR, ROYAL BIOGRAPHER

interest in being tied down, and would continue to be one of the world's most eligible bachelors into his 30s.

At his father's insistence, Charles pursued a career in every branch of the military, arguably enjoying Royal Air Force the most. In January 1969, Charles made his first solo flight, and later recalled, "... it was absolutely

of Cornwall, he owns massive estates (see pp.256–57), leading to one memorable quip from his father, who, on being asked whether he was familiar with the Scilly Isles, remarked, "I think my son owns them." Charles pursues organic farming, and started the multimillion-dollar Duchy Originals brand to market his own produce.

Organic farming methodology is just one of a number of hobby horses for which the Prince is famous. He promotes alternative medicine, especially homeopathy. He famously admitted to talking to his plants to help them grow. He holds strong views on architecture, outspokenly criticizing buildings he finds distasteful—when he labeled a proposed National Gallery extension "a monstrous carbuncle on the face of a much-loved and elegant friend", the extension was scrapped. To further his own taste in architecture, Prince Charles has developed a village at Poundbury in Dorset, with buildings that follow his architectural principles.

Forging a new style of monarchy
With advancing years, the Queen has increasingly looked to Charles to serve as a sort of co-monarch. He has moved center stage in guiding royal strategy,

Prince's Foundation
Charles speaks at the annual conference of the Prince's Foundation for the Built Environment—now known as the Prince's Foundation for Building Community—in 2010. Charles established the charity in 1986.

pursuing a "slimming" agenda that sees the Royal Family pared down to a core of his parents and his own direct family, moving his siblings and their offspring to the margins. Charles himself promises to be a new style of monarch, outspoken and an activist, but this has raised serious political and constitutional issues. These came to a head in the 2015 court battle over the release of the "black spider" memos, the letters in the Prince's distinctive spidery handwriting that he regularly fires off to government ministers to argue policy or push an agenda. "In defining his role as heir apparent," says Catherine Mayer, his biographer, "the Prince has signaled a redefinition of the monarchy. Some courtiers—and the sovereign herself—fear that neither the crown nor its subjects will tolerate the shock of the new."

TIMELINE

- **November 14, 1948** Born Charles Philip Arthur George at Buckingham Palace to Princess Elizabeth and the Duke of Edinburgh.
- **November 14, 1951** Celebrates his third birthday without his parents, who are in Canada on a royal tour.
- **February 6, 1952** King George VI dies; Charles becomes Duke of Cornwall, Duke of Rothesay, Earl of Carrick and Baron of Renfrew, Lord of the Isles, and Prince and Great Steward of Scotland.
- **June 2, 1953** Attends coronation of his mother.
- **November 7, 1956** Starts school at Hill House in central London.
- **July 26, 1958** Charles is created Prince of Wales.

PRINCE OF WALES COAT OF ARMS

- **May 1, 1962** Starts school at Gordonstoun in Scotland.
- **June 17, 1963** Causes media storm by ordering cherry brandy at a hotel in Stornoway, Scotland.
- **February–July 1966** Spends two terms at Timbertop, a remote annex of Geelong Church of England Grammar School in Australia.
- **October 8, 1967** Starts studying archeology and physical and social anthropology at Trinity College, Cambridge.
- **July 1, 1969** Charles is invested as Prince of Wales at Caernarfon Castle.
- **June 23, 1970** Becomes first heir to the throne to earn a university degree.
- **July 29, 1981** Marries Lady Diana Spencer.
- **June 21, 1982** Birth of Prince William.
- **September 15, 1984** Birth of Prince Harry.
- **December 9, 1992** Separates from Diana.
- **August 28, 1996** Divorces Diana.
- **August 31, 1997** Diana dies in a car crash.
- **November 1998** Charles's press secretary provokes a furore after an interview in which he suggests that the Prince would like the Queen to abdicate in his favor.
- **April 9, 2005** Marries Camilla Parker Bowles.
- **November 2012** During a visit to Dumfries House in East Ayrshire, Charles reportedly says, "Impatient? Me? What a thing to suggest! Yes, of course I am... I'll run out of time soon."
- **September 20, 2013** Passes the age of 64 years, 10 months, and 5 days to become the likely holder of the record for oldest person to be crowned in British history, when he eventually succeeds the Queen, surpassing William IV, who became king in 1830. Charles is also the longest serving heir apparent.

DUCHESS OF CORNWALL

CAMILLA

The Duchess of Cornwall was born Camilla Rosemary Shand on July 17, 1947, in London, into a well-connected, though not aristocratic, family. In 1973, she married Brigadier Andrew Parker Bowles, and had two children, but they got divorced in 1995. In 2005, she married Charles in a civil ceremony, followed by a service of prayer and dedication in St. George's Chapel, Windsor Castle, presided over by the Archbishop of Canterbury, followed by a reception hosted by the Queen. The Palace also announced that if Prince Charles becomes King, Camilla will use the style HRH Princess Consort.

The **Launch** of the **QE2**

The construction of the *Queen Elizabeth 2 (QE2)*—the mighty new flagship of the famous Cunard Line—signaled both the end of one era and the start of a new one. The last great passenger ship to be built on the Clyde River in Scotland, it marked the beginning of cruisers replacing liners.

Just a few days before the launch of the shipping company Cunard's latest and greatest ocean liner, the previous holder of that title, the *Queen Mary*, had made her last transatlantic crossing. This marked the transition from the old era of pre-aviation passenger shipping to a new age. In the early 1950s, liners carried over one million passengers a year across the Atlantic. By 1967, sea traffic had almost halved to around 500,000 journeys, while the airlines were carrying more than five million people each year. Accordingly, the 59,000-ton new ship was built to be very different from its predecessors. It was equipped for cruising as an end in itself, with nearly 1,000 cabins, restaurants on the upper decks with sea views, cocktail bars, nightclubs, and a theater. As Sir John Brocklebank, chairman of Cunard, had announced in 1962, "She must be a top flight cruise ship... with a concept in advance of any existing ship."

The great mystery to be revealed on the day of the launch was the name of the vessel, known up to that point simply as *Q4*. The presence of the Queen's sister at the launch led many to conclude it would be named the *Princess Margaret*. However, written on the slip of paper that was handed to the Queen with the name of the ship on it was simply "Queen Elizabeth." It was she who chose, by the act of declaring it aloud, that the ship would be known as the *Queen Elizabeth the Second.*

The Queen pressed the button to release a bottle of white wine (which Cunard always uses in preference to champagne) to smash against the bow. Soon the huge ship began to gather pace down the slipway, reaching 22 mph (35.4 kph) before entering the water stern-first and sending a 2-ft- (60-cm-) high wave washing across the Clyde.

> **"** Like her great predecessors, the **new liner** will write a **further chapter** in the **history of ocean travel."**
>
> **BRITISH PATHÉ NEWSREEL COMMENTATOR,** 1967

Ready for launch
The *QE2*, with its vast bulk of the hull and lower superstructure, is poised for its launch on September 20, 1967. Thousands of tons of drag chains were used to slow the mighty ship's descent and prevent her from crashing into the far bank of the Clyde.

Royal Family

One of the television events of the postwar era, the remarkable 1969 behind-the-scenes documentary *Royal Family* changed the way the world saw the monarchy and was subsequently broadcast in 140 countries.

Traditionally, Buckingham Palace had been very wary of the media, at best keeping them at arm's length, but Philip, the Duke of Edinburgh, had long advocated a more open approach for the Royal Family. He recognized that the ever-increasing clamor for access would need a higher degree of proficiency in dealing with the media, especially in the younger royals. He was supported by a few of the more progressive Palace staff, who recognized that the monarchy itself might be threatened as young people increasingly came to see them as irrelevant and old-fashioned.

It was against this background that the idea for a documentary was planned by the Queen's new Press Secretary, William Heseltine. In the wake of the announcement of the forthcoming investiture of Prince Charles, Heseltine recalled, there was "an unsolicited rush of requests from the media for... features about the young Prince... The Queen and Prince Philip decided that a biography of such a young man was not likely to be a very interesting one." Instead it was suggested that a more general documentary would be an "icebreaker."

Then then BBC Controller David Attenborough worried that a documentary of the Royal Family would "kill the monarchy" by "damaging the mystique" upon which it relied. However, the project went ahead nonetheless, with producer Richard Cawston and his team following the family at official engagements and in private from June 1968 to May 1969. The resulting film was first broadcast on June 21, 1969, when it was watched by an audience of 23 million, and repeated on commercial television eight days later.

> "A **television film designed to show** something of the role for which **the heir to the throne** was **being educated and prepared...**"
>
> **WILLIAM HESELTINE,** PRESS SECRETARY TO THE QUEEN

Filming the documentary
The Royal Family, observed by a camera, try to act natural. Princess Anne looks less enthusiastic than the others. She later said "I never liked the idea of *Royal Family*... The attention which had been brought upon one ever since one was a child... you just didn't need any more."

The **Royal Tour**

Today it seems the most natural thing in the world for any royal visit to be marked by an informal meet and greet with a crowd of well-wishers. However, when Elizabeth II first went "walkabout" in New Zealand in 1970, it signalled a radical break with centuries of tradition.

Elizabeth II's 1970 visit to New Zealand and Australia was particularly notable for inaugurating what has now become an integral royal tradition—the "walkabout," an event where royals meet and greet crowds in person. In fact, the first royal walkabout was arguably not Elizabeth's, but one led by her father and mother in Canada in 1939. On May 21 of that year, they charmed the Canadian people when, after unveiling the national war memorial in Ottawa, they plunged into a crowd of over 6,000 veterans and spent 30 minutes interacting with them in person. Lord Tweedsmuir, Canada's governor general, related how: "One old fellow said to me, 'Aye, man if Hitler could just see this.' It was wonderful proof of what a people's King means."

The official story of Elizabeth II's walkabout in New Zealand was that the Queen spontaneously broke protocol when she spied a group of schoolchildren waiting to greet her. However, the walkabout was in fact far from impromptu. "It didn't happen by accident," admitted William Heseltine, who had just been appointed the new press secretary to the Queen. "We were thinking, 'How can we make this a bit different so it's not just a repeat of the rather anticlimactic visit in 1963?' Out of our deliberations came the idea of closer contact with the public at large—who'd mostly been the recipients of little more than a wave or smile—rather than just mayors, councillors, and politicians."

Back home in England, the Queen did her first walkabout in Coventry, and it was a huge success. A new royal tradition had been born, and soon politicians were emulating it, and have done so ever since.

> **"** The most important thing
> of all was that it got a name—
> **'the walkabout'... ** it had
> a **romantic aura...** **"**
>
> **WILLIAM HESELTINE,** PRESS SECRETARY TO THE QUEEN

Breaking traditions
The Queen, with her trademark bag on her arm, goes "walkabout" among a crowd of schoolchildren in New Zealand in 1970. The choice of a bright primary color for her dress is very deliberate, as the Queen has always believed that part of her role is to be visible.

Full kilt
This Royal Family portrait—taken in 1972, on their annual summer vacation at Balmoral—is part of a series to mark the silver wedding anniversary of the Queen and the Duke of Edinburgh.

« BEFORE

In 1976, Charles spent nearly 10 months in command of minesweeper HMS *Bronington*, following a lieutenant's course at the Royal Naval College, Greenwich.

RETIRING FROM MILITARY SERVICE
In December, Charles **retired from active military** service, although he **continued to be promoted** in all three branches of the armed forces. By 2006 he was an Admiral in the Royal Navy, General in the Army, and Air Chief Marshal in the Royal Air Force.

IN CHARGE ON HMS *BRONINGTON*

The Prince's Trust

In the early 1970s a young, idealistic prince saw the opportunity to make a real, sustained difference to the lives of young people who had not enjoyed similar advantages to his own. He set up the Prince's Trust and, 40 years on, it is still changing lives.

In 1972 a young Prince Charles heard something on the radio that grabbed his attention. On BBC Radio 4's *Today* program, he listened to an interview with George Pratt, the second-ranked probation officer in London, talking about the challenges facing troubled youngsters. Prince Charles believed firmly that it was his duty to help those less fortunate than he was. He also had a strong sympathy for people of his own generation who needed support and to believe in themselves.

Enthusiastic and idealistic
Not long after the radio broadcast, Pratt received a phone call from the Prince's private secretary to arrange a meeting. Pratt later recalled how he "met this young, enthusiastic, and idealistic person." Charles told him that he wanted to do something to help young people like those Pratt had talked about.

At this point the Prince was still serving in the navy, and he started off on a small scale, channeling his efforts through Pratt, who put the word out for funding applications. These applications would be sent in a diplomatic bag to the Prince, wherever he was stationed. Charles would read nearly every one, and where he thought he could help, he would disburse, via Pratt, anonymous small gifts of cash and equipment. On one occasion, for instance, to help a group of young offenders go camping in the Peak District, Derbyshire, Charles paid for their train fares and sent camping equipment that he had borrowed from the Armed Forces.

Birth of the Trust
This went on for some time with Charles remaining incognito but, eventually, the Prince was encouraged to come out of the shadows when it was suggested to him that his public involvement would help raise the

Keeping it real
Prince Charles poses for a photograph with local young people who take part in the Prince's Trust activities during a visit to Surrey County Cricket Club. The Trust helps over 100 young people a day.

profile of the program. Accordingly, in December 1976, Charles formally launched the Prince's Trust. Looking back in 2013, Charles explained, "The belief that every young person deserves a chance to succeed, no matter what their background, led me to set up the Prince's Trust back in 1976." The Trust started with 21 pilot projects around the UK. Examples included a grant for a 19-year-old woman to run a social center for the Haggerston Housing Estate (a housing project) in east London; a grant for two ex-offenders to start a fishing club; funds to rent swimming pools in Cornwall to train young lifeguards; and money to set up a self-help bicycle repair program.

Since these modest beginnings, the Prince's Trust has flourished, becoming one of the most important charities in Britain. Part of its success has been due to its fund-raising ability, with a

> # 750,000 The number of young people helped directly by the Prince's Trust since 1976.

particular emphasis on using rock music to raise money. In 1982 the Trust held its first fund-raising concert, with Status Quo. The same year the first Prince's Trust Rock Gala was held at the Dominion Theatre on London's Tottenham Court Road, featuring Madness, Joan Armatrading, Phil Collins, Kate Bush, and Pete Townshend. In 1996 the Trust held a huge rock concert in Hyde Park—the first one allowed there in over 20 years.

Milestones

In 1983 a key platform of the Trust was launched with the business start-up program for unemployed

Prince's Trust

Three feathers

The logo of the Prince's Trust is based on the Prince of Wales's badge, specifically the insignia of the three ostrich feathers, which comes from the "shield of peace" of the Black Prince in the 14th century.

young people—a program to help young people put together the business model and initial funding to start their own businesses. Within three years, 1,000 businesses were trading, and 80 percent survived the first year of existence (a high success rate compared to normal start-ups). Since the launch of the start-up program, the Prince's Trust has helped more than 80,000 young people set up a business.

In 1998, the Trust marked the Prince's 50th birthday year with a £40 million ($64 million) appeal. This amount was matched by the government to raise a total of £80 million ($128 million). In 1999 a reorganization saw various Trust charities brought under one umbrella as the Prince's Trust, and the Queen granted the Trust a Royal Charter, generally regarded as the stamp of approval of a stable and successful institution embedded in public life. In 2000 the organizational structure of the Trust changed, with the introduction of a director and council for each region. By 2001 the total number of young people helped in some way by the Trust reached 400,000, and in 2003 the 10,000th Development Award was made.

Standing up for young people

The personal involvement of the Prince makes a real difference to the work of the charity. Martina Milburn, the chief executive of the Trust, explains, "I've sat with him in prisons, I've sat with him on sink estates, I've sat with him in classrooms when he's been talking

to young people. And he really cares about making a difference to them. You talk to young people—somehow they understand it, because he has been the one person over the last 37 years that has consistently stood up for them." Charles himself reflects: "You can see how it is possible to turn young people's lives around and give them self-confidence, self-worth, and self-esteem."

Success stories

Among all the statistics of the Trust's good work, individual success stories stand out. Arnold Sebutinde was sent to jail at the age of 22 and faced a difficult path when he was released. He recalls, "I'd seen a television report about how the Trust supports young people, but I was worried it might turn me away as soon as I mentioned my criminal record. Instead, they invited me to join their Enterprise program." Workshops, a loan, and a business mentor helped him to start a successful business capitalizing on his artistic talent. "The Trust was there for me at a time of greatest need and has opened so many doors for me." Arnold has since been invited to Clarence House as a Trust ambassador,

and reflects, "I've gone from being the guy whom society didn't think was safe to walk our streets to being a guest at one of our finest palaces. I'm proof that with the right help you can make it back from the brink. That is what the Prince's Trust has done for me."

> ## "Every **young** person deserves a **chance to succeed**, no matter what their background..."
>
> PRINCE CHARLES, 2013

A higher-profile Trust alumnus is Hollywood star Idris Elba, who was only able to attend theatre school thanks to a grant from the Prince's Trust. "It was the Prince's Trust that made it possible," he says. "It was a life-changing experience for me and taught me the importance of charity—of being there for people when they need it most."

Investing in the future

Prince Charles spoke on the subject of "Invest in Futures" at the Prince's Trust Gala in February 2013. In 2007, a £20 million ($30 million) loan was taken out from his foundation for the purchase of Dumfries House, Ayrshire, for the nation. This loan was repaid in full by 2012.

Meeting the people
The Queen on a royal walkabout in Camberwell, South London, greeting well-wishers young and old, all brandishing flags, during her Silver Jubilee year, in June 1977.

The **Silver Jubilee**

As with her coronation in 1953, the Queen's Silver Jubilee offered the nation a chance to forget gloomy headlines and enjoy a day of national celebration, with street parties being held across the land.

《 BEFORE

Five years before the Jubilee festival, Queen Elizabeth II and Prince Philip celebrated another royal milestone: their silver wedding anniversary.

SILVER WEDDING ANNIVERSARY
To **commemorate** the Queen and Prince Philip's silver wedding anniversary, a special **25 pence** coin was minted, and a **thanksgiving service** was held at Westminster Abbey. In her Christmas message for the year, the Queen spoke of how, "My whole family has been deeply touched by the affection you have shown to us when we celebrated our silver wedding…"

As the Queen's reign approached its jubilee year, she might have been forgiven for wondering whether things had improved much since the start of her rule, a time of rationing, bitter winters, and grim economic news. The notorious "winter of discontent" was just a couple of years away, and Britain was riven with recession, civil strife, and the looming prospect of the weakening or breakup of the Union in the face of imminent devolution referenda. There were strikes, the oil crisis, the three-day week, runaway inflation and, by 1977, mass unemployment. The UK was in such dire economic straits that the country had to get a loan from the International Monetary Fund after the

value of sterling plunged. Just as at the time of the coronation, the approaching Silver Jubilee was seen as a chance to distract the nation from its misery.

Theme of unity

The celebrations began on February 6, 1977, the anniversary of the Queen's accession to the throne. The palace and the government together had planned an ambitious series of events and tours for the jubilee year. The Queen declared that unity was the theme of the Jubilee, and that she wanted to be seen by as many of her subjects as possible, both in the UK and

around the Commonwealth. On February 10, she embarked on a world tour, starting in Fiji.

On May 4, the Queen received a loyal address from both Houses of Parliament, and in her controversial, forthright, and heartfelt reply she ignored her advisers' counsel to avoid addressing the topic of the possible breakup of the Union. Making direct reference to those agitating for devolved

Commemorative coin

This coin is unique in featuring no inscription or date on the reverse. Vast numbers were minted and issued for the Jubilee, and despite its size the coin only had a face value of 25 pence.

"The **cheerful crowd** was **symbolic** of... **people** who greeted us **wherever we went** this Jubilee year."

QUEEN ELIZABETH II, CHRISTMAS MESSAGE, 1977

national assemblies, she told the combined Houses of Parliament: "I number Kings and Queens of England and of Scotland and Princes of Wales among my ancestors and so I can readily understand these aspirations. But I cannot forget that I was crowned Queen of the United Kingdom of Great Britain and of Northern Ireland. Perhaps this Jubilee is a time to remind ourselves of the benefits which the union has conferred, at home and in our international dealings, on the inhabitants of all parts of the United Kingdom."

Home tours
On May 17, the Queen began a series of home tours, designed, as she told Members of Parliament, to demonstrate that she was "Queen of the whole United Kingdom." In six tours, over three months, she covered all parts of the UK, from Scotland to Northern Ireland, clocking up 7,000 miles (11,200 km). No other sovereign had visited so much of the country in so little time. The Queen toured 36 counties, starting in Glasgow, with the

Golden miles
The Gold State Coach passing Buckingham Palace on the way to St. Paul's Cathedral for the Silver Jubilee service of thanksgiving, with members of the Queen's Guard in the background.

biggest crowds ever seen there, and continued to draw vast numbers wherever she went. In Lancashire, over a million came out to see her in a single day.

Light the beacons
The climax of the Jubilee year came on June 7, proclaimed a public holiday by royal decree, with a glorious procession to St. Paul's for a thanksgiving service. The day before, the Queen herself initiated the Armada beacon chain, an homage to the beacons lit across the nation in the time of Elizabeth I to warn of the approach of the invading force of the Spanish Armada. The Queen lit a huge bonfire in Windsor Great Park, which was followed by 100 other beacons being lit from Land's End to Shetland, many on the sites of the original beacons.

On Tuesday, June 7, over a million people watched the Royal Family progress to St. Paul's Cathedral. At the Cathedral a service of thanksgiving was attended by guests, including international heads of state and current and former prime ministers of Britain. The service began with Ralph Vaughan Williams's arrangement of the hymn "All People That on Earth Do Dwell," which was played at the Queen's coronation in 1953.

After the service, at a Corporation of London lunch at the Guildhall, the Queen gave another heartfelt speech, thanking "all those in Britain and the Commonwealth who through their loyalty and friendship have given me strength and encouragement during these last 25 years," and also "to the many thousands who have sent me messages of congratulations on my

Jubilee service
Queen Elizabeth II and Prince Philip, with other members of the Royal family, joined 2,700 other guests at St. Paul's Cathedral during the service of thanksgiving.

silver jubilee, that and their good wishes for the future." As thousands celebrated with street parties across the nation, the Queen went on: "My Lord Mayor, when I was 21, I pledged my life to the service of our people and I asked for God's help to make good that vow. Although that vow was made in my salad days, when I was green in judgment, I do not regret nor retract one word of it." Later, the Royal Family made an appearance on the balcony of the palace, to the acclaim of a vast crowd.

Anarchy on the Thames
But not all of Britain was in a mood to celebrate. The Sex Pistols, who had burst onto the scene with their anarchic punk rock, and their iconic antiestablishment song "God Save the Queen" had been banned from radio stations. Their manager Malcom Mclaren had the idea of combining a piece of "situationist" performance art with a publicity stunt, and teamed up with Richard Branson, whose Virgin label was the only one who would sign the Sex Pistols, to hire a

Family affair
The Queen and the entire Royal Family greeted the crowds from the balcony at Buckingham Palace on June 7, 1977. By contrast, 35 years later Prince Charles insisted on a "slimmed down" family group on the balcony for the Diamond Jubilee.

boat. Accordingly, the Sex Pistols tried to crash the royal party by sailing down the Thames while playing their controversial single, but they were eventually forced to shore where they were arrested.

Continued celebrations
On June 9 came the final event of the main week of the Jubilee celebrations, with a river procession along the Thames, from Greenwich to Lambeth. At Lambeth, the Queen opened the Silver Jubilee Walkway and the new South Bank Jubilee Gardens, and then, following a magnificent fireworks display, the Queen traveled back to Buckingham Palace by carriage and appeared several more times on the balcony to delight the waiting crowds.

Soon afterward the Queen visited Wimbledon for the tennis championships, and her presence is widely credited with inspiring the British player Virginia Wade to win the ladies' singles title.

AFTER »

The extraordinary scenes in London in early June did not mark the end of the Jubilee events. After the UK celebrations, the Queen was soon back on the road, visiting Canada to open Parliament, and then on to the West Indies.

A SPECIAL YEAR
The **combined distance** of the Queen's Jubilee year itinerary is estimated at **56,000 miles** (89,600 km). But perhaps the best event of this special year, from a personal perspective, had come on November 15, when the Queen was delayed on her way to an investiture by a phone call from her daughter Anne, telling her that she had **just become a grandmother** for the first time **296–97** »

Party like it's 1977
Residents of Fulham, southwest London, show their support for the Queen (affectionately dubbed "Betty") during her Silver Jubilee year, 1977. Street parties were held across the country.

Princess Anne's Equestrian Career

Princess Anne's grit and determination drove her to prove herself at the grueling sport of equestrian eventing. She went on to achieve glory in Britain as well as in Europe.

Princess Anne first tasted eventing success in 1969 at age 18, riding Queen Elizabeth II's horse Royal Ocean. She had started training just a year earlier under coach Alison Oliver. Anne saw eventing as "a way of proving that you had something that was not dependent on your family, a way of being judged on what you did rather than having even more assumptions made."

In 1971, after coming fifth at the Badminton horse trials in April, Anne was selected to ride in the European championships at Burghley in September. However, her buildup to the competition was threatened by an operation on an ovarian cyst. Despite this, Anne won the three-day eventing championship on September 4. Riding the horse Doublet, she achieved a clear round in show-jumping to win the gold.

Anne capped a year of remarkable personal achievement by winning the national press accolade for Sportswoman of the Year in November, followed by being voted BBC Sports Personality of the Year in December. She went on to win silver at the European Championships in 1975, before being selected for the British Olympic team in Montreal in July 1976. Although Anne did not win a medal at Montreal, she completed the course despite being knocked out and concussed in a fall during the cross-country.

The Princess's response to accusations that she sometimes lacked royal decorum at events was blunt: "Horses and eventing are part of my private life—that's outside working hours. If people choose to think that I'm going to behave in the same way at a highly competitive event, where the pace is fast and the hazards are testing… they expect too much." Anne's achievements would be matched 34 years later by her daughter Zara Phillips (see pp.286–87).

> **"** [Eventing] is the one thing… that has got **nothing to do** with my **position,** my **money** or **anything else.** **"**
>
> PRINCESS ANNE

The Princess's horse
Anne crosses an obstacle on her horse Doublet at the 1972 Crookham Horse Trials. Doublet was a gift to the Princess from her mother Elizabeth II. The horse's career ended when he broke one of his legs during routine exercise in 1974 and had to be destroyed.

ROYAL RESIDENCE

St. James's Palace

Although no monarch has lived in St. James's Palace since George III moved his family to Buckingham House in 1762, it remains the official residence of the sovereign and is the home of several members of the Royal Family. It is also used for many official functions.

St. James's Palace was built on the orders of Henry VIII between 1531 and 1536, on the site of a leper hospital dedicated to St. James the Lesser, one of the more obscure members of the Catholic canon. At the time, Henry was evidently much in love with his wife, Anne Boleyn—the initials "H" and "A," entwined in a lover's knot, are a common motif at the palace, carved into fireplaces.

Queen's Chapel
The Queen's Chapel at St. James's Palace was the brainchild of James I, who commissioned the architect Inigo Jones to design it. The chapel, which was completed in 1626, was used by Queen Henrietta Maria, the Catholic wife of his son Charles I.

King James was also responsible for ordering the draining and landscaping of the palace grounds, now St. James's Park, creating lakes, and introducing exotic animals, such as camels, crocodiles, and an elephant.

Religious conflict
Existing tensions between Catholics and Protestants in England were exacerbated when, in 1638, Charles I gave St. James's Palace to his mother-in-law, Marie de Medici. She was not only the former queen of France, a recent enemy, but also a Catholic.

The gift proved deeply unpopular with Parliament and she was soon asked to move from the palace.

Charles I was tried for high treason in 1649 during the English Civil War. He stayed at St. James's Palace the night before his execution in nearby Whitehall. With the monarchy abolished, the Protestant Oliver Cromwell, Lord Protector of England, turned the palace into a barracks.

Restoration
Following the restoration of the English monarchy in 1660, Charles II, who had been born in St. James's Palace, had it restored. Inspired by the extravagant royal gardens he had seen during his exile in France, he had the gardens landscaped around a long canal. He also opened the park to the public, and it became a notorious rendezvous spot for secret lovers' trysts, including that of Charles and his mistress Nell Gwynn.

In 1698 the palace became the administrative center of the monarchy after Whitehall Palace was destroyed in a fire. Years later, George I and George II found it convenient to keep their mistresses here.

Chapel Royal
The Chapel Royal at St. James's was built by Henry VIII from 1531 for his marriage to Anne of Cleves in 1540.

Since then, it has been used for a number of royal weddings, including those of Queen Victoria and George V.

Both chapels have been used for the lying-in-state of members of the Royal Family—the coffins of the Queen Mother and Princess Margaret were laid in the Queen's Chapel, while the coffin of Diana, Princess of Wales, was set before the altar in the Chapel Royal, so family and friends could pay their respects in private.

Weekly Sunday services take place at either the Chapel Royal or the Queen's Chapel, which remain active places of worship. They are the only parts of the palace open for services.

Working palace
In addition to being used for a number of official functions, St. James's Palace contains the London residences of the Princess Royal and Princess Alexandra. Various royal offices are also based here.

The Palace and the Chapel Royal
The exterior of St. James's Palace today has changed little from the time of this illustration from 1812 (below left). A general view of the interior of the Chapel Royal, where the christening of Prince George of Cambridge took place in 2013 (below right).

ST. JAMES'S PALACE

CHAPEL ROYAL

BEFORE

Mountbatten spent decades at the very highest levels of British statecraft, involved in machinations relating to many major issues of post-war British history.

PLOTS AND SCHEMES
Having served as First sea lord and chief of the defense staff, Mountbatten was approached allegedly in the late 1960s by rogue MI5 agents plotting a right-wing coup to overthrow a possible Labour government under Harold Wilson. More pertinently to his assassination, Mountbatten was also involved in making **peace advances to representatives of Ireland,** approaching the Irish ambassador to the United Kingdom.

THE WRONG MAN?
According to papers in the National Archives in Dublin, Mountbatten told the Irish ambassador to London, Donal O'Sullivan, "that he hoped the policies of Edward Heath's government would ultimately **achieve Irish unity.**" If it is true that Mountbatten supported the policy of reunification, it makes his death at the hands of the IRA a particularly bitter irony.

EARL MOUNTBATTEN OF BURMA

LOUIS MOUNTBATTEN

Born on June 25, 1900, Mountbatten was Queen Victoria's great-grandson, Elizabeth II's second cousin, and Prince Philip's uncle. He had a distinguished naval career in both World Wars, after which he was appointed by Winston Churchill to take a lead role in Combined Operations, a special executive developing radical ideas and technologies to help the war effort. As Supreme Allied Commander in Southeast Asia, he oversaw the reconquest of Burma. After the war, he was appointed the last Viceroy and First Governor General of India.

The **Assassination** of **Lord Mountbatten**

A tragedy that rocked the Royal Family to its core, the 1979 assassination of Louis Mountbatten on his boat took the lives of one of the great figures of postwar British history, along with those of his grandson and son-in-law's mother, and a young Irish crew member.

Louis Mountbatten was a fascinating character in some of the great dramas of the 20th century, from World War II to Indian independence and the partition, but his final act would prove to be part of the grim tragedy of the Northern Irish Troubles—the period of unrest and terror attacks arising from the ongoing political and sectarian conflict in Northern Ireland.

Mountbatten had a home in Ireland (in Eire), just across the border from Northern Ireland. "I have a place in Eire, Classiebawn Castle in County Sligo," Mountbatten told the Empire Club of Canada in 1967, "and I and my family could not be treated with greater friendship by the Irish." This may have been true, but many questioned the wisdom of one of the highest grandees in the British establishment residing in a part of the country where his presence was likely to be seen as a provocation. As early as 1960, Mountbatten's estate manager, Patrick O'Grady, raised questions with the Irish police, the Garda, about the Earl's safety. "While everything points to the fact that no attack of any kind on the Earl by subversive elements

Family affair
The entire Royal Family was present for the funeral of Mountbatten. Here the Queen and Prince Philip lead the Queen Mother and Charles; behind them are Andrew in his midshipman's uniform and Edward.

was at any time contemplated," the reply went, "it would in my opinion be asking too much to say in effect that we can guarantee his safety while in this country." Mountbatten refused to heed warnings anyway, protesting that he was used to giving orders, not taking them. But, according to his biographer Richard Hough, "Second only to his cousin, Queen Elizabeth II, there was no more attractive victim for the IRA (Irish Republican Army)—a militant

organization that wanted a united independent Ireland—than this widely admired and much loved Englishman."

Attack on the boat
At the height of the Troubles, an audacious plot was hatched by the IRA. Early on August 27, 1979, Thomas McMahon—one of the IRA's experienced bombmakers—planted a huge bomb on Lord Mountbatten's 29-ft (9-m) fishing boat *Shadow V*, which was moored in the harbor at Mullaghmore, near Classiebawn Castle. Shortly afterward, McMahon was stopped at a police checkpoint and taken into police custody on suspicion of driving a stolen vehicle. He was later found to have on his clothes flakes of green paint from Lord Mountbatten's boat and traces of nitroglycerine.

At around 11 a.m., Mountbatten and five others—his elder daughter, Patricia, her husband, Lord Brabourne, Brabourne's 83-year-old mother, the Dowager Lady Brabourne, and the 14-year-old identical-twin sons of the Brabournes, Timothy and Nicholas Knatchbull—joined 15-year-old local crew member Paul Maxwell on board the *Shadow V*. Maxwell took the helm

Happier times
Mountbatten and his family enjoy a quiet day's fishing on board his fishing boat, *Shadow V*, nine years before it would become the scene of his grisly death.

and set off around Mullaghmore Head to the fishing ground. A routine Garda police patrol followed the progress of the boat out of the harbor.

The scene

At 11:39 a.m., a bomb on board the boat was detonated by radio control, just as it cleared the harbor wall.

50 LB (23 KG) **The weight of explosives in the bomb.**

Richard Hough described what happened next: "The boat disintegrated in a cloud of smoke and spume, and countless fragments of timber and metal, rope and cushions, life jackets and shoes, filled the air and fell in an oval pattern of splashes in the sea." Mountbatten, his legs blown off, was pulled from the water still alive but died shortly after. Nicholas

Knatchbull and Paul Maxwell were killed instantly; Timothy was seriously injured, while the Dowager Lady Brabourne died the day after. A few hours later, two bombs went off at Warrenpoint in County Down, ambushing an army convoy and killing at least 18 soldiers, in the single worst loss of life during the Troubles. A statement from the IRA said: "This operation is one of the discriminate ways we can bring to the attention of the English people the continuing occupation of our country."

State funeral

The death of such a highly placed individual in such an appalling manner called for a show of state strength and solidarity, an opportunity amply afforded by Mountbatten's state funeral on September 5, 1979. Mountbatten had left copious notes

on the details for his funeral as many members of the Royal Family are expected to do. He had outlined everything from the roles of more than 500 Royal Navy and Royal Marines personnel to his choice of hymns. Interviewed on television not long before his death, and asked what kind of funeral he would like to have, Mountbatten replied that he would wish it to be "a happy occasion." The funeral parade, with the coffin borne on a gun carriage, was led by his horse Dolly, riderless with her master's boots reversed in their stirrups, as was tradition.

Mountbatten's daughter Patricia, who had become Countess Mountbatten of Burma on her father's death, and her husband, Lord Brabourne, were still too badly injured to attend either this funeral or that of their son, Nicholas.

> ## "Life will never be the same now that he has gone."
>
> PRINCE CHARLES, DIARY ENTRY AFTER LEARNING OF THE DEATH OF HIS BELOVED GREAT-UNCLE

Final journey
Mountbatten's funeral procession, with police and military escorts for the coffin, makes its way from Westminster Abbey to Waterloo Station.

The events of August 27, 1979 elicited shock and condemnation. As the world became aware of the situation in Ireland, the Royal Family reeled under the weight of their loss.

DEEP IMPACT
At a memorial service held in December that year, Prince Charles **condemned the IRA** as "the kind of subhuman extremist that blows people up when he feels like it."

In 2009, on the 30th anniversary of the assassination, **Timothy Knatchbull** published *From a Clear Blue Sky*—an account of surviving the bombing. A narrative of loss, trauma, and reconciliation, it won the **Christopher Ewart-Biggs Memorial prize** for promoting peace and understanding in Ireland.

TIMOTHY KNATCHBULL
From a Clear Blue Sky
Surviving the Mountbatten Bomb

KNATCHBULL'S BOOK

The **Decolonization** of **Africa** and the **Caribbean**

The British Empire had already embarked on a transition to something new and different when Elizabeth came to the throne—a transition that she stewarded into a Commonwealth family that she has always cherished and nurtured.

When Elizabeth was growing up her father still ruled territory that, viewed on a map, colored a large proportion of the world pink: the lands of the British Empire. Much had changed by the time she acceded to the throne—most notably the independence of the Indian subcontinent—yet even in 1952 she could travel around the world without leaving her own territories. But this was a world in rapid transition; the Empire was transforming into a Commonwealth of nations, which, as the Queen herself said, "bears no resemblance to the Empires of the past. It is an entirely new conception..."

A bridge across the world

In the 1950s, the former empire comprised the Commonwealth—nations such Canada, Australia, and India—plus many other realms and protectorates, many of which were in Africa and the

Caribbean. The Commonwealth was vast and populous; it covered a quarter of the world's habitable surface and its population exceeded one-quarter of the human race. A large proportion of it was not yet independent. Territories that were still British colonies or protectorates included Northern and Southern Rhodesia, Malta, Malaya, Singapore, Jamaica and the British West Indies, Kenya, Nigeria, Uganda, Tanganyika, the Sudan, Nyasaland,

Zanzibar, the Gold Coast, and Somaliland. But from the very start of Elizabeth II's reign, the changing relationship between the monarch and former and current British dominions was made plain; the cabinet decided that Elizabeth's accession proclamation would not refer to the British Dominions or the Imperial Crown, and that she would not be "Queen of the British Dominions beyond the seas" but "Queen of her other Realms and Territories."

The magic of the moment
Harold Macmillan giving the "winds of change" address to the South African parliament, in which he spoke against the host country's policy of apartheid.

In its early days the Commonwealth seemed to be a successful and vibrant project. In October 1957, *Reader's Digest* magazine was able to reflect that the Queen "is as proud as her countrymen that, while the Communists have been holding 100 million foreign people

« BEFORE

The Commonwealth had existed in some form since 1924, but the independence of India meant that the former constitution of the Commonwealth would have to change.

THE LONDON DECLARATION
Issued on April 28, 1949, the **London Declaration marked the birth of the modern Commonwealth** « 64–65. Recognizing the "impending constitutional changes in India," the Declaration stated: "Accordingly the United Kingdom, Canada, Australia, New Zealand, South Africa, India, Pakistan and Ceylon hereby declare that they remain united **as free and equal members of the Commonwealth of Nations,** freely cooperating in the **pursuit of peace, liberty, and progress.**"

The last dance
Queen Elizabeth II and the first president of Ghana, Kwame Nkrumah, dance the shuffle at a ball held at State House, Accra, in November 1961.

behind the Iron Curtain and giving them the treatment of Hungary, Britain has been freeing 500 million people from colonial ties, investing £100 million ($280 million)a year in their local industries, helping them to organize complete self-government, no strings attached." By 1957, Britain's trade with her former territories had nearly doubled and the territories' own local revenues increased by 1,200 percent. That same year the Queen, in a speech to the young people of the Commonwealth, said, "You are growing up in a world which is as full

In October 1960, a few months after a tense Commonwealth premiers' conference held at Windsor in May, where apartheid was criticized, South African whites voted to jettison the Queen as head of state and the new republic left the Commonwealth.

Meanwhile the "wind of change" Macmillan had talked about in his speech was pushing over a dozen black-majority regions from across Africa and the Caribbean into nationhood. Nigeria and Somalia gained independence in 1960, Sierra Leone and Tanzania in 1961;

Fly the flag
The Commonwealth flag features a stylized globe surrounded by a crescent of golden spears making up the letter "C."

told him, "Danger is part of the job." After arriving at Accra airport, her route into town had to be lit by torches because of a power failure. Royal correspondent Audrey Russell recalled, "I was very anxious for the Queen. To carry on in those circumstances showed her tremendous courage.

Contentious opinions
After Northern Rhodesia was granted independence as Zambia in 1964, the mostly white government of Southern Rhodesia pushed hard for sovereignty, a demand that was refused by Britain under its policy of "no independence before majority rule." While African premiers were strongly urging Britain to initiate immediate action against Southern Rhodesia, Prince Philip, in a speech given to students in Edinburgh, shared his personal views on the crisis: "... it is better to spin out the solution of these difficulties with patience, and with a bit of luck get a better result than risk a bloodbath by forcing a pace." The Labour Party MPs tabled a motion stating that "royalty should not give expression to contentious political opinions," and Kenyan politicians joined in the criticism.

In 1994, South Africa held the first free and fair elections in its history, after Nelson Mandela was freed and apartheid dismantled. That same year it rejoined the Commonwealth.

QUEEN AND COMMONWEALTH
According to Kenneth Kaunda, a nationalist in Northern Rhodesia, **the transformation from Empire to Commonwealth** was only possible "because of the personality of the Queen. Without that, many of us would have left." During her reign, the Queen has paid more than 200 visits to Commonwealth countries and has visited **every country of the Commonwealth** except Cameroon, which joined in 1995, and Rwanda, which joined in 2009.

The August 1979 Commonwealth conference was dominated by a row over the future of Southern Rhodesia. British Prime Minister Margaret Thatcher backed a proposal for the independence of Zimbabwe—the name Southern Rhodesia would take on after independence—under Bishop Abel Muzorewa. The proposal excluded the

11,566,870 The **combined land area in square miles (29,958,050 sq kilometers) of current Commonwealth nations.**

nationalists under Robert Mugabe and Joshua Nkomo, but it was argued that a lasting peace was impossible without them. The Queen played a significant backstage role in brokering a proposal for a conference in London to devise a new constitution for Zimbabwe.

> "The **wind of change** is blowing… **whether we like it or not…** growth of national consciousness is a political fact."
>
> HAROLD MACMILLIAN, SPEECH TO THE SOUTH AFRICAN PARLIAMENT, 1960

of possibilities of adventure as it was in the days of my predecessor, Queen Elizabeth I. What the world now needs most is a solid bridge between East and West. The British Commonwealth is surely such a bridge."

The wind of change
It was in Africa, where British dominions and protectorates covered a huge proportion of the continent, that the reign of Queen Elizabeth II would see the most profound changes. From the late 1950s onward, a wave of newly independent nation states spread across the continent, in many cases peacefully but sometimes resulting in desperate struggles and violent upheaval. In 1957, the Gold Coast, in West Africa, became independent as the Republic of Ghana and joined the Commonwealth; it was the first majority-ruled African country to join.

The independence movement was gaining momentum across Africa when on February 3, 1960, British Prime Minister Harold Macmillan gave a famous speech to South African Members of Parliament in Cape Town. At the time, the ruling Nationalists were pursuing apartheid, and Macmillan had aroused criticism by agreeing to visit the country as their guest. But Macmillan disappointed the white politicians as he told them bluntly that a "wind of change" was blowing through Africa. "Whether we like it or not," Macmillan warned, "this growth of national consciousness is a political fact." The Nationalists were outraged; "We are the people who brought civilization to Africa," blustered South African Prime Minister Dr. Verwoerd.

Jamaica, Trinidad and Tobago, and Uganda in 1962; Kenya in 1963, Malawi and Zambia in 1964; the Gambia in 1965; Botswana and Lesotho in 1966; Mauritius and Swaziland in 1968; and after a long and bitter struggle, Zimbabwe in 1980. Most of these countries immediately joined the Commonwealth.

Danger is part of the job
In 1961, the Queen defied security risks and bomb threats to visit Ghana, previously the Gold Coast, the first "black" colony in Africa to become independent. The stakes were high; a bomb blast five days before the visit cast it into doubt, but British diplomats feared that cancellation would drive the new country into the Soviet sphere of influence. The Queen reportedly said, "If I were to cancel now, Nkrumah [the Ghanaian president] might invite Khrushchev, and they wouldn't like that, would they?" When Macmillan objected that it was too dangerous, she

Honor guard
The Queen inspects an honor guard at Entebbe, on arrival in Uganda for the Commonwealth Heads of Government Meeting on November 21, 2007. These meetings are the principal policy and decision-making forum for the Commonwealth.

QUEEN AND GRANDMOTHER

1980–2000

QUEEN AND GRANDMOTHER
1980–2000

1980		1984		1988	

OCTOBER 17, 1980
The Queen makes a state visit to the Vatican to meet Pope John Paul II.

JUNE 13, 1981
A 17-year-old youth fires shots at the Queen in the Mall as she rides to the Trooping the Color ceremony.

≫ Trooping the Color

APRIL 17, 1982
The Queen and Canadian Premier Pierre Trudeau sign the Proclamation of the *Constitution Act, 1982* giving Canada the power to amend its own Constitution.

JUNE 7–9, 1982
US President Ronald Reagan visits the UK.

MAY 30, 1984
Prince Charles critiques modern architecture in a controversial speech made during the 150th anniversary celebrations of the Royal Institute of British Architects (RIBA). The speech would lead to the proposed plan for an addition to the National Gallery being scrapped.

SEPTEMBER 15, 1984
The Princess of Wales gives birth to Prince Harry, her second son.

APRIL 3, 1987
The late Duchess of Windsor's jewels sell for £31 million at an auction in Switzerland; the entire proceeds of the sale are donated to the Pasteur Institute in Paris.

MARCH 10, 1988
Prince Charles escapes an avalanche in Switzerland that kills one of his companions, Major Hugh Lindsay, former equerry to the Queen.

≫ Birth of Princess Beatrice

SEPTEMBER 19, 1990
RAF flyby over Buckingham Palace commemorates the 50th anniversary of the Battle of Britain.

APRIL 29, 1986
The Queen attends the funeral of the Duchess of Windsor, widow of Edward VIII.

JULY 23, 1986
Prince Andrew marries Sarah Ferguson in Westminster Abbey. They become the Duke and Duchess of York.

AUGUST 8, 1988
The Duchess of York gives birth to Princess Beatrice, her elder daughter.

NOVEMBER 28, 1990
Margaret Thatcher resigns as Prime Minister. The Chancellor of the Exchequer, John Major, becomes the new Conservative Prime Minister.

JULY 29, 1981
Prince Charles marries Lady Diana Spencer in St. Paul's Cathedral.

JUNE 21, 1982
The Princess of Wales gives birth to Prince William, her elder son and second in line of succession.

JULY 9, 1982
An intruder finds his way into the Queen's bedroom in Buckingham Palace.

OCTOBER 12–18, 1986
The Queen and the Duke of Edinburgh make a state visit to China. The Queen becomes the first British monarch to visit the country.

≫ Marriage of Prince Andrew and Sarah Ferguson

JUNE 15, 1987
Prince Edward, Princess Anne, and the Duke and Duchess of York take part in TV gameshow *The Grand Knockout Tournament*.

AUGUST 31, 1989
Princess Anne and Captain Mark Phillips separate after 16 years of marriage.

JANUARY 16– FEBRUARY 28, 1991
British forces join a US-led coalition army to drive Iraqi troops out of Kuwait during the Gulf War.

25P

29 July 1981

≫ Commemorative stamp

FEBRUARY 9, 1983
The British £1 coin, with the Queen's head on the obverse, replaces the pound note.

MARCH 1983
Prince and Princess of Wales take 9-month-old William along on their official tour of New Zealand and Australia.

APRIL 1987
The Princess of Wales is photographed holding the hand of an AIDS-infected man at the Middlesex Hospital, London.

NOVEMBER 8, 1987
Irish Republican Army (IRA) bomb kills 11 in a Remembrance Day service in Enniskillen, Northern Ireland.

MARCH 23, 1990
The Duchess of York gives birth to Princess Eugenie, her second daughter..

MAY 17, 1991
The Queen addresses a joint session of the US Congress in Washington, D.C.

The 1980s opened brightly with the marriage of the Prince of Wales to Lady Diana Spencer, followed by the birth of their sons, William and Harry. By the end of the decade, the Queen had six grandchildren, but the divorces of three of her children and the bitter quarrel between the Prince and Princess of Wales were highly damaging, as the press declared open season on the privacy of the Royal Family. At a time of economic recession, the royal finances came under fire, leading to the Queen's offer to pay income tax. Diana's tragic death was met with an outpouring of public grief. Toward the end of the 1990s, the conflict in Northern Ireland finally came to an end.

1992

FEBRUARY 7, 1992
Britons become citizens of the European Union (EU) with the signing of the Maastricht Treaty.

MARCH 19, 1992
The Duke and Duchess of York separate.

APRIL 23, 1992
Princess Anne and Captain Mark Phillips divorce.

JUNE 7, 1992
Andrew Morton's controversial biography *Diana: Her True Story* is published.

NOVEMBER 20, 1992
Windsor Castle is badly damaged by fire.

NOVEMBER 24, 1992
The Queen gives her *annus horribilis* speech at London's Guildhall.

NOVEMBER 26, 1992
Parliament is informed that the Queen will pay income tax from April 1993.

» The Green Room at Buckingham Palace

DECEMBER 9, 1992
The Prince and Princess of Wales separate.

DECEMBER 12, 1992
Princess Anne marries Commander Timothy Laurence, former equerry to the Queen.

⌄ Fire ravages Windsor Castle

DECEMBER 23, 1992
The Sun publishes the text of the Queen's Christmas Day speech two days before the event.

1993

AUGUST 1993
Buckingham Palace opens its doors to the public for the first time.

DECEMBER 3, 1993
Diana announces her withdrawal from public life.

MARCH 12, 1994
The Church of England ordains its first women priests.

MAY 6, 1994
The Queen and President Mitterrand of France formally open the Channel Tunnel.

JUNE 1, 1994
South Africa rejoins the Commonwealth following the end of apartheid.

JUNE 5–6, 1994
The Queen leads the national commemorations of the 50th anniversary of the D-Day landings.

MARCH 19–25, 1995
The Queen visits South Africa after a gap of 48 years.

NOVEMBER 16, 1995
The Queen Mother has a hip replacement operation at the age of 95.

NOVEMBER 20, 1995
The Princess of Wales gives a revealing interview to Martin Bashir on BBC TV.

⌄ Diana tells all in a BBC interview

DECEMBER 20, 1995
The Queen writes to the Prince and Princess of Wales urging them to divorce.

MAY 30, 1996
The Duke and Duchess of York divorce.

AUGUST 28, 1996
The Prince and Princess of Wales divorce.

1997

MAY 2, 1997
Tony Blair becomes Prime Minister after Labour Party wins a landslide victory.

JUNE 30, 1997
Prince Charles represents the Queen at the return of British-ruled Hong Kong to China.

AUGUST 31, 1997
Diana is killed in a car accident in Paris.

SEPTEMBER 6, 1997
Funeral of Diana takes place in Westminster Abbey after a week of mourning.

NOVEMBER 20, 1997
The Queen and Prince Philip celebrate their Golden Wedding anniversary.

DECEMBER 11, 1997
The Royal Yacht *Britannia* is decommissioned after 44 years in service.

APRIL 10, 1998
Good Friday Agreement brings peace to Northern Ireland after 30 years of conflict.

⌄ Commemorative mug issued at Diana's death

JUNE 15, 1999
Prince Edward marries Sophie Rhys-Jones.

JULY 1, 1999
The Queen opens the Scottish Parliament in Edinburgh. The parliament would look after devolved domestic matters of Scotland, such as education, health, agriculture, and justice.

NOVEMBER 6, 1999
In a referendum, Australians vote to retain the Queen as monarch.

"The very essence of compassion, of duty, of style, of beauty"

≪ BEFORE

Charles and Diana had been seeing each other for about six months before he proposed on 6 February 1981. The engagement was announced on 24 February. Charles was 33 and Diana was 19.

A SUITABLE MATCH

Prince Charles's name was linked with several possible brides during the 1970s, including Lady Sarah Spencer, Diana's elder sister. He **met Diana** at a country weekend **in 1980**. With her connections to the monarchy – her sister was married to the Queen's assistant secretary, and Diana had spent her early childhood on the Sandringham Estate **206–07 ≫** – Diana seemed a **suitable wife for the future king.**

ENGAGEMENT RING

Diana chose her engagement ring from a selection at Garrards, the royal jewellers. Her engagement ring was made of **14 solitaire diamonds** surrounding an **oval sapphire** and was said to be worth £30,000.

THE ENGAGED COUPLE

> "It was an **easy decision.** I am looking forward to being a **good wife.**"

LADY DIANA SPENCER, INTERVIEWED BEFORE HER WEDDING, JULY 1981

Fairy-tale wedding
The radiant bride is seen here leaving St Paul's Cathedral on her husband's arm. Millions around the world watched the splendid ceremony unfold. The day was declared a national holiday in Britain.

The **Marriage** of **Charles** and **Diana**

The marriage of Prince Charles to Lady Diana Spencer on 29 July 1981 held the promise of a bright new future for the Royal Family. For the British public, it offered a welcome distraction from a gloomy summer of strikes, social discontent, and riots.

The question of a future wife for Prince Charles had long been a subject of speculation, but few had predicted that his choice would fall on a young English aristocrat, the daughter of a duke, rather than a suitable European princess. Press and public quickly fell in love with Lady Diana Spencer, 13 years the Prince's junior and the first Englishwoman and commoner to marry the heir to the throne since 1660. With her ready smile and fleeting downward glance, she was thought to bring something completely new and fresh to the Royal Family. As preparations for the "wedding of the century" got underway, Diana went to live with the Queen Mother in Clarence House, supposedly to gain an insight into royal life.

The choice of venue was a departure for a royal wedding. St Paul's Cathedral, Sir Christopher Wren's masterpiece at the heart of London's commercial centre, is the site for important national commemorations. It had never before held a royal wedding, but its long nave and magnificent dome provided a theatrical setting for the ceremony. The cathedral can house 3,500 guests, and was large enough for the wedding of a Prince of Wales, a major event attended by heads of state, Commonwealth leaders, politicians, and diplomats, as well as foreign royalty. An estimated 650,000 people lined the long route from the Mall to St Paul's, and some 750 million people worldwide watched the ceremony on television.

Nervous bride

When shortly before the wedding Diana confessed to her sisters that she was having cold feet, they are said to have replied, "Too late, your face is already on the tea-towels". She later described her wedding day as "the most emotionally confusing day" of her life and that she felt "like a lamb to the slaughter" as she saw the crowds camped in the Mall.

Diana made the journey from Clarence House in the Glass Coach (from the collection at the Royal Mews) with her father, the 8th Earl Spencer. The coach proved too small to accommodate them both, and the train of her wedding dress, which was 8 m (25 ft) long, emerged rather crumpled at St Paul's. It took her two senior bridesmaids – Lady Sarah Armstrong Jones (daughter of Princess Margaret) and India Hicks (granddaughter of the late Lord Mountbatten) – some time to disentangle and arrange the train before the bride mounted the red-carpeted steps of the cathedral on her father's arm. A stroke had left the Earl unsteady on his feet but he was determined to lead his daughter down the aisle.

Diana's nerves showed during the ceremony, which was conducted by the Archbishop of Canterbury, when she muddled up the Prince's names, calling him "Philip Charles Arthur George" rather than "Charles Philip Arthur George". Three of the Prince's favourite orchestras – the Philharmonia, the English Chamber, and the Royal Opera – played during the wedding, and the world-renowned New Zealand-born soprano Kiri Te Kanawa sang a Handel aria. One of the hymns, "I vow to thee my country", would be sung again in the less happy circumstances of Diana's funeral in 1997.

The kiss and the honeymoon

Smiling and waving at the cheering crowds, the newly married couple returned to Buckingham Palace in an open carriage. Later they appeared on the balcony and, egged on by the crowd, exchanged a kiss. The balcony kiss has now become an established part of the ritual of royal weddings, but this was the first. After a wedding breakfast with 120 family guests, the couple were driven in a landau sporting a "Just Married" sign to Waterloo Station to travel by train to Broadlands, the Mountbatten family home in Hampshire, where the Queen and Prince Philip had also spent the first part of their honeymoon.

Mismatched couple

At the time, and for a while afterwards, Charles and Diana's marriage was seen as a true love match and a fairy-tale romance. However, the gulf between their ages and their separate interests – Charles liked classical music, Diana liked Duran Duran; Charles loved the country, Diana preferred city life; Charles liked formality, Diana rebelled against it – made them a highly mismatched couple.

> **10,000** The number of pearl sequins sewn on to Diana's dress.

Commemorative stamp
Postage stamps featuring Charles and Diana were released a week before the wedding. The stamps were designed by Jeffrey Matthews, and the photograph was taken by Lord Snowdon.

AFTER

Although the stresses in Charles and Diana's relationship did not become obvious until the late 1980s, it is clear the marriage came under strain as Diana struggled with the pressures of royal life.

COLLAPSE OF A MARRIAGE

In November 1981 it was announced that Diana was expecting a baby, and Buckingham Palace asked the press to allow her greater privacy. We now know she was suffering from **depression and bulimia.** Charles and Diana maintained a united front while their sons William (born 1982) and Harry (born 1984) were young, but Charles appears to have **resumed his relationship** with Camilla Parker Bowles by 1985. That was followed by Diana's affair with James Hewitt. By 1992 the marriage was to all intents and purposes over. They were divorced in 1996 **230–31 》**.

The balcony appearance
The Royal Couple exchanges a public kiss. Giving them company on the balcony are, left to right, Prince Philip, the Queen Mother, the page boys, the bridesmaids, the Queen, Prince Edward, and Prince Andrew.

Visiting the Vatican

Following several previous visits by British royals to the Vatican, including her own as princess and as queen, Elizabeth went to Rome in 1980 for the first ever state visit by a British monarch—a trip she hoped would "support the growing movement of unity between the Christian Churches throughout the world."

One of the key moments in the history of British royalty was the break with Rome in the 16th century (see pp.28–29). For centuries the monarchs were at loggerheads—and sometimes at war—with the Papacy. Only in 1914 were diplomatic relationships reestablished, and since then the Windsor dynasty has made great efforts to improve relations with the Vatican, and the Queen's 1980 state visit to the Vatican must be seen in this context.

The Queen's first meeting with the Pope as head of her own state came in May 1961. She and Prince Philip had flown to Sardinia, cruised across the Mediterranean, and visited the island of Vulcano. There they strolled incognito among the fishermen and dined on grilled shrimp, veal, and strawberries. Traveling by train to Rome, she was met by crowds cheering "Bella! Viva la regina!," while 20,000 people chanted outside the Quirinale Palace for an hour, as Elizabeth and Philip attended a state banquet and a glittering reception for 3,000 members of Italian high society. The next day the Derby Italiano horse race was run, the date having been deliberately set to coincide with her visit. After meeting with Pope John XXIII, and enjoying a rendition of "God save the Queen!" by 1,000 nuns and priests, the royal couple went on to Venice, where Elizabeth won the hearts of gondoliers by declaring "I would love to ride in a gondola."

The Queen's 1980 trip to meet Pope John Paul II was marked by an exchange of gifts. The Pope presented her with a copy of Dante's *Divine Comedy* with its illustration of the Order of the Garter in the time of Edward IV. The Queen responded with a book about Windsor Castle by St. John Hope and two signed photographs.

"Meetings between popes and British sovereigns... serve to push back... political and bilateral obstacles..."

MARK PELLEW, FORMER UK AMBASSADOR TO THE HOLY SEE

Heads of state and church
The Queen, dressed in black according to Vatican protocol, chats with Pope John Paul II. At this meeting she invited him to the UK to visit "the Roman Catholic community in Great Britain where some four million of my people are members of the Roman Catholic Church."

Born 1961 Died 1997

Diana, Princess of Wales

"Hugs can do great amounts of good, especially for children."

DIANA, PRINCESS OF WALES

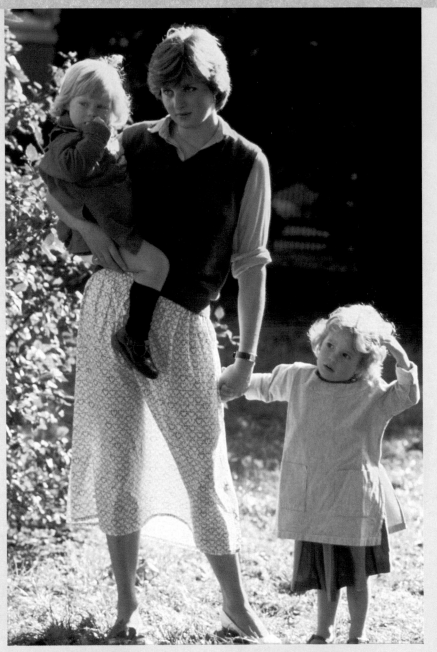

Diana Spencer was the fourth child and the youngest daughter of Viscount and Viscountess Althorp. Her father, Edward John Spencer, was a former Equerry—officer attendant—to King George VI and Queen Elizabeth II; her mother, Frances Roche, was the daughter of Baroness Fermoy, Lady-in-Waiting to the Queen Mother. Diana grew up at Park House, on the Queen's Sandringham estate in Norfolk. Diana's parents divorced when she was 8 years old.

In 1975, after the death of her grandfather, Diana's father became the 8th Earl Spencer, and the family moved into the family seat of Althorp in Northamptonshire. As the daughter of an earl, Diana became Lady Diana Spencer (she was previously the Honourable Diana Spencer). In 1976, her father married Raine, Countess of Dartmouth, daughter of the best-selling romantic novelist, Barbara Cartland.

Diana was first educated at Riddlesworth Hall near Diss, Norfolk, and later at West Heath Girls' School in Kent, but she left school without passing her O-level exams. At school, she showed a particular talent for music and dance – she was an accomplished pianist and was very keen on ballet. After a brief spell at finishing school at the Institut Alpin Videmanette in Rougemont, Switzerland, Diana moved to London, where she shared a flat with three other girls and held a variety of jobs including that of a nursery (pre-school) assistant.

Engagement

Diana first met Prince Charles, who was older than her by 13 years, in 1977, when he was going out with her elder sister Sarah. They met again in 1980, when Diana was 19, and the affair between Charles and Sarah had been over for more than two years. Their relationship developed over the

English schoolgirl
Diana enjoyed sport as a girl, especially swimming, and she dreamed of becoming a ballet dancer until she grew too tall for it. This photo was taken the year after her parents divorced.

Diana's flat, she got an early taste of the relentless paparazzi attention she would have to live with for the rest of her life.

Prince Charles proposed on 6 February 1981, and the engagement was officially announced on 24 February. When asked by a reporter on the day of the engagement if they were in love, Diana replied in tones of mock rebuke, "of course", and Prince Charles added, "whatever 'in love' means".

"… the unique, the complex, the extraordinary Diana."

CHARLES, EARL SPENCER, WHEN GIVING DIANA'S FUNERAL EULOGY, 1997

summer of 1980, and that same year the Queen invited Diana to Balmoral Castle, the Queen's private holiday home in Scotland. The Royal Family, too, approved of Diana. As the press got wind of the affair and photographers set up camp outside

Royal bride-to-be
The shy, naïve nursery assistant was about to become engaged to the heir to the throne when this famous photo was taken. Diana was always warm and spontaneous with children.

Soon after the wedding, Diana became involved in her official duties as a member of the Royal Family.

On 5 November 1981, Diana's first pregnancy was announced, and the couple's eldest son, William, was born just 11 months after the wedding. She flouted tradition by deciding that 9-month-old Prince William should accompany her and Prince Charles to Australia and New Zealand rather than be left in the care of nannies.

Their second son, Harry, followed two years later in 1984. Diana was a devoted and protective mother who declared, "I live for my sons. I would be lost without them."

Marriage and children
Charles and Diana's wedding (see pp.200–01) attracted a great deal of public interest. The couple made their homes at Kensington Palace and at Highgrove House, the Gloucestershire estate Prince Charles acquired in 1980.

Divorce and death
The marriage, under strain from very early on, fell apart in the early 1990s (see pp.230–31). Diana continued to

live in Kensington Palace after her separation and divorce, and gave much of her time to her charities (see pp.208–09). In the last year of her life she used her status as an international figure to call for a ban on the manufacture and use of landmines, a move that was seen by some as being out of step with government policy. Her tragic death in a car crash at the age of 36 (see pp.242–43) shocked and stunned the world.

Sparkling princess
Princess Diana is seen here wearing a beautiful tiara featuring 19 fabulous pearls hanging from diamond-encrusted lover's knots. Part of the Royal Collection, it was lent to her by the Queen.

> "I'd like to be a **queen of people's hearts,** in people's hearts, but **I don't see myself** being **Queen of this country.**"

DIANA, IN BBC1 PANORAMA INTERVIEW WITH MARTIN BASHIR, 1995

THE 9TH EARL SPENCER
CHARLES SPENCER

Born in May 1964, Charles was the youngest of Diana's siblings – she had two older sisters, Sarah and Jane. Charles became the 9th Earl Spencer on the death of his father in 1992. As Diana's closest male relative, Charles gave the eulogy at her funeral in Westminster Abbey. He described her as "the very essence of compassion, of duty, of style, of beauty", and recalled how she had mothered him when, as young children, they were shunted back and forth between their parents' homes.

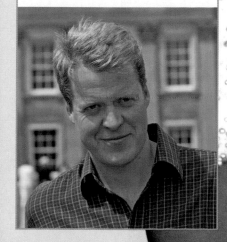

TIMELINE

- **1 July 1961** Born Diana Frances Spencer in Norfolk, England, to Viscount and Viscountess Althorp.

- **1969** Her parents divorce; her father gains custody of the children.

- **1970** Goes to her first boarding school – Riddlesworth Hall in Norfolk.

- **1974** Goes to West Heath Girls' School, Kent.

- **1975** Her father succeeds as 8th Earl Spencer.

- **1977** Leaves West Heath and goes to finishing school in Switzerland for a few months.

- **Summer 1977** Meets Prince Charles at a country weekend.

- **24 February 1981** Official announcement of engagement to Prince Charles.

- **29 July 1981** Marries Prince Charles at St Paul's Cathedral, London.

- **21 June 1982** Birth of Prince William.

- **September 1982** Represents the Queen at the State funeral of Princess Grace of Monaco on her first official visit overseas on her own.

- **March–April 1983** Charles and Diana take William with them on a 6-week visit to Australia and New Zealand.

- **February 1984** Attends a performance of *Carmen* by the London City Ballet in Norway, during her first solo overseas tour.

- **15 September 1984** Birth of Prince Harry.

- **9 November 1989** Dances with John Travolta at the White House (see pp.240–41).

- **19 April 1987** Shakes hands with an AIDS patient on a visit to Middlesex Hospital, London, in an effort to rid the disease of social stigma.

- **June 1992** Andrew Morton publishes her biography, *Diana: Her True Story*.

- **9 December 1992** Charles and Diana agree to separate.

- **December 1993** Announces that she will be reducing the extent of her public life.

- **20 November 1995** Appears in an interview by Martin Bashir on BBC television.

- **28 August 1996** Divorce of Charles and Diana.

- **January 1997** Backs international anti-landmine campaign on a visit to Angola.

- **25 June 1997** Auction of her dresses at Christies' New York raises money for cancer and AIDS charities.

- **21 July 1997** Visits the children's accident and emergency unit in Northwick Park Hospital, London, on her last official engagement.

- **31 August 1997** Dies of injuries sustained in a car accident in Paris, France.

- **6 September 1997** Funeral in Westminster Abbey, followed by burial at Althorp.

Diana
Princess of Wales Memorial Fund

DIANA'S SIGNATURE

BEFORE

Royal patronage goes back a long way. Queen Victoria was the patron of many hospitals, including Great Ormond Street Hospital and the Royal Free Hospital in London.

QUEEN ALEXANDRA ROSE DAY
Queen Alexandra launched the Alexandra Rose Day Appeal on June 26, 1912, to mark the 50th year of her arrival in Britain to marry the Prince of Wales, later King Edward VII **‹‹ 72–73.** The goal was to raise money for

POSTCARD FROM ROSE DAY, JULY 11, 1914

hospitals through the sale of silk roses. The first appeal raised £32,000 and was such a success that it became an annual event. By 1920, Rose Days had raised more than £775,000 ($2.9 million) for London hospitals. **Rose Days still take place every year.** Princess Alexandra, great-granddaughter of Queen Alexandra, is the present royal patron. Traditionally, the **prime minister buys the first rose.**

The Caring Princess

The Princess of Wales threw herself into charity work in a very personal way. She is best remembered for her natural warmth and compassion, and for the time and energy she spent supporting humanitarian causes around the world.

" Anywhere I see **suffering**, that is where I want to be, **doing what I can."**

DIANA, PRINCESS OF WALES, 1997

Caring for sick children
This picture from the 1996 National Heart Week shows Diana posing with young patients at a children's hospital ward in London. The Princess was known to take time to sit by patients' beds, hold their hands, and listen to their individual stories and problems.

On marrying the heir to the throne, Diana was expected to give her patronage to charities and philanthropic organizations. Visiting hospitals, opening buildings, and hosting receptions had long been seen, particularly since World War I, as a key function of the monarchy, and a means of bringing it into contact with ordinary people. Much of this work was high profile—Philip, Duke of Edinburgh, was president of the World Wildlife Fund; Charles founded the Prince's Trust and functioned as its president since 1976; and Princess Anne worked extensively for Save the Children. But, for the most part, royal charity work meant acting as a figurehead for fund-raising. To the public, it seemed that the royals' work mostly involved shaking hands, making speeches, receiving bouquets, and cutting ribbons.

Personal touch

That, however, was not Diana's style. Her natural empathy with sick people broke the mold of royal hospital visits. She had a special way of connecting with vulnerable young people, stemming from her own unhappiness during and after her parents' divorce and from her battles with bulimia and depression.

It is sometimes suggested that, after the breakdown of her marriage, Diana used her charity work to promote her own image at the expense of her husband's. There may be some truth in this, just as there is in the charge that she colluded with the press to give them the best photo opportunities. However, the individual stories that emerged after her death bear moving testimony to her ability to reach out to people in pain. She privately visited the Royal Brompton Hospital in London up

to three times a week, befriending some of the sickest patients. She painted the fingernails of one little girl on a dialysis machine a different color every week. Discovering that another was fascinated by ballet, she had a birthday cake made for her in the shape of pink ballet shoes.

Diana used her relationship with the press to help change public attitudes. In April 1987, she opened Britain's first ward for HIV (human immuno-deficiency virus) infection and AIDS (acquired immune deficiency syndrome) patients at London's Middlesex Hospital, and was photographed shaking hands with someone suffering from the disease. At that time, AIDS was still greatly feared and misunderstood, and her gesture helped to break down the prejudice surrounding the disease.

Role model

Diana is regarded by many as a role model for the way she spoke publicly about her unhappy marriage and about having sought psychiatric help for her depression and eating disorders, thereby enabling other women to talk openly about these problems.

Meeting Mother Teresa
Diana meets Mother Teresa at the Missionaries of Charity in the South Bronx, New York, in 1997. The Princess's visit to Mother Teresa's hospice for the sick and dying in Kolkata, India, in 1992 left a lasting impression on her.

Chosen charities

As a working royal, Diana was patron of more than 100 charities. After her separation from Charles, she gave nearly all of them up, retaining only six. These were: the Centrepoint charity for homeless young people, English National Ballet, Great Ormond Street Hospital for Children, Royal Marsden Hospital for cancer, National AIDS Trust, and the Leprosy Mission.

Diana had become patron of the Leprosy Mission, the only international charity on the list, after visiting a leprosy hospital in Indonesia in 1989. Leprosy is easily treatable if caught early enough, but sufferers are often regarded with revulsion because of the disfiguring effects. Officials advised Diana not to make the visit but she chose to ignore them. Instead, she was filmed holding hands with leprosy patients and touching their bandaged wounds, actions that were highly influential in tackling the age-old taboos. On later tours, she went out of her way to visit the Leprosy Mission's projects in India, Nepal, and Zimbabwe.

International star

Diana used her fame to support humanitarian causes all over the world. She was photographed holding a baby with AIDS at a paediatric unit in Harlem, New York. In June 1997, she auctioned a large number of her dresses at Christie's in New York in aid of AIDS and cancer charities. In the last year of her life, she campaigned extensively to ban landmines. It was on a visit to New York to promote this cause that Diana met Mother Teresa for the second time.

Landmine victims
Diana is photographed with young landmine victims during a visit to Angola in January 1997. She visited war-torn Bosnia just two weeks before her death, calling for a ban on these weapons.

AFTER ≫

Diana's humanitarian work continued to be remembered after her death. A fund was set up in response to donations that poured in spontaneously from the public.

The goal of the Diana, Princess of Wales Memorial Fund was to create a **lasting memorial to Diana's humanitarian work** by supporting charities for disadvantaged people. A sum of £38 million ($65 million) was raised from CD sales of the version of *Candle in the Wind* that singer Elton John performed at Diana's funeral. The general public gave £34 million ($58 million), and the princess's brother, Charles Spencer, donated proceeds from the Diana: A Celebration exhibition, which showcased 150 objects, including dresses and mementoes. By the time the Fund closed in 2012, it had awarded 727 grants to 471 organizations and **spent over £112 million ($180 million) on charitable causes.**

CONCERT FOR DIANA
Hosted by William and Harry, the Concert for Diana was held at London's Wembley Stadium in July 2007. The concert **raised money for Diana's charities** and for those of her sons.

Treading carefully
In the last year of her life, Diana, Princess of Wales, campaigned actively for an international ban on landmines. This famous picture of her walking through a minefield in Huambo, Angola, was taken in January 1997.

ROYAL RESIDENCE

Kensington Palace

Originally a modest Jacobean mansion in a rural village, Kensington Palace became the Royal Family's favorite London residence for almost 70 years. It was acquired by William and Mary, who wished to escape chilly Whitehall Palace and the fogs and floods of the Thames Rivers.

In 1688 when William III and Mary II assumed the throne, the King was in frail health, and his asthma was exacerbated by the cold, humid rooms of Whitehall Palace. Their search for a suitable alternative ended in 1689 with the purchase of Nottingham House—a two-story mansion in the village of Kensington—for £20,000. Christopher Wren, Surveyor of the King's Works, was hired to transform it into a palace.

The royal couple was anxious to move in, so speed was of the essence. Using bricks rather than stone to keep costs down, Wren's first step was to build a three-story pavilion at each corner of the mansion to accommodate the monarchs and their retinue, with a series of grand rooms—the State Apartments—for audiences and state ceremonies. Wren reoriented the house toward the west, and the north and south wings were added to flank a courtyard accessed through an archway that pierced the clock tower. The grounds were landscaped with lawns and formal gardens laid out in the Dutch fashion with geometrical paths and flower beds.

By Christmas 1689—just six months after work began—the royal court was able to move in, although building work continued. In 1694, tragedy struck the palace when Mary died of smallpox, with a devastated William at her bedside. Eight years later, in 1702, William also died at Kensington Palace after falling from his horse and then contracting pneumonia as he recuperated in the King's Gallery.

William's successor, Anne, continued to improve the palace, commissioning a staircase from Wren to link her apartments with the gardens. However, it was in the grounds that Anne made her mark: she redesigned the garden as a baroque parterre with elaborate topiary and erected a magnificent Orangery to protect her orange trees over winter. Designed by Nicholas Hawksmoor and John Vanbrugh, with carvings in pear- and pinewood by Grinling Gibbons, the Orangery served an additional purpose as an enchanting venue for royal receptions.

Georgian heydey

After Queen Anne died in 1714, the throne passed to her closest Protestant relative, George, Elector of Hanover. A survey discovered that the palace was in need of repair, but the new King "lik'd it very much" and proceeded to spend vast amounts on Kensington. Three additional state rooms—the Cupola Room, the Privy Chamber, and the Withdrawing Room—were created in the process. The existing State Apartments were given a makeover by the unknown artist and designer, William Kent, who undercut the expected choice—the established painter Sir James Thornhill—on price.

George II and his consort Queen Caroline presided over a glittering time for the palace. They loved to entertain, and the court attracted a fashionable set of intellectuals, politicians, writers, philosophers, and poets. Outside, the old-fashioned parterres were replaced with gardens designed in a romantic "natural" style by the royal gardener Charles Bridgeman. He created many features still seen in Kensington Gardens today, such as the Serpentine, the Round Pond, and the Broad Walk. The gardens were opened on Saturdays when the Royal Family decamped to Richmond; they soon became a center of high society, as the great and good gathered to parade the latest fashions.

After Caroline's death in 1737, the palace declined. George II died there in 1760; his successor, George III, elected to live at Kew, Windsor, and newly purchased Buckingham House. »

Palatial heights
The palace complex sits at the edge of Kensington Gardens. A statue of Queen Victoria by her daughter, Princess Louise for the 1887 Golden Jubilee celebration marks the main public entrance, while the bronze figure of William of Orange guards the south front.

WILLIAM OF ORANGE AT THE SOUTH FRONT

KENSINGTON PALACE FROM THE SOUTH

The Sunken Garden
The 17th-century Dutch style garden is a relatively modern development. It was created by Ernest Law in 1909 at the behest of Edward VII, to replace an unsightly cluster of greenhouses and potting sheds.

THE KING'S GALLERY

THE KING'S STAIRCASE

>> Kensington thenceforth became a home for minor royals and monarchs-in-waiting. One of the more colorful denizens was George III's sixth son, Prince Augustus Frederick, Duke of Sussex, whose menagerie of songbirds flew freely around his apartments. His brother, Prince Edward, Duke of Kent and Strathearn, also had rooms in the palace; Edward's daughter, Alexandrina Victoria, was born at Kensington nine months before his death, on May 24, 1819. Her childhood was lonely: educated under the "Kensington System" she was confined to the Palace with every move monitored by her mother and her equerry, Sir John Conroy, who strove to keep the

the palace in which she was born should not be destroyed." Eventually Parliament agreed to fund the palace's restoration. Subsequently the state rooms opened to the public on the Queen's birthday in 1899, launching the palace's dual role as a private home to royalty and public museum.

Kensington Palace was hit by a bomb in 1940, which severely damaged many of the surrounding buildings, including the Queen's Apartments. The garden was full of antiaircraft guns, sandbags, and trenches. After the war, the palace entered another period of neglect, but in the 1960s its fortunes revived when Princess Margaret and Antony Armstrong-

The King's State Apartments

Kensington was at the heart of Georgian society: well-dressed courtiers were immortalized by Kent on the staircase leading to the sumptuous rooms. William III's wind dial, connected to a weather vane on the roof, was retained when Kent redesigned the King's Gallery.

"normal" childhood, with visits to the local barbers, Kensington Odeon, and McDonalds on Kensington High Street. Kensington Palace remained the official residence of Diana, Princess of Wales until her untimely death on August 31, 1997, when the Golden Gates at the south entrance became the focus of public mourning. Over one million bouquets, reaching 5ft (1.5m) deep in places, were left in tribute. The Princess's coffin spent its last night in London at Kensington Palace, departing on the morning of September 6, 1997, on a gun carriage, to Westminster Abbey.

In 2011, it was announced that the Duke and Duchess of Cambridge would move from Nottingham Cottage, in the grounds of Kensington Palace, into the former residence of Princess Margaret. The following year Prince Harry also moved back into the palace: the long-established tradition of combining private royal residences at the palace with a public space looked set to continue for years to come.

Meanwhile, the State Rooms have also seen a major renovation. They were reopened in 2012, in time for Elizabeth II's Diamond Jubilee, as a museum with digital presentations, interactive experiences, and audio sequences bringing to life the State Apartments and the people who lived there, and making the rich collections of royal fashion, antique furniture, and other memorabilia accessible to visitors from around the world.

> "I have gone through **painful and disagreeable scenes** here, 'tis true, but still **I am fond of the poor old Palace.**"
>
> QUEEN VICTORIA, 1837

Princess under their control. Victoria's first request, when she became 18, was that she be allowed an hour by herself each day, and one of her first acts upon her accession to the throne was to banish Conroy forever from the royal apartments, and to evict her mother from the palace.

A palace for everyone

By the end of the 19th century, the State Rooms were severely neglected. With the brickwork decaying, and the woodwork infested with dry rot and rising damp, calls came for the palace to be demolished. However, Queen Victoria declared that "while she lived,

Jones, 1st Earl of Snowdon moved in. They lived in Apartment 10—"the doll's house" as Margaret described it, while they renovated and redecorated Apartment 1A in Margaret's favorite pink and kingfisher blue with the help of theater designer Carl Toms, adding a photographic darkroom for Lord Snowdon.

In 1981, the newly married Prince of Wales and his wife, Diana, moved into a part of the palace that George I had created for his mistress. Princes William and Harry were raised there, attending local preschool and pre-preparatory schools in Notting Hill. They were given occasional tastes of

The Cupola Room

Queen Victoria was christened in the magnificent Cupola Room, William Kent's first commission for George I. The King liked his work so much, he was commissioned to redecorate other State Rooms.

Prince Andrew in the Falklands

On April 2, 1982, Argentina invaded the British overseas territory of the Falkland Islands, a remote, windswept archipelago in the South Atlantic. Prince Andrew, a sub-lieutenant in the Royal Navy, was serving on board the aircraft carrier HMS *Invincible* as Britain set about assembling a task force to retake the islands.

The hastily assembled fleet of 127 ships that set sail in mid-April included two aircraft carriers, one of them being the HMS *Invincible*. Prince Andrew was a Sea King helicopter pilot, trained for operational flying. He was also second in line to the throne. It was widely assumed that he would be kept out of harm's way and given a safe desk job, as several members of the Cabinet urged, but Andrew, backed up by the Queen, insisted on being allowed to remain with his ship.

The battle to regain the islands began on May 1. As a Sea King copilot, Prince Andrew flew on missions that included antisubmarine and anti-surface warfare. One task of the Sea King helicopters was to act as decoys against the deadly Exocet missiles launched by Argentinian jets against British warships. By hovering near the rear of the carrier, the helicopter created a large radar target that diverted the missile away from the ship. Prince Andrew copiloted a Sea King that helped save seamen from the requisitioned merchant navy ship SS *Atlantic Conveyor* after it had been hit by two Exocets. He later described the experience as "probably the most frightening moment of my war." He also revealed that his biggest worry was being hit by friendly fire from the Royal Navy's Sea Wolf defense missiles: "It is not much fun having one of those fellows pick you out as a target."

Port Stanley, the capital of the Falkland Islands, was retaken on June 14. When HMS *Invincible* returned to Portsmouth on September 17, the Queen and Prince Philip joined other families of the crew in welcoming the ship carrying their son home.

> # "It's **not particularly nice** being **shot** at and I can attest to that. You **look at life** in a **different way.**"
>
> **PRINCE ANDREW**, ON THE FALKLANDS WAR, AUGUST 2014

Action man
Prince Andrew, seen here with the Sea King helicopter in the background, returns to Portsmouth on board HMS *Invincible* after the cessation of the Falklands War. The first royal to see frontline action in modern times, he served 22 years in the Royal Navy.

Born 1960

The **Duke** of **York**

> "I'm **not** even going to say that was **a piece of cake.** I will **never do it again.**"

PRINCE ANDREW, AFTER ABSEILING DOWN THE SHARD, SEPTEMBER 2012

Naval officer
In his 22-year-long naval career, Prince Andrew participated in the Falklands War and commanded HMS *Cottesmore*. He retired from active service in 2001.

Prince Andrew is the second son and third child of Queen Elizabeth II and Prince Philip. Born on February 19, 1960, in Buckingham Palace, he was the first child to be born to a reigning monarch since the birth of Queen Victoria's youngest child, Princess Beatrice, in 1857. At the time of his birth, he was second in line of succession to the throne; he is now sixth. He was christened Andrew Albert Christian Edward, Andrew being the name of his paternal grandfather, Prince Andrew of Greece, who died in 1944.

Prince Andrew was educated at Heatherdown Preparatory School, Ascot, in Berkshire, from the age of 8 to 13, before going on to Gordonstoun School in Scotland, where both his father and his elder brother, Charles, had been educated. After taking his O-levels, he spent two terms at Lakefield College School in Ontario, Canada, before returning to Gordonstoun to take his A-levels. Unlike his brothers, he did not go to university, but entered the Britannia Royal Naval College at Dartmouth (BRNC, popularly known as Dartmouth), Devon, where he began training to become an officer in the Royal Navy.

Naval career

After graduating from Dartmouth, Andrew learned to fly Gazelle and Sea King helicopters and was appointed to 820 Naval Air Squadron, serving aboard the aircraft carrier HMS *Invincible*. Six months later, in April 1982, he sailed in HMS *Invincible* as

Farewell to Hong Kong

Prince Andrew undertakes many military duties. He is seen here visiting a British army unit based on Stonecutters Island in Hong Kong as preparations are made for the transfer of sovereignty from Britain to China in 1997.

part of the Task Force sent to the South Atlantic to regain the Falkland Islands (see pp.216–17). On his return, he converted to flying Lynx helicopters. He was made a Commander in 1999, and retired with the rank of honorary Captain. In 2010 he was promoted to Honorary Rear Admiral, and five years later to Vice Admiral.

Marriage and children

Andrew was known to have had many girlfriends, including American actress Koo Stark, before his engagement to Sarah Ferguson. The redhead was a great success with the press and was soon universally known as Fergie. Prince Andrew was created Duke of York, a dukedom traditionally reserved for the second son of the monarch—on his marriage to Sarah on July 23, 1986 (see pp.222–23). The Queen built a 12-bedroom, ranchlike house for them at Sunninghill Park, Berkshire. Andrew and Sarah have two daughters, Princess Beatrice and Princess Eugenie.

Separation and divorce

As a serving naval officer, Andrew was frequently away, and during one of his absences Sarah took lessons in helicopter flying. This experience led her to write a series of children's books about Budgie, a little helicopter, which later became an animated television series. Sarah's popularity started to fall about this time, when the press began to publish pictures of her in the company of other men. The couple separated in March 1992, and divorced in May 1996, just three months before Charles and Diana. Like Diana, she was no longer styled Her Royal Highness.

Andrew and Sarah agreed to have joint custody of their daughters and shared Sunninghill Park as their family home until 2004, when Andrew moved into Royal Lodge, the Queen Mother's former home. Since 2008 Sarah has lived there as well. She spends much of her time in New York, where she pursues various commercial interests. In 2010 she was caught in a newspaper sting offering access to Andrew for

> "There is **something about** going to **sea.** A little bit of **discipline** and **humility** is required."
>
> PRINCE ANDREW, IN AN INTERVIEW

£500,000 ($750,000) and was forced to apologize. She and Andrew remain on good terms and often speak affectionately of each other.

Life after the navy

On leaving the navy, Prince Andrew was appointed Special Representative for International Trade and Investment, promoting British business interests abroad. He resigned from this role in 2011, following criticism about his friendly relations with controversial figures, including one of Libyan leader Colonel Gaddafi's sons, and a wealthy American financier convicted of sex offences.

Prince Andrew supports many charities, and is the chairman of the Outward Bound Trust, an educational charity. He is colonel-in-chief of several regiments in the British Army, and in Canada and New Zealand.

SARAH FERGUSON

Born in 1959, Sarah Ferguson is the daughter of the late Major Ronald Ferguson, polo manager to the Duke of Edinburgh and later to the Prince of Wales, and his wife Susan. After Sarah's parents divorced in 1974, her mother married an Argentinian polo player, Hector Barrantes. Sarah and Andrew knew each other as children, but their romance began after she was asked to join the royal party at Windsor Castle during Royal Ascot in 1985, reportedly at Princess of Wales's suggestion. Sarah was working in publishing at the time of their engagement. Andrew designed an engagement ring for her consisting of ten diamonds surrounding a ruby, chosen to complement her fiery red hair.

TIMELINE

- **February 19, 1960** Born at Buckingham Palace, the first child born to a reigning monarch for 103 years. Christened Andrew Albert Christian Edward.

- **1973** Attends Gordonstoun School in Morayshire, Scotland.

- **1979** Joins the Royal Navy on a short-term commission as a Seaman Officer with the goal of becoming a helicopter pilot.

- **April 1981** Receives his flying brevet (wings) from the Duke of Edinburgh as well as winning an award as best pilot.

- **April 5, 1982** Sails on board HMS *Invincible* as part of the Task Force to regain the Falkland Islands; flies several frontline missions.

- **May 1984** Promoted Lieutenant and serves as Flight Pilot in the Type 22 Frigate HMS *Brazen*. [...] the Queen's household and has personal aide-de-camp.

- **July 23, 1986** Marries Sarah Ferguson at Westminster Abbey and is created Duke of York.

- **August 8, 1988** Birth of first daughter, Beatrice.

- **March 23, 1990** Birth of second daughter, Eugenie.

- **March 1992** Duke and Duchess of York separate; divorce follows four years later.

- **November 20, 1992** Helps to rescue treasures from the Windsor Castle fire.

- **1993** Appointed Commander to command the anti-mine vessel HMS *Cottesmore*.

- **1999** Appointed Commander in the Diplomatic Directorate of the Naval Staff.

- **July 2001** Retires from active service with the Royal Navy.

PRINCE ANDREW AT CERN, GENEVA

- **2001–11** Serves as Special Representative for International Trade and Investment, promoting British business interests abroad. His tours included a trip to the European Organization for Nuclear Research (CERN), Geneva.

- **July 2005** Promoted to Captain. Appointed Commodore in Chief of the Fleet Air Arm the following year.

- **February 2010** Promoted to Rear Admiral.

- **September 3, 2012** Abseils down the Shard, London's tallest skyscraper, to raise money for the Outward Bound Trust.

- **February 2015** Promoted to Vice Admiral.

Queen visiting Canada
The Queen inspects a guard of honor of the
Governor General's Foot Guards outside
the Parliament Building in Ottawa while
on a visit to Canada in 1984.

« BEFORE

Trooping the Color dates back to the 1700s when a battalion's flag, or color, was carried slowly (trooped) along the ranks of soldiers so it could be seen and recognized.

BIRTHDAY PARADE

The Trooping the Color ceremony was first used to mark the sovereign's birthday in 1748, when **George II** was on the throne. Since this time the Trooping the Color ceremony has **celebrated the sovereign's official birthday** on a Saturday in June in the expectation of good weather.

KING GEORGE V AT THE PARADE, 1925

The Queen's 60th Birthday

The Queen celebrates two birthdays every year—her actual birthday on April 21, and the official one in early June, when she attends the Trooping the Color ceremony. Her 60th birthday in 1986 was marked by special tributes at home and around the Commonwealth.

The two royal events that took place in 1986—the marriage of Prince Andrew and Sarah Ferguson in July (see pp. 222–23) and the Queen's 60th birthday celebrations—were welcome interludes in what was otherwise a challenging year for the monarchy. There was talk of differences between the Queen and Prime Minister Margaret Thatcher over Britain's stance with regard to the apartheid regime in South Africa. In July, a newspaper report claimed that the Queen was dismayed with the government's harsh social policies

in the wake of the miners' strike the year before, but this was instantly denied by the palace. The Royal Family was frequently caricatured on the satirical TV puppet show *Spitting Image*—something that would have been unthinkable a few years earlier. There were also worries over security—in 1981, a pistol had been fired from the crowd as the Queen rode down the Mall for the Trooping the Color, and the IRA (Irish Republican Army) terror campaign in mainland Britain was an ever-present threat. However, these

concerns did not deter the crowds from turning out to celebrate the Queen's birthday.

Bagpipes and daffodils

Queen Elizabeth's 60th birthday on April 21, 1986, started with an early morning rendition of "Happy Birthday to You," played on the bagpipes by the Queen's Piper outside her apartment at

Say it with flowers

Radiant in springtime yellow, a smiling Queen Elizabeth collects bunches of daffodils from a group of children in the forecourt of Buckingham Palace.

Birthday procession
The band and troops of the Household Division, headed by five Drum Majors in ceremonial state dress, return along the Mall towards Buckingham Palace at the end of the Trooping the Colour ceremony in June 2014.

Windsor Castle. The Piper is a member of the royal household. His principal duty is to play under the Queen's window every morning at 9 a.m., a tradition started by Queen Victoria. This was followed by a 21-gun salute

"We **saw your car,** Hurrah! Hurrah! We saw you **wave,** the **smile you gave,** We saw **your horse,** of course, of course."

THE QUEEN'S BIRTHDAY SONG, BY CHRISTOPHER LOGUE, 1986

in Windsor Great Park, a service of thanksgiving in St. George's Chapel, Windsor, and a carriage procession through the town.

That afternoon the Queen was driven to Buckingham Palace, where she was greeted by a parade of 6,000 children from all over Britain and the Commonwealth who processed the length of the Mall in the steady rain, each carrying a daffodil. Standing on the balcony of the Palace, she listened to them sing a song specially composed for the occasion, "Happy Birthday Ma'am, God Bless You," before going down into the palace forecourt to collect bunches of daffodils from the children. She was helped by Prince Andrew and Sarah Ferguson, who were due to be married in three months' time. In the evening the entire Royal Family attended a gala at the Royal Opera House with a cast headed

by Placido Domingo. It included a ballet portraying the Queen and Princess Margaret as young girls.

Last appearance for Burmese
The Trooping the Color parade held on June 14 was notable for being the last public appearance of Burmese, the Queen's favorite black parade horse. Burmese, a mare, had been presented to the Queen by the Royal Canadian Mounted Police in 1969 and had

Inspecting the Terra-cotta Army
Queen Elizabeth II visited the now world-famous excavation site of the "terra-cotta warriors" at Xi'an in Shaanxi province in October 1986. She was the first British monarch to set foot in China.

carried the Queen, who always rode her side-saddle, at every Trooping the Color for 18 years. The Queen had been mounted on Burmese in 1981 when the horse reared after five blank shots were fired from the crowd. The Queen quickly brought the mare under control, winning great praise for her presence of mind. She later explained that Burmese had not heard the shots above the noise of the crowd, but was reacting to the

6,000 The number of children in the Mall who sang "Happy Birthday" as part of the Queen's 60th birthday celebrations.

movement of the Household Cavalry's horses who had immediately turned to protect the sovereign. "Burmese felt that the Household Cavalry was going to attack me, so she attacked them first," she was reported as saying. The assailant was a 17-year-old boy who did it, he said, because "I wanted to be famous. I wanted to be somebody."

Burmese was retired after the 1986 Trooping the Color and put out to pasture in Windsor Castle's Home Park. She died in 1990. The Queen decided not to replace her. In 1987, the Queen was driven to the Trooping the Color in a phaeton (light carriage) and took the salute from a dais, a procedure she has followed ever since.

Commemorative stamps
The Queen's 60th birthday was celebrated at home and around the Commonwealth with the issue of commemorative stamps and coins. The British set of four stamps carried portraits, three on each stamp, of the

Twenty years on, the Queen celebrated her 80th birthday with a royal tour in Windsor, where she was greeted by thousands of well-wishers.

SAY IT WITH EMAILS
Buckingham Palace announced that the Queen had received **20,000 cards** and **17,000 emails,** sent via her 80th-birthday website. Tributes included a visual greeting from the **500 members** of the crew of **HMS *Illustrious,*** on deployment in the Indian Ocean, who lined up to spell out "Happy 80th." The **Cabinet** presented the Queen with a **Spode china tea set.** In the evening **Prince Charles,** who had earlier broadcast a **tribute to his mother** on BBC Radio, **hosted a family dinner** for the Queen at Kew Palace, before a fireworks and laser display over Kew Gardens in southwest London. On June 25, a party for 2,000 children, chosen through a national ballot, was held in the garden of Buckingham Palace.

THE QUEEN'S 80TH BIRTHDAY, 2006

Queen at different times of her life, from the earliest portrait of her as a two year old to the present time. Eleven Commonwealth countries also issued commemorative stamps. However, when the Queen opened the 13th Commonwealth Games in Edinburgh on July 24, 32 of the 59 countries that were eligible to compete stayed away in protest against the British government's policy of maintaining sporting links with South Africa and its refusal to apply economic sanctions against the apartheid regime. The Queen rounded off her 60th birthday year with a state visit to China in October. It was the first time a British monarch had ever visited China, ending years of enmity dating back to the 19th century.

Come reign, come shine
Elizabeth rides through pouring rain on to
Horse Guards Parade for the 1983 Trooping
the Color. The ceremony is held each year
on her official birthday in June.

Diana's Dresses

Diana was famous throughout the world for her glamorous dress-sense. Shortly before her death, she selected 10 dresses to be auctioned for charity. Her other dresses occasionally feature in royal exhibitions.

1 Victor Edelstein dress The Princess of Wales wore this midnight blue velvet dress to a state dinner at the White House in 1985. At this event she danced with American actor John Travolta to music from the movie *Saturday Night Fever* (see pp.240–41). It became known as the Travolta dress, and raised £240,000 ($360,000) at an auction in 2013. Diana also wore it in her last official portrait photograph, taken by the Earl of Snowdon, former husband of Princess Margaret, in 1997. **2 Bruce Oldfield evening dress** This dress was worn by Diana while on royal tour of Saudi Arabia in 1986. This dress was included in the "Fashion Rules" royal clothing exhibition held at Kensington Palace, London, in 2013. **3 Murray Arbeid dress** Diana wore this dress—a midnight blue creation with diamanté

stars and a dramatic fish-tail skirt of layered tulle—to a dinner held at Claridge's Hotel for the President of Greece in 1986. A stamp issued in Togo to commemorate her charity work features the Princess of Wales wearing this dress. **4 Catherine Walker evening gown** This sea green sequined evening gown is by one of Diana's favorite designers, Catherine Walker. It was worn by Diana on a variety of occasions ranging from a state visit to Austria in 1989 to the premier of the film *Biggles* in 1993. **5 Catherine Walker gown and jacket** This opulent Mughal-inspired dress was made for Diana's official visit to India in 1992. Made of pink slubbed silk, the bolero jacket and bodice are encrusted with opulent embroidery. The sleeveless dress is lined in ivory satin.

1 VICTOR EDELSTEIN DRESS

Long bodice embroidered with beads

2 BRUCE OLDFIELD EVENING DRESS

Blue tulle skirt lined with purple silk

3 MURRAY ARBEID DRESS

Gathers running down the center seam at the front of the dress

Bolero jacket with floral embroidery in corded silk, embellished with pink sequins and colored beads

Gold chain-stitched leaves on bodice

5 CATHERINE WALKER GOWN AND JACKET

4 CATHERINE WALKER EVENING GOWN

Charles and Diana Divorce

The marriage of the Prince and Princess of Wales fell apart publicly in the early 1990s. Their mutual accusations—fanned by press speculation and rumor—scandalized, entertained, and divided the nation. The media came to call the divorce "the war of the Waleses."

The cracks that appeared early in the marriage of the Prince and Princess of Wales did not become obvious to the public for a few years. To the outside world, they seemed like a united couple and the caring parents of two young sons. But they began to appear together less frequently, and when they did, Charles often seemed peevish and unhappy that Diana was more popular with the crowds than he was, whereas in the early days of their marriage he had been proud to show her off.

Rumors about the failing marriage first broke when Charles and Diana were on a official visit to India in February 1992. When Diana went on her own to the Taj Mahal, she was photographed sitting alone in front of the white marble mausoleum, built by the Mogul emperor Shah Jahan as a memorial to his wife and widely regarded as a monument to love. The pose was clearly intended to signal her loneliness and isolation.

Revelations

Three months later, English writer Andrew Morton published *Diana: Her True Story*. This book revealed details of Diana's bulimia and her attempted suicide while pregnant with William by throwing herself down a staircase at Sandringham. It also exposed Charles's long-running affair with Camilla Parker Bowles (see pp.264–65). Diana undoubtedly cooperated in the writing of the biography and encouraged her friends to do so too. The book had a devastating effect on public opinion by portraying the Royal Family as cold and dysfunctional.

In the past, the Royal Family might have hoped to cover up the marital difficulties of the heir to the throne—a situation that was not without precedent—but there was a new factor to be reckoned with: the media. Over the coming months, it proved impossible to keep the couple's increasingly bitter estrangement out of the headlines.

A series of leaked phone calls, first between Diana and a close friend, James Gilbey, and then between Charles and Camilla, horrified and enthralled the nation. Meanwhile, rumors began to surface that Diana was having an affair with her children's former horse riding instructor, James Hewitt.

In December 1992, Prime Minister John Major announced to the House of Commons that Charles and Diana

Unhappy couple

Charles and Diana attend the State Opening of Parliament in October 1991. Increasingly, photographs of the couple showed them staring in different directions, suggesting a rift in the relationship.

BEFORE

Prince Charles and Camilla Parker Bowles, then Camilla Shand, got to know each other in the early 1970s. They frequently met at polo matches and soon began dating.

THE THIRD IN THE MARRIAGE
Charles's relationship with Camilla ended abruptly in 1973, and she **married Andrew Parker Bowles,** a cavalry officer with whom she had had an on-off relationship for some time. It is doubtful that Camilla would have been thought a suitable wife for Charles at this time, even if she had wished to marry him.

CHARLES AND CAMILLA AT A POLO MATCH, 1975

The friendship between Charles and Camilla appears to have revived in the late 1970s or early 1980s, before his engagement to Diana Spencer, who became aware of it just before or soon after their marriage. Camilla and Andrew Parker Bowles had two children. They were **divorced in 1995,** a year after Charles admitted to his relationship with Camilla in his interview with Jonathan Dimbleby.

"Well, there were **three of us** in this **marriage**, so it was a bit **crowded**."

DIANA, TO BRITISH JOURNALIST MARTIN BASHIR, ON BBC'S PANORAMA, NOVEMBER 20, 1995

Panorama interview
Diana was able to make her controversial interview on BBC's *Panorama* by keeping the broadcast a secret from Buckingham Palace until just before the program was aired

After the separation was announced, discussion centred on whether Diana would be allowed to retain the style of Her Royal Highness, reserved for members of the royal family.

LOSS OF TITLE
In July 1996, a joint statement issued by Buckingham Palace and Diana's lawyers announced that Diana would receive a **lump-sum financial settlement**. Just before the divorce was made absolute in August, letters patent were issued **regulating royal titles** after divorce. As she was no longer married to the Prince of Wales, Diana would in future be styled "Diana, Princess of Wales," without the Her Royal Highness (HRH). She would continue to live at Kensington Palace and, as the mother of the second and third in line to the throne, would be "regarded as a member of the Royal Family." Upset by the loss of his mother's HRH, Prince William is reported to have said he would give it back to her when he became king.

were to separate amicably but had no plans to divorce, adding that, "there is no reason why the Princess of Wales should not be crowned Queen of England in due course."

Diana turned down an invitation to spend that Christmas at Sandringham with the Royal family, but the couple continued to attend some functions together. Decisions had to be made about their sons, now at boarding school. It was arranged that they should spend part of each school vacation at Highgrove, with their father, and part at Kensington Palace, with their mother. In December 1993, Diana announced her withdrawal from public life.

Swaying public opinion
A large proportion of the British public sided with the Princess—she was young and attractive, and a devoted mother. They could not understand why Charles should prefer an older woman, and questioned why he always seemed so glum. In June 1994, in an apparent attempt to make himself seem more appealing, the Prince gave a television interview to journalist Jonathan Dimbleby as part of a documentary on his life and work. In it he publicly admitted that he had been unfaithful to Diana "once the

> **15** MILLION The number of people who tuned in to watch Diana's BBC interview.

marriage had irretrievably broken down." His words caused an instant furore and undid any chance the program might have had of restoring his reputation. In November, the publication of Dimbleby's authorized biography of the Prince of Wales confirmed he was having an affair with Camilla.

A year later, Diana had her revenge by giving an hour-long interview on BBC's *Panorama*. Millions tuned in to watch ashen-faced Diana, wearing minimal makeup except for kohl around her eyes, confess to her adultery with James Hewitt, her depression and bulimia, and her hurt over Charles's affair with Camilla. Perhaps the most damaging exchanges came late in the interview when Diana said she did not think she would ever be queen, and that she doubted that Charles would adapt to the demanding role of being king. She also said she had no wish for a divorce.

Damage limitation
The Queen, however, thought otherwise. Too much harm was being done to the monarchy to allow this undignified warfare between her son and her daughter-in-law to continue. After consulting the prime minister and the Archbishop of Canterbury, she wrote to both the Prince and the Princess, advising them to seek an

The Prince's biography
For the completion of the biography, Dimbleby was given access to the Prince's own archives—more than 10,000 letters, private journals, and diaries, none of which had ever been made public before.

early divorce. Charles issued a statement saying he took the same view, and declared he had no intention of remarrying. Diana took longer to agree, but eventually announced that she had instructed her lawyers to begin negotiating a divorce settlement.

> **£17** MILLION ($26 million) The amount of Diana's financial settlement.

The terms were agreed upon in July 1996, and the couple divorced on August 28 after 15 years of marriage.

Changing times
Sixty years earlier, a constitutional crisis had erupted over Edward VIII's decision to marry a twice-divorced woman (see pp.90–91). He chose to abdicate rather than give her up. Now, when Charles eventually becomes king, he will do so as a divorced and remarried man—a sign of how much public opinion and the Royal Family have changed through the years.

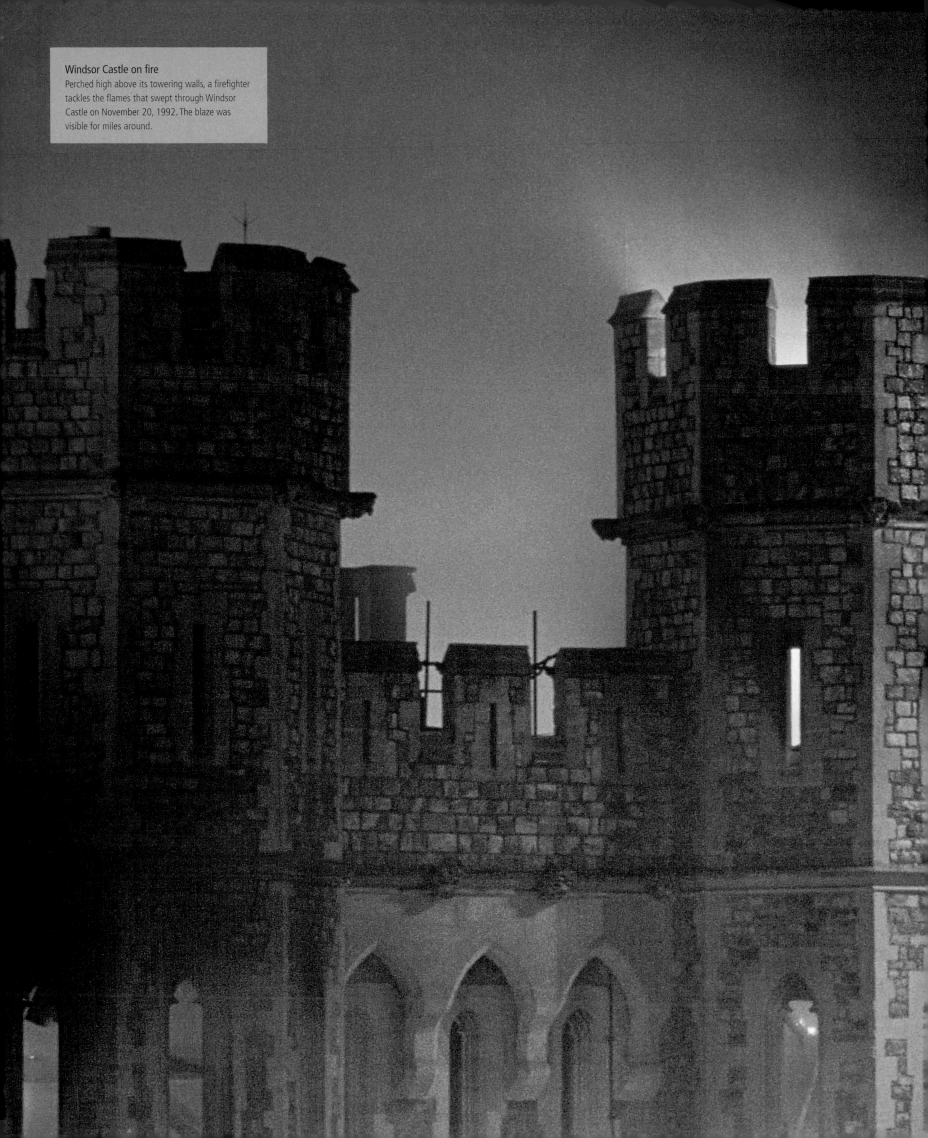

Windsor Castle on fire
Perched high above its towering walls, a firefighter tackles the flames that swept through Windsor Castle on November 20, 1992. The blaze was visible for miles around.

Buckingham Palace opens to the Public

Buckingham Palace had never before been put on public show. The urgent need to raise funds to pay for the restoration of Windsor Castle after the fire prompted the Queen's decision to open the State Rooms, with their priceless collections of paintings, furniture, and porcelain, for two months each summer while she was resident in Scotland.

The decision to invite the public into the heart of Buckingham Palace came about after a period of intense soul-searching and debate within the royal household following the Windsor Castle fire (see pp.232–33) and other events that took place in the annus horribilis (see pp.234–35). Taken aback by the strength of opposition to the idea that the taxpayer should help fund the repairs, the Queen's advisers hoped that this move would help bring the monarchy closer to the people and show its willingness to modernize.

On the first day of the opening, 4,314 people paid £8 ($15) each to visit the palace's State Rooms, including the 155-ft (47-m) long Picture Gallery, the State Dining Room, the Green Drawing Room, and the Throne Room. All group visits—booked in advance—had been sold for the next three years. The scheme, originally intended to last five years, proved a huge success, regularly drawing in around 400,000 visitors a year, and the palace continued to open its doors even after the Windsor Castle restorations had been paid for.

In the early years, there was some criticism that the tour was dull and uninformative. Since then, more rooms have been opened up and visitors can now see part of the palace gardens, as well as an exhibition on a particular theme each year. Buckingham Palace, together with the Royal Mews and the Queen's Gallery, which displays items from the Queen's fabulous art collection, is now one of London's top tourist attractions. The income it generates is plowed back through the Royal Collection Trust into the upkeep of the royal palaces and their contents.

"It is indeed **not easy to conceive** anything **more splendid.**"

ALLAN CUNNINGHAM, ART CRITIC, ON JOHN NASH'S DESIGNS
FOR BUCKINGHAM PALACE, 1830

The Green Drawing Room
Visitors are given an extensive tour of the State Rooms, designed by architect John Nash for King George IV. The people enter the Throne Room, used by the Queen for state and ceremonial entertaining, through the Green Drawing Room.

Diana: A Star is Born

It was at a gala dinner at the White House that Diana took to the dance floor with Hollywood actor John Travolta. Images of the princess in a figure-hugging, dark blue velvet gown being swung around the floor by the world's most famed disco dancer announced Diana's glittering arrival on the international scene.

The dinner hosted by President Ronald Reagan and his wife Nancy came at the beginning of Charles and Diana's first visit to the US after their marriage. There was a moment of embarrassment when the President welcomed her as "Princess David… er, Princess Diane," but this was soon forgotten because, in the days that followed, Diana took the US by storm.

From the naive preschool assistant, who avoided looking directly at the camera, and the young bride and mother with an uncertain taste for frills and puffed sleeves, Diana had transformed herself into a beautiful and self-confident fashion icon, sure of her own taste. Her favorite designers were Bruce Oldfield, Catherine Walker, Victor Edelstein, and Versace. In the mid-1980s, she adopted the "Dynasty" style, named after the popular TV series, which called for wide shoulders and big hairstyles, but she later championed the slim sheath dress, stamping it with her individual style and elegance. Despite her fraught relationship with the paparazzi, no one understood the power of the image better than she did or could control the camera more effectively. Whether posing alone in front of the Taj Mahal, wearing a dazzling evening gown for a gala movie premiere or a demure white suit to meet Mother Teresa, or dressed in a crisp chambray shirt and chinos on a minefield in Angola, she filled the pages of the world press for more than a decade.

> **"As [Diana] matured, she was less concerned about fashion and followed her own sense of style even more."**
> **VICTOR EDELSTEIN**, DRESS DESIGNER

Iconic gown
Diana included this Edwardian-inspired gown, by the British designer Victor Edelstein, in the collection of dresses she auctioned for charity in New York in June 1997. It was bought for £137,000 ($233,000).

The **Death** of **Diana**

On Sunday, August 31, 1997, Britons awoke to the news that Diana, Princess of Wales had died in Paris from injuries sustained in a car crash. They reacted with shock and disbelief as they struggled to comprehend that the life of this vibrant, beautiful woman had ended so tragically.

Diana was in Paris with Egyptian heir and film producer Dodi Al Fayed, her boyfriend of only a few weeks. They had just returned from vacationing on a luxury yacht belonging to Dodi's father, Mohamed Al Fayed, owner of Harrods department store in London and the Ritz hotel in Paris. Henri Paul, deputy head of security at the Ritz, was driving the couple in a Mercedes-Benz from the hotel to Dodi Al Fayed's private apartment. They were being pursued by photographers on motorcycles and in cars. At around 12:23 a.m., the car entered an underpass at an estimated speed of 65 mph (105 kph). Paul lost control of the car and it hit a pillar before spinning off to crash into the tunnel wall. Al Fayed and the driver died at the scene of the accident. Diana died in Paris's Pitié-Salpêtrière Hospital a few hours later.

The people's princess

As news of the tragedy spread, one of the first to pay public tribute to Diana was British Prime Minister Tony Blair. Addressing the press before he entered church for the Sunday morning service in his northern constituency, he said, "We are a nation in a state of shock… she was the people's princess." His words struck an immediate chord with thousands of grieving Britons, many of whom were already laying floral tributes to Diana outside Kensington Palace (see pp.244–45). They began to ask why the Royal Family was still at Balmoral, their summer home, instead of returning to London, and why the Queen had made Princes William and Harry attend church

BEFORE

Diana's affair with Dodi Fayed is said to have started in July 1997, when the Princess and her sons vacationed on board Mohamed Al Fayed's yacht.

DIANA ON BOARD AL FAYED'S YACHT *JONIKAL*

VACATION SNAPSHOT
A **photo of Diana and Dodi kissing** on board his father's yacht *Jonikal*, taken in late August, made **headline news** around the world. It was the first that most people knew of the affair. There are suggestions that Diana herself may have **alerted the paparazzi** to her presence on the yacht.

Coming home
Draped in the Royal Standard, the coffin containing Diana's body arrives at Royal Air Force Northolt airfield, close to London. Prince Charles and Diana's sisters were in the plane that carried her back from France.

response did not satisfy the tabloids, which judged that the monarchy was out of touch with the people.

The Queen had never before come under such direct criticism. One headline read, "Speak to us, ma'am, please speak," while another demanded "Show us you care." On September 5, the Queen returned to Buckingham Palace, stopping to look at the floral tributes to Diana outside the gates. Once inside, she made a live broadcast from the Chinese Drawing Room, in which she paid her own personal tribute to Diana as "an exceptional and gifted human being." Her dignified words were well received, suggesting that the storm of hostility whipped up by the press was beginning to abate.

> " There are **lessons** to be drawn from her life and from the **extraordinary** and moving **reaction** to her **death**."

ELIZABETH II, FROM A LIVE BROADCAST, SEPTEMBER 5, 1997

straight after learning of their mother's death (the fact is that they had asked to do so). Reflecting the people's mood, the press—a portion of which had been highly critical of Diana only a short while before—joined in the attacks. These came to focus on why the Union Jack was not flying at half-mast over Buckingham Palace. According to royal protocol, the only flag that ever flies over the palace is the Royal Standard, and only when the monarch is in residence. It is never flown at half-mast. This official

Flowers for Diana

The Queen and Prince Philip examine the floral tributes outside the gates of Buckingham Palace. They were said to have been deeply moved by the expressions of love for Diana following her death.

Diana's funeral

Diana's funeral took place on Saturday, September 6. Over a million people lined the 4 mile (6 km) route along which her coffin, draped with her personal standard, was carried on a gun carriage from Kensington Palace to Westminster Abbey. At St. James's Palace, the Duke of Edinburgh, the Prince of Wales, his two sons, and their uncle Charles Spencer joined the procession to walk behind the coffin the rest of the way. At Buckingham Palace, the Union Jack was flying at half-mast on the Queen's

United in grief
Prince William and Prince Harry walk behind their mother's coffin, flanked by their father, grandfather, and uncle. The princes were ages 15 and 12 when their mother died.

orders. She was waiting at the gates with other members of the Royal Family and bowed her head as the coffin passed by.

Some 31.5 million viewers watched the funeral in Britain, while an estimated 2.5 billion people viewed it live worldwide. During the traditional Church of England funeral service, Elton John performed a version of his song *Candle in the Wind* dedicated to Diana. In his eulogy, Charles Spencer took the opportunity to criticize the press and, indirectly, the Royal Family for their treatment of his sister. Many in the congregation applauded. Afterward, the coffin was driven to the Spencer family home of Althorp where, in a private ceremony, Diana was laid to rest on an island in the middle of a lake.

Cause of the accident
Immediately after the crash, the paparazzi who had been pursuing the car were blamed for the accident. However, the official French report concluded that the driver, Henri Paul,

was driving at excessive speed under the influence of both prescription drugs and alcohol. None of the photographers arrested after the crash were charged with manslaughter. Mohamed Al Fayed was not satisfied with this verdict. He claimed that Diana and his son were

£12.5 MILLION ($20 million) The cost of the inquiry into Diana's death.

250 The number of witnesses that were interviewed during the inquiry.

about to announce their engagement, and that they had been killed by the British secret service to prevent this from happening. He even accused Prince Philip of masterminding the plot. In 2004, a British inquest was opened into their deaths, but it did not begin hearing evidence until 2007. In April 2008 the jury delivered its verdict that Diana and Fayed had been killed by the grossly negligent driving of Henri Paul and the vehicles in pursuit.

In the years that followed her death, several memorials were erected in different locations to commemorate Diana's life and work.

REMEMBERING DIANA
The **Princess of Wales Memorial Playground** in Kensington Gardens, close to her former home, celebrates Diana's love of children. It encourages children to explore and follow their imagination, and has a wooden pirate ship as its centerpiece. The playground also features toys and play sculptures.

Nearby in Hyde Park, the **Diana Memorial Fountain** is formed as a stone oval made from slabs of Cornish granite. It was opened by the Queen in 2004.

The **Flame of Liberty,** built in 1989 in Paris, stands not far from the entrance to the tunnel where Diana died. It became

an unofficial memorial when people began leaving flowers and messages there soon after the Princess's death.

Her memory is commemorated by a **classical temple** built close to the site of her island grave at Althorp. One of the most extraordinary memorials was the **bronze statue of Diana and Dodi** placed by Mohamed Al Fayed at Harrods.

DIANA MEMORIAL FOUNTAIN, HYDE PARK

Farewell to Diana

Diana's death was met with an unprecedented wave of emotion from the public. Within hours of the news breaking, people of all ages began to leave bouquets of flowers and other mementos outside the gates of Kensington Palace. In places, the pile of flowers was 5 ft (1.5 m) high.

The spontaneous outpouring of grief over Diana's death was extraordinarily intense. Many people attached heartfelt messages to the bouquets explaining that, although they had never met her, it was as if they had lost a close family member. The waiting time to sign books of condolence at St. James's Palace grew to five hours, then to 11, and the Salvation Army provided free cups of tea to the lengthening lines. The displays of emotion were not confined to London—floral tributes sprang up in cities throughout the country, and people lined up to sign books of condolence all around the world, from Sydney to New York. In Paris, messages and flowers were placed at the foot of the Flame of Liberty memorial at the Pont d'Alma, close to where Diana had died. On the day of her funeral, more than three million people waited silently on the streets to watch Diana's coffin being taken to Westminster Abbey.

In retrospect, the heightened emotions that accompanied Diana's death seem inexplicable. Several commentators at the time put the reaction down to mass hysteria, but there was no doubt that Diana's projected personality had struck a chord with the public, and many people experienced genuine feelings of loss. A large number of the personal notes written by the public contrasted her warmth and spontaneity with the supposed coldness of the Royal Family. The press picked up on this theme. They helped fuel accusations that the Royal Family was uncaring by questioning why the Union Jack was not flying at half-mast over Buckingham Palace.

> **"I can't understand** this feeling of **pain** for someone who **never** even **knew my name."**
>
> ONE OF THE THOUSANDS OF HANDWRITTEN MESSAGES LEFT FOR DIANA

Floral tributes
Thousands of people left flowers outside Kensington Palace, Diana's home. It was later estimated that Londoners had spent £25 million ($42 million) on 1.3 million bouquets. The bottom layer had started to compost before they were cleared away.

ROYAL RESIDENCE

Balmoral Castle

Built of local granite and bristling with towers and turrets, Balmoral epitomizes the romantic vision of Scotland prevalent in Victorian England. The Aberdeenshire estate has been the private property of the Royal Family since 1852, when it was acquired by Prince Albert.

Queen Victoria and Prince Albert first visited Scotland in 1842, two years after their marriage. Captivated by its beauty, which Albert felt was "very Germanic," it was the first of several visits. Their enthusiasm undampened by their experience of the rainy weather, they set about finding a highland retreat of their own.

A highland paradise

The search began in Deeside at the suggestion of the royal physician, who recommended the area for its gentler climate. Advised by Lord Aberdeen—who had inherited the lease on the estate from his brother—the royal couple bought the lease on Balmoral blind. Both instantly loved the estate when they arrived there for the first time in September 1848. "All seemed to breathe freedom and peace, and to make one forget the world and its sad turmoils," wrote Victoria in her diary. Albert, on the other hand, found that the landscape reminded him of his Thuringian roots, and prominent artists including Edwin and Charles Landseer were soon commissioned to paint Balmoral landscapes.

The house was deemed pretty, but it was far too small to meet the needs of their growing family and a stream of official visitors. The initial plan to extend the house was soon abandoned:

ever more enamored of the property, they began negotiations to buy out the landowner in 1849, with a view to building a completely new house. Meanwhile, Albert came up with an interim solution to their space issue. Inspired by a display at the Great Exhibition of 1851, he ordered a prefabricated iron building to serve as a temporary ballroom and dining room, which remained in use until 1856.

Albert and Victoria finally managed to buy the Balmoral estate, and that of neighboring Birkhall, outright in 1852. On September 28, 1853, Victoria laid the foundation stone of their new house on a site just to the north of the existing building. It was designed by local Aberdeen architect William Smith with "amendments" by Prince Albert. The result was an extremely cleverly planned country house formed of two quadrangular blocks, broadly arranged on a diagonal, each with its own courtyard, and a passage linking them together. One block was devoted to the kitchen, household offices, and the ballroom (the only public room); the other provided the family and intimate guests with the privacy they craved.

The royal apartments were ready in time for the fall visit in 1855; the old house was used by the servants until the construction finished the following year, then it was demolished. Finally, a

bridge designed by Isambard Kingdom Brunel was erected over the Dee providing a direct link between Balmoral and the village of Crathie, home to many of the estate workers.

Victoria and Albert's fondness for all things Scottish had a powerful impact on the castle interior. Tartan appeared everywhere: carpets were woven in red Royal Stewart and green Hunting Stewart; curtains and upholstery covers in Dress Stewart. They even designed their own tartans, the Queen creating Victoria tartan, and Albert, Balmoral; both are still used as royal tartans today. The decor was not to everyone's taste: visiting in 1855, the Duchess of Kent's lady-in-waiting, Lady Augusta Bruce, admired many of the ornaments, but felt "a certain absence of harmony of the whole," adding that the tartans were all "highly characteristic and appropriate, but not all equally *flatteux* to the eye." »

Vacation home

The Queen spends about 10 weeks at the castle every year, from August to October, relaxing on horseback in the seclusion of the estate. She occasionally appears at local events: here she is pictured in 1967 at the North of Scotland Gun Dog Association's Open Stake Retriever Trials—held at Balmoral—with trial judge Lord Porchester and head gamekeeper James Gillan.

THE QUEEN FOLLOWING GUN DOG TRIALS IN 1967

ELIZABETH II ON VACATION AT BALMORAL IN 1971

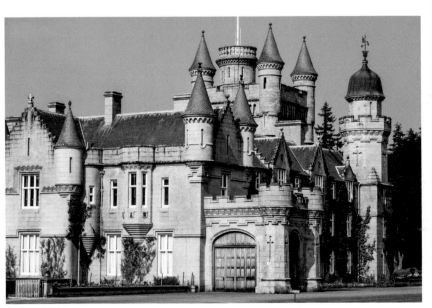

TURRETS AND CRENELLATIONS ARE TYPICAL OF SCOTTISH BARONIAL ARCHITECTURE

Balmoral south front
The walled garden laid out by Queen Mary in the 1920s, complete with monogrammed gates, enhances the castle's fairy-tale setting at the heart of the Cairngorm National Park.

>> Balmorality

An advocate of the benefits of fresh air, Victoria reveled in the freedom of the secluded surroundings, often going for long walks while Albert hunted deer and game. The Queen observed a strict interest in country pursuits. According to Henry Campbell-Bannerman it was just like a convent: "We meet at meals, breakfast at 9:45, lunch 2, dinner 9, and when we have finished each is off to his cell." Czar Nicholas II had hoped

> " The **weather is awful**, rain and wind every day and, on top of it, **no luck at all**—I haven't killed a stag yet."

NICHOLAS II, CZAR OF RUSSIA, IN A LETTER TO HIS MOTHER, 1896

daily routine of walking, answering State correspondence, and writing her diaries that continued after Albert's death, when she spent increasingly long periods at Balmoral. Castle guests were expected to adhere to a similarly rigid timetable—Victoria simply assumed her visitors shared the same

to enjoy some family time with his new wife (Victoria's granddaughter) and infant daughter when they visited Balmoral in 1896; instead he endured long days hunting with the Prince of Wales followed by heavy discussions on European affairs with the Queen and Prime Minister, Lord Salisbury.

Today, the 50,000 acre (20,000 hectares) estate remains the private property of the royal family, who continue to spend summer vacations there. It is a working estate, rich in wildlife, with grouse moors, forest, and farmland, as well as managed herds of Highland cattle, ponies, and deer, but the grounds, gardens, and ballroom are open to visitors at specified times of year. With landscapes ranging from the Dee river valley to lochs and open mountains including seven Munros—hills over 3,000ft (910m)—it is one of the most beautiful parts of Scotland.

Artists in residence

James Giles and James Roberts were two of many artists commissioned by Victoria and Albert to capture interiors and landscapes before and after the new castle was built. Old Balmoral was demolished in 1856; a stone in the lawn marks the position of its front door.

DINING ROOM, OLD BALMORAL (JAMES GILES,1855)

BILLIARD ROOM AND LIBRARY, OLD BALMORAL (JAMES GILES,1855)

PRINCE ALBERT'S SITTING ROOM, OLD BALMORAL (JAMES ROBERTS, c.1860)

Queen Victoria's bedroom, *c.* 1880–1890
Balmoral was intended as a private house, and was
fairly simply furnished. With no one to please but
themselves, Victoria and Albert indulged a passion
for all things tartan—from carpets to tablecloths.

Born 1964

The Earl of Wessex

"I love... **show business.** It's a wonderful **world of fantasy.**"

PRINCE EDWARD, 1987

The Queen's youngest son was born on March 10, 1964, at Buckingham Palace and christened Edward Antony Richard Louis. At the time of his birth he was third in line of succession; he is currently ninth. His first public appearance was at the age of 3 months, when the Queen carried Edward in her arms on the balcony of Buckingham Palace after the Trooping the Colour ceremony.

At the age of 13 Prince Edward went to Gordonstoun school in Scotland, following in his father's and brothers' footsteps. He was elected guardian (head boy) for his last term and left with A-levels in History, English Literature, and Economic and Political Studies. After a gap term spent teaching at a school in Wanganui, New Zealand, he went to Jesus College, Cambridge, to study history—his admission caused some controversy at the time because his grades were below the standard normally required for entry. During his time at Cambridge he acted in and produced a number of student shows.

Real tennis player
Edward took up real tennis at university. Also known as royal tennis, the game is much older than lawn tennis. He met his future wife Sophie at a real tennis charity competition he had organized.

Choice of career

After leaving university in 1986, Prince Edward joined the Royal Marines as a university cadet but dropped out after completing one-third of the grueling 12-month training course. Some in the media criticized his decision to quit, and Prince Philip was said to be

Stage-struck prince
Prince Edward's decision to follow a career in entertainment rather than the army, as was royal tradition, was criticized at the time but it revealed that he had a streak of quiet determination.

furious with Edward for breaking with royal tradition by not following his brothers into the armed services.

Edward opted instead for a career in entertainment, but his first foray plunged him into fresh controversy when he helped stage *The Grand Knockout Tournament*—nicknamed *It's a Royal Knockout*—for charity on British television in June 1987. In the show, four members of the Royal Family— Prince Edward, Princess Anne, and the Duke and Duchess of York—each captained a team of celebrities, urging them on to greater feats in rough-and-tumble games. The press panned the show, and it is remembered as an embarrassment; however, it succeeded in raising over £1 million ($1.5 million) for charity.

Home office
At one time, Ardent Productions was housed in the stable block of Bagshot Park in Surrey, the family home of the Earl and Countess of Wessex.

In January 1988, Buckingham Palace announced that Prince Edward was joining the Really Useful Group, the theater company founded by composer Andrew Lloyd Webber. His job of production assistant was described as being on "the very lowest rung" of the theatrical ladder. Five years later, in 1993, Prince Edward formed Ardent Productions, which produced a number of television documentaries and dramas but failed to make a profit. In 2002, not long after an Ardent film crew was alleged to have invaded

Prince William's privacy during his time at St. Andrews University, Edward left the company to support the Queen during her Golden Jubilee year.

Marriage

In January 1999, Edward announced his engagement to Sophie Rhys-Jones, a public relations executive he had met in 1993. Their wedding on June 19 was a low-key event compared with those of his elder siblings. It was held in St. George's Chapel at Windsor Castle, rather than in Westminster Abbey, and the guest list was much smaller—not even the then Prime Minister Tony Blair was invited. In another break with tradition, the Queen made Edward an earl, rather

than a royal duke, on marriage. Edward's choice of Wessex as his title showed his love of theater—he is said to have borrowed the title from a fictional character in the movie *Shakespeare in Love* (1998).

At first, Sophie, who became Her Royal Highness the Countess of Wessex on marriage, continued to work for her own public relations agency, but she resigned in 2002 to devote more time to her royal duties. She has performed more than 3,250 public engagements since joining the Royal Family. Edward and Sophie frequently travel abroad on behalf of the Queen and the Foreign Office. They made a tour of the Caribbean during the Queen's Diamond Jubilee year, and often act as the Queen's personal representatives at events involving foreign royalty. In recent years, Edward has taken on many of his father's causes and organizations, particularly the Duke of Edinburgh's Award program. It is known that the Queen would like him to succeed to the title of Duke of Edinburgh when it reverts to the Crown in due course.

The couple have two children, Lady Louise Windsor and James, Viscount Severn. Both were born in Frimley Park Hospital, a National Health Service (NHS) hospital. They are styled as the children of an earl, rather than a royal duke, so do not use the HRH style The family home is at Bagshot Park, a royal residence in Surrey that Prince Edward rents from the Crown. A 19th-century palatial country house of Anglo-Indian style, it was once the home of Queen Victoria's son Arthur, the Duke of Connaught.

THE COUNTESS OF WESSEX

SOPHIE RHYS-JONES

Born on January 20, 1965, Sophie Rhys-Jones is the daughter of Christopher and Mary Rhys-Jones. Her father was a businessman and she was brought up in Kent. Upon graduation, she embarked on a career in public relations, working for a time for Capital Radio before launching her own agency, RJH Public Relations, in 1996. She met Prince Edward at a real tennis charity event in 1993. Their relationship began soon afterward, and they were married six years later. In 2001, an undercover reporter recorded her appearing to use her royal status to gain clientele for her agency. This was firmly denied. She is said to get along very well with the Queen.

EDWARD AND SOPHIE WITH THEIR CHILDREN

6
TODAY'S ROYAL FAMILY
2000–PRESENT

TODAY'S ROYAL FAMILY
2000–PRESENT

2000

2003

2006

JANUARY 1, 2000
Queen Elizabeth II officially opens the Millennium Dome in Greenwich, London.

AUGUST 4, 2000
The Queen Mother celebrates her 100th birthday.

» Mug commemorating the Queen Mother's 100th birthday

MARCH 20, 2003
British land troops take part in the US-led coalition invasion of Iraq.

Chapel, Windsor Castle.

JULY 1, 2007
Princes William and Harry host Concert for Diana at Wembley Stadium to mark the forthcoming 10th anniversary of their mother's death.

« Prince William and Prince Harry hosting "Concert for Diana"

SEPTEMBER 21, 2001
The Queen's message— "Grief is the price we pay for love"—is read by the British ambassador to the US, Sir Christopher Meyer, at the prayer service for the 67 British victims of the 9/11 terrorist attack in New York.

APRIL 2002
The Queen Mother's funeral is held on April 9, at Westminster Abbey, followed by burial at St. George's

29 APRIL 2002
The Queen attends dinner with the five living prime ministers who have served under her.

NOVEMBER 2003
A *Daily Mirror* reporter reveals he faked references to obtain a job as footman at Buckingham Palace.

NOVEMBER 8, 2003
Lady Louise Windsor, the daughter of the Earl and Countess of Wessex, is born.

APRIL 9, 2005
Prince Charles and Camilla Parker Bowles are married in a civil ceremony, followed by a service of blessing in St. George's Chapel, Windsor. Camilla becomes the Duchess of Cornwall.

⌄ Family photograph after Prince Charles and Camilla's wedding

MARCH 1, 2006
The Queen opens the Senedd—the debating chamber of the National Assembly for Wales—in Cardiff.

APRIL 2006
Prince Harry is commissioned into the Household Cavalry on April 12. The Queen celebrates her 80th birthday on April 21.

DECEMBER 2007
James, Viscount Severn, son of the Earl and Countess of Wessex, is born on December 17. The Royal Channel, the official channel of the British monarchy goes live on YouTube on December 23.

OCTOBER 7, 2001
Britain joins the US invasion force to drive out the Taliban and expel Al-Qaeda from Afghanistan.

DECEMBER 2001
Lucian Freud's controversial portrait of the Queen is exhibited. It is widely criticized as unflattering.

JUNE 1–4, 2002
The Queen's Golden Jubilee is celebrated with a weekend of events, including "The Party in the Palace" in the Buckingham Palace garden.

⌄ The Queen en route to St. Paul's Cathedral for a Golden Jubilee service

JANUARY 6, 2004
The coroner's inquest into the deaths of Diana and Dodi Al-Fayed opens in London.

JANUARY 8, 2004
The Queen names the *Queen Mary 2*, the first major transatlantic liner built in more than 30 years.

JULY 6, 2004
The Queen opens the Diana Memorial Fountain in Hyde Park, London.

FEBRUARY 9, 2002
Princess Margaret dies peacefully in her sleep at the age of 71.

MARCH 30, 2002
The Queen Mother dies at the age of 101.

JULY 25, 2002
The Queen opens the Commonwealth Games in Manchester.

NOVEMBER 1, 2002
Paul Burrell, former butler to Diana, the Princess of Wales, is cleared of stealing from her estate.

JANUARY 30, 2005
Pictures of Prince Harry wearing a swastika armband to a private costume party appear in the press.

JUNE 23, 2005
Prince William graduates from the University of St. Andrews, Scotland.

DECEMBER 10, 2006
Zara Phillips, the daughter of Princess Anne, is voted BBC Sports Personality of the Year.

DECEMBER 15, 2006
Catherine Middleton attends Prince William's passing out parade at Sandhurst.

MARCH 26, 2008
The Queen welcomes French President Nicolas Sarkozy and his wife, Carla Bruni, on a state visit to the UK.

APRIL 7, 2008
The inquest into the death of Diana records a verdict of accidental death.

The first decade and a half of the 21st century saw public affection for Queen Elizabeth II soar with every milestone she passed—her Golden and Diamond Jubilees were both national celebrations. Her son Charles, the Prince of Wales, married again, and the royal grandchildren began to take center stage, with Prince William and Prince Harry taking on greater responsibilities. Both pursued army careers. The wedding of Prince William and Catherine Middleton in 2011 was a worldwide event, as was the birth of their first son, George, two years later. In 2015, the Queen became the longest-reigning monarch in British history.

2009

2012

2014

JANUARY 2009
Prince William begins training as an RAF helicopter pilot.

SEPTEMBER 2009
The Princes set up their own charitable foundation: Foundation of Prince William and Prince Harry, renamed the Royal Foundation of the Duke and Duchess of Cambridge and Prince Harry in 2011.

FEBRUARY 2011
Prince William makes a special visit to New Zealand following the Christchurch earthquake.

APRIL 29, 2011
Prince William and Catherine Middleton get married in Westminster Abbey.

FEBRUARY 6, 2012
The Queen marks the 60th anniversary of her accession to the throne.

APRIL 1, 2012
The Civil List is replaced by the Sovereign Grant—a single annual government grant.

JUNE 2–5, 2012
The Queen's Diamond Jubilee is celebrated with a pageant of boats on the Thames River and a pop concert outside Buckingham Palace.

« Wedding portrait of William and Catherine with the little attendants

AUGUST 30, 2012
The Queen opens the Paralympic Games in London.

⌄ Commemorative collection for the Queen's Diamond Jubilee

JANUARY 17, 2014
Mia, the daughter of Zara Philips and Mike Tindall, is born.

APRIL 7–23, 2014
The Duke and Duchess of Cambridge tour New Zealand and Australia with Prince George.

OCTOBER 16, 2014
The Queen visits the ceramic poppy installation at the Tower of London remembering the dead of World War I.

OCTOBER 24, 2014
The Queen sends her first tweet.

SEPTEMBER 2012
Prince Harry is deployed to Afghanistan as an Apache copilot gunner.

JUNE 5–7, 2014
The Queen visits France for the 70th anniversary of the D-Day landings.

JULY 23, 2014
The Queen opens the Commonwealth Games in Glasgow.

MAY 2, 2015
Duchess of Cambridge gives birth to her second child, Charlotte.

JUNE 24–26, 2015
The Queen and Duke of Edinburgh make a state visit to Germany.

MAY 11, 2010
After the general election on May 6 results in a hung parliament, David Cameron becomes Prime Minister in a Conservative-Liberal coalition government.

JUNE 15–21, 2010
Princes William and Harry make their first joint tour to southern Africa.

MAY 17–20, 2011
The Queen makes a state visit to Ireland.

JULY 2011
Duke of York relinquishes role as UK Special Representative for Trade and Investment.

JULY 30, 2011
On Zara Phillips marries English rugby player Mike Tindall.

JULY 2012
The Queen officially opens the Summer Olympic Games in London on July 27. Zara Phillips wins a silver medal with the British eventing team on July 31.

APRIL 17, 2013
The Queen and Duke of Edinburgh attend Margaret Thatcher's funeral in St. Paul's Cathedral.

NOVEMBER 16, 2010
Prince William and Catherine Middleton are engaged.

DECEMBER 9, 2010
Student protesters attack a car carrying Prince Charles and the Duchess of Cornwall in London.

DECEMBER 29, 2010
The Queen's first great grandchild, Savannah Phillips, is born.

⌄ Zara Phillips competes in the London 2012 Olympics

JULY 22, 2013
Duchess of Cambridge gives birth to her first son, George.

» Harry and Zara at the Invictus Games

SEPTEMBER 10–14, 2014
The first Invictus Games for wounded soldiers are held in London.

SEPTEMBER 19, 2014
Scotland rejects independence by voting in a referendum.

SEPTEMBER 9, 2015
The Queen becomes the longest reigning monarch in British history.

«

BEFORE

The Duchy was founded in 1337 by Edward III for his eldest son, Edward, the Black Prince, who became the first Duke of Cornwall at just 7 years of age.

THE BLACK PRINCE

As an adult, the Black Prince spent much of his time in France—**fighting to reclaim the French crown** for his father. However, in Cornwall he was considered to be a **benevolent landlord.** When Cornwall and the rest of England were in the grip of the **Black Death,** he **alleviated suffering** by letting his tenants live **rent free,** and commanded that the Duchy animals grazing on Dartmoor be given to the poor.

The Isles of Scilly
The Duchy of Cornwall owns most of the Scilly Isles, and is the archipelago's port authority, based at St. Mary's. Several of its properties are vacation homes, run on environmentally friendly principles.

> " My whole **aim** was to **repair the damage,** to **heal the wounds,** as it were, of the countryside."
>
> PRINCE CHARLES, MAY 2006

The **Duchy** of **Cornwall**

In addition to being the Prince of Wales, Prince Charles is also the Duke of Cornwall. Founded as a source of private income for the heir to the throne, the Duchy of Cornwall's revenues today support the public, private, and charitable activities of Prince Charles and his immediate family.

Although Cornwall is often referred to as "The Duchy," the estate actually includes land throughout the southwest of England – only 13 percent of the estate is in Cornwall. Since it was founded by Edward III, the extent of the estate has varied, as lands were bought and sold. Today the Duchy includes 131,297 acres (53,134 hectares) of land spread over 24 counties. Almost half of the holdings are in Devon, with others in Herefordshire, Somerset, and Wales. The Oval cricket ground in London is also part of the Duchy—dating back to the days when it was a market garden. The Duchy includes arable and livestock farms, residential and commercial properties, forests, rivers, quarries, coastline—and the new town of Poundbury, created in the 1990s.

Many of the Duchy's holdings and laws date back to the medieval era – indeed, some have their origin in ancient Celtic and Anglo-Saxon law—prompting accusations of anachronistic feudalism. The Duchy has the right of *bona vacantia*—a right to the estates of anyone in Cornwall who dies without a will or surviving relatives. This is paid into a charitable account that funds environmental and community projects. It also has the right to appoint the county's High Sheriff, is the port authority for the Isles of Scilly, and owns about three-fifths of the Cornish foreshore. The Duke has "right of wreck" on all ships wrecked on Cornish shores, as well as to any "royal fish," such as whales, porpoises, and sturgeon, washed up on its beaches.

The origins of the Duchy
In Saxon times, Cornwall and Wales were not ruled by England—indeed King Athelstan (see p.12) set the English border along the Tamar River—and their independence survived the Norman Conquest. William the Conqueror's half-brother, Robert of Mortain acquired Cornwall in 1072, and the Domesday Book, compiled 14 years later, shows that Cornish landowners owed allegiance only to Mortain, not, as in the rest of the country, to the King.

Educating the next duke
Prince William and Prince Charles check on their rare-breed Ayrshire dairy cattle on the Highgrove estate. Prince William will inherit the Duchy of Cornwall when his father accedes to the throne.

When in 1337, Edward III created the Duchy of Cornwall for his son, the Black Prince, and for all future "first-begotten" sons and "heirs apparent to the kingdom of England," its charter renounced the King's rights to tax revenues within the Duchy, and stated that royal ministers, sheriffs, or bailiffs had no right to enter the territory. Although Prince Charles has volunteered to pay income tax (see p.235), the Duchy estate is not subject to corporation tax on the grounds that it is a private estate; the Duchy retains the right to appoint a High Sheriff; and although the first-born child of a monarch—whether girl or boy—will inherit the throne, a woman cannot inherit the Duchy of Cornwall. If the monarch has no male children, the rights and responsibilities of the Duchy belong to the Crown and there is no Duke.

The Duchy today
Prince Charles is the longest-ever serving Duke of Cornwall, having inherited the Duchy of Cornwall on the death of King George VI in 1952. He became the 24th Duke of Cornwall at just 4 years old on the Queen's accession to the throne. In 1969, at the age of 21, he became responsible

for the managing of the Duchy—and entitled to its income.

The Duchy of Cornwall's portfolio of land and property is valued at £763 million ($1.1 billion). In 2013 the Duchy generated £28.8 million ($43.2 million),

205 The total extent of lands in square miles (531 sq kilometers) held by the Duchy of Cornwall.

and Charles received an income of £19 million ($28.5 million)—up 4 percent on the previous year. The Prince pays income tax on the money left after costs—around £9.2 million ($13.8 million) in 2013—so his tax bill was £4.4 million ($6.6 million). The vestiges of the ancient laws defining the Duchy mean that only the Royal Family, its advisors, and HM Revenue and Customs currently know what the Prince claims as his expenses before tax.

Prince Charles has silenced some critics by offering to pay tax, but the demand for more transparency continues. Labour MP Margaret Hodge, chairing the House of Commons Public Accounts Committee, said, "The Duchy enjoys an exemption from paying tax even though it engages in a range of commercial activities. This tax exemption may give it an unfair advantage over its competitors who do pay corporation and capital gains tax." There have consequently been calls for the Duchy's centuries-old charter, which confers it its tax-exempt status, to be reformed.

Sustainable farming

The Duchy of Cornwall has given Prince Charles the opportunity to put his passions for sustainable agriculture and organic farming into practice. The Duchy Home Farm, in the grounds of Highgrove House, has been entirely organic since 1985, making the Prince

a pioneer in the field. Managed hands-on by Prince Charles, the estate has been built and is run on the philosophy that commercial success can be balanced with environmental and social responsibility. The commercial success has been huge—with the Duchy's income doubling between 2012 and 2013. One success story is the Duchy Originals brand—set up in 1990 to market its produce. Now owned by Waitrose, a chain of British supermarkets, the brand is known as Duchy Originals from Waitrose. It pays royalties of around £1 million ($1.5 million) each year back to the Prince's Charitable Foundation.

Home Farm is the Duchy's flagship, playing an important role in preserving rare indigenous breeds such as Tamworth pigs, Irish Moiled, Gloucester, Shetland and British White cattle, as well as Hebridean and Shropshire sheep. When British farmers complained about how hard it was to sell mature sheep, Prince Charles headed the Mutton Renaissance campaign, to encourage British families to eat more mutton.

The Duchy includes many areas of outstanding natural beauty and gives much support to conservation projects. It makes regular contributions to projects such as the Fishing for Litter initiative, which encourages fishermen to bring ashore litter caught in their nets at sea. It also works with English Heritage to manage the

New Highgrove Farm shop
Prince Charles and the Duchess of Cornwall opening the new Highgrove Farm Shop on the High Street, Tetbury. The shop sells gifts inspired by Highgrove or made from organic produce cultivated on the estates and farms of the Duchy of Cornwall.

Visit to Waitrose store
Prince Charles and the Duchess of Cornwall visited the Waitrose store in Belgravia, London, on September 10, 2009. Duchy Originals was set up by Prince Charles to promote sustainable organic food and to raise money for his charities.

many ancient and historical sites and monuments on its lands. The Duchy also owns most of the land, and almost one-third of the residential buildings on the Scilly Isles, where it promotes sustainable tourism. It even has its own environmentally friendly vacation cottages on the islands, in Cornwall, and also in Wales.

The future of the Duchy
The Duchy has also given Prince Charles the opportunity to put into practice the architectural and social theories in his book, *A Vision of Britain*. In 1994 the Duchy created Poundbury, an experimental new town outside Dorchester. With houses built in a mix of traditional and classical styles, the town was designed as a "walkable community," with stores, leisure facilities, and residential areas integrated, rather than segregated as they are in many modern towns and cities. The Duchy has undertaken similar projects in Truro and Newquay, while in Kennington, London—where it has owned land since

Oat biscuit with the Duchy crest
Oat biscuits are part of a brand of organic food sold in Waitrose stores in Britain. The Duchy Originals company was set up by Prince Charles in 1990.

When Prince Charles accedes to the throne, the Duchy of Cornwall will pass to Prince William.

DUCHY OF LANCASTER
As **King,** Charles will become **Duke of Lancaster** in succession to the Queen. Similar to the Duchy of Cornwall, the Duchy of Lancaster is **held in trust** for a Royal Family member, in this case the Sovereign. **Revenues** from its properties **provide** his or her **main source of income.**

THE FUTURE DUKE
Prince Charles has already taken measures to **prepare Prince William** to take over the Duchy of Cornwall. Since 2011, Prince William has attended the twice-yearly meetings of the **Prince's Council,** which controls the Duchy. According to a Clarence House spokesman, William"… has been learning about the Duchy for a number of years with a view to getting a greater understanding of how it all works."

1337—rents on its properties have been frozen to make them affordable for elderly tenants. The Duchy—a complex mix of arcane ancient tradition and contemporary ecological and social responsibility—will likely to continue to cause controversy, but the commitment of Prince Charles to his estate remains unquestionable.

> "I have **tried to break** conventional **molds** because **I think** they are **mistaken.**"
>
> PRINCE CHARLES, MAY 2006

« BEFORE

As the Queen Mother became celebrated for her longevity, well-wishers would gather outside Clarence House every year on August 4, her birthday, to congratulate her.

100TH BIRTHDAY
More than **40,000 people were in the Mall** on the Queen Mother's 100th birthday in 2000 to greet her as she stepped out onto the balcony of Buckingham Palace, accompanied by her daughters. That morning, the Queen, following her practice of congratulating all centenarians on their birthday, had a handwritten telegram delivered to Clarence House, the Queen Mother's residence. The Queen Mother was **one of 12 centenarians celebrating their birthdays that day.**

Other 100th birthday celebrations for the Queen Mother included a lunch at Guildhall, London, on June 27. A pageant in her honor was held at Horse Guards Parade on July 19. It included marching bands, carnival floats, choirs, racehorses, Aberdeen Angus bulls, and even camels. The Queen Mother, accompanied by Prince Charles, arrived at the pageant in an open carriage. At the end of the hour-long festivities, she thanked all who had attended, saying the **parade had been "a great joy" to her.**

Mother and daughters
This portrait of the Queen Mother with the Queen and Princess Margaret was taken by celebrated fashion and portrait photographer Norman Parkinson for the Queen Mother's 80th birthday in 1980.

Two Royal Farewells

The year 2002—the 50th of her reign—began on a sad note for Her Majesty the Queen. Within the space of eight weeks she lost her sister, Princess Margaret, on February 9, followed by her mother, the Queen Mother, on March 30, at the age of 101.

Princess Margaret, four years younger than Queen Elizabeth II, died while hospitalized at the age of 71. She had been ill for many years and had suffered the first of a series of strokes in 1998. To those born after 1960, Princess Margaret seemed like a remote figure, but an older generation remembered the young princess of the 1950s who loved nightclubs and the theater. In the light of recent royal divorces and scandal, it was now hard to believe she had been prevented from marrying the man she loved, Captain Peter Townsend, because he was divorced (see pp.154–55). Margaret's subsequent marriage to the successful

photographer Antony Armstrong-Jones (Lord Snowdon), their stormy relationship and divorce, and gossip about her private life dominated the newspaper headlines in the 1960s and 1970s. Margaret had sometimes seemed bored by her royal duties and was judged by some to have been haughty and extravagant, but she was always unfailing in her loyalty to her sister. Despite their different lifestyles, she and the Queen remained very close.

Margaret's funeral
Princess Margaret's funeral service was held at St. George's Chapel, Windsor, on February 15, which was also the

50th anniversary of the burial of her father, King George VI. The mourners were headed by the Queen and Prince Philip, and by Princess Margaret's children, Viscount Linley and Lady Sarah Chatto, and Lord Snowdon, her former husband. The Queen Mother, who had had a chest infection since Christmas, attended the service in a wheelchair, having been flown by helicopter from Sandringham the day before. Princess Margaret had planned many details of the funeral herself, including the choice of hymns, and had also requested that her body be cremated. After the service, her coffin was driven by hearse to Slough

Centennial menu
The roundels on the menu for the Queen Mother's centennial lunch show four places connected with her life (clockwise from top left): Clarence House, Royal Lodge, Glamis Castle, and the Castle of Mey.

"My mother... had an infectious zest for living."

FROM THE QUEEN'S TRIBUTE, APRIL 5, 2002

municipal crematorium, and her ashes were later returned to St. George's Chapel for interment in the Royal Vault.

Death of the Queen Mother

After attending the funeral of Princess Margaret, the Queen Mother returned to the Royal Lodge, Windsor, her country residence since 1931. Her health steadily deteriorated, and she died peacefully in her sleep at 3:15 p.m. on March 30, with Queen Elizabeth II at her bedside. She was 101 years old. Prince Charles, her eldest grandson to whom she was particularly close, immediately returned to England from Klosters in Switzerland, where he was on a skiing trip with Princes William and Harry.

On hearing the news of her death, crowds immediately began to gather outside Buckingham Palace and Clarence House, the Queen Mother's London home. Although the Queen Mother's death could by no means be described as unexpected, she was nevertheless deeply mourned. Born in 1900, she represented continuity throughout a century of change. Her popularity with the public, forged in the days of World War II (see pp.102–103), remained as strong as ever, and she was loved and admired by millions for her good spirit, ready smile, and devotion to duty. Her last official engagement had been on 22 November, only four months before her death, when she was guest of honor at the recommissioning ceremony of the aircraft carrier HMS *Ark Royal*. As

Famous for her hats
The portrait on this 100th birthday commemorative mug shows the Queen Mother wearing one of the broad-brimmed feathered hats for which she was famous.

tributes to the Queen Mother poured in from members of the public as well as national and international leaders, books of condolence were opened at locations including St. James's Palace, the Palace of Holyroodhouse in Edinburgh, and Windsor Castle.

Lying-in-state and funeral

On Friday, April 5, the Queen Mother's coffin was borne on a gun carriage in a solemn procession from St. James's Palace to Westminster Hall, where it would lie-in-state for four days until the funeral. Fifty years earlier, King George VI had also lain in state in Westminster Hall, the medieval hall that is the oldest part of the Palace of Westminster.

Fourteen members of the royal family walked behind the coffin. In a break with precedent (traditionally it was only men who followed the coffin), Princess Anne, the Princess Royal, was among their number. The Queen attended a short service as the coffin, draped with the Queen Mother's personal Royal Standard and bearing the crown she had worn for George VI's coronation in 1937, was placed on a 7ft- (2m-)

Silent vigil
Wearing the dress uniform of a Rear Admiral, Prince Charles mounts guard at a corner of the Queen Mother's catafalque. Her three other grandsons stood at the other corners in a shared moment of solemn tribute.

high catafalque (coffin support) in the hall. Over the next three days, more than 200,000 people filed past the catafalque to pay their last respects, where soldiers stood guard at each corner throughout the vigil. On the eve of her funeral, the Queen Mother's four grandsons—the Prince of Wales, the Duke of York, the Earl of Wessex, and Viscount Linley—mounted the guard as a mark of mourning and respect.

On the eve of the funeral, the Queen made a televised speech in which she paid tribute to her mother's "resolve, dedication, and enthusiasm for life." Before the start of the funeral service on April 9, the tenor bell of Westminster Abbey tolled 101 times for every year of the Queen Mother's life, and her coffin was carried from Westminster Hall to the Great West Door of the Abbey to the sound of 128 pipers. Over a million people crowded the area outside the Abbey and the surrounding streets, as more than 2,100 mourners, including 35 members of the British Royal Family and representatives from 25 foreign royal families, attended the 55-minute-long service, which

included two of the Queen Mother's favorite hymns, "Immortal, invisible, God only wise," and "Guide me, O thou great Redeemer."

After the service, as her coffin started on its final journey to Windsor Castle, the Royal Air Force Battle of Britain Memorial Flight of vintage Spitfires, Hurricanes, a Dakota, and a Lancaster flew over Buckingham Palace and the Mall. Large crowds lined the 23-mile (37-km) route. Later that day, in a private service of committal, the Queen Mother's body was interred next to that of her husband in the black marble vault of the George VI Memorial Chapel in the north aisle of St. George's Chapel. The ashes of Princess Margaret were placed with them.

Gun salute
Gunners of the 105 Royal Artillery Regiment fire a 41-gun salute from the walls of Stirling Castle in Scotland to honor the Queen Mother. Similar gun salutes were sounded in several other cities in the UK.

AFTER

After the Queen Mother's death, **Prince Charles moved into Clarence House, her former London home, and Prince Andrew into the Royal Lodge at Windsor.**

WORKS OF ART
The Queen Mother left her entire **estate to the Queen,** her only surviving daughter. She had previously established a **trust fund for her great-grandchildren.** Reported to be worth an estimated £70 million ($110 million), the Queen Mother's fortune came mainly from paintings, china, jewelry, and other works of art, including a valuable Fabergé collection. These now form part of the Royal Collection, and many can be seen on display in the Queen's Gallery.

MEMORIAL STATUE
In 2009, a 9½-ft- (3-m-) high **bronze statue of the Queen Mother** was unveiled beside the statue of King George VI on the steps overlooking the Mall. The statue, which cost £2 million ($3.2 million), was paid for from the sales of the £5 ($11) coin issued to celebrate the Queen's 80th birthday in 2006.

The Golden Jubilee

Millions of people throughout the UK and the Commonwealth joined in celebrating the Queen's Golden Jubilee in 2002. During the year-long commemorations the Queen and Prince Philip traveled more than 40,000 miles (nearly 64,000 km) to all parts of the globe.

The Queen wanted to celebrate her Golden Jubilee year by visiting and being seen by as many of her subjects as possible—at home and around the world—to thank them for their support and loyalty during the 50 years of her reign. Although the death of Princess Margaret in February and that of the Queen Mother in March (see pp.258–59), coming so close to the 50th anniversary of the Queen's accession on February 6, 2002, cast a deep shadow over the start of the celebrations, the Queen went ahead with the program as planned. Just nine days after the death of her sister, she was welcomed to Jamaica as its Queen, and over the course of the next few months she and Prince Philip would make extensive tours of New Zealand, Australia, and Canada.

Between May and August, the Queen visited more than 70 cities and towns in all four countries of the United Kingdom, and took part in scores of "meet the people" tours. The predictions made by several British newspapers that the Golden Jubilee

« BEFORE

Vast numbers of those taking part in the Golden Jubilee celebrations were too young to remember the Queen's Silver Jubilee, or had been born after it.

TWENTY-FIVE YEARS BEFORE

The Golden Jubilee commemorations reprised many elements of the **Silver Jubilee « 182–83,** most notably the ceremonial procession in the **Gold State Coach** from **Buckingham Palace** to **St. Paul's Cathedral** for the national service of thanksgiving. The nation in 1977 was in festive mood, and street parties were very much a theme of the earlier celebrations. **Millions greeted the Queen,** who made several appearances on the balcony of Buckingham Palace. There was a **Royal Progress by boat along the Thames River** and a **fireworks display.** But worldwide television was not yet the phenomenon it became by 2002, and nothing was organized quite on the scale of the two Palace music events.

Wave of affection
The Queen waves to the crowds as she rides to the service of thanksgiving at St. Paul's Cathedral. She is said to have been amazed by the vast numbers who turned out to see her.

would turn out to be a flop as the public had lost its enthusiasm for royal events proved to be very wide of the mark.

Golden Jubilee weekend

Thousands of adults and children took part in the celebrations organized in London over the Golden Jubilee weekend at the beginning of June, and millions more watched on television. Among the highlights of the weekend's events were two concerts in the gardens of Buckingham Palace. The "Prom in the Palace" on June 1, attended by 12,500 guests, featured classical music performed by the BBC Symphony Orchestra and the BBC Symphony Choir. The "Party at the Palace" on June 3 showcased 50 years of British pop, and was led by Brian May, guitarist in the rock band Queen, playing his arrangement of "God Save the Queen" from the roof of the Palace. The concert, which included performances by Paul McCartney, Eric Clapton, Cliff Richard, and Tony Bennett, attracted over 200 million viewers around the world and was particularly enjoyed by the younger members of the Royal Family. Between two Paul McCartney numbers, the Queen lit the National Beacon in front of the Queen Victoria Memorial in the Mall. It formed part

of a chain of more than 2,000 beacons lit throughout British territories and Commonwealth countries around the world and covering the length and breadth of the United Kingdom.

Jubilee Day

On Monday, June 4, the Queen rode in the Gold State Coach in a procession from Buckingham Palace to St. Paul's Cathedral for a national service of thanksgiving led by the Archbishop of Canterbury. Leaders of the Roman Catholic and Methodist churches, the Church in Wales, and the Church of Scotland also took part, as did representative leaders from the Commonwealth.

After a luncheon in the Guildhall hosted by the Lord Mayor of London, the Queen and Royal

Commemorative plate
This blue-and-white Wedgwood plate was one of many commemorative items produced to celebrate the Queen's Golden Jubilee.

Royal salute

Concorde and the Red Arrows bring up the rear of the 22 km- (14 mile-) long flypast over the Mall and Buckingham Palace that brought the Jubilee Day celebrations to a close.

As part of her Golden Jubilee celebrations the Queen founded the Queen's Award for Voluntary Service (originally known as the Queen's Golden Jubilee Award).

HELPING THE COMMUNITY

The Queen's Award for Voluntary Service is given for **outstanding achievement by groups of volunteers** who regularly give up their time to helping others in the community, improving the quality of life and opportunity for others, and providing an outstanding service. **The first awards were given in 2003.** The Cabinet Office announces the names of the winning groups on June 2 each year, the **anniversary of the Queen's coronation.** Examples of the kind of service recognized include such things as providing support to victims of crime, driving cars for the elderly, or organizing community sport projects.

Family returned to Buckingham Palace for the Jubilee Parade involving more than 20,000 people. Numerous floats illustrating aspects of British life in the 50 years since the Queen's accession paraded down the Mall and in front of the Palace. Later, an ocean of people, nearly all of them waving Union Jacks, packed the entire length of the Mall to cheer the Queen and the Royal Family as they appeared on the balcony of Buckingham Palace at the end of the day's celebr.ations.

People held their own street parties and events to celebrate the Jubilee, including a cricket match played on sea ice by members of the British Antarctic Survey. In New York, the Empire State Building was lit up in purple and gold on the evening of June 4 in honor of the Queen—a rare compliment to an overseas figure.

Back to School

Prince William and his fiancée Catherine Middleton returned to the University of St. Andrews in Scotland, where they had met as students 10 years earlier, to launch the university's 600th anniversary commemorations. It was fitting that one of their first official engagements together was at the place where their romance began.

William and Catherine first met in September 2001 as students at St. Andrews University, on the east coast of Scotland. St. Andrews, home to the world-famous Royal and Ancient Golf Club, founded in 1764, is a small seaside town. Its university, the oldest in Scotland, has 6,000 undergraduates, who wear a distinctive red gown. William and Catherine lived in St. Salvator's Hall (affectionately known as Sallies), the university's oldest hall of residence, during their first year. Both were studying for an honors degree in the History of Art, though William later switched to Geography.

While at university, William had reached an agreement with the media that once he had given them an interview and a photo opportunity, they would leave him alone to lead a normal student life. He enjoyed shopping in the local supermarket and going out to student pubs and bars. William captained the collegiate water polo team and represented the Scottish national universities at the Celtic Nations tournament in 2004.

Catherine is said to have caught William's eye when she was modeling at a student fashion show early in their first year of studies. They shared an apartment in the center of St. Andrews with two friends during their second year, and moved into a cottage a little way outside the town for their final year. Both graduated on the same day: June 23, 2005.

Speculation that the couple were about to get engaged intensified around the time of Catherine's 25th birthday in January 2007, and caused them to split up for a time. They eventually got engaged in October 2010 while on vacation in Kenya.

"It feels like coming home."

PRINCE WILLIAM, AT THE LAUNCH OF ST. ANDREWS'S 600TH ANNIVERSARY CAMPAIGN, FEBRUARY 25, 2011

First official visit as a royal couple
Wearing a scarlet coat to match the scarlet gowns worn by St. Andrews's undergraduate students, Catherine waves to a crowd of well-wishers. During their visit, the engaged couple unveiled a plaque to mark the launch of the university's 600th anniversary.

BEFORE

Following the death of Diana, Camilla was rarely seen in public. The campaign to rehabilitate public perception of her as Charles's chosen companion was carefully managed.

STEP BY STEP

Charles and Camilla's **first appearance as a couple** was at the 50th birthday party for her sister Annabel at the Ritz Hotel, London.

The press had been informed that the Prince would be present, and 200 photographers were on hand to record them leaving the event. In 2002, in her capacity as President of the National Osteoporosis Society, **Camilla greeted Charles with a kiss**—their first in public—as he arrived at a reception for the charity. Much was made of **her commitment to raising awareness of osteoporosis,** a disease that had affected her mother and grandmother, as part of the campaign to boost her public profile.

CHARLES AND CAMILLA LEAVE THE RITZ

The Marriage of Charles and Camilla

More than 30 years after their romance first began, a decade after their affair was first made public, and nearly eight years after Diana's death, the Prince of Wales and Camilla Parker Bowles finally became husband and wife on April 9, 2005.

Clarence House announced the engagement of the Prince of Wales and Camilla Parker Bowles on February 10, 2005. Charles gave his bride-to-be a ring belonging to his grandmother Queen Elizabeth the Queen Mother, as an engagement ring. The Queen immediately issued a statement expressing her and Prince Philip's good wishes for the couple's future, and Princes William and Harry were said to be delighted.

Following his divorce, Prince Charles had publicly said that his relationship with Camilla Parker Bowles was "non-negotiable," but Diana's popularity, and the swell of emotion after her death, had made it hard for him to win the public over to his side. Press opinion was uniformly hostile to the woman it blamed for causing Diana's unhappiness.

In 2000 the Queen met Camilla for the first time since the relationship had became known. This was seen as a sign that she had come to accept Camilla, who was invited to sit in the royal box at the 2002 Golden Jubilee celebrations. Camilla moved into Clarence House when it became Charles's household and official residence in 2003, though she kept (and still keeps) her own house in Wiltshire. The climate of opinion had gradually changed, making it possible for the couple to legitimize their relationship.

Constitutional questions

Camilla's divorced status raised potential constitutional difficulties in view of Charles's future rule as Supreme Governor of the Church of England, and aroused memories of the

arrangements for the remarriage were consistent with the Church of England guidelines, "which the Prince of Wales fully accepts as a committed Anglican and as prospective Supreme Governor of the Church of England." Some constitutionalists argued that the heir to the throne could not legally be married in a civil ceremony, but the Lord Chancellor, Lord Falconer, made it clear in a statement to the House of Lords on February 24 that the Human Rights Act of 1998 superseded any laws concerning royal marriages.

Two ceremonies

The marriage had originally been set for April 8, but was postponed for one day, so that Charles could represent the Queen at the funeral of Pope John

> ## "The Duke of Edinburgh and I are **very happy** that the Prince of Wales and Mrs. Parker Bowles are to **marry.**"
>
> QUEEN ELIZABETH II, IN A STATEMENT ISSUED BY BUCKINGHAM PALACE

abdication crisis of Edward VIII in 1936 (see pp.92–93). A traditional Church of England wedding service was ruled out because Camilla was a divorcée with a husband still living; although Charles had been divorced, his first wife was no longer alive and so he was a widower in the eyes of the Church. It was decided that the couple would have a civil wedding at the Windsor Guildhall, the nearest register office to Windsor Castle, followed by a service of blessing in St. George's Chapel, Windsor. The Archbishop of Canterbury, Dr Rowan Williams, issued a statement saying that the

Highland Games

Charles and Camilla are seen here in relaxed mood at the Caithness Highland Games in Scotland in August 2003. By now the public was becoming used to seeing them together.

Paul II. A crowd of more than 20,000 people greeted the couple as they arrived for their private register office wedding at 12:30 p.m. It took place in front of a small group of family guests, who were driven from Windsor Castle to the Guildhall in a hired minibus. The guests did not include the Queen and Duke of Edinburgh—the Queen had earlier announced her decision not to attend on the grounds that the couple wanted to keep it low-key and her presence would not allow that to happen. The legal witnesses to the marriage were Prince William and Tom Parker Bowles, Camilla's son.

The bride wore a cream-colored dress and coat with a wide-brimmed, cream-colored hat for the civil ceremony. She changed into a blue and gold silk coat and dress with a gold headdress for the televised service of blessing in

Family portrait

In this official wedding portrait, the newly wed royal couple is seen with the Royal Family (left) and Camilla's father Major Bruce Shand and her children Tom and Laura (right).

St. George's Chapel, which was attended by the Queen and Prince Philip. Other guests included Charles's biographer Jonathan Dimbleby, broadcaster Sir David Frost, and actors Kenneth Branagh and Joanna Lumley.

Charles and Camilla entered the chapel arm-in-arm and stood facing the Archbishop of Canterbury to reaffirm their vows. Afterward they walked around and chatted with the crowd gathered outside the chapel before returning to the State Apartments at Windsor Castle for a reception hosted by the Queen. In a speech at the reception, Elizabeth

said how very proud she was of her son who "despite Becher's Brook and The Chair [a reference to the Grand National steeplechase being run that same day] and all kinds of other terrible obstacles… has come through."

Duchess of Cornwall

Camilla became Her Royal Highness the Duchess of Cornwall (the Duchess of Rothesay in Scotland) on her marriage instead of the Princess of Wales. This was out of deference to public opinion, which still associated Diana with the title. For similar reasons it was announced that Camilla would become Princess Consort on Charles's accession rather than Queen Camilla. An opinion poll taken at the time found that while 65 percent of people were in favor of the marriage, only 7 percent thought that Camilla should eventually become queen.

Grand Cross of the Royal Victorian Order

The Queen created Camilla a Dame Grand Cross of the Royal Victorian Order in 2012. Admission to the Order is in the Queen's personal gift, and is given in recognition of distinguished personal service and as a sign of her affection and trust.

Camilla has taken on significant new duties in recent years and played a prominent part in the Diamond Jubilee celebrations in 2012.

The Duchess made her **first overseas tour** with Charles a few months after their wedding, when they visited the US in November and met with President George W. Bush in the White House. She attended the **Trooping the Color** in London, in June 2005, making her first appearance on the balcony of Buckingham Palace.

In December 2010 **students protesting against increased tuition fees** and cuts in further education surrounded the car in which Prince Charles and Camilla were traveling along Regent Street on their way to the Royal Variety Show.

FUTURE QUEEN CONSORT?

As the Prince of Wales took on more of the Queen's public duties, Camilla appeared more frequently at State events. On May 8, 2013,

she attended the **State Opening of Parliament** for the first time. Dressed in full regalia, she sat beside Charles at the side of the throne as the Queen addressed Parliament. This was taken by many as a sign that she was being seen as a future Queen Consort. According to a poll conducted in 2015, 49 percent of people now believed Camilla should become Queen Consort upon Charles's eventual accession to the throne.

CAMILLA IN REGAL DRESS, 2013

The **Diamond Wedding**

Another milestone was passed when the Queen became the first monarch in British history to celebrate 60 years of marriage. She and Prince Philip were married in 1947 at a time of austerity in Britain. Sixty years later they came together to Westminster Abbey to renew their wedding vows in a special service of celebration.

The service took place on November 19, the day before the actual wedding anniversary. It was attended by more than 30 members of the Royal Family and 2,000 guests. Among them were five choristers who had sung in the Westminster Abbey choir in 1947 and 10 couples who had married on the same day. The service included psalms and hymns chosen by the couple for their wedding, and during the prayers the Archbishop of Canterbury, Dr. Rowan Williams, asked the Queen and Duke of Edinburgh "to renew in your hearts promises you made to one another." Prince William gave a reading from the Bible, and the Oscar-winning actress Dame Judi Dench read a poem specially written for the occasion by the Poet Laureate Andrew Motion. Afterward the Queen and Duke chatted with some of the waiting crowds in Parliament Square.

The day before the service, the couple revisited Broadlands, the former home of the late Lord Mountbatten where they had spent their honeymoon 60 years before. Then on November 20, the day of their wedding anniversary, the Queen and Duke of Edinburgh flew to the Mediterranean island of Malta where they had lived from 1949 to 1951, when Prince Philip was serving in the Royal Navy. The Queen is known to have especially fond memories of her years on the island. It was the only period of their marriage when she and Philip were able to enjoy a relatively normal life away from the "full light of publicity… and the pressure this brings." These were the words used by the Archbishop of Canterbury the day before in thanking the couple for the public character of their 60 years of service and dedication to the country and the Commonwealth.

> **"Some couples** have to **live** more than others in the **full light of publicity."**
>
> DR. ROWAN WILLIAMS, SERMON, NOVEMBER 19, 2007

Happy memories
As part of their Diamond Wedding celebrations the Queen and Duke of Edinburgh revisited Broadlands, the house where they spent their honeymoon. This photograph of the couple was taken while they were walking in the grounds together, remembering old times.

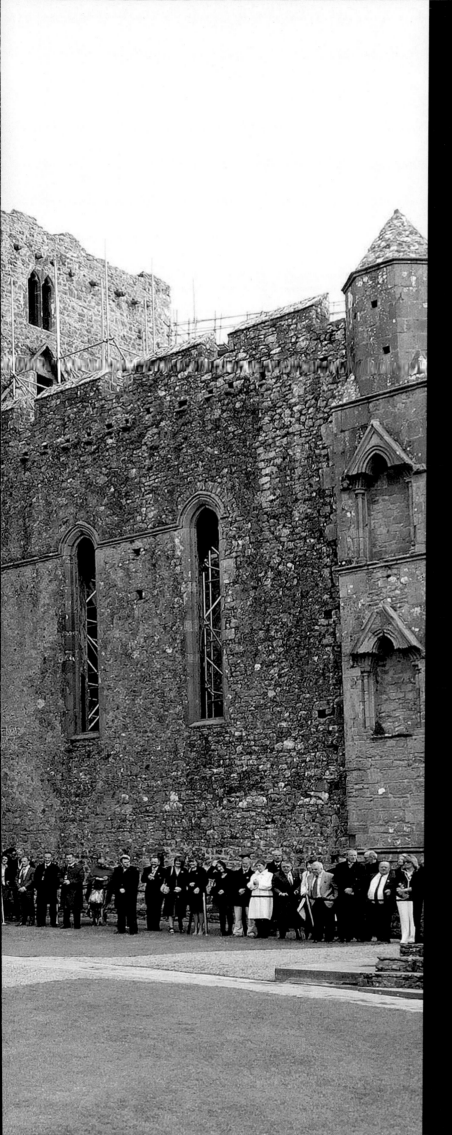

State Visit to Ireland

The Queen's state visit to the Republic of Ireland, made at the invitation of its President, Mary McAleese, was the first by a British monarch since 1911. It marked a historic turning point in the troubled relations between the United Kingdom and the Republic of Ireland.

The last British monarch to visit Ireland was the Queen's grandfather, George V, when the whole of Ireland was still part of the United Kingdom. Since then, the two countries had been divided by a long history of hostilities stemming from the Easter Rising of 1916, the bloody struggle for Irish independence, and the subsequent bitter conflict over the island's partition into the Irish Free State (later the Republic of Ireland) and Northern Ireland, which remains part of the United Kingdom. The signing of the Good Friday Agreement in 1998, by which the Republic gave up its territorial claim to Northern Ireland, helped to pave the way for the royal visit, which was seen as a symbol of reconciliation.

Dublin was on full security alert throughout the Queen's visit. On the first day, Elizabeth laid a wreath in the Garden of Remembrance, which was dedicated to the memory of "all those who gave their lives in the cause of Irish freedom." She visited Croke Park, where British troops had fired on Irish civilians at a Gaelic football match in 1920. Speaking later that evening at a state banquet in Dublin Castle, the Queen delighted her audience by beginning in Irish, a notoriously difficult language: "A Uachtarain agus a chairde" (President and friends). On hearing this, Mary McAleese was seen to mouth "Wow." The Queen spoke feelingly of the troubled past and the building of bridges to a better future. Her mention of the personal pain suffered by those who had lost family members was a clear reference to the murder of her cousin, Lord Mountbatten, by the Irish Republican Army (IRA) in 1979 (see pp.192–93).

"With the **benefit** of **historical hindsight** we can all see things we would wish had been **done differently,** or **not at all.**"

QUEEN ELIZABETH II, AT THE STATE BANQUET IN DUBLIN CASTLE, MAY 18, 2011

Coat of emerald green
The Queen wears Irish green for a tour of the historic Rock of Cashel in County Tipperary. Coming at the end of her visit, this was a more relaxed day, giving her time to visit the famous Coolmore Stud for racehorses.

« BEFORE

William is the fourth pilot in the Royal Family, following in the footsteps of his grandfather, his father, and his uncle, the Duke of York.

LIKE FATHER, LIKE SON

William owes his **passion for flying** to his father. Prince Charles had already earned his **private pilot's license** when he flew himself to RAF Cranwell in 1971 to start advanced training as a jet pilot. Three years later, he trained as a helicopter pilot with the **Royal Navy** at Yeovilton in 1974. He frequently took the controls when flying on aircraft belonging to the Queen's Flight—a unit that until 1995 operated aircraft for the transportation of members of the Royal Family.

4-YEAR-OLD WILLIAM STEPS OUT OF A HELICOPTER

FALKLANDS STORIES

Andrew, the Duke of York, then second in line to the throne, served as a **Sea King helicopter copilot** on board HMS *Invincible* during the **Falklands War.** He would have inspired William with stories of how he lured Argentinian Exocet missiles away from the ships of the British Task Force « 216–17.

The **Pilot Prince**

Flying is in the royal blood. William earned his pilot's badge, the RAF wings, during his time in the military. He went on to become a dedicated Search and Rescue (SAR) pilot. On leaving the armed forces, he planned to continue flying helicopters alongside his royal duties.

In 2007, the Ministry of Defence announced that William was to serve a four-month tour of duty with the Royal Air Force (RAF). Lieutenant Wales, as he was known in the army, had recently completed a training course as a troop commander in an armored reconnaissance unit. He had signed up for a three-year army commission, but once it became clear he would not be allowed to see frontline action in Afghanistan, it was decided he should spend time experiencing life in the other two services (the RAF and the Royal Navy). Time with the RAF would allow him to realize his lifetime ambition of learning to fly, and familiarize him with the use of modern air power.

William underwent an intensive 12-week course learning to pilot helicopters and fixed-wing aircraft at Cranwell, the RAF's flying college in Lincolnshire. After eight and a half hours' flying time, he made his first solo flight. "It was an amazing feeling," he said afterward. On April 11, 2008, Prince Charles, who had trained at Cranwell in the 1970s, presented William with his RAF wings. At the

end of his stint, William even made it to the frontline when he flew (though not at the controls) in a C-17 Globemaster military transport plane on a 30-hour round trip to Kandahar air base in Afghanistan to repatriate the body of a fallen soldier. The news broke after his return to RAF Lyneham in Wiltshire; he said he was "deeply honored" to have been part of the crew that brought the body home.

William also served a short attachment to the Royal Navy. While deployed on HMS *Iron Duke* in the Caribbean, he took part in a joint operation with the United States Coast Guard to seize a speedboat carrying 1,984 lb (900 kg) of cocaine worth approximately £40 million ($60 million).

Search and Rescue pilot

In 2009, William extended his commission and transferred to the RAF to train to become a helicopter pilot with their Search and Rescue (SAR) Force. This branch of the service provides round-the-clock air search-and-rescue cover throughout the UK, Cyprus, and the Falkland Islands. It developed out of the air-sea rescue squadrons formed during World War II to pick up aircrew downed in the sea. Although its role remains military, today most of SARF's operational missions are undertaken to rescue civilians from emergencies at sea or on mountainsides, which it carries out in cooperation with Her Majesty's Coastguard.

Service with the SARF would allow William to continue flying and have an active role in the armed forces without being deployed on combat operations. Promoted to Flight Lieutenant, he completed a 12-month course in advanced

helicopter flying at the Defence Helicopter Flying School based at RAF Shawbury in Shropshire. During this course he completed around 80 hours of training on the Griffin HT1 helicopter, covering advanced handling, night flying, emergency handling, and tactical and formation flying.

In January 2010, Flight Lieutenant Wales transferred to the Search and Rescue Conversion Course at RAF Valley on the island of Anglesey in North Wales. For the first six weeks

> ## 1,765
> **The number of incidents to which William's Search and Rescue unit from RAF Valley responded in 2012.**

he continued to train in the Griffin helicopter before moving on to the Sea King Operation Conversion Unit, where he trained on a mixture of simulators and RAF Sea King helicopters.

The busiest SAR unit

In September 2010, at the end of his training, William was assigned to C Flight No. 22 Squadron based at RAF Valley—the busiest SAR unit in the country—to fly the Sea King Mark 3 helicopter. His operational tour was expected to last from 30 to 36 months.

An SAR duty shift is 24 hours. The crew must be ready for takeoff within 15 minutes of receiving an emergency call (45 minutes at night). There is a morning briefing session to pass on information about weather conditions and other operational factors, and to report on the state of their aircraft. The crew is responsible for carrying out preflight checks, but much of the time on base is spent in the crew room.

The standard SAR crew includes two pilots, one of whom is the aircraft captain. Additionally, there is a radio operator who operates the winch that is used at the rescue scene to lower the winchman on a rope, and to lift

Billy the Fish

William's RAF name badge states his name as Will Wales. He earned the nickname Billy the Fish during his training because "Wales" sounds like "whales."

SAR graduates

Along with six fellow students, Flight Lieutenant Wales (middle back row) displays his graduation certificate after completing his SAR training course at RAF Valley in September 2012.

"**I really enjoy my time** in the **Air Force.**
And **I'd love to continue it.** But the
pressures of my **other life are building.**"

WILLIAM, BEFORE LEAVING ACTIVE SERVICE IN 2013

In August 2014, it was announced that William would return to flying by training to become an air ambulance pilot.

A NEW CAREER IN THE AIR
After a period of training, William began work with the **East Anglian Air Ambulance (EAAA),** based at Cambridge and Norwich airports, in March 2015, shortly before the birth of his second child. He intends to fit his new role around his royal duties, and will **donate his salary to charity.** His **official contract of employment** is with the civilian company Bond Air Services.

The EAAA operates two EC145 T2 helicopters and employs three pilots in Norwich and three in Cambridge. Each helicopter carries a pilot, a doctor, and a paramedic. While working for EAAA, he and Duchess of Cambridge mostly live at Anmer Hall, their country house on the Sandringham estate in Norfolk.

At the controls
Described as "a highly professional and competent pilot," William took part in many daring rescue missions over the stormy waters of the Irish Sea and the mountains of Snowdonia in North Wales.

the injured person to safety. The winchman is normally trained to paramedic standard and supplies immediate first-aid and recovery services at the rescue site. William's first mission as copilot took place on October 2, 2010, when he was part of a team airlifting a casualty from an offshore gas rig to the hospital. Over the next three years, the Prince would take part in a total of 156 Search and Rescue operations with C Flight, resulting in 149 saved lives. In 2012, he passed the required tests to become an operational captain, in charge of the four-man crew.

No greater feeling
William's pleasure in flying helicopters is obvious. A BBC TV documentary in 2013, *Helicopter Rescue,* showed him as the aircraft captain on a flight to rescue a boy from a quarry. In the documentary, William spoke about his role: "There's no greater feeling than when you've actually done some good and saved someone's life."

Before their marriage, William and Catherine made their first home together in a rented farmhouse on Anglesey. Catherine has spoken of the fears she had for his safety when he was flying dangerous missions. When William's period of active service in the RAF ended in September 2013, he had completed more than 1,300 flying hours.

The **Wedding** of **William** and **Catherine**

In a break with tradition, a commoner and a member of the middle class, Catherine Middleton wed the future king of England. Catherine had won the public's heart and a million people turned out to cheer the couple after their wedding in Westminster Abbey on April 29, 2011.

Comparisons with the wedding of Prince Charles and Lady Diana Spencer, 30 years earlier, were inevitable. That, too, had been heralded as "a fairy-tale wedding" and preceded by months of eager anticipation. Their wedding had been a state occasion held amid the baroque splendors of St. Paul's Cathedral. Westminster Abbey, though grand enough and with closer connections to the monarchy, seats less than 2,000 people. William had insisted that he and Catherine should be allowed to have a say in who was invited. As a result, more than half the guests were family and friends of the couple, and the number of invitations traditionally issued to heads of state, politicians, diplomats, and other dignitaries was greatly reduced.

It was announced on the morning of the wedding that the Queen had created her grandson the Duke of Cambridge, Earl of Strathearn, and Baron Carrickfergus, and that Catherine (Kate) would assume the title of Her Royal Highness the Duchess of Cambridge immediately upon the marriage. William's new titles were drawn from England, Scotland, and Northern Ireland respectively.

Floral theme
The medieval nave of Westminster Abbey had been transformed into an avenue of trees, some of them standing up to 25 ft (7.5 m) high, and decorated with 30,000 flowers, including azaleas and other blossoms from Windsor Great Park. Prince William, in the full-dress scarlet uniform of the Irish Guards, and Prince Harry, his best man, in the bold blue of the Blues and Royals, stood out against this English floral background.

The bride, attended by her sister Pippa as maid of honor, four bridesmaids, and two pageboys, made the three-and-a-half minute journey from the Great West Door of the Abbey to the choir on her father's arm. Her dress, designed by Sarah Burton at Alexander McQueen, was made of ivory and white satin, and both the bodice and skirt incorporated lace floral motifs appliquéd by workers from the Royal School of Needlework. The skirt formed a Victorian-style semi-bustle at the back and finished in a short train measuring just under 10 ft (3 m) long. The veil was held in place by a tiara loaned by the Queen. Catherine carried a small bouquet of white spring flowers.

The Dean of Westminster, John Hall, led the traditional Church of England service and the Archbishop of Canterbury, Rowan Williams, married the couple. Richard Chartres, the Bishop of London, gave a sermon, and the bride's brother, James Middleton, read the lesson.

The newly married couple left the abbey to a peal of bells. They returned to Buckingham Palace in the 1902 State Landau (pp.136–37) drawn by four Windsor grays. It was followed by a procession of carriages carrying the Queen and other members of the Royal Family back to Buckingham Palace.

Lunchtime reception
The Queen hosted a lunchtime reception for about 600 guests, made up of friends of the couple as well as representatives from the many organizations they are associated with.

72 MILLION The number of people who viewed the royal wedding on YouTube.

3 The number of hours the bells of Westminster Abbey were rung after the royal wedding.

Eight-tiered cake
It took cake-maker Fiona Cairns and her team five weeks to create the magnificent eight-tiered wedding cake. The groom also requested a chocolate biscuit cake made to a favorite recipe.

William and Catherine, together with their families, appeared on the balcony of Buckingham Palace to greet the thousands of people gathered below. The crowd roared their approval as the couple exchanged the by now traditional royal marriage kiss, and then repeated it. Overcome by the noise, one of the tiny bridesmaids, William's three-year-old goddaughter Grace van Cutsem, covered her ears. The traditional Royal Air Force flyby over the palace included Lancaster, Spitfire, and Hurricane planes from World War II.

Just after 3:30 p.m., William drove his bride in a classic Aston Martin convertible to Clarence House, his official residence. The couple returned to the Palace in the evening for a private dinner given by Prince Charles for close friends and family. It was followed by dancing, with a small fireworks display in the palace grounds.

Public celebrations
The wedding day, a Friday, was declared a national holiday in the UK. Millions of people watched the day's events on television. It was broadcast live to millions more around the world. More than 5,000 permits were issued to hold street parties, including one hosted by Prime Minister David Cameron in Downing Street. Union Jacks and bunting decorated the streets of London and other cities. The cost of the event was estimated at £20 million ($30 million), most of which was paid for by Prince Charles, although the Middletons also made a contribution.

« **BEFORE**

The engagement of Prince William, who is second in line to the throne, to Catherine Middleton was announced on November 16, 2010.

DIANA'S RING
William gave Catherine the sapphire and diamond engagement ring belonging to the **Princess of Wales « 200**. William told reporters that the ring was "very special to him" and was "my way of making sure my mother didn't miss out on today."

Wedding portrait
The bride and groom, surrounded by Catherine's young attendants, pose in the Throne Room of Buckingham Palace after the wedding.

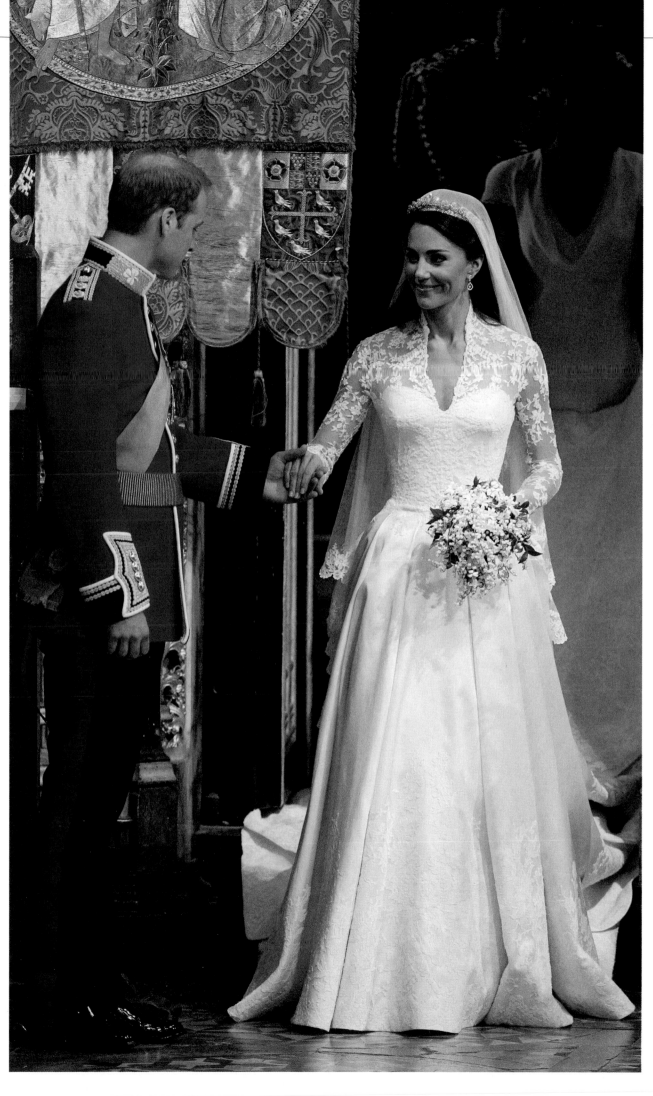

Husband and wife
Catherine has a special smile for Prince William as he takes her hand as the newly married couple prepare to lead the procession out of Westminster Abbey after the wedding.

"When we go for it, **we really go for it.**"

DAVID CAMERON, BRITISH PRIME MINISTER, ON THE ROYAL WEDDING CELEBRATIONS

Leaving in style
Prince William drives his wife from the reception in a classic Aston Martin convertible belonging to his father. It was decorated with balloons, and the license plate had been altered to read "JUST WED."

AFTER

Prince William returned to duty as an RAF Search and Rescue pilot the day after the wedding. The couple did not leave for their honeymoon in the Seychelles until May 9.

WORKING ROYAL
The Duchess's official duties began soon after their honeymoon. In May, she and William attended a private meeting at Buckingham Palace for **US President Barack Obama** and his wife, Michelle. In July the couple made their first overseas tour together to **Canada and the US 294–95 »**.

CHARITY FUND-RAISER
Catherine's wedding dress was put on display in Buckingham Palace throughout the summer, where it attracted a record number of visitors. It helped to raise £8 million ($12 million) for the Duchess of Cambridge's own charity fund.

Two entwined "A"s—the initials of Prince Albert and Princess Alexandra

Double portrait of King Edward VII and Queen Alexandra

1 WEDNING SOUVENIR

2 EDWARD VII CORONATION BEAKER

Royal Memorabilia

Since the days of Queen Victoria, many people have shared a passion for collecting royal memorabilia, ranging from fine china commemorating coronations to mass-produced items such as sweet tins, mugs, and posters.

1 **Wedding souvenir** A rare silver gilt and enamel medal, it was given to a Royal Entertainments committee member after the wedding in 1863 of Prince Albert of Wales and Princess Alexandra. 2 **Edward VII coronation beaker** This Royal Doulton porcelain cup was presented to guests invited to the official coronation dinners. 3 **Edward VII coronation vase** Another Royal Doulton creation, this 1902 vase has painted floral motifs on a gilt and blue ground. 4 **George V coronation cup** The Royal Crown Derby miniature loving (two-handled) cup was created to commemorate George V's coronation. 5 **George V Silver Jubilee medal** This commemorative medal was given by J. J. Cash, Coventry, to its employees. 6 **George V Silver Jubilee ribbon pin** Attached with a pin at the back, this embroidered ribbon was designed to be worn on a jacket. 7 **George V coronation souvenir tin** Rowntree & Sons released this unusual coronation casket containing chocolates in 1911. 8 **George VI coronation cup** The blue and gold Coalport loving cup commemorates the coronation of George VI and Elizabeth on May 12, 1937. 9 **Elizabeth II diamond wedding anniversary presentation tin** Complete with a piece of cake inside, this cake tin commemorates the 60th wedding anniversary of Queen Elizabeth II and Prince Philip. 10 **Prince of Wales wedding cake tin** This wedding cake tin bears the crests of the Prince of Wales and the Duchess of Cornwall along with the date of their wedding. 11, 12 **Miniature loving cups** The births of Princes William and Harry were marked by the release of a miniature loving cup. 13 **Elizabeth II Diamond Jubilee teapot** The limited edition bone china teapot is from a collection officially approved by the Queen. The proceeds from sales go towards the upkeep of the Royal Collection of art and antiquities. 14 **Royal wedding mug** This souvenir mug formed part of the official range of fine bone china commemorating Prince William's marriage to Catherine Middleton.

Edward VII's royal cypher, ERVII, standing for Edward Rex (king)

6 GEORGE V SILVER JUBILEE RIBBON PIN

5 GEORGE V SILVER JUBILEE MEDAL

22-carat gilding

3 EDWARD VII CORONATION VASE

4 GEORGE V CORONATION CUP

Scenes from the King's vast empire, which includes India, and parts of Africa and Australasia

7 GEORGE V CORONATION SOUVENIR TIN

9 ELIZABETH II DIAMOND WEDDING ANNIVERSARY PRESENTATION TIN

10 PRINCE OF WALES WEDDING CAKE TIN

8 GEORGE VI CORONATION CUP

11 MINIATURE LOVING CUP—WILLIAM

12 MINIATURE LOVING CUP—HENRY

Royal coat of arms

13 ELIZABETH II DIAMOND JUBILEE TEAPOT

Embellishments in burnished gold and platinum

The initials of "C" and "W" for Catherine and William appear below Prince William's coronet

14 ROYAL WEDDING MUG

Born 1982

The Duchess of Cambridge

"I really hope I can **make a difference**, even in the smallest way."

CATHERINE MIDDLETON, POST-ENGAGEMENT INTERVIEW, NOVEMBER 16, 2010

Catherine Elizabeth Middleton was born in Reading, Berkshire, on January 9, 1982, the first child of Carole and Michael, who met while working with British Airways (BA). In 1984 the family moved to Jordan, where Michael continued to work for BA, and Catherine attended an English nursery school. The Middletons returned to England in time for Catherine to start at St. Andrew's prep school in Pangbourne. Carole started one of the UK's first internet mail-order companies, Party Pieces, selling childrens' party supplies. It became a huge success.

Graduation day
Catherine Middleton received her degree in 2005, graduating with an upper-second class Bachelor of Arts. There she had already impressed fellow student Prince William, who was to become her husband.

Tall and shy, Catherine excelled at sports, and was among the spectators when Prince William, then age 9, visited her school to play hockey. After leaving St. Andrew's in 1995 she went briefly to Downe House school, an elite girls' school, where it seems she was badly bullied for being skinny, unpolished, and middle class. Her parents withdrew her, and her mother helped rebuild her self-confidence, partly through learning how to groom and present herself. She then went to Marlborough College, where she was not yet perceived as a beauty: the school's older boys publicly ranked new girls on a scale of 1 to 10; she received only ones and twos. Catherine did well at school, getting two As and a B at A level, and she was offered a place at Edinburgh University to study, but decided to take a gap year in Italy, and applied instead to study History of Art at the University of St. Andrews for the following year. Her decision may have been influenced by the announcement that her peer, Prince William, was going to take a gap year and then study the same course at St. Andrews.

University life

Both William and Catherine went to St. Andrews in the fall of 2001 and were placed in the same residence hall. Despite close monitoring of the Prince by the ever-voracious press, it was not until the following spring that Catherine first attracted attention. She had agreed to model at a student fashion show, and it was discovered that William had paid £200 ($300) for a front row seat. Catherine appeared several times on the catwalk, her costumes ranging from a vibrant, voluminous sweater to a transparent

Attending the Jubilee
Catherine, seen here during the Queen's Diamond Jubilee celebrations, had become a fashion icon, her every move, outfit, and even slightest fluctuation in weight scrutinized.

Wedding portrait
The official family photograph shows Prince William and Catherine with Queen Elizabeth II and Prince Philip; the Duke and Duchess of Cornwall; Prince Harry; Carole, Michael, James, and Pippa Middleton.

black shift dress. The Prince, so the story goes, was most intrigued. A discreet romance began, and the next year they moved into a row house in the center of St. Andrews with two other students.

Leaving university
In 2006, after graduating, Catherine began to work part-time for the fashion company Jigsaw. Press speculation about the future of her relationship with William was revered. Jigsaw founder Belle Robinson remembers that there were days when the road outside the office was clogged with TV crews. "We'd say: 'Listen, do you want to go out the back way?' And she'd say: 'To be honest, they're going to hound us until they've got the picture. So why don't I just go, get the picture done, and then they'll leave us alone.' I thought she was very mature for a 26-year-old." In April 2007, William and Catherine caused a press furore by calling a pause in their relationship. Clarence House refused to comment, and press speculation was rife. But the couple soon began to be seen in public together again and there were reports that their relationship had rekindled.

Royal wedding
The couple eventually became engaged in October 2010, while on vacation in Kenya to celebrate Prince William passing his RAF helicopter Search and Rescue course. Prince William gave Catherine the engagement ring that had belonged to his mother, Diana, Princess of Wales. They married in Westminster Abbey on April 29, 2011, and moved to a remote farmhouse on the island of Anglesey, where William worked as a Search and Rescue pilot. They had no domestic staff, and friends reported that they wanted to live as normal a life as possible, with Catherine cooking dinner, buying groceries in the local store, and having a bath run for William by the time he came home.

Their carefully guarded private life provided much-needed respite from the constant attention of the press. Catherine had become a fashion icon, although bucked royal tradition in selecting her own clothes—from UK chain stores

> **"The best dressing up outfit I ever had was a pair of clown dungarees my Granny made."**
>
> DUCHESS OF CAMBRIDGE, IN AN INTERVIEW

as well as from exclusive designers. It was enough for Catherine to appear in a dress for it to sell out.

New generation
In December 2012, Catherine was admitted to the hospital. Buckingham Palace announced that she was pregnant and suffering from an extreme form of morning sickness. After the birth of Prince George on July 22, 2013, William and Catherine spent several weeks living with the Middleton family in Berkshire before moving back to

The new princess
Princess Charlotte made her first public appearance 10 hours after she was born. The following evening London landmarks such as Tower Bridge and the London Eye were illuminated in pink.

Anglesey, along with Catherine's mother and the Queen's former housekeeper. The following October they moved into Kensington Palace. In 2015, William took on a new position as an air ambulance pilot in Norfolk, and they relocated to Anmer Hall, on the

Sandringham estate. On May 2, 2015, Catherine and William's second child, Princess Charlotte Elizabeth Diana was born at St. Mary's Hospital, London. Fourth in line to the throne, she was the first girl to be born so high in the line of succession since Princess Anne was born 65 years ago.

TIMELINE

- **January 9, 1982** Born Catherine Elizabeth, the eldest child of Michael and Carole Middleton, at Royal Berkshire Hospital, Reading.
- **May 1984** The Middletons move to Amman, Jordan, where Michael Middleton works as a flight dispatcher for British Airways. Catherine attends an English-language nursery school.
- **September 1987** The Middletons return to England and Catherine is enrolled at St. Andrew's School, Berkshire.
- **1987** Carole and Michael Middleton found Party Pieces, a mail-order company selling party supplies.
- **September 1995** Catherine briefly attends Downe House school.
- **April 1996** Begins attending Marlborough College, a coeducational boarding school.
- **2000** Studies at the British Institute in Florence during her gap year.

COMBINED COAT OF ARMS OF THE DUKE AND DUCHESS OF CAMBRIDGE

- **September 2001** Enrolls at St. Andrews University, Scotland, to study History of Art.
- **2003** Begins dating Prince William. They try to keep the romance discreet in an attempt to avoid press coverage.
- **February 2006** Catherine is given 24-hour security by the Royalty and Diplomatic Protection Department.
- **December 15, 2006** Attends Prince William's Passing Out Parade at Sandhurst as an official royal guest.
- **April 2007** The couple split up for a short time.
- **October 2010** William and Catherine become engaged during a 10-day trip to Kenya.
- **April 29, 2011** Marries the Duke of Cambridge at Westminster Abbey and is created the Duchess of Cambridge.
- **December 6, 2012** St. James's Palace announces that the Duchess is pregnant after she is admitted to King Edward VII Hospital with severe morning sickness.
- **July 22, 2013** Gives birth to first child, George Alexander Louis.
- **September 2014** Cancels two-day visit to Malta, where she was due to represent the Queen on the 50th anniversary of Malta's independence, because of early pregnancy.
- **May 2, 2015** Catherine's second child, Princess Charlotte Elizabeth Diana, is born.

Aerial salute
A Hurricane fighter plane of the Royal Air Force (RAF) Battle of Britain Memorial Flight passes over Buckingham Palace during the flypast to mark the Queen's Diamond Jubilee celebrations.

« BEFORE

The only other monarch in British history to have had a Diamond Jubilee was Queen Victoria, who celebrated her 60 years as Queen in 1897.

BANDANNA COMMEMORATING THE GOLDEN JUBILEE OF QUEEN VICTORIA

VICTORIA'S JUBILEES

While **Queen Victoria's Diamond Jubilee** celebration was **grander than** that of her **Golden Jubilee,** the Queen kept in poor health **« 67**. Crippled with arthritis, she was unable to climb the steps of St. Paul's Cathedral for the service of thanksgiving, and so it was decided to hold it outside. Dressed as usual in black, she remained seated in her carriage throughout.

The Diamond Jubilee

In 2012, Queen Elizabeth II celebrated her Diamond Jubilee. The event came less than a year after the excitement of the marriage of the Duke and Duchess of Cambridge, and the nation and the Commonwealth were in a mood to celebrate 60 years of her reign.

The Diamond Jubilee provided the occasion for her subjects to reflect upon the Queen's lifetime of service to her country through 60 years of change. Prime Minister David Cameron echoed these sentiments when, addressing the House of Commons on March 7, he said, "While the sands of culture shift and the tides of politics ebb and flow, Her Majesty has been a permanent anchor… grounding us in certainty."

> **400,000** The number of Diamond Jubilee medals awarded in the UK to the armed forces, prison police, and emergency services.

Weekend of celebrations

The government announced in January that the focal point of the Queen's Diamond Jubilee celebrations would be the first weekend in June. Monday, June 4, and Tuesday, June 5, were designated as public holidays, giving people throughout the country the chance to hold street parties or picnics or to join in one of the hundreds of public events organized in every region.

The Queen began her Diamond Jubilee celebrations by attending the Epsom Derby horse races on Saturday, June 2. In London, the celebrations were marked on Sunday, June 3 with a spectacular pageant on the Thames, an event inspired by a painting by the 18th-century artist Canaletto, *The Thames on Lord Mayor's Day*, depicting gilded barges and a flotilla of river craft against the backdrop of St. Paul's Cathedral. More than 1,000 boats, old and new, from all over the country and further afield, assembled on the river. They included vessels that had taken part in the Dunkirk evacuation during World War II in 1940, an early 19th-century Maori war canoe, and a wooden gig (rowboat) believed to have ferried Queen Victoria on a visit to Cornwall. *Gloriana*, a rowing barge specially commissioned for this event, was powered by an 18-man team of rowers, including Olympic oarsmen Sir Steve Redgrave and Sir Matthew Pinsent.

The Queen and Duke of Edinburgh, and other members of the Royal Family, were on board the royal barge—MV *The Spirit of Chartwell*—lavishly got up with

Pageant on the Thames
As scores of tiny rowing boats stream under Westminster Bridge, the high-rise buildings behind are testament to how much the London skyline has changed during Queen Elizabeth II's reign.

The Queen's Diamond Jubilee was marked in many different ways to provide a lasting legacy of her 60 years on the throne.

JUBILEE TRIBUTES

Among the permanent tributes to the Queen were the **60 Jubilee woodlands planted by the Woodland Trust.** The clock tower of Westminster Palace that houses Big Ben was renamed the Elizabeth Tower, the main gate to Kew Gardens became the Elizabeth Gate and in December 2012, the British Foreign Office announced that a portion of **the British Antarctic Territory would be known as Queen Elizabeth Land.** The Queen bestowed city status on Chelmsford in England, Perth in Scotland, and St. Asaph in Wales, while Armagh in Northern Ireland was granted a Lord Mayor. The borough of Richmond in southwest London became a Royal Borough.

DIAMOND JUBILEE MEDAL

Three versions of the **Queen Elizabeth II Diamond Jubilee medal** were issued, one each by the UK, Canada, and the Caribbean Commonwealth realms. It was awarded for honorable service in the armed forces, police, prison, and emergency services, or for outstanding achievement or public service.

Diamond Jubilee china
The official range of commemorative china for the Diamond Jubilee was modeled on the Rockingham Service, first used at the coronation banquet of Queen Victoria in 1838.

gold and velvet awnings. In cold, chilly rain they watched the early part of the 7.5-mile (12-km) long flotilla of boats pass by before the royal barge joined the procession to the pageant's finale at Tower Bridge.

Concert at the palace
The next day a concert organized by singer and songwriter Gary Barlow took place in front of Buckingham Palace on a stage built around the Queen Victoria

Barge fit for a Queen
The rowing barge *Gloriana*, which was privately built as a tribute to the Queen, was modelled on the Lord Mayor's guilded barge pictured in Canaletto's painting of the River Thames.

Memorial. A total of 10,000 free tickets had been made available to the public and distributed by ballot. An afternoon picnic, with a menu designed by top chef Heston Blumenthal was laid on for ticket-holders in the palace gardens beforehand. The concert included headline performances by Elton John, Stevie Wonder, and Paul McCartney. Prince Philip, who had been admitted to hospital earlier that day with a bladder

infection, could not attend the concert. At 10:30 p.m., the Queen placed a crystal glass diamond into a special pod to activate a laser that lit the last in a chain of more than 4,000 beacons

stretching around the world from Tonga and New Zealand to Sydney, New Delhi, Hong Kong, and Canada, and from John O'Groats to the Channel Islands.

On the final day of the celebrations, the Queen and other members of the Royal Family attended a national service of thanksgiving at St. Paul's Cathedral. Also present were the governors general and prime ministers of the Commonwealth, together with

> ## "In this special year… I **dedicate myself anew** to your service."
>
> THE QUEEN, ON THE 60TH ANNIVERSARY OF HER ACCESSION, FEBRUARY 2, 2012

representatives of many branches of national life. After a lunch with 700 guests in Westminster Hall, the Queen returned in an open-top carriage to Buckingham Palace. The celebrations ended with the customary appearance of the Royal Family on the balcony of Buckingham Palace for a flyby by the Red Arrows, the RAF aerobatic display team, and other aircraft.

Overseas tours
Ten years before, for the Golden Jubilee, the Queen and Prince Philip had visited every country of the Commonwealth, but now the 86-year-old monarch called upon the support of other members of the Royal Family. Overseas tours undertaken on behalf of the Queen included visits by the Prince of Wales and the Duchess of Cornwall to Australia, Canada, New Zealand, and Papua New Guinea; the Duke and Duchess of Cambridge to Malaysia, Singapore, the Solomon Islands, and Tuvalu; and Prince Harry to Belize, Jamaica, and the Bahamas.

Lighting the National Beacon
The Queen manipulates the crystal glass diamond into position to light the National Beacon. Seconds later, the brilliant white flare rose high into the sky in front of Buckingham Palace.

Other events held in the Diamond Jubilee year included an overseas sovereigns' lunch hosted by the Queen at Windsor Castle on May 18. In all, 22 reigning and former monarchs attended, including the Emperor of Japan, two queens, nine kings, three princes, one grand duke, and one sultan.

Opening the Olympics

Early in the morning of July, 28 Queen Elizabeth II stepped up to the microphone to declare the 2012 London Olympic Games officially open. Her brief words came in the midst of a lavish opening ceremony—created by Oscar-winning director Danny Boyle—that had begun five hours before.

For many, the highlight of the show came at around 10:30 p.m. when the huge audience packed into the stadium, and the millions viewing at home, were treated to a short film showing Daniel Craig as James Bond arriving at Buckingham Palace. Followed by the Queen's corgis Monty, Willow, and Holly, he is shown into the royal study where the Queen, with her back to the camera, is writing at her desk. Is it really her? All doubts are put aside when she turns and greets the famous spy: "Good evening, Mr. Bond."

The monarch and spy are then seen leaving the Palace and apparently climbing aboard a helicopter, which flies across London to the Olympic Stadium, where they leap out. At that moment, in real time, two skydivers, one dressed as the Queen, appeared above the stadium. And minutes later, the Queen, wearing the same outfit as in the film, accompanied by the Duke of Edinburgh arrived to take her seat. The Queen's starring role was one of the best-kept secrets of the night. According to Lord Coe, chairman of the Games' organizing committee, Princes William and Harry were as stunned as anyone to see the Queen in her first movie role. As the skydiver started to descend, the Princes were heard to shout, "Go, Granny!"

The Queen's surprise cameo, which had taken three hours to film under Danny Boyle's direction, gave the royal seal of approval to a hugely successful summer Olympic Games, in which Great Britain finished third in the medal rankings. It crowned a triumphant regal summer, following on from the enormous success of the Queen's Diamond Jubilee in June (see pp.282–83).

> "I declare open the **Games of London,** celebrating the **30th Olympiad** of the modern era."
>
> **QUEEN ELIZABETH II,** OPENING THE OLYMPIC GAMES, JULY 28, 2012

Crown of light
Her Majesty the Queen, in a peach-colored cocktail dress and a headpiece with handmade porcelain flowers, formally opens the London Olympic Games. Seconds later an explosion of fireworks appeared to enfold the stadium in a scintillating crown of light.

Born 1984

Prince Harry

"There are **three** parts of **me**—one wearing a **uniform,** one being **Prince Harry**, and the other... **private.**"

PRINCE HARRY, ON RETURN FROM AFGHANISTAN, JANUARY 2012

Prince Harry is the younger son of Charles, Prince of Wales and Diana, Princess of Wales, and is currently fifth in line of succession to the throne—after Prince Charles, Prince William, and William's two children. Harry was born on September 15, 1984, at St. Mary's Hospital, in Paddington, central London, and named Henry Charles Albert David. A good-looking toddler with striking red hair and an impish grin, Harry seems to have a developed a cheeky, happy-go-lucky attitude to life from an early age, in contrast to his shyer, more serious older brother.

Death of Diana
Harry was 12 at the time of his mother's tragic death. A diminutive figure in an unfamiliar black suit, he walked bravely behind his mother's coffin with his grandfather, father, brother, and maternal uncle, Earl Spencer, as it made its way to Westminster Abbey. As an adult, Harry has spoken openly about the pain of losing his mother—"To us, she was quite simply the best mother in the world"—and it cannot be doubted it is this experience that allows him to empathize with children in his charity work and official engagements. A trip that Harry made to Botswana and South Africa with Prince Charles in the winter after Diana's death gave him his first taste of Africa, a continent he has visited many times since.

Eton and after
In September 1998, Harry joined Prince William at Eton College—an independent secondary school in Berkshire, near Windsor. Although he did not shine academically, he excelled at sports, particularly polo and rugby union, and joined the school Combined Cadet Force (CCF), reaching the rank of Cadet Officer. He did not escape getting into teenage scrapes—when the press published reports that he had taken part in underage drinking and

Cute boy
Prince Harry peers out of the back door of Highgrove, Prince Charles's country home. Harry and William divided school vacations between Highgrove and Diana's Kensington Palace apartment.

The people's prince
People have tended to identify more with Prince Harry than any other royal. His very public transformation from a cheeky young boy to a vociferous advocate for various charities has endeared him to the public.

smoking pot, his father arranged for him to visit a South London drug rehabilitation center.

After graduation in 2003, and before embarking on a military career, Harry took a gap year to travel in Australia, Argentina, and Africa. In Africa, he made a documentary about the plight of orphans in Lesotho. He also spent part of the year training as a coach with the Rugby Football Union, visiting schools and teams around the country to promote the sport.

Prince Harry entered the Royal Military Academy at Sandhurst, Berkshire, in May 2005 and after completing his training course was commissioned as a second lieutenant into the Blues and Royals, part of the Household Cavalry. He was deployed twice to Afghanistan and is a qualified Apache helicopter commander (see pp.290–91). In an interview to the press about life on the

frontline, he said "I haven't really had a shower for four days, I haven't washed my clothes for a week."

A talent for caring

As with William, Diana, Princess of Wales's influence shows in many of the charities and causes Harry supports. In 2006 he founded Sentebale with Prince Seeiso of Lesotho. Sentebale, which means

For love of Africa
On a 2014 trip to Lesotho, Prince Harry shows a group of boys the photo he has just taken of them on his camera. The boys go to a night school built by Sentebale, Prince Harry's African charity.

raise money for the charity Walking With the Wounded. He also championed the hugely successful Invictus Games for wounded service personnel in October 2014 (see pp.300–301).

Harry has had many brushes with the paparazzi. He apologized after a photograph appeared in the press of him wearing a uniform with a swastika armband to a costume party. In 2012 he was photographed naked in Las Vegas with an unknown woman, apparently taking part in a game of strip billiards. Incidents such as these helped to build his image as a fun-loving prince, especially in his younger days, and they have not dented his popularity—in 2014 he was voted the nation's favorite royal. In very large part, this is due to his ability to reach out to ordinary people, a gift he has inherited from his mother.

The future

Prince Harry is known to have had two long-term relationships. Although he has expressed the wish to marry and have children, for the time being he remains single. Although he stated "I am definitely not a diplomat," in a CBS interview, Harry has taken on a greater role in performing official duties for the Queen and the Duke of Edinburgh. This aspect of his royal duties will grow as he develops new responsibilities following his departure from the army, announced in March 2015.

> # "We're **very privileged** in the **position** that we are. But… with privilege comes **great responsibility.**"
>
> PRINCE HARRY, INTERVIEWED ON CBS NEWS, MARCH 13, 2012

"forget-me-not" in the Sesotho language, helps care for vulnerable children who are the forgotten victims of poverty and the HIV/AIDS epidemic. The "Concert for Diana," organized by William and Harry at Wembley Stadium in July 2007, was held to aid Sentebale, along with Diana's favorite charities. In 2010, Harry and William visited Sentebale during their official joint tour of South Africa, Botswana, and Lesotho (see pp.294–95).

Harry's personal experience of the huge risks and suffering arising from warfare has led him to take an ever more active role in supporting those injured in the line of duty. He trekked part of the way with teams of injured servicemen to the North Pole in 2011 and to the South Pole in 2013 to

Prince Harry's coat of arms
The Queen gave Prince Harry his own coat of arms on his 18th birthday. The red escallops (shells) on the collars of the lions, unicorn, and shield are from the Spencer coat of arms of his maternal family.

CONCERT FOR DIANA

The **Birth** of **George**

Prince William was at Catherine's side when, on the afternoon of July 22, 2013, their son entered the world weighing 8 lb 6 oz (3.8 kg). The birth took place in the Lindo Wing of St. Mary's Hospital, Paddington, close to Kensington Palace, where William had been born 31 years before.

In a break with royal tradition, the news of the birth was given through an email press release and immediately tweeted around the world, even before the customary bulletin had been posted on an easel in the forecourt of Buckingham Palace: "Her Royal Highness The Duchess of Cambridge was safely delivered of a son at 4.24 p.m. today. Her Royal Highness and her child are both doing well."

The next day, gun salutes were sounded in Green Park and the Tower of London, the bells of Westminster Abbey rang for three hours, and the fountains in Trafalgar Square were illuminated in blue in honor of a boy. A large crowd joined the hundreds of journalists who had camped outside the hospital for several days. They waited patiently for a sight of the baby prince as first Catherine's parents, and then the Prince of Wales and the Duchess of Cornwall, arrived to greet their first grandchild. Just before 8 p.m. the next day, Catherine and William emerged through the doors of the hospital cradling their son. They posed for pictures and spoke briefly to the crowd—like any proud father, William commented that the baby had a good set of lungs, while Catherine revealed that William had already done a diaper change.

The next day they announced their choice of names—George Alexander Louis. Meanwhile, the baby at the center of the drama, now formally known as HRH Prince George of Cambridge, remained unaware that his great-grandmother was the reigning monarch, and that one day in the distant future he was destined to be king. Not since Queen Victoria's death in 1901 had there been three generations alive in direct line of succession to the throne: the Queen's son, grandson, and great-grandson.

" He's got **her looks, thankfully."**

PRINCE WILLIAM, SPEAKING TO THE WAITING PRESS
OUTSIDE THE HOSPITAL, JULY 23, 2013

Proud father
William and Catherine show off their son to the waiting photographers. The couple decided not to employ a full-time nanny for Prince George during his first weeks, preferring to care for him themselves with the help of Catherine's mother.

◀◀ BEFORE

As children, William and Harry accompanied their parents on several overseas visits.

SEASONED TRAVELERS
In 1983, Diana took 9-month-old William on a long official visit with Charles to **New Zealand and Australia.** Her decision was questioned because of the risk of having the first and second in line to the throne aboard the same plane ◀◀ **206.** In 1985, William and Harry joined their parents for a few days at the end of an **official visit to Italy.** Both sons accompanied their parents on an official visit to **Canada** in 1993.

ROYAL TOUR OF NEW ZEALAND

William, Catherine, and Harry Abroad

Like other members of the Royal Family, William and Harry act as ambassadors for Britain. In recent years, they have both made several successful overseas tours. Catherine travels with William when she can, and Prince George has already made his first visit abroad.

Royal overseas tours have several purposes—they boost Britain's interests by showcasing its creativity and innovation and help develop business partnerships. They also help establish goodwill between Britain and other countries and, in the case of Commonwealth nations, foster and develop friendships.

William and Harry represent the Queen at important events and ceremonies on official overseas tours. Their relaxed and friendly manner with crowds wins them admirers wherever they go. On more informal visits, the Princes promote the work of the charities and organizations that they support.

In June 2010, William and Harry made a joint goodwill tour of southern Africa. In Botswana, the brothers saw firsthand the work of the Tusk Trust—a wildlife conservation organization that William supports. They then traveled on to Lesotho, where Harry showed his brother some of the projects undertaken by Sentebale—the charity he cofounded with Prince Seeiso of Lesotho to help vulnerable children and orphans. The tour ended in South Africa, where William, in his capacity as president of the English Football Association, and Harry saw England draw with Algeria in a second-stage match in the World Cup.

Going solo
William made his first solo visit overseas in July 2005, soon after graduating from university. He was invited by the British and Irish Lions rugby team to join them on their tour of New Zealand. While there, the Prince represented the Queen at official events in Auckland and Wellington to mark the 60th anniversary of the end of World War II. He returned to New Zealand for a two-day visit in January 2010, when he represented the Queen at the opening of the Supreme Court building in Wellington. William then paid an unofficial visit to Australia, his first since visiting the country at the age of 9 months, on a mission to get to know the country and its people.

Barely a year later, a powerful earthquake struck the city of Christchurch on New Zealand's South Island, killing 185 people and causing widespread damage. William flew there to attend a national memorial service on behalf of the Queen. After inspecting the devastated area and speaking with victims and rescuers,

Bidding goodbye
The Duke and Duchess of Cambridge, with Prince George, wave farewell to Australia as they board a flight in Canberra at the end of their triumphant tour of the country in 2014.

he traveled to Greymouth, the site of a coal-mining accident that had killed 29 miners a short while before. The Prince then flew to Australia, where he visited flood-damaged areas of Queensland and Victoria.

Traveling together
Two months after their wedding, William and Catherine visited Canada on their first overseas tour together. During their nine-day visit, the royal couple attended the Canada Day Parade on Ottawa's Parliament Hill in searing temperatures of 90°F (32°C). Catherine's striking red hat was decorated with maple leaves—Canada's national emblem—and she wore a diamond maple leaf brooch that had been loaned to her by the Queen. William and Catherine also visited Prince Edward Island and the Northwest Territories before watching the annual stampede—a 10-day rodeo, exhibition, and festival event—in Calgary, Alberta. At the end of the trip, they made a short visit to California, to

> " He's **cool,** very **down to earth...** you think it will be difficult but **he just wanted to laugh.** "

USAIN BOLT, ON HIS MEETING WITH PRINCE HARRY IN JAMAICA, 2012

In the running
Harry takes part in a race with sprint record holder Usain Bolt on the Usain Bolt [running] track in Mona, Jamaica. The Prince took advantage of a false start to sprint down the track, leaving Bolt behind.

AFTER

promote the British film industry at an event in Los Angeles. The couple's next long overseas tour was to Southeast Asia and the Pacific for the Queen's Diamond Jubilee in 2012. The tour covered four Commonwealth countries: Singapore, Malaysia, Solomon Islands, and Tuvalu.

In April 2014, the Prince and Princess of Wales embarked on a 19-day tour of New Zealand and Australia. They were accompanied by 9-month-old Prince George in a visit that replicated that of his father with the Prince and Princess of Wales 32 years earlier. The royal entourage included a full-time nanny, Maria Borrallo, whom Catherine had hired just before the trip to look after George. The little Prince's public appearances were carefully managed—he visited a playgroup with his mother in Wellington, and a zoo in Sydney, where he delighted the assembled photographers by throwing a stuffed toy to the ground.

Catherine was intending to make her first official solo visit to Malta in September 2014, when the onset of severe morning sickness at the start of her second pregnancy forced her to cancel the trip. William went instead as a last minute stand-in.

The couple made a highly successful visit to the US in December, when Catherine was five months pregnant. She stuck to a tight schedule in New York City, visiting child development projects and a National Basketball

> **671** The number of gifts Prince George received on his visit to New Zealand and Australia.

Association (NBA) game. Meanwhile, William traveled alone to Washington for a meeting with President Barack Obama and to attend a working lunch to discuss and to address a World Bank consortium on the fight against the illegal trade in ivory.

Catherine's pregnancy also caused her to be absent from the state visits William made to Japan and China in February 2015. In Japan, the Prince visited the northeast region of Fukushima, which was devastated by an earthquake and tsunami in 2011. The first member of the Royal Family to visit China for nearly 30 years, William met President Xi Jinping in Beijing, launched a festival promoting British businesses in Shanghai, and visited an elephant sanctuary in Yunnan province.

Harry's expeditions

Harry made his first official overseas tour in 2012 when he visited Belize, the Bahamas, and Jamaica on behalf of the Queen during her Diamond Jubilee year. In addition to carrying out his public duties, he delighted his hosts by entering completely into the spirit of the celebrations—joining in dances at street parties and playing soccer with local children. In Jamaica, he took part in a mock race against champion sprinter Usain Bolt. Prince Harry has also made official visits to Chile, Brazil, Estonia, and Italy, where he attended the 70th anniversary of the Battle of Monte Cassino, commemorating the heavy losses incurred by Allied troops in Italy during World War II.

Prince George proved so popular in Australia that some commentators even credited him with causing a slump in support for the republican movement.

GEORGE "THE REPUBLICAN SLAYER"
The republican movement in Australia aims to change the country's status from a constitutional monarchy to a republic. In 2014, in the wake of William and Catherine's tour of Australia with baby Prince George in tow, **support for the republic movement dropped** to its lowest level in three decades.

An Australian breakfast television show dubbed George "the Republican Slayer" after an **opinion poll** revealed that support for the republican movement was at 42 percent – its lowest in 35 years. Meanwhile, 51 percent were in favor of retaining the monarchy, a figure that rose to 60 percent among the 18–24 age group. Women were generally more pro-monarchy than men.

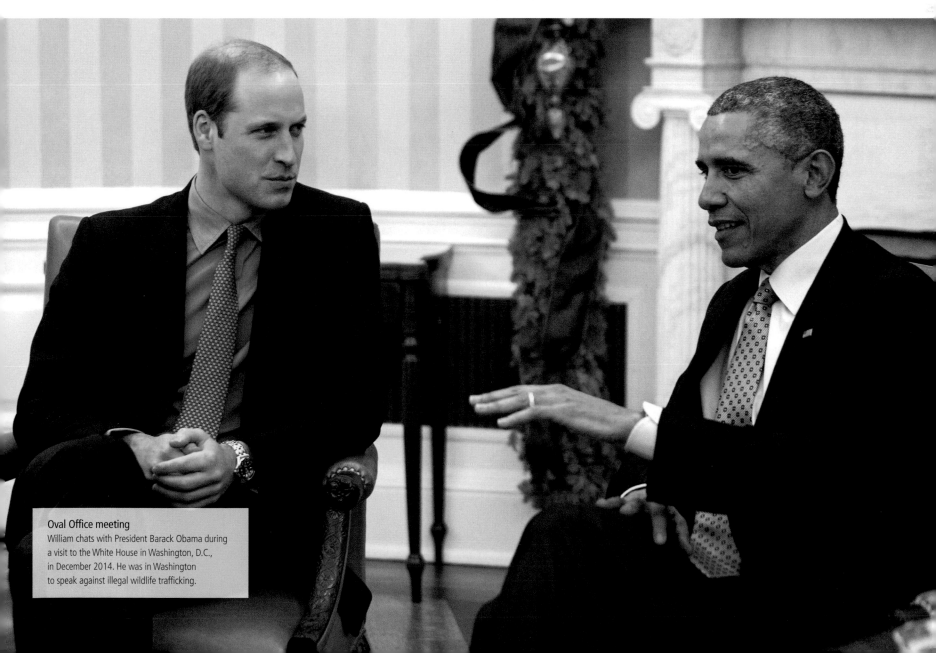

Oval Office meeting
William chats with President Barack Obama during a visit to the White House in Washington, D.C., in December 2014. He was in Washington to speak against illegal wildlife trafficking.

The Queen's Grandchildren

Queen Elizabeth II and Prince Philip, the Duke of Edinburgh, have eight grandchildren. The eldest, Peter Phillips, was born in 1977 and the youngest, James, Viscount Severn, in 2007. The Queen enjoys being in their company and is said to "light up" when they are around.

Family life is very important to Elizabeth II. Each year her children and grandchildren gather for summer vacation at Balmoral, where the younger cousins enjoy family picnics, pony trekking, and other outdoor activities. The family also gets together for Christmas at Sandringham and for Easter at Windsor Castle. The Queen has taught all her grandchildren to ride. She loves their jokes and, like so many grandparents, possibly allows them more leeway than she gave her own children, to whom she is sometimes said to have been a rather remote mother.

For Princes William (b.1982) and Harry (b.1984), second and fifth in line of succession, both grandparents provided stability, support, and protection, especially during the difficult years when their parents Charles and Diana, divorced, and after the painful loss of their mother. As they grew into adulthood, the Queen became an even more important part of the Princes' lives, and they both look to her for approval and advice. "My relationship with the Queen has gone from strength to strength," William has said, explaining that he sometimes found it hard to talk to her about weighty matters when he was younger, but now finds it much easier. Elizabeth's pride at William's passing out parade at Sandhurst in 2006, and her happiness at the wedding of William and Catherine in 2011 was plain to see. Prince Harry, too, has a good rapport with the Queen. Like his brother William, he undertook a series of overseas Commonwealth tours on

The Queen and her grandchildren
This family portrait—taken on vacation in the grounds of Balmoral in 1999—shows the Queen and Prince Philip with five of their grandchildren, left to right: Harry, Eugenie, William, Beatrice, and Zara.

BEFORE

The best-known royal grandmother in British history was Queen Victoria, who had a total of 20 grandsons and 22 granddaughters, the eldest born in 1859 and the youngest in 1891.

THE GRANDMOTHER OF EUROPE
Victoria's children married into many of Europe's royal houses **‹‹ 51.** Her grandchildren included King George V of Great Britain, the German Emperor Wilhelm II, the wife of Czar Nicholas II, the last ruler of Russia, and the consorts of the kings of Romania, Greece, Norway, and Spain. **Queen Victoria** was a **carrier of hemophilia,** a genetic disorder that prevents blood clotting. It is passed on by women but mostly occurs in men. Through three of Victoria's carrier daughters, hemophilia spread into many of the royal families of Europe.

VICTORIA WITH PRINCE ARTHUR AND PRINCESS MARGARET OF CONNAUGHT

AFTER »

Proud grandparents
The Queen and Prince Philip look on as their eldest grandson Peter Phillips leaves St George's Chapel, Windsor, with his bride Autumn Kelly after their wedding on 17 May 2008.

her behalf during the Diamond Jubilee year in 2012, and has spoken warmly of her sympathy and concern.

Princess Anne's children

The Queen's eldest grandchildren are Peter Phillips (b.1977) and Zara Phillips (b.1981), the son and daughter of

"When the Queen says well done, it means so much."

PRINCE WILLIAM, IN AN INTERVIEW WITH ROBERT HARDMAN, 2011

Princess Anne and her first husband, Captain Mark Phillips. They are currently 13th and 16th in the line of succession to the throne, but do not have a royal title because they are the grandchildren of the monarch through the female line. Both their parents were Olympic equestrians—Mark Phillips competed at Munich, Germany, in 1972, and Princess Anne at Montreal, Canada, in 1976 (see pp.186–87)—so it is not surprising that Peter and Zara both developed a strong interest in sport from an early age. They were kept out of the limelight as children, and are the only grandchildren of the Duke of Edinburgh to attend his old school, Gordonstoun, in Scotland so far (see pp.124–25).

Peter graduated with a degree in sports science from the University of Exeter before pursuing a career in sports sponsorship management, working for a time for the Williams Formula 1 racing team. He now works in event management. In 2008 he married Canadian-born business consultant Autumn Kelly, whom he

met at the Canadian Grand Prix in Montreal. She was a Roman Catholic but became a member of the Church of England so that Peter would not have to give up his place in the line of succession. At that time a clause of the 1701 Act of Settlement that made it illegal for anyone married to a Roman Catholic to succeed to the throne was still in force; the bar has since been removed by the Succession to the Crown Act, 2013. Peter and Autumn have two daughters.

Like her parents, Zara is an accomplished equestrian. She was Eventing World Champion in 2006 and part of the British eventing team that won the team silver medal at the 2012 Olympics in London. She is nearest in age to William and Harry among the royal cousins, and is godmother to William and Catherine's son, Prince George. As a young royal with a

rebellious streak (as a 17-year-old she sported a tongue piercing at Prince Charles's 50th birthday), she was frequently in the gossip magazines. In 2011 she married the former international rugby player and England captain Mike Tindall at Canongate Kirk in Edinburgh. They have one daughter.

The young Yorks

Princess Beatrice (b.1988) and Princess Eugenie (b.1990), the daughters of Andrew and Sarah, the Duke and Duchess of York, are currently seventh and eighth in line to the throne. They are both styled Her Royal Highness as the granddaughters of the monarch through the male line. The Duke and Duchess agreed to joint custody of their daughters after their divorce and shared responsibility for their upbringing.

Princess Beatrice, who is dyslexic, attended St. George's School, Ascot, an independent girls' day school, before going on to study history at Goldsmiths College, University of London, graduating in 2011. She was the first member of the Royal Family to complete the London Marathon and is patron of a number of charities and organizations, particularly those working to improve the lives of young people. She is famous for the unusual hat she wore to the wedding of Prince William and Catherine Middleton; she later offered it for auction on eBay, where it raised £81,000 ($120,000) for charity. In 2014–15 she interned at the London offices of Sony Pictures Television.

Princess Eugenie was a boarder at Marlborough College in Wiltshire. She graduated from Newcastle University in 2012 with a degree in English literature and history of art. She had corrective orthopedic surgery as a girl because of a congenital spinal condition, and is now closely involved

with the fundraising appeal for the Royal National Orthopaedic Hospital. Eugenie is currently working in New York for an online auction house.

The Earl of Wessex's children

The Queen's youngest grandchildren are Lady Louise Windsor (b.2003) and James, Viscount Severn (b.2007). The children of the Earl and Countess of Wessex, they are currently 10th and 11th in line of succession, but do not have a royal title—a decision made on their parents' marriage, when Prince Edward chose to become an earl rather than a royal duke (see p.251).

Louise was born prematurely at Frimley Park Hospital in Surrey after her mother was rushed there as a medical emergency. Louise was a bridesmaid at the wedding of Prince William and Catherine Middleton. She is frequently seen at royal occasions such as Trooping the Color and attended the Diamond Jubilee river pageant with her brother. James was born by Caesarean section at the same hospital. The Queen is said to be very fond of both children, and goes riding with them in Windsor Great Park.

> The Queen and the Duke of Edinburgh first became great-grandparents in 2010. At the present time, they are great-grandparents five times over.

THE NEXT GENERATION
Elizabeth II's eldest great-grandchild **Savannah Anne Kathleen,** the daughter of Peter and Autumn Phillips, was born on September 29, 2010. The Queen attended her baptism at Holy Cross Church, Avening, in Gloucestershire. A second daughter, **Isla Elizabeth,** was born to the couple on March 29, 2012. The Queen's **first great-grandson, Prince George of Cambridge,** son of the Duke and Duchess of Cambridge, was born on July 22, 2013 **« 292.** His third cousin, **Mia Grace Tindall,** daughter of Zara and Mike Tindall, was born on January 17, 2014. George's younger sister, Charlotte, was born on 2 May 2015.

PRINCE GEORGE

Plane spotting
The Queen's youngest grandchild James, son of Earl and Countess of Wessex (back), peers through cupped hands at the RAF flypast after the Trooping the Colour ceremony in 2013. His sister Louise is beside him on the Palace balcony.

Born 1926

Elizabeth II, the Later Years

"You can **do a lot** if you are **properly trained.**"

QUEEN ELIZABETH II

Queen Elizabeth II is said to have been taken aback by the degree of affection shown to her by the public during her Golden Jubilee year in 2002. The previous two decades had been difficult for the Royal Family, for the institution of monarchy, and for the Queen personally. She had seen three of her children's marriages fail under the glare of publicity, while she herself was subjected to an unprecedented storm of criticism after the death of Diana, Princess of Wales, in 1997. At the height of these troubles, the Royal Family was held up to ridicule in the satirical puppet show *Spitting Image*, one of the most popular television comedies of the 1980s and 1990s. It even featured caricatures of the Queen as well as the Queen Mother, and Prince Philip, something that would have been unthinkable in the early years of her reign.

The Queen successfully weathered all these storms, and public respect continues to grow from year to year for the way she carries out her role as monarch, for her devotion to duty, and for her personal qualities of steadfast strength, good humor, and courtesy. In part, of course, this is due

to the Queen's longevity—she is now 89 years old, yet still carries out a punishing daily work schedule, long after the age most people have opted for retirement. However, it can be attributed even more to the Queen's own willingness to adapt to change.

At dinner with the Queen
Queen Elizabeth and Prince Philip welcome US President Barack Obama and his wife, Michelle, to a state banquet at Buckingham Palace on May 24, 2011.

She has reformed the monarchy substantially. In 1992, she offered to start paying income tax and capital gains tax on her private wealth. She opened her official residences, including Buckingham Palace, to the

393 The number of the Queen's official engagements in 2014.

public in an effort to finance their upkeep. She supported measures to end the law of male primogeniture, which means that the eldest child of the sovereign can succeed to the throne, regardless of gender, as well as lifting the bar that prevents anyone

Octogenarian monarch
At 89, the Queen is an active monarch with a busy schedule. An avid horsewoman, she is seen here arriving for Ladies Day at the Royal Ascot race meeting in June 2014.

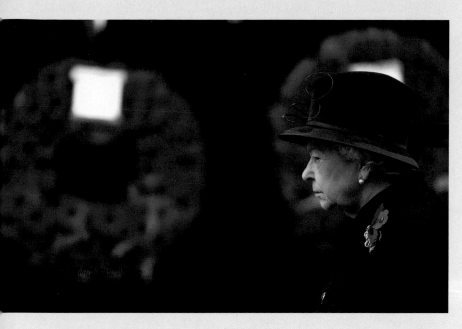

Act of remembrance
The Queen pays tribute to all those who died serving their country at the national Service of Remembrance held at the Cenotaph in Whitehall in November every year.

Her passion for horses is well known. She still rides, though she now prefers to be mounted on sturdy fell ponies from the north of England—known for their steady temperament and sure-footedness (she is patron of the Fell Pony Society). It is public knowledge that the Queen never wears a hard riding hat, preferring a silk headscarf. Her daughter Princess Anne, her grooms, and ROSPA (the Royal Society for the Prevention of Accidents) have all remonstrated with her about it, but she takes no notice.

The Queen loves horse racing, and has a deep knowledge of breeding and bloodlines. She owns 25–30 racehorses and tries to see them run as often as she can. She is at her most relaxed at a race meeting and has won all the major Classic races, except for the

who is married to a Roman Catholic from standing in the line of succession to the throne.

Personal style
The Queen has developed a personal style of dress that has served her well over the years. A two-piece suit, or dress and coat, for daytime engagements, usually in a single color and ending just below the knees. A large hat with swept-back brim to show her face, low-heeled shoes, and a handbag (no one knows what she keeps in it). She almost invariably wears a pearl necklace and has a brooch pinned to her lapel. On formal occasions, such as state banquets, she sparkles in beaded gowns, with a Garter Sash worn from the left shoulder, and diamond jewelry.

Queen Elizabeth took to wearing eyeglasses in public in 1982, when she put them on to read a speech, remarking at the time, "It's extraordinary, my mother doesn't need glasses at all and here I am—52, 56, well whatever age I am [she was 56]—and I can't see a thing." She has sometimes been accused of looking grumpy in public—she has said of herself that she has the kind of face that, when not smiling, tends to look cross. In recent years, however, she has been seen laughing and smiling more than she did formerly. She has sat for over 240 official portraits in the course of her reign.

Countrywoman
In 1986 the Queen told BBC producer Eddie Mirzoeff, who was making a documentary about the Royal

Family, that she did sometimes begrudge some of the hours she has to do when she could be outdoors instead. It was a refreshingly honest

> ## "The **true measure** of all our **actions** is how long the **good** in them **last… everything** we do, we do **for the young.**"
>
> QUEEN ELIZABETH II, 70TH ANNIVERSARY OF D-DAY, JUNE 2014

admission—the Queen is at heart a countrywoman, and likes nothing better than going for long country walks with her dogs at Balmoral. She loves being surrounded by her grandchildren (see p.296).

Epsom Derby, as an owner. In 2011, her horse Carlton House was favorite to win the Derby, but was beaten into third place. The Queen's excitement, and disappointment at the outcome, was plain to see.

First past the post
The Queen possesses a formidable knowledge of horse racing. She is seen here congratulating her filly Estimate, winner of the Gold Cup at Ascot in June 2013.

TIMELINE

- **1980** Makes a state visit to the Vatican.
- **April 17, 1982** Signs the Canadian Constitution Act in Ottawa, surrendering the right of the British Parliament to make laws affecting Canada.
- **July 9, 1982** An intruder, Michael Fagan, enters the Queen's bedroom in Buckingham Palace, raising questions about security.
- **1985** The Queen and members of the Royal Family are caricatured on the TV satirical puppet show *Spitting Image*.

THE QUEEN'S 60TH BIRTHDAY COMMEMORATIVE STAMPS

- **October 1986** Visits China, becoming the first British monarch to do so.
- **May 16, 1991** Becomes the first British monarch to address a joint meeting of the United States Congress.
- **November 20, 1992** Windsor Castle is damaged by fire at the end of the Queen's annus horribilis.
- **1993** Pays income tax for the first time.
- **December 20, 1995** Advises Charles and Diana that a divorce is desirable.
- **September 1997** Is criticized for her apparent lack of feeling on Diana's death by media.
- **December 1997** Attends the decommissioning ceremony of the Royal Yacht *Britannia*.
- **February 6, 2002** The 50th anniversary of the Queen's accession marks the start of her Golden Jubilee year.
- **November 20, 2007** The Queen and Prince Philip celebrate their 60th wedding anniversary.
- **November 8, 2010** Joins Facebook with the launch of a British Monarchy page.
- **December 29, 2010** Birth of the Queen's first great-grandchild, Savannah Phillips, daughter of Peter and Autumn Phillips.
- **May 2011** Visits the Republic of Ireland, a historic turning point in the troubled relations between Ireland and the UK.
- **October 2011** Carries out what is probably her last visit to Australia, the 16th of her reign.
- **June 2, 2012** Starts off the Diamond Jubilee celebrations by attending the Epsom Derby.
- **July 28, 2012** Opens the Summer Olympic Games in London.
- **June 2014** Makes a state visit to France on the occasion of the 70th anniversary of the D-Day landings.
- **April 21, 2015** Celebrates her 89th birthday.

The **Invictus Games**

Prince Harry was the driving force behind the Invictus Games, a Paralympic-style championship for wounded servicemen and women. After attending the Warrior Games in the US in May 2013, where he witnessed the courage and determination of those taking part, he decided to bring a similar event to Britain.

Modeled on the Warrior Games—an annual sports event for injured service members and veterans in the US—the Invictus Games were organized in only 10 months. Funding came equally from the Royal Foundation—established by the Duke and Duchess of Cambridge and Prince Harry—and from the Treasury.

At the official launch in March 2014, Harry said, "I have witnessed firsthand how the power of sport can actively impact the lives of wounded, injured, and sick servicemen and women in their journey of recovery." Six months later, Prince Charles, the Duchess of Cornwall, Prince William, and Prime Minister David Cameron were there to see Harry, as founder of the Games, welcome more than 400 competitors from 13 countries to the Queen Elizabeth Olympic Park in east London. The countries taking part included eight from Europe, one from Asia, two from North America, and two from Oceania. All had fought alongside Britain in recent military campaigns. Iraq was invited to send a team, but declined to do so.

Invictus is Latin for "undefeated." At the opening ceremony, actor Idris Elba read the short poem *Invictus* by the Victorian poet William Ernest Henley, with its inspiring lines: "My head is bloody, but unbowed… I am the master of my fate, I am the captain of my soul." Over the next four days, events were held at five different venues used during the 2012 London Olympics. Serving personnel as well as veterans injured in the line of duty competed in nine different adaptive sports: archery, indoor rowing, power lifting, road cycling, sitting volleyball, swimming, wheelchair basketball, and wheelchair rugby. Prince Harry attended every event. Planning is underway for a follow-up Invictus Games in 2016.

> **"**I have no doubt that **lives will be changed** this weekend.**"**
>
> **PRINCE HARRY,** IN HIS OPENING SPEECH AT THE INVICTUS GAMES, SEPTEMBER 10, 2014

Star-studded event
Harry and his cousin Zara Tindall, daughter of Princess Anne, compete in an exhibition game of wheelchair rugby. Other sports stars who took part in the Invictus Games included Zara's husband, Mike Tindall, and British Olympic legends Dame Kelly Holmes and Denise Lewis.

The Queen as Patron

Outside the pomp of a royal ceremony or state visit, the public is most familiar with the Queen in her role as patron, visiting a hospital, school, or organization, or hosting a reception in aid of one of her many charities.

Garden party event
The Queen greets Andy Reid, an injured Afghanistan veteran, at a garden party held at Buckingham Palace for the "Not Forgotten" Association—a charity that helps ex-service personnel.

Queen Elizabeth II is patron of more than 600 organizations and charities. These range from large medical charities such as Cancer Research and the British Red Cross to smaller organizations such as the Friends of the Elderly and the Fire Fighters Charity. Many scientific and professional institutions—such as the Royal Society, the Royal Institute of British Architects, and the Royal Society for the Protection of Birds—have royal charters that ensure that the reigning monarch is always their patron, but the Queen also supports scores of small charities such as the Reedham Trust, a Surrey-based charity that cares for children who have suffered parental bereavement, the Manchester Geographical Society, which encourages geographical research in the northwest of England, and the Society for Promoting Christian Knowledge, the Church of England's earliest missionary society, established in 1698 to support Christian education. Her Majesty is patron of the National Federation of Women's Institutes, founded in 1915 to revitalize rural communities and encourage women to play a part in food production. She attends the New Year meeting of her local branch at West Newton, Norfolk, while staying at Sandringham for her winter break. The Queen also supports a large number of animal welfare charities—from the Dog Trust and the Royal Society for the Prevention of Cruelty to Animals (RSPCA) to the Fell Pony Society and the Labrador Retriever Club.

Kinds of support
The support the Queen gives to each of her charities varies according to its type, setup, and the kind of work it does. As patron, she allows her name to be placed at the head of the organization's official communications, thereby helping to raise its public profile and promote its work. The officers of the organization may be invited from time to time to a meeting with the Queen or one of her private secretaries to report on its affairs, or she will send a representative to its annual general meeting—or even attend herself, if there is an important occasion such as a centenary to be observed. She visits national and regional headquarters, meeting staff and volunteers.

The Queen also allows individual charities to hold a lunchtime or evening reception at Buckingham Palace, Windsor Castle, or Holyrood Palace when she is in Scotland. It gives wealthy supporters of a charity the chance to meet their patron, and helps to attract donors and publicity. Sometimes the help the Queen gives a charity is of a strictly practical nature—for instance, the gift of a Land Rover to aid the work of the Leonard Cheshire Trust, which is involved with people with disabilities, in Zimbabwe. She invites representatives from the many organizations she supports to the garden parties she hosts each summer at Buckingham Palace as a way of showing her appreciation for the work they do. She also gives generously as a private individual to various charities.

Raising awareness
The Queen's presence at an event or organization attracts national attention. For example, she carried out a joint engagement with the Duchess of Cornwall to open the new headquarters of Barnardo's in 2013. The Queen has been patron of the society, which supports 200,000 vulnerable children in the UK each year, since 1983 and the Duchess of Cornwall is its president. Because their visit took place just before Christmas, they were invited to take part in the society's annual Giving Tree campaign by donating Christmas tree ornaments. The event received newspaper and television coverage, creating favorable publicity for the charity.

Sharing the work
Some 17 members of the Royal Family share the work of royal patronage with the Queen, supporting a total of 2,415 organizations in the UK, and almost 3,000 worldwide. Individual members of the Royal Family support those charities that they consider to be rewarding or important, and which fall within their own areas of interest and concern. Their endorsement of a charity helps to raise public awareness of its work. The Duke of Edinburgh alone is patron of more than 700 organizations, including more than 250 involved with sports and recreation initiatives, and 100 with the armed services. The Prince of Wales has an interest in environmental causes and the built environment, while the Duchess of Cornwall is concerned with programs to encourage literacy and reading, such as Booktrust and First Story. She is President of the National Osteoporosis Society, which researches the brittle bone disease that affected both her mother and grandmother.

£1.4 **BILLION ($2.1 billion)**
The amount Queen Elizabeth II has raised for the charities she supports.

<< **BEFORE**

The annual distribution of Maundy money by the Queen is a form of royal charity that has its origins in the Middle Ages.

ROYAL MAUNDY SERVICE
Every **Maundy Thursday** (the day in the church calendar before Good Friday) the Queen visits a **cathedral** to present local elderly people with two purses, one containing **modern** coinage, and the other, **specially minted** coins (Maundy money). The ceremony is based on Jesus Christ's command (*Mandatum*) to love one another when he washed his disciples' feet at the Last Supper and dates back to the 13th century when the sovereign would give money, food, clothing, and wash the recipient's feet.

MAUNDY MONEY OF GEORGE VI

Golden Jubilee Tour
As patron of the Royal National Lifeboat Institution (RNLI) the Queen names a new all-weather lifeboat, RNLB *Richard Cox Scott*, in Falmouth Harbour during her Golden Jubilee visit to Cornwall in May 2002.

The number of charities supported by the Queen and the other members of the Royal Family is increasing every year.

REQUESTS FOR PATRONAGE

Charities are aware that having **a royal patron helps to attract much-needed publicity and funds,** and gives it recognition and status. Buckingham Palace receives **hundreds of requests for patronage** each year. Individual members of the Royal Family can only take on a limited number of new requests, but the younger royals in particular are championing lesser-known causes, rather than the mainstream charities.

One of the hardest working members of the Royal Family is Princess Anne, who is currently patron of more than 300 organizations. As President of Save the Children since 1970, she has helped to raise awareness of the charity and its work, both at home and overseas. She makes at least two field trips a year to Africa to witness the work performed by the charity, often venturing into remote terrain.

Prince William and Prince Harry have both inherited Diana, Princess of Wales's compassionate concern. Prince William has taken over some his mother's favorite charities, including Centrepoint, which works with homeless young people, and the Royal Marsden Hospital. He and Catherine chose to support charitable causes as part of their wedding celebrations as well. They particularly support those causes concerned with children. The Duchess of Cambridge's growing portfolio of charities includes Place2Be, which works in schools to provide early-intervention mental health support, and the Art Room, an Oxford-based charity that offers art as therapy for children with behavioral difficulties. Prince Harry is patron of a smaller number of organizations, including Sentebale, the charity he cofounded in Lesotho (see pp.288–89). This number is likely to grow as Prince Harry finds more time for involvement now that he has left his life in the army.

Traditional charity
The Queen distributed Maundy money at Blackburn Cathedral in 2014. The number of recipients is determined by her age – as she was 88 that year, she gave Maundy money to 88 men and 88 women.

The centenary of World War I
Queen Elizabeth II visits the *Blood Swept Lands and Seas of Red* display of 888,246 ceramic poppies at the Tower of London in 2014. Each poppy represented a British fallen soldier from World War I.

« BEFORE

The working life of the sovereign has changed over the centuries. Many duties the Queen performs today have evolved in the last 100 years.

ROYAL MEDDLER
Queen Victoria « 50–55 interfered in government in a way that would be impossible now, peppering her ministers with letters of advice and admonition, especially over foreign affairs and public appointments. She did not like appearing in public and after the death of Prince Albert in 1861, hardly ever did so, attending only seven **State Openings of Parliament « 134–35** after that.

DUTIFUL MONARCH
Although **Edward VII « 72–73** played a more public role, opening hospitals and other institutions, the modern concept of the working monarch really developed in the reign of **George V « 78–79**. No great intellect, he emphasized the **idea of duty**, believing that the primary role of the monarchy was to maintain traditional values and customs.

The Royal Working Life

The Queen attends more than 300 official engagements a year, including the lengthy, often exhausting ceremonial duties she performs as head of state. Even in her 90th year, she still has a heavy and varied program of work.

On a normal day, the Queen devotes the first part of her morning to her correspondence. She receives some 200–300 letters a day. The Queen glances through this mailbag, selecting some to read, and tells her correspondence secretary or ladies in waiting how she wishes them to be answered. Virtually every letter receives a reply.

The Queen then meets with her two private secretaries and goes through the official papers that are sent each day in a government red box bearing the royal cypher. They include policy papers, Cabinet documents, and letters from government ministers and Commonwealth officials. They all have to be read and, where necessary, approved and signed. She may hold audiences (meetings) with overseas diplomats, British ambassadors, senior members of the armed forces, bishops, judges, and leading figures from the fields of science or literature. She sees each visitor alone, and the meeting usually lasts 20 minutes.

Around 25 times a year, and lately decreasing in number, the Queen holds an investiture at 11 a.m. in the ballroom at Buckingham Palace at which she invests a number of people who have been named in the Birthday or New Year's Honors List with their awards (around 2,600 are given out a year). Sometimes Prince Charles, Prince William, or Princess Anne will hold an investiture on her behalf.

Public engagements
The Queen usually attends public engagements such as visits to schools, hospitals, community centers, and places of work in the afternoon, though sometimes she spends a whole day, in which case the Duke of Edinburgh is likely to accompany her. The Queen chooses which places to visit from the many invitations she is sent each year, often by the Lord-Lieutenants—the Queen's personal representatives in each county of the United Kingdom.

50,000 The number of people who visit Buckingham Palace each year as guests of the Queen.

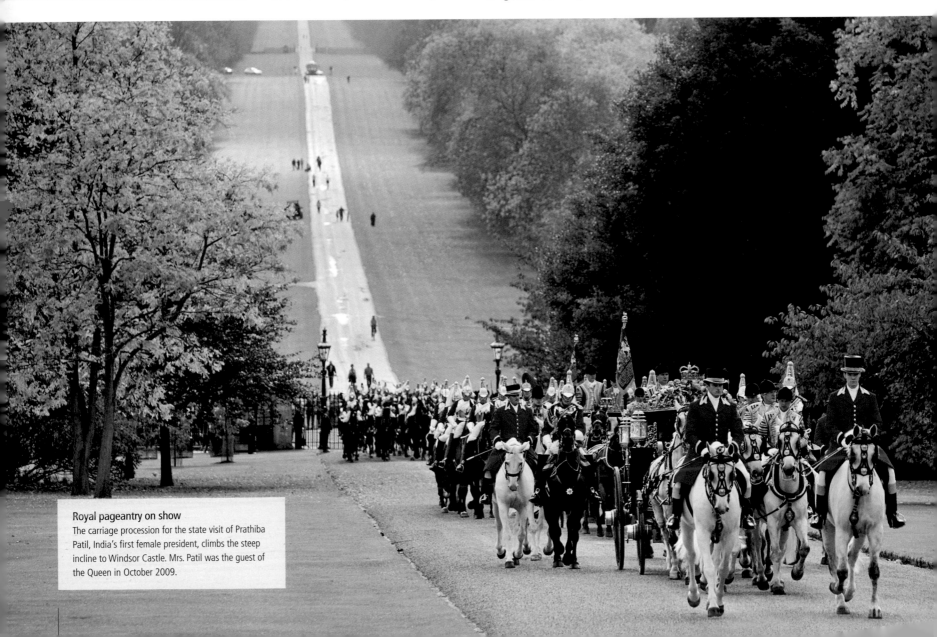

Royal pageantry on show
The carriage procession for the state visit of Prathiba Patil, India's first female president, climbs the steep incline to Windsor Castle. Mrs. Patil was the guest of the Queen in October 2009.

The Queen has recently begun to hand over some of her public duties, particularly overseas travel, to other members of the royal family.

SCALING DOWN

That the Queen undertook no overseas visits in her **Diamond Jubilee** year ❮❮ 280–83 was a sign that she is reducing long-distance travel due to her age. Most significant was her decision not to attend the **Commonwealth Heads of Government Meeting** held in Sri Lanka in 2013, the first time in 40 years she had not attended. **Prince Charles** went in her place, amid calls to boycott the event due to human rights violations in the host country. The Queen's overseas trips are now restricted to Europe: she visited Italy in 2014 and France, also in 2014, for the **70th anniversary of D-Day** ❮❮ 239, and plans to make a state visit to Germany in June 2015.

When she is in London, the Queen's weekly meeting with the Prime Minister takes place on Wednesdays at 6:30 p.m. When Parliament is sitting she receives a report of the day's proceedings written by one of the government's whips, which she reads the same evening. Later in the evening the Queen may, on rare instances, attend a film première, concert, or reception on behalf of one of the many organizations of which she is patron. She also hosts official receptions at the Palace, such as those held annually for the diplomatic corps and those for winners of the Queen's Award for Enterprise (formerly Industry), which promotes business excellence.

Duke of Normandy

The Queen is known as the Duke of Normandy in the Channel Islands—self-governing territories with their own legislative assemblies that have belonged to the English crown since 1106. Here her head appears on a Jersey pound note.

The Court Circular

A list of the Queen's engagements, and those of other members of her family, is published the next day in the Court Circular. This appears in *The Times*, the *Daily Telegraph*, and *The Scotsman* newspapers, and has been in existence since 1803 when George III appointed a "court newsman." His job was to provide the newspapers with accurate information about the court in order to counter the many false rumors in the press at that time. The Court Circular

is prepared in the Queen's press office, and she always approves it before it is sent to the newspapers.

State visits

Foreign heads of state are invited by the Queen to make a formal visit to Britain on the advice of the Foreign and Commonwealth Office, with the aim of strengthening ties and building economic links. There are usually two such visits a year. The visit normally begins with a ceremonial welcome by the Queen or other senior royal. If in London, the visitor inspects a guard of honor on Horse Guards Parade, then travels in a carriage procession to Buckingham Palace. In the evening the Queen hosts a state banquet in honor of the visitor. During the one-to-three-day visit, he or she will meet the Prime Minister, and perhaps visit a school, museum, or business that has links with their country. Recent visiting heads of state have included the President of Ireland in 2014, and in 2015, the President of Mexico.

Head of the armed forces

As sovereign the Queen is head of the armed forces, a duty she takes very seriously. Under the royal prerogative, only the monarch, acting on the advice of the Government, can declare war or peace. The Queen has never done so as there has been no formal declaration of war since 1939, though British troops have engaged in numerous armed conflicts during her reign. The Queen takes a keen interest in the armed forces of the UK and the Commonwealth. She visits army, navy,

Elizabeth II Visits The Highlanders

The Queen joins the Argyll and Sutherland Highlanders at their barracks in Canterbury, Kent. She was there as head of the army to witness the battalion's final parade.

"I… give my **heart** and devotion to **these islands**."

QUEEN ELIZABETH II, CHRISTMAS BROADCAST, 1957

and air force establishments to meet servicemen and servicewomen of all ranks, and holds audiences with the Chief of Defence Staff and other senior military figures. She and members of her family hold appointments and honorary ranks in the armed forces, and she attends the Remembrance Day service in Whitehall in November.

There are many other duties, such as the State Opening of Parliament (see pp.308–09), that the Queen carries out as head of state. Many are full of symbolism, such as the annual service for the Order of the Garter, which takes place at Windsor Castle in June. The Garter is Britain's senior order of chivalry, founded by Edward III in 1348, and the service is preceded by a procession of all the Knights of the Garter in their blue velvet mantles and plumed hats.

One event the Queen always enjoys is the Chelsea Flower Show. Held in the grounds of the Royal Hospital, Chelsea, since 1913, and

organized by the Royal Horticultural Society, it has become a regular fixture in the royal calendar. Every summer the Queen hosts at least three garden parties at Buckingham Palace and one at Holyrood Palace in Edinburgh. About 8,000 people attend each one, to enjoy tea and cakes and possibly to meet the Queen. They are drawn from all walks of life and have usually contributed in some way to their community or profession.

In these, and countless other ways, the Queen fulfills her role as the head of the nation. And of course she is ready to perform occasional tasks such as opening the Olympic Games. She has a truly formidable workload for anyone, let alone an octogenarian.

The Order Of The Garter

Four royal knights (Andrew, Edward, William, and Charles) attend the Order of the Garter service, Windsor Castle. The Queen is Sovereign of the Order, which has only 24 knights, plus the royal knights and ladies.

State Opening of Parliament
In her formal role as head of state, Queen Elizabeth II reads the Speech from the Throne at the State Opening of Parliament, a duty she usually performs once a year.

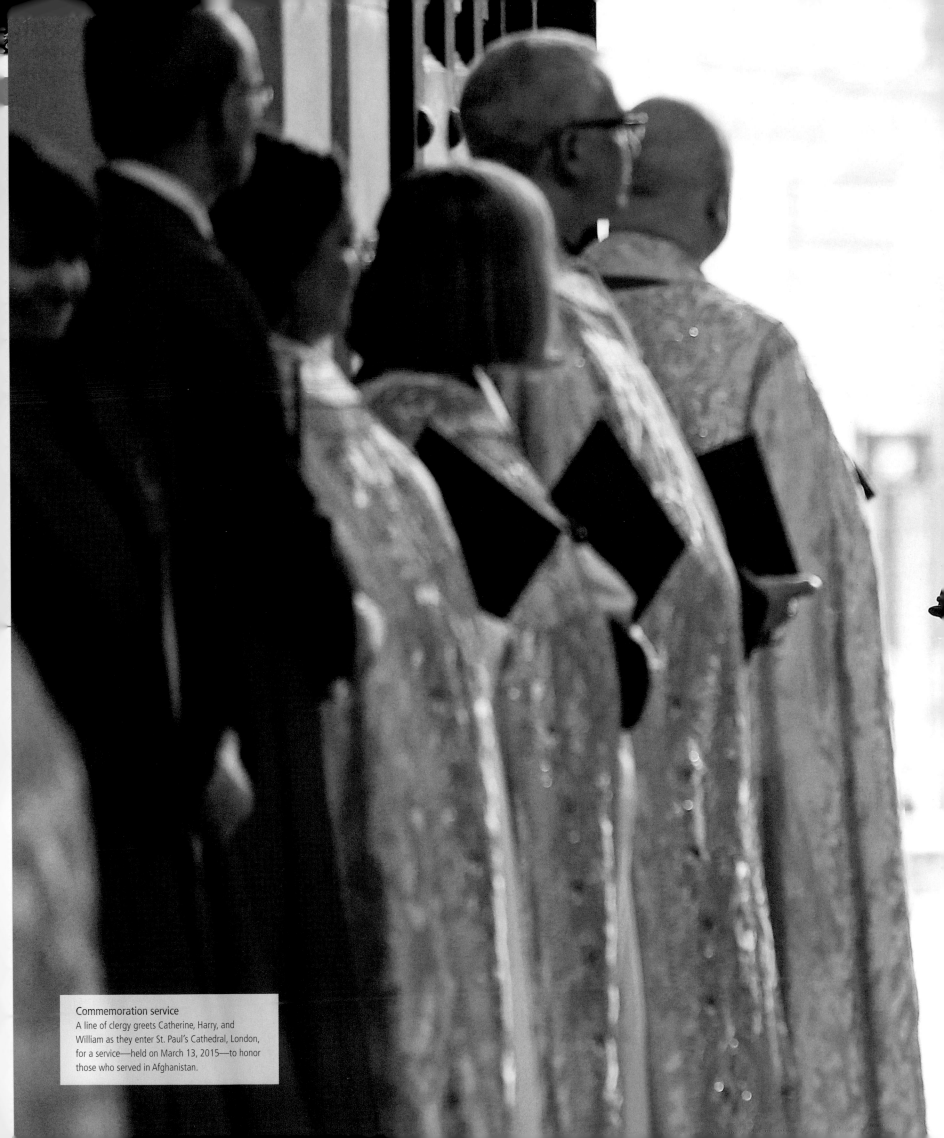

Commemoration service
A line of clergy greets Catherine, Harry, and William as they enter St. Paul's Cathedral, London, for a service—held on March 13, 2015—to honor those who served in Afghanistan.

Index

Acknowledgments

Dorling Kindersley would like to thank: Stefan Podhorodecki and Paul Self for photography; Sneha Sunder Benjamin, Arpita Dasgupta, Helen Bridge, Suefa Lee, Isha Sharma, Fleur Star, and Sonia Yooshing for editorial assistance; Devika Awasthi, Paul Drislane, Parul Gambhir, Roshni Kapur, Shahid Mahmood, and Amit Malhotra for design assistance; Monica Byles for proofreading; Colin Hynson for indexing; and Gill Pitts, Karen Self, Helen Spencer, and Sharon Bartlett for allowing us to photograph their royal memorabilia.

Special thanks go to Agata Rutkowska, Picture Library Assistant, Royal Collection Trust; Chris Barker, Assistant Curator, Royal Mint; and John Loughery for help and advice.

The publisher would also like to thank James Grinter at Reeman Dansie Auctioneers for allowing us to photograph their collections.

Reeman Dansie Auctioneers
No. 8 Wyncolls Road
Colchester CO4 9HU
www.reemandansie.com/

Picture Credits
The publisher would like to thank the following for their kind permission to reproduce their photographs:

(Key: a-above; b-below/bottom; c-center; f-far; l-left; r-right; t-top)

1 Royal Mint Museum. 2–3 Corbis: Reuters / Luke Macgregor. 4 Corbis: Hoberman Collection (cra). 5 Corbis: Bettmann (br); Hulton-Deutsch Collection (tr). Dorling Kindersley: Reeman Dansie Auctioneers (cla, bl). Getty Images: Hulton Archive (tl). The Royal Collection Trust © Her Majesty Queen Elizabeth II 2015: (cra). 6 Alamy Images: Holmes Garden Photos (ca). Corbis: Ralf-Finn Hestoft (br). Getty Images: Hulton Archive (bl); Central Press (tl); Chris Jackson (tr). Royal Mint Museum: (cra). 7 Corbis: Chris Ison / epa (br); Pool Photograph (tl). Getty Images: WPA Pool (tr). The Royal Collection Trust © Her Majesty Queen Elizabeth II 2015: (cla) 8–9 Corbis: Hoberman Collection. 10 Bridgeman Images: National Archives, UK (ca); Alecto Historical Editions, London, UK (bc); The Trustees of the Weston Park Foundation, UK (cr). By permission of The British Library: (cla). Dorling Kindersley: Ashmolean Museum, Oxford (cl) 11 Corbis: The Gallery Collection (clb); Leemage (bc). Dorling Kindersley: Reeman Dansie Auctioneers (cr). The Art Archive Ashmolean Museum (cla). 12 Dorling Kindersley: National Maritime Museum, London (b); Ashmolean Museum, Oxford (tr). 13 By permission of The British Library: (cr). The Art Archive: Musée de la Tapisserie Bayeux / Gianni Dagli Orti (c). 14–15 The Art Archive: Musée de la Tapisserie Bayeux / Gianni Dagli Orti. 16 Bridgeman Images: Chetham's Library, Manchester, UK. 17 Bridgeman Images: Alecto Historical Editions, London, UK (crb).

Corbis: The Gallery Collection (t). Photo SCALA, Florence: British Library board / Robana / Scala, Florence (bl). 18–19 Getty Images: DeAgostini. 20 By permission of The British Library: (tr). Dorling Kindersley: The Trustees of the British Museum (b). 21 Alamy Images: travelibUK (bl). Bridgeman Images: National Archives, UK (cr); Bibliothèque Nationale, Paris, France (tc). 22–23 Bridgeman Images: Bibliothèque Nationale, Paris, France. 24 Alamy Images: Mary Evans Picture Library (bl). 24–25 Bridgeman Images: The Trustees of the Weston Park Foundation, UK; National Portrait Gallery, London, UK (Henry V). 25 Corbis: Leemage (tr). 26–27 Bridgeman Images: De Agostini Picture Library. 28 Alamy Images: The Art Archive (cl). Corbis: Gianni Dagli Orti (r). 29 Corbis: Hoberman Collection (bc); Miles Ertman / All Canada Photos (tl); Leemage (cr). 30–31 Bridgeman Images: Musée de Blois, Blois, France. 32–33 Corbis: The Gallery Collection. 33 Bridgeman Images: Hoefnagel, Joris (1542–1600) / Private Collection (cb). Corbis: (tl, bc). 34–35 Corbis: Farrell Grehan (b). 34 National Museums of Scotland: (tr). 35 Bridgeman Images: His Grace The Duke of Norfolk, Arundel Castle (tr); National Library of Scotland, Edinburgh, Scotland (cl); Scottish National Portrait Gallery, Edinburgh, Scotland (cb). 36–37 The Royal Collection Trust © Her Majesty Queen Elizabeth II 2015. 37 Alamy Images: Realy Easy Star / Giuseppe Masci (bc); Rolf Richardson (crb). Corbis: Andrew Milligan / PA Wire / epa (br). 38 Corbis: Gianni Dagli Orti. 39 Alamy Images: Mary Evans Picture Library (bc). Corbis: The Gallery Collection (cl). Getty Images: DEA / G. Nimatallah (tr). 40 Corbis: (cra). 40–41 Bridgeman Images: Cheltenham Art Gallery & Museums, Gloucestershire, UK (b). 41 Alamy Images: The Art Archive (tl). 42–43 The Royal Collection Trust © Her Majesty Queen Elizabeth II 2015. 44–45 Corbis: Jason Hawkes (t). 44 Rex Features: Jonathan Hordle (bl). 45 Corbis: Philip Craven / Robert Harding World Imagery (bc). Dreamstime.com: Aagje De Jong (br). 46 Alamy Images: Steve Vidler (b). Getty Images: Tim Graham (tr, cra). 47 Rex Features. 48 Alamy Images: GL Archive (b). Getty Images: Apic (tr). 49 Corbis: The Gallery Collection (r). 50 Corbis: The Gallery Collection (bl); Hulton-Deutsch Collection (r). 51 Dorling Kindersley: Royal Green Jackets Museum, Winchester (crb); Thackray Medical Museum (cl). The Royal Collection Trust © Her Majesty Queen Elizabeth II 2015: (bc); (t). 52–53 akg-images: Archie Miles. ley: Reeman Dansie Auctioneers (cra). 54–55 The Royal Collection Trust © Her Majesty Queen Elizabeth II 2015. 55 The Royal Collection Trust © Her Majesty Queen Elizabeth II 2015: (br); (tl). 56–57 Bridgeman Images: De Agostini Picture Library / W. Buss. 57 Alamy Images: Graham Prentice (cb). Bridgeman Images: Historic England (br) Corbis: Corrie: Nigel / Arcaid (bc). 58–59 Corbis: Historical Picture Archive. 60 Corbis: (r). Getty Images: Universal History Archive (bl). 61 Getty

Images: Davide Cioffi (c). The Royal Collection Trust © Her Majesty Queen Elizabeth II 2015: (cra). 62–63 Bridgeman Images: Haig, Axel (1835–1921) / British Library, London, UK. 64 Alamy Images: The Art Archive (cl). Bridgeman Images: Harris, Albert E (fl.1917) / Roy Miles Fine Paintings (b). Getty Images: Arkivi (ca). 65 Alamy Images: David Coleman (br). Getty Images: Popperfoto (cb). Mary Evans Picture Library: Illustrated London News Ltd (t). 66 Dorling Kindersley: Reeman Dansie Auctioneers (t, bl, cr, br). 67 Corbis: (tr). Getty Images: Hulton Archive (b). 68 The Royal Collection Trust © Her Majesty Queen Elizabeth II 2015: (cl, clb, bl). 68–69 The Royal Collection Trust © Her Majesty Queen Elizabeth II 2015. 69 The Royal Collection Trust © Her Majesty Queen Elizabeth II 2015: (tl, bl). 70–71 The Royal Collection Trust © Her Majesty Queen Elizabeth II 2015. 72 The Royal Collection Trust © Her Majesty Queen Elizabeth II 2015: (l). V&A Images / Victoria and Albert Museum, London: (br). 73 Dorling Kindersley: Reeman Dansie Auctioneers (t, tc, cla, cr). Getty Images: Elliott & Fry (bc). 74–75 Dorling Kindersley: Reeman Dansie Auctioneers. 76 123RF.com: Scott Clarke (cb). Dorling Kindersley: Reeman Dansie Auctioneers (cla, cr). 77 Dorling Kindersley: Reeman Dansie Auctioneers (cl); The Wardrobe Museum, Salisbury (ca). Getty Images: Keystone (bc). Press Association Images: Topfoto / Topham Picturepoint (crb). 78 Alamy Images: (l). Corbis Hulton-Deutsch Collection (cr). 79 Corbis: Hulton-Deutsch Collection (br). Getty Images: Hulton Archive (bl). The Royal Collection Trust © Her Majesty Queen Elizabeth II 2015: (tc). 80 Getty Images: The Print Collector (cla); Central Press / Hulton Archive (tr). 80–81 Getty Images: Popperfoto (b). 81 Alamy Images: Universal Art Archive (bc). Mary Evans Picture Library: (tr). Royal Artillery Historical Trust: (c). 82–83 Corbis: Hulton-Deutsch Collection. 84 Getty Images: Tim Graham (b). 84–85 The Royal Collection Trust © Her Majesty Queen Elizabeth II 2015. 86 Press Association Images: Fiona Hanson (b). The Royal Collection Trust © Her Majesty Queen Elizabeth II 2015: (tr, cra). 87 The Royal Collection Trust © Her Majesty Queen Elizabeth II 2015. 88–89 Getty Images: Hulton Archive. 90 Bridgeman Images: Look and Learn / Elgar Collection (r). The Art Archive: Private Collection MD (bl). 91 Alamy Images: Hilary Morgan (bc); Ivan Vdovin (crb). Getty Images: Keystone (tc). 92 Corbis: Hulton-Deutsch Collection (br). Dorling Kindersley: Reeman Dansie Auctioneers (tr). The Art Archive: Mondadori Portfolio (bl). 93 Alamy Images: Keystone Pictures USA. Getty Images: Hulton Archive (crb). 94 Dorling Kindersley: Reeman Dansie Auctioneers (tl, tc). Getty Images: Fox Photos (cra). 95 Getty Images: Topical Press Agency (tc); Keystone. 96 Corbis: (r). Getty Images: The Print Collector (bl). 97 Dorling Kindersley: Reeman Dansie Auctioneers (tl). Royal Mint Museum: (bc). The

Stanley Gibbons Group plc: (cr). 98 Getty Images: Lisa Sheridan / Studio Lisa / Hulton Archive (cl). Press Association Images: (br). The Royal Collection Trust © Her Majesty Queen Elizabeth II 2015: (ca). 99 The Royal Collection Trust © Her Majesty Queen Elizabeth II 2015. 100–101 Corbis: Hulton-Deutsch Collection. 102 Corbis: Hulton-Deutsch Collection (tr). 102–103 Getty Images: Fox Photos / Hulton Archive. 103 Alamy Images: Pictorial Press Ltd (tc). Press Association Images: Topfoto / Topham Picturepoint (br). 104–105 Mirrorpix. 106 Getty Images: Topical Press Agency / Hulton Archive (bl). The Royal Collection Trust © Her Majesty Queen Elizabeth II 2015: (cra). 107 Getty Images: David E. Scherman / The LIFE Picture Collection. 108–109 Corbis: Hulton-Deutsch Collection. 110 Corbis: Bettmann (r). Getty Images: Rita Martin (bl). Mirrorpix: (bc). 111 Alamy Images: Heritage Image Partnership Ltd (bl). Corbis: Matthew Polak / Sygma (tc). Dorling Kindersley: Reeman Dansie Auctioneers (tl). 112–113 Getty Images: Popperfoto. 114 Getty Images: Popperfoto. 115 Getty Images: Popperfoto (bc). Mirrorpix: (cr). Press Association Images: AP Photo (tl). 116–117 The Royal Collection Trust © Her Majesty Queen Elizabeth II 2015. 118 Dorling Kindersley: Reeman Dansie Auctioneers (ca). Getty Images: Central Press (br); E. Round / Fox Photos (cr). Mirrorpix: (cl); NCJ – Kemsley (bl). 119 Alamy Images: Vintage Image (cla). Corbis: Bettmann (bl). Getty Images: Topical Press Agency (cl). Press Association Images: AP (cr). 120 123RF.com: tommroch (cl). Mirrorpix: NCJ – Kemsley (bl). Rex Features: Associated Newspapers / Daily Mail (cr). 121 123RF.com: © Stamp Design Royal Mail Group Ltd (br). Rex Features: Daily Mail. 122–123 Alamy Images: Arcaid Images. 123 Alamy Images: Arcaid Images (bl); Prixpics (bc); worldthroughthelens-UK (br). 124–125 Getty Images: Central Press. 124 Christopher Hogue Thompson: (bl). 125 Getty Images: Central Press (crb). Leo Reynolds: (c). Victor Kusin: (tc). 126 Dorling Kindersley: Reeman Dansie Auctioneers (bl). 126–127 Dorling Kindersley: Reeman Dansie Auctioneers. 127 Dorling Kindersley: Reeman Dansie Auctioneers (br). 128–129 Press Association Images: AP Photo / Max Desfor. 130 Corbis: Henri Bureau / Sygma (br). Getty Images: Lisa Sheridan / Studio Lisa (tr). 131 The College of Arms: The royal arms (the arms of Queen Elizabeth II). Reproduced by permission of the Kings, Heralds and Pursuivants of Arms (cr). The Royal Collection Trust © Her Majesty Queen Elizabeth II 2015. 132 Dorling Kindersley: Reeman Dansie Auctioneers (br). Mirrorpix: NCJ – Topix (t). 133 Dorling Kindersley: Reeman Dansie Auctioneers (tl). Getty Images: E Round / Fox Photos (br). 134 Getty Images: Central Press (bl). 134–135 The Royal Collection Trust © Her Majesty Queen Elizabeth II 2015. 135 Corbis: Pool Photograph (br). Press Association Images: Barratts / S&G Barratts / EMPICS Archive (tr). 136 The

Royal Collection Trust © Her Majesty Queen Elizabeth II 2015: (tl, cra, tr). 136–137 The Royal Collection Trust © Her Majesty Queen Elizabeth II 2015. 137 The Royal Collection Trust © Her Majesty Queen Elizabeth II 2015: (t, c). 138–139 Corbis: David Boyer / National Geographic Creative. 140 Dorling Kindersley: Reeman Dansie Auctioneers (clb, bl). Getty Images: Topical Press Agency. 141 Corbis: Bettmann (ca). Dorling Kindersley: Paul Self. 142–143 Alamy Images: V&A Images. 144 The Royal Collection Trust © Her Majesty Queen Elizabeth II 2015: All Rights Reserved (cla, bl, r). 145 The Royal Collection Trust © Her Majesty Queen Elizabeth II 2015: All Rights Reserved (tl, tr, r). 146 Alamy Images: Justin Kase (bl). Getty Images: Max Mumby / Indigo (bc); Picture Post (clb). 146–147 Alamy Images: The Print Collector (bc). Rex Features: Peter Richardson / Robert Harding (tl). 147 Alamy Images: Krys Bailey (bc); The Foto Factory (cb). 148 Bridgeman Images: English Photographer, (20th century) / Museum purchase with funds donated by Michael D Wolfe (br). The Royal Collection Trust © Her Majesty Queen Elizabeth II 2015: (bl). The Art Archive: Victoria and Albert Museum London / V&A Images (cl). 149 Bridgeman Images: English Photographer, (20th century) / © Country Life. 150 Getty Images: Cornell Capa / The LIFE Picture Collection. 151 Dreamstime.com: Creativehearts (c). Getty Images: Dan Kitwood (br). The Art Archive: Ashmolean Museum (clb). 152 Alamy Images: Vintage Image (cl). 152–153 Getty Images: Central Press (c). 153 Corbis: Bettmann (tc); Gideon Mendel (br). 154 Rex Features. 155 Corbis: Bettmann (bl, tr). Getty Images: Popperfoto (cl). 156–157 Press Association Images: AP. 158–159 Royal Mint Museum. 160 Alamy Images: V&A Images (ca). Bridgeman Images: Armstrong-Jones, Antony (b.1930) / Private Collection / Photo © Christie's Images (cr). Press Association Images: PA / PA Archive (bc). 161 123RF.com: © Stamp Design Royal Mail Group Ltd (c). Corbis: Norman Parkinson / Sygma (bl). Rex Features: Mike Hollist / Associated Newspapers (crb). Royal Mint Museum: (cra). 162 Alamy Images: V&A Images (cl). Corbis: Teresa Dapp / dpa (tr). TopFoto.co.uk: (bc). 163 Corbis: Norman Parkinson / Sygma (tr). Rex Features: Joan Williams (bl). 164–165 Getty Images: Jim Gray. 166 Getty Images: Mark Cuthbert (l); Tim Graham (cr). 167 The College of Arms: the arms of HRH the Prince of Wales. Reproduced by permission of the Kings, Heralds and Pursuivants of Arms (cr). Getty Images: Mark Cuthbert (bl); WPA Pool / Pool (c). Rex Features: Reginald Davis (tl). 168–169 Press Association Images: PA / PA Archive. 170 Corbis: Adam Woolfitt (cb). Rex Features: Joan Williams (cla). 171 Bridgeman Images: Armstrong-Jones, Antony (b.1930) / Private Collection / Photo © Christie's Images (bl). Corbis: Bettmann (crb). TopFoto.co.uk: PA (tl). 172–173 Getty Images: Hulton Archive. 174 Corbis: Norman Parkinson / Sygma (t) Getty Images: Central Press (bl). Press Association Images: Khan Tariq Mikkel / Polfoto (cr). 175 Corbis: Norman Parkinson / Sygma (c). 176–177 Rex features: Reginald Davis. 178–179 Getty Images: Lichfield. 180 Getty Images: Central Press (cla); WPA Pool / Pool (b). 181 Rex Features: (br). The

Prince's Trust: (tc). 182 Getty Images: Graham Wiltshire (t). Royal Mint Museum: (br). 183 Getty Images: Serge Lemoine (bl); Central Press (tr); Fox Photos / Hulton Archive (c). 184–185 Corbis: Hulton-Deutsch Collection. 186–187 Rex Features: Reginald Davis. 188 Corbis: Norman Parkinson / Sygma (br). Getty Images: Jacques Gustave (tr); Popperfoto (bl). 189 Alamy Images: Trinity Mirror / Mirrorpix. Getty Images: Hulton Archive (b). 190 Getty Images: Guildhall Library & Art Gallery / Heritage Images (bl). Press Association Images: John Stillwell / PA Archive (br). 190–191 Corbis: Stapleton Collection. 192 Alamy Images: Robert Estall photo agency (bc); Keystone Pictures USA (cra). Corbis: Hulton-Deutsch Collection (bl). 193 The Random House Group Ltd: (cr). Rex Features: Mike Hollist / Associated Newspapers (b) 194 Rex Features: Associated Newspapers (tr). TopFoto.co.uk: Topham / AP (br). 195 Corbis: Stephen Morrison / epa (br). 196–197 Royal Mint Museum. 198 123RF.com: © Stamp Design Royal Mail Group Ltd (bl). Alamy Images: Trinity Mirror / Mirrorpix (c). Corbis: Bettmann (cr); Quadrillion (cl). 199 Getty Images: Tim Graham (clb). Rex Features: (cb). The Royal Collection Trust © Her Majesty Queen Elizabeth II 2015: (ca). 200 Corbis: Atlan-Bureau-Dejean-Graham-Guichard-Karel-Melloul-Nogues-Pavlovsky-Rancinan. Getty Images: Tim Graham (cl). 201 123RF.com: Andy Lidstone / © Stamp Design Royal Mail Group Ltd (tr). Corbis: Douglas Kirkland (br). 202–203 Getty Images: Anwar Hussein. 204 123RF.com: © Stamp Design Royal Mail Group Ltd (8). Dorling Kindersley: © Stamp Design Royal Mail Group Ltd (t). The Stanley Gibbons Group plc: (14, 15); (1, 2, 3, 4, 5, 6, 7, 9, 10, 11, 12, 13). 205 Dorling Kindersley: © Stamp Design Royal Mail Group Ltd (1, 2, 3, 4, 5, 6, 7, 8, 9, 12, 13, 15). Dreamstime.com: © Stamp Design Royal Mail Group Ltd (10, 11, 14). 206 Getty Images: Central Press (bl). Rex Features: (tr). 207 Getty Images: Sion Touhig (bl). Press Association Images: PA Archive (br). Rex Features: David Levenson. 208 Alamy Images: Trinity Mirror / Mirrorpix (c). Rushden Research: (cla). 209 Mirrorpix: Gavin Kent (tr). Press Association Images: Bebeto Mattews / AP (bl). 210–211 Getty Images: Tim Graham. 212 Getty Images: Jason Hawkes (br); DEA / W. BUSS (bl). 213 SuperStock: Steve Vidler / Steve Vidler. 214 Alamy Images: Prisma Bildagentur AG (tl). Press Association Images: David Jensen / EMPICS Entertainment (tc). 215 Getty Images: Samir Hussein / WireImage. 216–217 Getty Images: David Levenson. 218 Rex Features: Glenn Harvey. 219 Corbis: Denis Balibouse / Reuters (crb); Michel Setboun (t); Hulton-Deutsch Collection (bc). 220–221 Corbis: Quadrillion. 222 Alamy Images: Trinity Mirror / Mirrorpix. 223 Getty Images: Tim Graham (tr). Rex Features: Glenn Harvey (bl). 224 Rex Features: Associated Newspapers (cla); Illustrated London News (b). 225 Getty Images: Chris Jackson (tl). Rex Features: Mauro Carraro (bc); (cr). 226–227 Corbis: Quadrillion. 228 Rex Features: Nils Jorgensen (l, c, r). 229 Rex Features: Tim Stewart News (tr, r). 230 Rex Features: (clb). 230–231 Press Association Images: Tony Harris / PA Archive. 231 Rex Features: (tc, cr). 232–233 Getty Images: Tim Graham. 234 Alamy Images: Heritage Image Partnership Ltd (bl). Bridgeman

Images: National Gallery of Canada, Ottawa, Ontario, Canada / Phillips, Fine Art Auctioneers, New York, USA (cl). Press Association Images: Anthony Devlin / PA Wire (ca). 235 Alamy Images: Terry Fincher (b). Rex Features: Simon & Schuster US (tl). 236–237 The Royal Collection Trust © Her Majesty Queen Elizabeth II 2015. 238–239 Rex Features: Steve Back / Associated Newspapers. 238 123RF.com: © Stamp Design Royal Mail Group Ltd (bl). Rex Features: Jeremy Selwyn / Associated Newspapers (tr). 239 Rex Features: (tl, cr). 240–241 Corbis: Courtesy of Ronald Reagan Library. 242 Getty Images: Anwar Hussein (cra). Mirrorpix: (bl). Rex Features: SIPA Press (cl). 243 Corbis: Jason Hawkes (br). Getty Images: AFP (t). 244–245 Corbis: Ralf-Finn Hestoft. 246 Alamy Images: Dennis Hardley (tl). Getty Images: Cowper / Central Press (cla); Lichfield (bl). 247 Corbis: Roger Antrobus. 248 Mary Evans Picture Library: (b). The Royal Collection Trust © Her Majesty Queen Elizabeth II 2015: Image English Photographer, (19th century) / Private Collection. 250 Getty Images: Tim Graham (l, cr). 251 Photoshot: (br). Rex Features: Glenn Harvey (tl). Tim Rooke (bc). 252–253 The Royal Collection Trust © Her Majesty Queen Elizabeth II 2015. 254 Corbis: Pool Photograph (clb, crb). Dorling Kindersley: Paul Self (tl). Getty Images: Stephen Hird / AFP (cra). 255 Getty Images: Alex Livesey (bl). Mirrorpix: Phil Harris / Daily Mirror (br). Rex Features: Hugo Burnand / Clarence House (cl). The Royal Collection Trust © Her Majesty Queen Elizabeth II 2015: (c). 256 Alamy Images: Skyscan Photolibrary (cl). Corbis: Michael Crabtree / Reuters (br). 257 Corbis: Demotix / Amer Ghazzal (tc). Getty Images: Matt Cardy (br). Rex Features: (tl). 258 Corbis: Norman Parkinson / Sygma (t). Dorling Kindersley: Reeman Dansie Auctioneers (br). 259 Corbis: Jeff J Mitchell / Reuters (bl); Reuters (tr). Dorling Kindersley: Paul Self (cla). 260 Rex Features: Tony Kyriacou. 261 Corbis: Pool Photograph (ca). Rex Features: (br). 262–263 Getty Images: Carl De Souza. 264 Corbis: Reuters (bl). Photoshot: UPPA (cl). 265 Corbis: Dave Evans / Demotix (br); Pool Photograph. 266–267 Getty Images: AFP. 268 Getty Images: Tim Graham (bl). 268–269 Corbis: Reuters (ca). 269 Press Association Images: David Jones / PA Archive (tc). 270–271 Corbis: POOL / Reuters. 272 Corbis: Phil Noble / Reuters (crb). Getty Images: Tim Graham (cl). Rex Features: SAC Faye Storer (bl). 273 Corbis: POOL / Reuters. 274 Corbis: John Stillwell / PA / POOL / epa (tr). Rex Features: Hugo Burnand / Clarence House (bl). 275 Corbis: Chris Ison / epa (cr). Press Association Images: Dave Thompson / PA Archive (l). 276 Dorling Kindersley: Reeman Dansie Auctioneers (tl, cla, cl, bl, bc, fbr, br). 276–277 The Royal Collection Trust © Her Majesty Queen Elizabeth II 2015. 277 Dorling Kindersley: Reeman Dansie Auctioneers (tl, tc, tr, ca, cra, br). 278 Getty Images: Tim Graham (bl). 278–279 Getty Images: Max Mumby / Indigo (c). 279 The College of Arms: The conjugal arms of the Duke and Duchess of Cambridge. Reproduced by permission of the Kings, Heralds and Pursuivants of Arms (cr). Rex Features: Ray Tang (bc). 280–281 Rex Features: Senior Aircraftsman Daniel Herri. 282 Corbis: (tl); Kerim Okten / epa (b). 283 Corbis: Rune Hellestad (crb).

Rex Features: Vickie Flores / LNP (bl). The Royal Collection Trust © Her Majesty Queen Elizabeth II 2015: (t). 284–285 Getty Images: WPA Pool / Pool. 286–287 Getty Images: Alex Livesey. 288 Getty Images: Tim Graham (bl). 288–289 Getty Images: Chris Jackson (c). 289 The College of Arms: The arms of HRH Prince Henry of Wales. Reproduced by permission of the Kings, Heralds and Pursuivants of Arms (bc). Getty Images: AFP (cr); Chris Jackson (tc). 290 Alamy Images: AF archive (cla). Corbis: John Stillwell / PA Wire / epa (r). 291 Getty Images: Max Mumby / Indigo (br). Press Association Images: John Stillwell / PA Archive (tr). Roland Smithies / luped.com: (clb). 292–293 Rex Features: Zuma. 294 Getty Images: Chris Jackson (cr). Rex Features: Tim Rooke (bl); (cl). 295 Rex Features: Globe Photos / ZUMA Press, Inc. (br). Getty Images: Hulton Archive (bl). 296 Alamy Images: Shaun Curry (tl); Max Mumby / Indigo (bc). Rex Features: TRH Duke & Duchess of Cambridge (cr). 298 Getty Images: Anwar Hussein (cr); Samir Hussein (l). 299 Dorling Kindersley: © Stamp Design Royal Mail Group Ltd (tr). Getty Images: Chris Jackson (tl). Rex Features: Tim Rooke (bc). 300–301 Mirrorpix: Phil Harris / Daily Mirror. 302 Dorling Kindersley: Reeman Dansie Auctioneers (bc). Getty Images: WPA Pool / Pool (tl). 302–303 Getty Images: WPA Pool / Pool (br). 303 Getty Images: Tim Graham (bl). 304–305 Getty Images: Chris Jackson. 306 Getty Images: WPA Pool / Pool (b). 307 Dorling Kindersley: Bank of Jersey (clb). Getty Images: WPA Pool / Pool (tl, br). 308–309 Corbis: Pool Photograph. 310 Corbis: Hulton-Deutsch Collection (cra). Royal Mint Museum: (br, bc). 311 Getty Images: WPA Pool / Pool (tr). Rex Features: Royal Mint (br). Royal Mint Museum: (tc, bl, tl, bc). 312–313 Getty Images: WPA Pool

All other images © Dorling Kindersley

For further information see:
www.dkimages.com